The Holocaust and Its Religious Impact

Recent Titles in
Bibliographies and Indexes in Religious Studies

The Holocaust and Its Religious Impact

A Critical Assessment and Annotated Bibliography

Jack R. Fischel and Susan M. Ortmann

Bibliographies and Indexes in Religious Studies, Number 54
G. E. Gorman, Advisory Editor

Westport, Connecticut
London

Library of Congress Cataloging-in-Publication Data

Fischel, Jack.
  The Holocaust and its religious impact : a critical assessment and annotated bibliography
/ Jack R. Fischel and Susan M. Ortmann.
    p. cm.—(Bibliographies and indexes in religious studies, ISSN 0742–6836 ; no. 54)
  Includes bibliographical references and index.
  ISBN 0–313–30950–7 (alk. paper)
    1. Holocaust, Jewish (1939–1945)—Causes—Bibliography.   2. Christianity and
antisemitism—History—Bibliography.   3. Holocaust (Christian theology)—Bibliography.   4.
Holocaust (Jewish theology)—Bibliography.   I. Ortmann, Susan M.   II. Title.   III. Series.
Z6374.H6F57 2004
[D804.3]
016.94053′181—dc22   2003068984

British Library Cataloguing in Publication Data is available.

Library of Congress Catalog Card Number: 2003068984
ISBN: 0–313–30950–7
ISSN: 0742–6836

First published in 2004

Praeger Publishers, 88 Post Road West, Westport, CT 06881
An imprint of Greenwood Publishing Group, Inc.
www.praeger.com

Printed in the United States of America

The paper used in this book complies with the
Permanent Paper Standard issued by the National
Information Standards Organization (Z39.48–1984).

10   9   8   7   6   5   4   3   2   1

Contents

Preface

Scholars will continue to debate the link between Christianity's "teaching of contempt" for Jews, and the Holocaust. Following the end of World War II, Pope John XXIII initiated a process that led the church to reexamine its liturgy and responsibility in creating an atmosphere that allowed the Nazis to capitalize on centuries of Christian anti-Jewish feeling in their war against the Jews. The Second Vatican Council (1964) subsequently repudiated the notion of the Jewish people as "rejected, cursed, or guilty of deicide." This effort by the Catholic Church to examine its responsibility for creating a climate that ultimately led to the Holocaust was joined by Protestant theologians and scholars who were similarly introspective about the nexus between Christianity and the destruction of European Jewry. In the decades since the Second Vatican Council, scholars have sought to determine the extent to which Nazi anti-Semitism represented the transformation of the anti-Judentum of the church fathers into the pseudo scientific stereotype of Jews based upon race. Also to be investigated is the question of how difficult it was for the Nazis to convince large numbers of Germans, and their supporters throughout the rest of Europe, that Jews were even more dangerous as race defilers, given the centuries of church teaching that Jews were Christ-killers and guilty of other sins against God.

These are some of the historical problems, which remain unsolved when it comes to understanding the relationship of Christian anti-Judentum to the Holocaust. Although it is apparent that Christian anti-*Judentum* created the preconditions for the acceptance of racial anti-Semitism, it would be an oversimplification to place blame for the destruction of European Jewry entirely upon Christianity The appeal of the Nazi Party was based on many factors including political and economic issues that made possible Hitler's appointment as chancellor of Germany in 1933. Furthermore, scholars continue to debate the circumstances that led to the Holocaust. Was the Nazi genocide of the Jews the result of a calculated plan that Hitler intended from the moment he took over leadership of the Nazi Party, or was the Holocaust a functional response to the nature of the warfare brought on by the German invasion of the Soviet Union in 1941?

What remains undisputed is that with few exceptions, the churches of Europe did not distinguish themselves in regard to opposing the excesses of the Nazi regime in general, and the persecution and genocide of the Jews in particular. Critical studies continue to be written about the reluctance, or what some called the "silence," of Pope Pius XII when it came to condemning the Nazi massacres, in light of his knowledge of the death camps. The flow of literature regarding the role of the churches during the war and its response to Jewish suffering and death shows no sign of abating. This annotated bibliography addresses the role of Christianity in regard to the Holocaust. The reference work is divided into four chapters plus an introduction, which provides the reader with an historical overview of the subject. Chapter one describes the literature dealing with Church anti-Semitism from the *New Testament* to the modern period. Chapter 2 starts with the Enlightenment and brings it up to the advent of the Nazi seizure of power in 1933. Chapter 3 deals with the role of Christians and the churches during the Nazi period, and Chapter 4 examines the way Jews and Christian have assessed the responsibility of Christianity for bringing about the Holocaust, and ways in which the "teaching of contempt" can be eliminated from church teaching and dogma.

This annotated bibliography is intended for non-specialists with some background in history. It should provide an accessible tool for research. Furthermore, it is hoped that teachers and students in both high schools and colleges might use the bibliography. In compiling the information for this volume, the author has received help from Gary Gorman, the book's advisory editor, in regard to structure and content. I would especially like to thank my student editorial assistant, Sue Ortmann, for whom no task was too difficult, and no source inaccessible, and without whom this book would not have been possible. I sincerely thank Maggie Eichler for the assistance that only a competent secretary can provide. My wife, Julie, displayed extraordinary patience and support for the project. My children, Joshua and Corrie, displayed encouragement for their father's efforts. Finally, I thank Millersville University for encouraging me to undertake this assignment, and for granting me funds, which allowed me to employ my student assistant.

Jack Fischel

I would like to thank Dr. Jack Fischel for giving me the opportunity to work with him on this book. He is truly everything a student could wish for in a teacher. My children, Jennie, Mindy, and Christopher have been very supportive of my participation in this project, and I am grateful for their understanding and affection. My parents, Joseph and Pauline Giandalia, taught me to love education and books. Their continued encouragement is appreciated.

Most of all I am grateful to my husband, PJ, for the inexhaustible pool of patience and love he gives to me. Hopefully he knows how important he is in my life.

Finally, thank you to all the authors who have written about the subject explored in this text. Your efforts have inspired new ideas, questions, and the motivation to continue searching for answers.

Sue Ortmann

Introduction

The Holocaust entailed the annihilation of six-million Jews and approximately five million other Europeans, including one and half million children. Proportionately, the starkness of the catastrophe was even worse when one considers that close to seventy percent of the Jews of Europe were exterminated by the Nazis in the period between the German invasion of the Soviet Union in 1941 and the end of the war in 1945. Unlike other groups targeted for destruction by the Nazis, the elimination of European Jewry was a major priority of those who led the Third Reich. Indeed, one could argue that World War II encompassed two wars; the conventional war between the Allies and Nazi Germany, and Hitler's war against the Jews.

As we distance ourselves from the events of the Holocaust, it becomes clear that the churches of Europe, as denominational institutions, failed to confront Hitler's Germany in regard to the Nazi genocide. This accusation focuses less, with regard to the Protestant churches, then it does to the Catholic Church, and in particular to the tenure of Pope Pius XII. The reign of Pope Pius XII, which began in 1939 and ended with his death in 1958, continues to rankle those who criticize the pope for failing to use his position as the pre-eminent moral leader of Europe to speak out against the Nazi barbarity. Indeed, the title of one controversial book about the pope's wartime role during the Holocaust refers to him as "Hitler's Pope." It is also true, however, that where possible both

Catholic and Protestant clergy were instrumental in saving the lives of countless number of Jews. One Israeli official, Pinchas Lapide, in his book *Three Popes and the Jews* (1967), has estimated that Pope Pius XII was responsible for saving the lives of approximately 800,000 Jews (although Lapide offers no documentation for his sources).

In Protestant countries, individual clergymen risked their lives to save Jews, however, at the same time many Protestant clergy supported the Nazi regime. This was true in Germany, where the Nazi government attempted to "Aryanize" all the Protestant churches by expelling from them any aspect of Jewish influence, including baptized Jews. The so-called "Confessing Church" arose in defiance of Hitler's efforts to subordinate the churches to the dictates of the government. Joined by such clergymen as Karl Barth, Dietrich Bonhoeffer, Martin Niemoller, and Heinrich Gruber, Protestant clerics issued the Barmen Declaration in May 1934, which attempted to counter the Nazi regime's imposition of racial superiority policies on the churches. These racial dictates included the expulsion of Jewish converts from the churches. Unfortunately, many of these clerics also harbored anti-Jewish attitudes, and their quarrel with Hitler had more to do with their efforts to protect the efficacy of baptism than concerns about the persecution of the Jews of Germany.

The idea that traditional Christian attitudes played a role in preparing the German people to support the Nazi measures against the Jews remains, for historians and others, an issue embroiled in controversy. The willingness of the German people to accept the Nuremberg Laws of 1935, which deprived Jews of their rights, could certainly be interpreted as a continuation of measures that have a long history in regard to the early churches response to the Jews. Historian Raul Hilberg has pointed out in his *The Destruction of European Jews* (vols.1-31985) that there is very little in the Nuremberg Laws that could not be found in the medieval church decrees, which banished Jews from the mainstream of the Christian world. At the Nuremberg Trials, one defendant invoked the writings of Martin Luther in defense of his actions towards Jews. Luther, in a series of essays, vilified the Jews and called for the burning of their synagogues. In one of his writings, *The Jews and Their Lies* (1543), Luther wrote that next to the devil, a Christian has "no enemy more cruel, more venomous and violent than a true Jew.

Adolf Hitler was adeptly tailored his speeches in a way that secularized religious imagery. This worked to garner support for his anti-Semitic program. Instead of the devil, the Jew was associated with bolshevism and international capitalism. Hitler accused the Jews of betraying Germany during World War I and argued Jews could never be true Germans because they were a Semitic people. The substitution of Aryan "blood" for baptism as a condition for citizenship, cast the Jew in the same light as their ancestors during the Medieval period--outcasts.

Hitler also used religious imagery when he characterized himself as someone sent by God to deliver the German people from the Jews. He was Saint George fighting the dragon of Jewish international finance, capitalism and bolshevism. Presenting himself as a political messiah, Hitler used the symbolism of religion to convince millions of Germans that the struggle was no longer one between Christ and the Devil, but between the Aryan race and the "parasitic" Jews. As taught in traditional Christian scenarios regarding the last days, Jesus' ultimate triumph would not occur until the defeat of the anti-Christ in battle. The triumph of the Aryan race over the Semites, similarly required a secular Armageddon, whereby, the Jews would be eliminated from the face of the earth. It is this history of latent Christian anti-Jewish hatred, metamorphosed into racial ideology that led historian Daniel Jonah Goldhagen to conclude in his book, *Hitler's Willing Executioners (1996)* that the Holocaust was as a national project of the German people.

Following the end of World War II, the humanity was shocked when the immensity of the Nazi genocide became public knowledge. As the evidence unfolded, through survivor testimony, documentaries, the trials of Nazi war-criminals, eyewitness accounts, and accounts taken directly from the Nazis themselves, the Holocaust elicited almost total disbelief. How could the murder of millions of people, simply because of their ethnicity and religion, occur on such a wholesale level in civilized and cultured Germany? How was it possible, it was asked, that a country that had produced Goethe, Kant, Beethoven and Heine, to name only a few of the great cultural figures of German history, could also construct Auschwitz and a method to systematically execute men, women and children?

The death camp at Auschwitz-Birkenau, where between one and a half million Jews were gassed, has become synonymous with the Holocaust, and has also raised many existential questions. For example, many have wondered how an omnipotent God permitted millions of innocent people to be murdered. How are we to explain the phenomena of the Holocaust? Can one still believe in the God of the Hebrew and Christian testaments after Auschwitz? These are some of the troublesome questions that have occupied the scholarship of many theologians, survivors and philosophers since the end of World War II. In his influential book, *After Auschwitz (1966)*, Richard Rubenstein, a theologian, argued that the existence of the death camps and the simultaneous silence of God must be considered in any relevant discussion of the relationship between God and man. The question of maintaining faith in a beneficent God after Auschwitz, however, has not been the concern of Jews alone, but has also resonated throughout much of the Christian world. Vatican II and the subsequent dialogue between Christians and Jews about the church's "teaching of contempt" in regard to the Jews, was a direct result of the Holocaust. A survey of the many books written in the decades since the end of World War II indicate that the philosophical and theological questions regarding the Holocaust have yet to be fully answered.

A byproduct of the discussion surrounding the religious implications of the Holocaust is the reappearance of the word "evil" as a means of describing the barbaric behavior of Nazi Germany. Long discarded by social scientists because of its connection to religion, the word evil was used by Hannah Arendt to describe Adolf Eichmann, the Nazi official responsible for implementing the "Final Solution." Arendt's, *Eichmann in Jerusalem: A Report on the Banality of Evil* (1964) promoted the controversial idea that Nazis, like Eichmann, were caught up in a regime which legitimized genocide, and that these men were merely functionaries carrying out orders. Many scholars took Arendt to task for having, in their opinions, provided an excuse for the "desk murderer". Holocaust historians also took issue with her charge that the leaders of the Jewish Councils were responsible for collaborating with the Germans, and that given their cooperation the deportation to the death camps proved that much easier to implement. While the book remains controversial, it also continues to be influential in drawing our attention to the issue of personal responsibility in the time of genocide. Arendt's book has revived the concept of evil by depicting the excesses of the Third Reich.

Were the events, which culminated in the Holocaust the logical result of a tradition that had united Germany through " blood and iron," or was Hitler an aberration, a historical accident, that permitted the most extreme elements in Germany to seize power? This too has become part of the ongoing debate with regard to how we evaluate Hitler's appeal to the German people. Did the German people strike a Faustian bargain, whereby, they condoned the persecution and later annihilation of the Jews in exchange for the restoration of national honor and the promise of world domination in the name of Aryan superiority?

The Holocaust has been recognized by both the Catholic and many Protestant churches as a watershed event in regard to our understanding of God's intentions in allowing the Nazi genocide to occur. In vain do we seek answers as to the meaning of the murder of six-million Jews. Some suggest that it was divine providence that allowed the Jews to be murdered, so that the State of Israel could be founded. Others find this connection beyond contempt. Some Orthodox Jews have contended that the Holocaust was God's punishment for Jews deviating from the tenets of Judaism. Forgotten in this argument, however, is that the Nazis murdered the cream of Orthodox Jewry, by executing many of the great rabbis of Europe, and destroying a number of the most prominent Yeshivas (Jewish religious academies). So the search for meaning goes on as scholars, ranging from Emil Fackenheim, to the late Harry James Cargas, to Franklin Littell, have attempted to grapple with the issues in their scholarship.

The questions raised by the Holocaust, however, are not limited to the past. More than fifty years after the *Shoah*, strained exchanges between Catholics and Jews continue to mark their bittersweet relationship. In recent years, for example, Polish Catholics and Jews confronted one another over the establishment of a convent on the grounds of Auschwitz. For Poles, Auschwitz was a place where many Catholics were killed. For Jews, Auschwitz represents a large Jewish burial ground, and they found it a desecration for the Carmelite nuns to establish a convent on holy soil. It took all of his gifts for Pope John Paul II to mediate these differences. Similarly, Jewish organizations protested the canonization and the elevation to sainthood of Edith Stein, a Jewish convert to Catholicism. For Catholics, Stein was a Christian martyr, whereas, for Jews, Edith Stein was murdered in Auschwitz because the Nazis considered her a Jew. Perhaps the most divisive strain between Catholics and Jews resulting from the Holocaust is the promotion by the Vatican of Pope Pius XII to sainthood. For many Jews, the pope's silence in the face of Jewish annihilation is interpreted as a great moral failure. The controversial legacy of Pius XII' papacy, during the Holocaust, received worldwide attention with the debut of Rolf Hochuth's scathing play *The Deputy* (1964). The drama accuses the pope of being callous, if not indifferent, to the conditions of the Jews at the very time that millions of them were being murdered in the death camps. For Hochuth and the scholars who have adopted his view, such as James Carroll, John Cornwell, Daniel Goldhagen, John Morley, Michael Phayer, Gary Wills, and Susan Zuccotti, Pius XII is accused of moral culpability in the destruction of European Jewry. The pope's defenders, however, view Pope Pius XII as a leader who attempted to use his moral authority to mitigate the worst excesses of Nazism. Scholars, such as Pirre Blet, Father Frank A. Graham, Sister Marguerite Marchione, Ronald Rychlak and Jose Sanchez, have argued that the pope feared that confronting Hitler directly would have resulted in the persecution of Catholics, and the seizure of church property in German occupied Europe. In addition, they cite evidence that Pius XII saved hundreds of thousands of Jews, and point out that in Israel there was a move to list him among the Righteous Gentiles (those who risked their person to help Jews during the Holocaust.).

The purpose of this annotated bibliography is to provide the reader with a comprehensive survey of writings about the Holocaust. This presents the audience with an overview of the issues discussed above, as they have appeared in the thousands of books and articles published on the Holocaust in the decades since the end of World War II. The expectation is that the reference work will be user-friendly. Towards that end, the bibliography is listed under four topics with introductory comments, which frame the theories put forward in the books and articles included in each section. The First Chapter, *Christian Anti-Judaism*, introduces the reader to the roots of anti-Semitism as it manifested itself as anti-

Judaism in the formative years of Christianity. Chapter Two, *From Anti-Judentum to Anti-Semitism*, familiarizes the reader with the literature recounting the evolution of negative feelings and stereotypes about Jews in the Medieval world through to the emergence of racial anti-Semitism during the nineteenth century. The Third Chapter, *The Moral and Religious Response to the Nazi Persecution and Genocide of the Jews*, deals with the literature of the Holocaust and the many interpretations of the religious responses to the Nazi genocide. Chapter Four, *Post-World War II Responses to the Holocaust*, provides the reader with a view of the responses of both Jews and Christians to the Holocaust, including the efforts of the churches to deal with the legacy of the "teaching of contempt" for Jews, as found in the Gospels.

Given the vast selection of literature dedicated to these issues, and the fact that there is more released each day, there is little chance that everything published could be included. However, the books and articles listed offer a broad array of past and recent scholarship, from a variety of venues and points of view.

1

Christian Anti-Judentum

In 1879 Wilhelm Marr, a member of the Reichstag, first used the term anti-Semitism to describe *Völkisch* (racial nationalists) opposition to the place of Jews in German life. Unsurprisingly Marr found an audience already prepared to listen to his racial attack, for Christian hatred of Jews had a history as old as Western civilization itself. The Christian contempt for Jews was grounded in the Jewish religious belief system rather than in their people hood. From the institutionalizing of Christianity at the Council of Nicea in 325 a.d. to the advent of the Nazi seizure of power in 1933, Jews had the choice of becoming Christian and therefore have had the choice to overcome the hatred they experienced by the majority population. Racial anti-Semitism in the late-nineteenth century drew upon this traditional contempt for Jews and added the argument that it was not simply the Jewish religion which threatened Christian civilization but the Jewish people as a racial group. Jewish converts to Christianity were believed to be as much a threat to Germany as those who maintained their Jewish identity. German racial nationalists rejected the efficacy of baptism and declared that their war was as much against Jewish converts as Jews themselves. Nazi anti-Semitism, born in the racial *Völkisch* nationalism of the late nineteenth century, promoted the idea that the Jewish race threatened the racial purity of the German race. Their solution was to advocate purging all persons of Jewish ancestry from German life, even if they were practicing Christians.

What separated Nazi anti-Semitism from traditional Christian anti-*Judentum* was, therefore, a matter of definition. Despite differences, Christian anti-*Judentum* and *Völkisch* racism shared several commonalities including the belief that Jews deserved persecution. In enacting the Nuremberg Laws of 1935, with its many exclusionary provisions against Jews, the Nazi's matched measures enacted by the papacy during the Middle Ages. In medieval Europe, Jews were demonized, and charged with the most fantastic crimes. Jews were condemned as Christ-killers, accused of using the blood of Christian children in baking unleavened bread for Passover (ritual murder), charged with torturing the Host, condemned for poisoning the wells of Europe during the Great Plague of 1350, and denounced as agents of the anti-Christ or Satan. During the Nazi years, many of the medieval accusations made against Jews were secularized. Jews were no longer demonized, but instead, were accused of being bent on world domination through their leadership of the Bolshevik Revolution, and their control of international finance. Nazi ideology defined Jews in biological terms. They were condemned as sub-human parasites feeding off the wealth of the countries that they inhabited.

Minus two centuries of Christian teaching of contempt about Jews, it is possible that Nazi ideology would have found little fertile ground among Europeans. Nazi anti-Semitism built upon already established attitudes about Jews and placed them in a modern context. Never has the expression, "old wine in new bottles" been as appropriate as when used to connect traditional anti-Judaism and modern anti-Semitism. The bibliography, which follows, invites the reader to survey books that deal with the roots of Nazi anti-Semitism that are found in the early church teaching about Jews.

Abulafia, Anna Sapir. *Christians and Jews in the Twelfth Century Renaissance.* **Routledge Publishers, 1995, 196 pp.**
The author argues that Christians came to identify reason with their own faith so fully, that it became inconceivable to them that anyone could reasonably doubt its truth and authority; consequently the refusal of Jews to convert increasingly appeared to be deliberate and perverse.

Allen, Ronald and John C. Holbert. *Holy Root, Holy Branches; Christian Preaching From the Old Testament.* **Nashville: Abingdon Press, 1995, 211 pp.**
The authors make the point that a difficulty in Christian-Jewish relations stems from the fact that Christianity's beginnings are based upon a Biblical interpretation that denigrates Jews and Judaism and highlights Christianity as a superior religion. This view has been reiterated in Christian teachings, liturgy and sermons for centuries. The authors have undertaken work that is at best difficult, for it is their intent to produce a text, which not only preserves Christian dogma, but also avoids any trace of negatively stereotyping Jews. The chapters of their book deal with methods for proclaiming the Gospels without attacking the Jews or their faith.

Almog, Shmuel, ed. *Anti-Semitism Through the Ages.* **Oxford: Pergamon**

Press, 1988, 419 pp.
This collection of essays addresses the subject of Jew-hatred from classical antiquity to the present, through its many forms and manifestations in history. It also includes the interpretations of contemporary historians.

Amos, Anne." The Parting of the Ways." Jewish-Christian Relations (2001), http://www.jcrelations.net/articl11/amos.htm, 9 pp.
Amos argues, that the split between Judaism and Christianity was gradual and took place at a differing pace in various locations. He also notes two distinct stages in the separation. The first was concerned with self-definition and who was and was not Christian. The second moved beyond the need for self-definition to establishing a legitimate basis for the new faith that would make it more attractive than Judaism. As a result of this "competition" for followers Christianity portrayed Jews as the "other", and spread anti-Jewish invectives.

Augustine, Cardinal Bea. "The Jewish People in the Divine Plan of Salvation." Thought (Spring 1966), Volume 41 Issue 160, pp. 9-32.
The Cardinal insists, that the Gospel texts of Sts. Peter, Paul and Steven do not indict the entire Jewish community for the death of Christ. Rather, if any guilt is to be placed it rests upon the leaders of the Sanhedrin. Yet the author points out that even the leaders who participated in the trial of Jesus may be deemed innocent because it is possible that they did not fully understand the divine nature of Christ. Therefore the charge of deicide cannot be leveled at the Jews as a whole, or quite possibly even at their leaders.

Baron, Salo W. "Changing Patterns of Anti-Semitism. " Jewish Social Studies (1976), Volume 38 Issue 1, pp. 5-38.
This article examines the basic causes of anti-Semitism in a variety of historical time periods. The author traces the anti-Jewish attitudes of non-Jews through the centuries during which Christians persecuted Jews. Baron studies the way in which Jews were regarded during the European quest for national homogeneity. He also examines the development of racial hatred of Jews in the nineteenth century.

Barth, Markus. "Was Paul an Anti-Semite?" Journal of Ecumenical Studies (1968), Volume 5, pp. 78-104.
The author insists that Paul did not lead the Church in the direction of anti-Semitism. Rather, Paul's writings were used by later Christians to slander Jews and Judaism. Barth claims that recent research has shown Paul in a new light and that his later writings indicate that he never intended to eliminate Jews from salvation. Instead he moved to open up God's redemptive plan for his chosen people to include Gentiles. Additionally, any disagreements Paul had with Judaism were not exceptional in nature. They were simply part of the overall dialogue that Jews, with differing opinions, have always expressed about their beliefs.

Beck, Norman. *Mature Christianity: The Recognition and Repudiation of the*

Anti-Jewish Polemic of the New Testament. **Selinsgrove: Susquehanna University Press, 1985, 325 pp.**
Beck explains Christian anti-*Judentum* as phenomena not unusual in the evolution of groups or religions, which spring from the parent church. In this situation, the sect writing the text attempts to justify its existence against an older and more firmly entrenched theology. It is Beck's contention, that the anti-Jewish polemics of the *New Testament* can be understood in this context. Beck finds some of most defamatory passages in the *New Testament,* in the *Gospel of Luke* and in the *Book of Acts*. In *Acts*, for example, the argument is made that Jews who did not repent and follow Jesus lost their right to be called the people of God. Furthermore, Judaism was described as an empty shell to be discarded, inasmuch as followers of Jesus were now the people of God.

____. **"Removing Anti-Jewish Polemic from Our Christian Lectionaries: A Proposal." http://www.jcrelations.net/artic11/beck.htm, December 28, 2001, 15 pp.**
In this article, the author contends, that over the past few decades Christians increasingly recognize the anti-Jewish polemic that is contained within *New Testament* texts. Beck lists the most offensive texts in each of the *New Testament* books. For example, the *Gospel According to Saint Matthew* contains eighty verses of defamatory anti-Jewish polemic, many of which are utilized in the Catholic *Lectionary for Mass* during its three-year cycle. Beck makes a case for revising the *Lectionary* and extending it to a four-year cycle, in which the use of Anti-Jewish texts could be avoided.

Benhayim, Menachem. *Jews, Gentiles and the New Testament Scriptures: Alleged Anti-Semitism in the New Testament.* **Jerusalem; Yanetz, 1985, 74 pp.**
The focus of this article is on the origins of anti-Semitism among Gentiles. Benhayim insists that while the authors of the *New Testament* disagreed with aspects of Judaism, they were not anti-Jewish. He claims that interpreting passages of the Gospels in an anti-Jewish manner came about when non-Jewish converts to Christianity felt a need to prove their superiority over the Jews. The author prompts Jews and Christians to overcome any intolerance of one another and help eradicate anti-Semitism.

Berdiaev, Nikolai Aleksandrovich. *Christianity and Anti-Semitism.* **New York: Philosophical Library, 1954, 58 pp.**
The author, one of twentieth century Russia's most important philosophers, explores the role that Christianity played, and continues to play, in promoting anti-Semitism.

Berger, David, ed. *History and Hate: The Dimensions of Anti-Semitism.* **Philadelphia, Pa.: Jewish Publications Society, 1986, 140 pp.**
Berger has compiled a group of essays written by scholars engaged in the study of the roots and development of anti-Semitism. This volume covers such subjects as

anti-Semitic attitudes in the ancient world, the Middle Ages, and throughout Western civilization. In each time period and in every location, the author identifies the role Christianity played in promoting hostility toward the Jews.

Boksar, Ben Zion. *Judaism and the Christian Predicament.* **New York: Knopf Publishers, 1966, 384 pp.**
This volume traces the Jewish reaction to the long, hostile history of Christian anti-Semitism. Rabbi Boksar emphasizes how Christianity's prejudice towards Judaism obscured its roots in the Jewish tradition.

Bondi, Richard A. "John 8: 39-47: Children of Abraham or of the Devil?" Journal of Ecumenical Studies (Fall 1997), Volume 34 Issue 4, pp. 473-498.
Bondi addresses the *New Testament* Biblical text of John 8:39-47, which includes some of the most offensive stereotypes of Jews. For example, over the centuries passages such as "you are of the devil" and "you are not of God" have been supposedly directed toward Jews. Bondi insists, that these lines have been misused because they have been read outside the historical context of their time. He contends that the sting of these words cannot be totally removed. Yet if they are read as the words of a humanly fallible apostle, speaking passionately as he tried to win the struggle for converts from Judaism and not as a direct quote from the Savior, then they can be better understood.

Bonfil, Robert. *Jewish Life in Renaissance Italy.* **Oldcorn, Anthony, Translator. University of California Press; 1994, 320 pp.**
Bonfil agues, that the romantic visions of Renaissance Italy put forward by some other historians are too simplistic. He reports that Jews living in Italy suffered relentless persecution mostly as a result of anti-Jewish attitudes held by the Christian majority. Copies of the *Talmud* were burned, friars promoted hate-filled propaganda, and Jews were pressured to convert to Christianity. According to Bonfil the Jews were regarded as the "other" in Renaissance Italy and in this context they were forced to develop their own identity.

Boyarin, Daniel. *A Radical Jew: Paul and the Politics of Identity.* **Berkeley: University of California Press, 1994, 366 pp.**
The author contends, that while Paul's ideas may not have been anti-Judaic and were not the origin of anti-Semitism, his arguments "are the origin of the Jewish question." By studying Pauline teachings in the *New Testament*, the author supports his own contentions and demonstrates that others have used Paul's work to shore up theological anti-Judaism. He suggests a new reading of Paul's message is due and proposes looking at Paul as a proponent of human equality.

___. "Justin Martyr Invents Judaism." Church History (September 2001), Volume 70 Issue 3, pp. 427-465.
In this article Boyarin explores the development of the concept of "heretics" in Christianity as well as the beginnings of Jews perceiving members within their own

community as "deviant outsiders." Justin Martyr claimed Jews cursed and labeled Jewish Christians as heretics. According to Martyr, Jews "pronounced a curse on Christians in their prayers." This development, and Martyr's recording of it, has been regarded by some scholars as an aspect of the "parting of the ways" between Jews and Christians. The author insists that there is scant evidence to support Martyr's claim of a curse by Jews upon Christians and therefore it cannot be used as a reason for the separation of the two groups. Boyarin proposes that once the simplistic and linear accounts of Judaism and Christianity are discarded, one can begin to take a scholarly look at the contacts and relationship between the two faith communities that produced notions of heresy in both groups. The author puts forward his theories about Jewish and Christian interactions as they occurred over through the first three to four centuries.

Braham, Randolph L. *The Vatican and the Holocaust: The Catholic Church and the Jews During the Nazi Era.* **New York: Columbia University Press, 2000, 330 pp.**
The long history of Christian anti-Judaism and its links to Nazi anti-Semitism are the focus of Braham's book.

_____**ed.** *The Origins of the Holocaust: Christian Anti-Semitism.* **New York: Columbia University Press, 1986, 85 pp.**
Braham serves as the editor of this book, which explores the issue of anti-Semitism and its impact on the Holocaust. The book focuses on Hyam Maccoby's theory that anti-Semitism resides at the very core of the Christian myth of redemption. The Jews, according to Maccoby, became the necessary executioner in the sacrificial death of Jesus, a role that underlies their subsequent demonization. The five Jewish and Christian contributors (including Eugene J. Fisher, executive secretary, Catholic-Jewish relations of the National Conference of Catholic Bishops) agree that there is a linkage between Christian anti-Semitism and the Holocaust.

Bratton, Fred Gladstone. *The Crime of Christendom: The Theological Sources of Anti-Semitism.* **Boston: Beacon Press, 1969, 241 pp.**
A Congregational minister, Bratton considers the roots of anti-Semitism, the Jewish background of Jesus, and the influence of other traditions upon formative Christianity. The author states, that it is unrealistic to believe that if Christians would give up their notion of Jesus' divinity, anti-Semitism would disappear. Much of the book, however, details how secular anti-Semitism evolved from Christian theology.

_____. *The Theological Sources of Christian Anti-Semitism.* **Boston: Beacon Press, 1969, 241 pp.**
The early chapters of the work focus on the anti-Judaism of the *New Testament* and the Church Fathers. This is followed by chapters assessing the medieval Christian hatred of Jews, as expressed in restrictive legislation, forced conversions and systematic persecution. A special feature of the survey is Bratton's informed

chapter on literary sources of anti-Semitism. Bratton's historical survey, however, is bound together with a controversial thesis, which argues that ethnic and cultural anti-Semitism, which has an even longer history than the theological type, was originally provoked and continuously nourished by the Orthodox Jewish dogma of uniqueness.

Brown, Father Raymond. *The Death of the Messiah.* **New York: Doubleday, 1994, 1,608 pp.**
This two-volume work explores aspects of the Crucifixion of Christ. Brown, a *New Testament* scholar, argues that one cannot just dismiss the role that Jews played in the death of Jesus. He defines that role as implicating Jewish leaders, not ordinary Jews. Brown also claims, that Christians have mishandled the Gospels and used Jesus' death as grounds for unfairly attacking Jews and persecuting them. He insists, that both sides must come to a better understanding of the true events surrounding Christ's execution and the ways in which history has shaped views of the Crucifixion.

____. **"The Narratives of Jesus' Passion and Anti-Judaism."** *America* **(April 1,1995), Volume 172 Issue 11, pp. 8-13.**
The author explores ways that *New Testament* readings, which deal with Christ's Crucifixion, have been interpreted by Christians, in order to vilify Jews. Brown rejects literal readings of these passages because they slander Jews as liars, who schemed to put Christ to death. He insists, that the Church must right the wrong done to the Jews by these untruths, and that work be undertaken to help Christians understand the rich and valuable heritage of Judaism.

Carmichael, Joel. 'Anti-Semitism Misunderstood." *Midstream* **(November 1992), Volume 38 Issue 8, pp. 15-17.**
Carmichael's article focuses upon how Christian doctrine developed the idea of the "evil of Jews." He insists there is a difference between the run-of-the-mill xenophobia that consists of insults and slurs and the mystical anti-Semitism that was projected by Christianity through stereotyping Jews as non-human and/or evil beings possessing some uncanny source of power. Jews, though horrified at this depiction of themselves as evil, have maintained an air of indifference to Christian doctrine. However, the image of the "inhuman, evil Jew" has served over time as the linchpin between theological and biological anti-Semitism.

___. **"Extracting Anti-Semitism from Christianity."** *Midstream* **(April 1988), Volume 34 Issue 3, pp. 3-4.**
This article contends, that the teachings of Paul serve as the source for demonizing the Jews. Carmichael maintains, that Paul took the Jews rejection of Jesus as the Messiah as proof that they were the devil's agents. When they did not recognize their error in refusing Christ's redemption, their punishment by God came to be viewed as eternal. The author insists, that we must revise our reading of Paul so that the poison of anti-Judaism can be removed from Christian teaching.

___. 'Mystical Anti-Semitism and Xenophobia." Midstream (April 1986), Volume 32 Issue 4, pp. 14-18.
The author notes the difference between the more "ordinary" antagonisms directed at Jews and Christianity's mystical anti-Judaism, which holds, that the Jews' refusal to accept Christ as the Messiah provided proof of their evil. While this ant-Semitic attitude justified violence against Jews, the Church also understood the need to preserve the Jews, for their suffering gave evidence of Christianity's religious superiority. The Christian portrayal of the Jews as "an enemy" fit the needs of the Nazis and the Bolsheviks, so both adopted it and tailored it to their agendas.

___. The Satanizing of the Jews: Origin and Development of Mystical Anti-Semitism. New York: Fromm International Publishing Corp., 1992, 210 pp.
According to Carmichael, although Christians viewed Jews as a powerless people, they, nevertheless, bestowed upon them an immense supernatural power as the agents of Satan in this world. Emanating in the hostile atmosphere of the Middle Ages, mystical anti-Semitism, argues Carmichael, evolved from this contradiction. He claims the anti-Semite, on the one hand, often saw his Jewish countrymen as disadvantaged, marginalized, and often without power. On the other hand, Jews were viewed collectively as the personification of cosmic evil on the verge of triumph. This dual image of the Jew, contends the author, links the anti-*Judentum* of the Middle Ages with the anti-Semitism of modernity.

Carroll, James. *Constantine's Sword: The Church and the Jews.* New York: Houghton Mifflin, 2000, 752 pp.
Carroll's book traces the record of anti-Semitism and anti-Judaism in the Catholic Church, suggesting that centuries of teaching hatred of the Jews culminated in the Holocaust. The author also offers examples of anti-Jewish sentiment throughout European history, from blood libel to the Dreyfus affair, and from the Inquisition to Auschwitz. Carroll rejects the simple Christian distinction between itself and Judaism whereby the God of the Jews is depicted as judgmental and concerned with law, whereas Jesus is concerned with love, a contrast, which Carroll argues, contributed to the growth of anti-Semitism. The author maintains, that Jesus' emphasis on love was his most Jewish attribute.

Chazan, Robert. *European Jewry and the First Crusade.* Berkeley: University of California Press, 1987, 380 pp.
The author argues, that both our historical and moral understanding will be enhanced if medieval Jews and Christians are understood, even in the crucible of persecution and massacre, as dwellers within the same cultural world. Chazan focuses on the massacres of 1096, when some of those Christians fighting in the Crusades interpreted their mission as requiring the slaughter and forced conversion of the Rhineland Jews. Chazan rejects the view, that the massacre of the Jews was an exceptional instance of aberrant behavior, which had little to do with the essential objective of the Crusade.

___. *Medieval Stereotypes and Modern Anti-Semitism.* **Berkeley: University of California Press, 1997, 189 pp.**
During the eleventh and twelfth centuries, Jews prospered in Northern Europe, and their communities spread to England, the German lands, and Poland, where the Christian majority tolerated them. Chazan focuses on the rise of anti-Jewish sentiments in twelfth century Northern Europe. It is during this century that a new charge was added to the older negative images of Jews persisting throughout Christendom. Christians accused Jews of inflicting harm on followers of Christ because of their animosity to Christianity. Chazan argues, that the decline of the Ashkenazi Jewish communities of northern Europe can be traced to the creation of these new and highly charged negative images and stereotypes of Jews.

Cherlin, Leonard. "The First Thousand Years of Christian Anti-Semitism." Humanistic Judaism (Spring 1985), Volume 13 Issue 1, pp. 21-23.
The author insists, that the foundations for Christian endorsed anti-Semitism can be found in ecclesiastical rulings that maligned the Jews and Judaism. The tradition of Christian anti-Semitism, according to Cherlin, was well in place by the fourth century when hating Jews had become part of a Christian's duty to his faith.

Cohen, Jeremy. *The Friars and the Jews: the Evolution of Medieval Anti-Judaism.* **Ithaca and London: Cornell University Press, 1982, 301 pp.**
Cohen deals with the reasons why the mendicant friars abandoned the medieval Augustinian principle of grudging toleration of Jews and Judaism. He finds that prior to the thirteenth century, Jews in Christian Europe were not viewed by the Church as heretics, but as a stubborn people, punished by God for not accepting Jesus as the Christ. However, when churchmen came to learn of the Talmud and to an understanding that Judaism was something more than a Biblical religion, the friars concluded that Talmudic Judaism was a perversion of the Bible. Thus it was deemed a quasi heresy. Subsequently, the friars became the prime movers in condemning and publicly burning the *Talmud*, as well as using the Talmud as a tool to convert Jews. The public burning of the *Talmud* by Dominican and Franciscan friars foreshadowed the Nazi's 1933 burning of books authored by Jews. Cohen argues, that Dominican and Franciscan theologians rejected Augustine's position, that the Jews must be tolerated as guardians of the Hebrew Scriptures, who continue to observe the letter of the law. Cohen analyzes the major attack against Judaism and the Talmud from investigations of the 1230's through the early fourteenth century.

____. *Essential Papers on Judaism and Christianity in Conflict: From Late Antiquity to the Reformation.* **New York: New York University Press, 1991, 577 pp.**
Nineteen essays examine the time period concerned with late Judaism and early Christianity. The articles cover a variety of subjects that include late antiquity, Christianity's separation from the Jewish community, problems in dealing with the trial of Jesus, anti-Judaism, the Middle Ages and the Reformation.

Cohn-Sherbok, Daniel. *The Crucified Jew: Twenty Centuries of Christian Anti-Semitism.* **Eerdmanns, 1997, 258 pp.**
The volume is a survey of the Christian roots of historical and institutional anti-Semitism, in which the author has popularized the material for a general audience. Cohn-Sherbok provides examples of religious leaders like Martin Luther, who perpetuated anti-Semitic attitudes. He also recounts the forced conversions of Jews during the Middle Ages. Much of the work in this eighteen chapter historical survey is a compilation of information gleaned from more scholarly accounts of the subject.

____. **"Jews, Christians and Liberation Theology." Jewish Christian Relations (March 1984), Volume 17 Issue 1, pp. 3-11.**
Cohn-Sherbok studies both the anti-Semitism and anti-Judaism that has long been present in Christianity's actions and teaching. He also examines anti-Christianity as it has manifested itself over time in Judaism. For the author the idea of "liberation theology" allows for Jews and Christians to find ways to relate to one another and to close the gap that exists between the two communities by returning to genuine "scriptural sources."

Crossan, John Dominic. *The Birth of Christianity: Discovering What Happened in the Years Immediately after the Execution of Jesus.* **Harper San Francisco, 1999, 688 pp.**
The author sheds new light on the rise of Christianity in the years before and following Christ's Crucifixion. Crossan argues, that the meaning of the "resurrection" is different for today's traditional Christian than it was for early followers of Jesus. He also contends, that Christianity would have developed without the efforts and teachings of Paul. His study includes the role played by Jews in the early church and tensions that arose over time between the two groups.

___. *The Roots of Anti-Semitism in the Gospel Story of the Death of Jesus.* **San Francisco: Harper Publishers, 1995, 238 pp.**
Crossan argues, that the roots of anti-Semitism spring from Gospel narratives of the death of Jesus, and that the Romans, not the Jews, killed Jesus because he was viewed as a revolutionary agitator who threatened their continued rule over Judea.

___. *Who Killed Jesus? Exposing the Roots of anti-Semitism in the Gospel Story of the Death of Jesus.* **San Francisco: Harper San Francisco, 1995, 238 pp.**
According to Crossan, the roots of anti-Semitism spring from the Gospel narrative of the death of Jesus, which blame the Jews and not the Romans for the Crucifixion. The author distinguishes between two types of historical writing; the first is the writing of history as it actually happened and the other is prophecy historicized, or history written to conform to ancient prophecies. According to Crossan, the passion accounts blaming Jews for Jesus' arrest and Crucifixion are based on the second type of historical writing.

Cutler, Harris and Helen Elmquist Cutler. *The Jews as Ally of the Muslims: Medieval Roots of Anti-Semitism.* **South Bend,IN: University of Notre Dame Press, 1986, 577 pp.**
The authors contend that medieval anti-Semitism was an outgrowth of medieval anti-Muslimism. Christians tended to view Jews as hostile agents of Islam based on the reading of a handful of pro-Arab medieval Jewish texts. The Cutlers argue, that the image of a Jewish-Muslim alliance could have been transmitted through these texts to medieval Christendom, which, in turn, led to the great revival of anti-Semitism in Western Europe. The authors also point out that the decree of the Fourth Lateran Council of 1215, which compelled Jews and Muslims to wear a distinctive mark on their clothes. In German occupied Europe, the Nazis would require Jews to wear the Yellow Star of David derived from the anti-Muslim eschatological concerns of Pope Innocent III.

Danniel, Benjamin. *Jesus, Jews, and Gentiles: the True Story of Their Relationship as Recorded in the Bible.* **Arco Books, 1948, 296 pp.**
Anti-Semitism, the author maintains, is rooted in *New Testament* teaching, whereby, Jews are accused of crucifying Christ and, therefore, are condemned until they accept Jesus and are converted by baptism. Based on a careful reading of the King James version of the *New Testament*, Danniel concludes, that Christian anti-Semitism is fundamentally based on misquotations, misinterpretations and fabrications, which over the centuries have been incorporated into traditional church teaching about Jews.

Darr, John A. and Joanna Dewey. "Responses: Is There Anti-Semitism in the Gospels?" Biblical Interpretation (November 1991), Volume 1 Issue 3, pp. 353-367.
The article responds to Rene Girard's argument that the Gospels are not anti-Semitic take issue with his contentions. Darr insists that the Gospels did in fact reflect the anti-Jewish polemics of the first century that were deemed necessary for the survival of Christianity. He claims, that later interpretations added to the danger for Jews because the context in which the Gospels were written was forgotten. Removed from their historical significance the anti-Jewish passages became a justification for oppressing the Jews. The author concludes, that Girard's theories asserting there is no anti-Semitism in the Gospels is unsupported and may well encourage anti-Semitism.

Davies, Alan T. ed. *Anti-Semitism and the Foundations of Christianity.* **New York: Paulist Press, 1979, 288 pp.**
This volume presents essays responding to Rosemary R. Ruether's argument in *Faith and Fratricide* that anti-Judaism springs from the very heart of Christian faith; the negative side of affirming Jesus as the Messiah. All of the contributors agree that anti-Judaism is indeed embedded in Christianity but they deny, especially those who discuss anti-Judaism in the *New Testament*, that it is implied by the Christian faith itself.

Dietrich, Donald J. *God and Humanity in Auschwitz: Jewish-Christian Relations and Sanctioned Murder.* **New Jersey: Transaction Press, 1995, 355 pp.**
Although Christian anti-*Judentum* alone was not a sufficient cause for the Holocaust, the author concludes, it nevertheless was a necessary one. Dietrich tracks the development of Christian anti-*Judentum* within its various historical contexts. The author discusses how Christian theologians have sought to welcome the legacy of the church's misinterpretations of Judaism and issues raised by the Shoah. He traces the development of Christian anti-Semitism within its various historical contexts and examines in detail the ways in which Christian and Jewish theologians have been forced to rethink their view of themselves and of each other in the post-Holocaust era.

Dolan, Edward F. *Anti-Semitism.* **Watts Franklin, 1985, 135 pp.**
Dolan contends, that there are three roots of anti-Semitism; a religion that separates them from others, the fact that they have been without a homeland, and the role they have played in the economic concerns of nations. The author attempts to find the origins of these so-called roots and provides a historical overview of the violent and restrictive experiences that have befallen the Jews because of these ideas.

Dudley, Martin. "The Jews in the Good Friday Liturgy." **Anglican Theological Review (Winter 1994), Volume 76 Issue 1, pp. 61-71.**
The author presents three texts used by Christian denominations in the Good Friday liturgy. He shows the anti-Semitic interpretations that have historically been associated with these readings and details the problems involved with revising those texts in a way that meets the needs of Christians and Jews.

Eakin, Frank Edwin, Jr. "The Bible and Anti-Semitism." *The Conflict:: Biblical versus. Secular Ethics.* **Eds. R. Joseph Hoffmann and Gerald R. Larue. Buffalo, NY.: Prometheus, 1988, pp. 47-56.**
This was a paper presented at a 1986 conference. Eakin addresses several aspects of the problem of traditional Christian anti-Semitism. First he is critical of the uninformed readings of the *New Testament* that have promoted anti-Jewish sentiment and he claims, that the writings of Paul have been particularly inflammatory even though the author may not have intended to denigrate Jews. Eakin also notes the pervasive use of anti-Semitic imagery during the Middle Ages in the Christian Cathedrals. Finally, he examines the recent scholarly writings that deal with the subject of Christianity's historic hostility toward the Jews.

_____ . *What Price Prejudice? Christian Anti-Semitism in America.* **Mahwah, NJ.: Paulist Press, 1998, 208 pp.**
Because the Christian Churches have regarded the Scriptures as their own and have tried to establish their superiority over other religions Christianity has throughout the centuries developed a "contempt for Jews." Eakin claims, that Christianity gave up its claim to its own doctrine of love once it began preaching hostility toward

Jews. Specific chapters within this volume deal with issues concerning Christian anti-Semitism during the early and middle ages while others address Christianity's role in creating anti-Semitic attitudes in America. The author also explores the recent attempts by Christian Churches to enter into a dialogue with Jews and suggests ideas for improving the relationship between the two religious communities.

Eckardt, Alice. "The Reformation and the Jews." Shofar (Summer 1989), Volume 7 Issue 4, pp. 23-47.
Eckardt contends, that the Reformation continued Christianity's long held tradition of anti-Judaism and that though most of the effects upon Jews were negative, there was a positive aspect. The author also reports on the mostly negative attitudes held by Reformation leaders. For example, Martin Luther moved from a determination to convert Jews to strong condemnations of them. Yet despite the continued persecution, Jews viewed the Reformation and the conflict it created between groups of Christians as God's punishment directed against Christianity.

Eckstein, Jerome. "Luther's Legacy in the Jewish Community." Viewpoints (April-May1984), Volume 12 Issue 10, pp. 5-6.
This examination focuses on the anti-Jewish attitude of Martin Luther and the effect his writings had upon proponents of National Socialism. The author also discusses the origins of Christian anti-Semitism and how Luther's ideas contributed to the continuation of prejudice against Jews. He contrasts the recent attempts by Christian theologians to reject the negative stereotyping of Jews and Judaism by Christianity.

Edelstein, Alan.   *An Unacknowledged Harmony: Philo-Semitism and the Survival of European Jewry.* Westport: Greenwood Press, 1982, 247 pp.
The author argues that the survival of medieval European Jewry and the basis for their emancipation in the eighteenth century can be attributed to the legacy of Christian philo-Semitism. It manifested itself in the past two centuries through a variety of forms including: economic, religious, social, nationalistic, intellectual, democratic/liberal, and humanistic. Edelstein reviews Western European Jewish history from the Roman Empire through the Holocaust, asserting that the absence of anti-Jewish feelings at particular times and places amounted not merely to neutral tolerance, but to an intrinsically positive dimension of the Western ethos. This tradition accounts for the willingness of some Christians during the Holocaust, to hide and protect Jews, despite the considerable risk to their own person.

Evans, Craig A., Donald A. Hagner, eds. *Anti-Semitism and Early Christianity: Issues of Polemic and Faith.* Fortress Press, 1994, 304 pp.
The compilation of works contained in this volume, include both ancient and modern writings Evans and Hagner have selected writings that address among other things; "Jesus and the Question of Anti-Semitism", "Paul's Quarrel with Judaism", "Anti-Semitism in the Gospel of John", "Anti-Semitism and/or Anti-

Judaism in Mark", "Anti-Judaism in the Early Church Fathers", and "Polemic in the Hebrew and Catholic Epistles."

Falk, Gerhard. *The Jew in Christian Theology: Martin Luther's Anti-Jewish "Vom Schem Hamphoras," Previously Unpublished in English, and Other Milestones in Church Doctrine Concerning Judaism.* **Jefferson: McFarland and Company, Inc., 1992, 304 pp.**
Falk briefly surveys anti-Jewish teachings in Christian theology from the second to the twentieth centuries, including a reproduction of the St. Louis Walch edition (in modern German) of Martin Luther's anti-Jewish essay, *Vom Schem Hamphhoras.* The author argues that the Holocaust was "the outcome, the extension of the theological teachings and Christian laws." He contends that, because Christianity was unable to achieve internal consensus it needed an external threat (the Jews) to survive. Falk concludes, that Christianity "grew to maturity upon renouncing anti-Judaism in the early 1960s."

Farmer, William R., ed. *Anti-Judaism and the Gospels.* **New York: Trinity Press, 1999, 394 pp.**
The essays compiled for this text deal with the topic of when and under what circumstances, the Gospel texts began to serve as tools for disseminating anti-Jewish teachings. It examines whether or not the evangelists were anti-Jewish. The contributors to this text include leading *New Testament* scholars, who share the common objective of presenting the Jewish Jesus against a Jewish background.

Feldman, Louis H. *Studies in Hellenistic Judaism.* **Leiden: E.J. Brill, 1996, 677 pp.**
This collection of essays contains several that note the Christian origins of anti-Jewish attitudes. The anti-Semitic content of the *New Testament* is examined, as are other sources of anti-Jewish feelings. Other Christian, anti-Jewish polemics are studied in an attempt to understand the reasons for and the extent of Christianity's development of hostility toward the Jews in the early period.

Finzi, Roberto. *Anti-Semitism.* **Maud Jackson, Translator. Interlink Publishing Group, Incorporated, 1998, 128 pp.**
Historian, Roberto Finzi, investigates the spread of anti-Semitism over more than one thousand years. He concludes, that this hatred of Jews developed from religious origins, which, over time assumed more secular and modern features. The author asserts, in this succinct history, that for centuries Jews have suffered bloody persecutions borne of prejudice and that even the Holocaust has not completely eradicated the hostility directed at the Jews escape the Nazis.

Flannery, Edward H. *The Anguish of the Jews: Twenty-Three Centuries of Anti-Semitism.* **New York: Paulist Press, 1964, 369 pp.**
This classic account written by a Catholic priest, traces the conflict between Christians ᴄᴏd Jews from the anti-Jewish slanders of St. John Chrysostom in the

fourth century, to the Christian charges of ritual murder, through to the vituperations of Martin Luther against the Jews. The study concludes with the failures of Christians during the Holocaust to help the Jews escape the Nazis.

Foa, Anna. Translated by Andrea Glover. *The Jews of Europe after the Black* *Death.* **Berkeley: University of California Press, 2000, 276 pp.**
Foa focuses on the historical relationship between Christianity and the Jews and the Church's conversionary mission. She argues, that anti-Semitic stereotypes of Jews were first fixed in the fourteenth century, in the aftermath of the Black Death, when a wave of hatred against Jews spread through Europe. Jews were accused of well-poisoning, bearers of syphilis, and other negative fantasies, which carried over to the modern age.

Freudmann, Lillian C. *Anti-Semitism in the New Testament.* **Lanham: University Press of America, 1994, 358 pp.**
The book details how the *New Testament,* for two centuries, has contributed to anti-Jewish attitudes among Christians. It examines the context in which the Gospels were written and how the circumstances of the times affected the content of the *New Testament.* The volume also includes an excellent chapter on Christians using Jews as scapegoats for the Crucifixion of Jesus. Freudmann accuses Paul, as the creator of a new faith divorced from Judaism, with fostering the hatred of Jews.

Fricke, Weddig, *The Court-Martial of Jesus: A Christian Defends the Jews* *Against the Charge of Deicide.* **Grove-Atlantic, Incorporated, 1990, 296 pp.**
Originally published in Germany in 1986, the author, an attorney, argues that most likely the Gospel accounts that recount Jesus' trial before the Jewish Sanhedrin are false. He attempts to finally put an end to the malicious charge of deicide leveled at the Jewish community and insists that those writing the *New Testament* were so eager to smooth relations with the Romans that they played down the role the Romans played in Christ's execution. He also theorizes that Jesus was sentenced and crucified by the Roman's in a "military type proceeding."

Friedman, Jerome. "Jewish Conversion, the Spanish Pure Blood Laws and Reformation: A Revisionist View of Racial and Religious anti-Semitism." Sixteenth Century Journal (1987), Volume 18 Issue 1, pp. 3-30.
According to Friedman, Protestant religious reformers, like Martin Luther, and Jewish rabbis laid the sixteenth century foundations for European anti–Semitism when forming their response to Jews who converted to Christianity. Christian leaders regarded these 'New Christians" as different from themselves and the rabbis rejected them because of their conversion. At the same time the Spanish Inquisition and Spain's pure blood laws from that period gave a firm basis to the idea of racial anti-Semitism.

Gager, John. *The Origins of Anti-Semitism: Attituades Towards Judaism in* *Pagan and Christian Antiquity.* **New York and Oxford: Oxford University**

Press, 1983, 320 pp.
Gager rejects the argument that the roots of anti-Semitism can be found in the ancient world. Instead, he locates the origin of Christian anti-Judaism not in the pervasive hatred of Jews in the Roman world, but in the misinterpretation of Paul by later Christian theologians. The misinterpretation of Paul stems from a reading of his letters by various Christian theologians whereby the Jewish observance of the *Torah* was seen as incompatible with the Christian faith claim of Christ's exclusivity. Gager claims this "exclusivity" is not present in Paul's writings. The author argues, that in its early stages the debate was never between Christians and Jews, but among groups of Christians. Eventually, those promoting the anti-Jewish reading of Paul's works won, and anti-Jewish theology became the normative reading for Christianity as well as for Western culture.

Gavriel, Mardell J. *The Anti-Semitism of Martin Luther: A Psycho-historical Exploration.* Dissertation-Chicago School of Professional Psychology, 1997, 126 pp.
Gavriel proposes that Luther's superstition, "characterological" anger, and anal personality traits may have predisposed him to develop prejudice." The author examines the status of Jews in the medieval era and identifies them as "internal foreigners", those who rejected Christ and were allies of the devil. Gavriel suggests that this depiction of Jews made them attractive targets for Luther, who was beset by unconscious internal conflicts. Luther moved from tolerance for Jews to rage against them, once he realized that his personal constructions about them no longer held since he proved unable to convert them to Christianity.

Gilliard, Frank D. "The Problem of the Anti-Semitic Comma Between 1 Thessalonians 2: 14 and 15." New Testament Studies (October 1989), Volume 35 Issue 4, pp. 481-502.
This article contends that Paul's ideas of Christianity were not meant to be anti-Semitic and today's Christians can reject this interpretation of his teachings. The author maintains, that in the *New Testament* text of Thessalonians, dealing with Paul's condemnation of Jews for their guilt in the Crucifixion of Christ there are two lines in which a comma appears. This comma, argues Gilliard, is the crux of the charge of deicide against "all" Jews, instead of against a particular group within the Jewish community. Gilliard proposes, that these linguistic and grammatical problems can be solved, by simply omitting the comma.

Girard, Rene. "Is There Anti-Semitism in the Gospels?" Interpretation (November 1991), Biblical Volume 1 Issue 3, pp. 339-352.
Girard maintains that the role of the "scapegoat" in religions has historically been used to control violence within society and that Christianity has chosen to reject the "scapegoat" process. Therefore it is not the Gospels, which project anti-Semitism. Rather it is the interpretations of them that promoted anti-Jewish attitudes and this happened because interpreters throughout the centuries have continued to misunderstand the messages.

Goetz, Ronald. "A Precarious Righteousness." Christian Century (August 13, 1997), Volume 114 Issue 23, pp. 725-726.
Goetz reviews the criticisms Jesus reportedly directed at Jews as these are recounted in the Gospel of Mark. The author explains that Christians have used these verses to justify persecuting the Jews. Goetz, however, asserts that Christ never meant for the Jews to suffer and that any mistreatment of them is actually in direct opposition to what he taught.

Goguel, Maurice . *The Birth of Christianity*. H.C. Snape, Translator. New York: Macmillan, 1954, 560 pp.
This volume provides a comprehensive study of the early development of Christianity as a separate religion. Goguel addresses the reasons why Christianity could not continue within the framework of Judaism, and the emergence of the conflict between Christians and Jews once there was a "parting of the ways."

Gold, JudithTaylor and Joseph Gold. *Monsters and Madonnas: The Roots of Christian Anti-Semitism.* New York: New Amsterdam Publishers, 1990, 288 pp.
The authors take an original approach in trying to determine the roots of Christian anti-Semitism by comparing archetypal elements of the Christ story with pre-Gospel religion and classic horror literature. Through these comparisons, they challenge the view of many Biblical scholars that attributes the source of Christian anti-Semitism to the negative and hostile portrayals of Jews in the *New Testament*.

Gow, Andrew Colin. *The Red Jews: Anti-Semitism in an Apocalyptic Age, 1200-1600*. Leaden, and New York: E.J. Brill Publishers, 1995, 420 pp.
Apocalyptic thinking is connected to intensified anti-Jewish feelings in late medieval Western Europe, by the author. The "Red Jews", an imaginary people described in vernacular sources of medieval and early modern German literature, were viewed as a threat to Christendom.

Hall, Sidney G. *Christian Anti-Semitism and Paul's Theology*. Minneapolis: Fortress Press, 1993, 192 pp.
The author maintains that, a great deal of anti-Semitism can be gleaned from the Gospels, and that the roots of the Holocaust can be found in Christian theology as a result of misreading Paul's intentions towards the Jews. In the post-Holocaust era, contends Hall, a new understanding in regard to Paul's theology concerning the Jews is necessary. Hall denies that Paul sought to preach Christ to the Jews but accepted the salvation of the Jews as a fixed pillar in his Christological thinking. Overall, the book traces twentieth-century anti-Semitism back through centuries of Christian use of Paul's letters and theology.

Hare, Douglas R.A. "The Relationship Between Jewish and Gentile Persecution of Christians." Journal of Ecumenical Studies (1967), Volume 4,

pp. 446-456.
The evidence, according to Hare, does not support the thesis that Jews were responsible for inciting Gentiles to persecute the earliest Christians. Additionally, any violence against Christians that may possibly be argued as inspired by Jews was restrained and very limited in scope. The author claims that the accusations of Jews promoting hostility toward Christians were used to further the efforts of Christian leaders, who wished to marginalize Jews and Judaism.

Harkins, Paul W., ed. *St. John Chrysostom: Discourses Against Judaizing Christians.* **Baltimore: Catholic University of America Press, 1979, 299 pp.**
This book reflects the post-Vatican II understanding that Jews bear no collective guilt for the Crucifixion of Jesus. Harkins is condemnatory of Chrysostom's anti-Jewish excesses, but shows no ability to separate Christian triumphalistic claims about the Jews from critical history. This leads him to condemn Chrysostom's anti-Judaism, while at the same time accepting some of the premises upon which it was based.

Hay, Malcolm. *Europe and the Jews: The Pressure of Christendom on the People of Israel for 1900 years.* **Chicago: Academy Chicago Publishers, 1991, 352 pp.**
Using Hitler's concentration camps as a point of departure, Hay leads the reader on a tour of the various ways in which Christianity's hatred for the Jews has affected them for 1900 years. The author demonstrates the slanderous falsehoods that were developed about the Jews throughout the centuries and maintains that sloppy historical scholarship has helped to perpetuate these lies.

Heer, Friedrich. *God's First Love: Christians and Jews Over Two Thousand Years.* **London: Weybright & Talley, 1969, 529 pp.**
To support his thesis that the concepts of Jew-hating and Jew-killing were based upon Christian theology, and taught by the most eminent church fathers, Heer cites anti-Jewish selections from the writings of St. John, St. Paul, St. Augustine, and Martin Luther.

Hellig, Jocelyn L. "The Doctrine of Chosenness: Its Relation to Anti-Semitism." *Waters out of the Well: Essays in Jewish Studies.* **Eds. Reuben Musiker and Joseph Sherman. Johannesburg: University of Witwatersrand, 1988, pp. 11-28.**
Hellig claims, that the "doctrine of chosenness" in Judaism provides a source for anti-Semitism because it is so often misunderstood. Most non-Jews believe that Jews see themselves as "chosen" for God's favor, when in reality they have been chosen for service and suffering. The "doctrine of chosenness" has played an important role for both Jews and Christians. Christianity, in an effort to overcome the idea of the Jews as a "chosen people," provided the foundations for the development of many of the negative stereotypes that are bound up in anti-Semitism. This demonization of Jews eventually led to the Holocaust and persists

even in current times.

___. "The Myth of Jewish Chosenness in the Modern World." Dialogue and Alliance (Fall 1989), Volume 3 Issue 3, pp. 5-16.
The author makes the case, that the "doctrine of Jewish chosenness" has caused the Jews great suffering, for the world perceived them in ways that were destructive. Christianity, in Hellig's view, has distorted this concept and used it to create the theory that it has surpassed Jews and replaced them in God's favor. Christian superiority and hatred of the Jews was founded on the idea that the Jews were responsible for the death of Christ the Redeemer. This hostility toward Jews culminated in the Holocaust. Hellig suggests a connection between the anti-Semitism of the past and the more vocal and violent anti-Zionism of the present.

Holmgren, Fredrick. *The Old Testament and the Significance of Jesus: Embracing Change – Maintaining Christian Identity.* Grand Rapids: Eerdmans, 1999, 204 pp.
This study examines Christianity's claims that Jesus Christ's activities and identity are rooted in *Old Testament* scriptures. It also highlights the Jewish origins of Christianity, and studies the Biblical underpinnings of the Jews existence as a religion that stands on an equal footing with other religious communities.

Hsia, R. Po-Chia. *The Myth of Ritual Murder: Jews and Magic in Reformation Germany.* New Haven: Yale University Press, 1988, 248 pp.
This book examines the persecution of Jews in the Holy Roman Empire from 1470 to 1600. Hsia argues, that during these decades, legends, balads, legal procedures, letters and theological treatises provided the framework for the charges made against Jews of ritual murder, and that these discourses can be best understood as fundamentally contesting Jewish magic to Christian anti-magic. The author concludes, that the charges of ritual murder began to decline during the Reformation, as new discourses in theology and law challenged the ideological foundation of the older ritual murder discourse.

Indinopulos, Thomas A. and Ray Bowen Ward. " Is Christology Inherently Anti-Semitic?" Journal of the American Academy of Religion (June 1977), Volume 45 Issue 2, pp. 193-214.
In their critical review of Rosemary Ruether's book *Faith and Fratricide* Indinopulos and Ward note the positive contribution Ruether has made to the ongoing dialogue between Christians and Jews. However, they take issue with her conclusion that Christianity's anti-Judaic and anti-Semitic attitudes were inspired by the church's Christology and therefore can be changed on an intellectual or theological basis. According to Ward and Indinopulos, political and historical events lay at the heart of Christianity's ongoing struggle with the Jews and the solution to the conflict is practical and can be achieved by deed not intellect.

Isaac, Jules. *Jesus and Israel.* Paris: Albin Michel, 1948, and New York: Holt

Publishers, 1971, 405 pp. (Translated from French)
Isaac argues, that Christianity prepared the way for the Holocaust. In presenting his indictment of Christianity, Isaac reminds us that Jesus was a Jew and that Christianity is the offspring of Judaism. Furthermore he contends, that Jesus did not denounce Judaism in general and that the Christian charge that Jews are collectively guilty of deicide is unfounded.

___. *The Teaching of Contempt: Christian Roots of Anti-Semitism.* **New York: Holt Publishers, 1964, 164 pp.**
This is a companion piece to the author's *Jesus and Israel* (French edition, 1948, translated in English, 1971). In tracing the history of Christian anti-*Judentum*, Isaac finds, that the anti-Jewish trends found in Christian teaching about Jews have no Biblical justification. This is a shorter version of many of the arguments presented in *Jesus and Israel*.

Jocz, Jakob. *Jewish People and Jesus Christ After Auschwitz: A Study in Controversy Between Church and Synagogue.* **University Press of America, 1991, 274 pp.**
According to Jocz,, the end of World War II opened the way to a new era for Jews, the Christian Church and the world. In his view the creation of an Israeli State and the Second Vatican Council are two major events that mark this new beginning. The author claims, that Judaism has gained a new tolerance for Jesus as Jew, just as the Christian world has come to devote its efforts to improving its relationship with the Jews.

Jordan, William Chester. "The Last Tormentor of Christ: An Image of the Jew in Ancient and Medieval Exegesis, Art and Drama." Jewish Quarterly Review (July-October 1987), Volume 78 Issue 1-2, pp. 21-47.
The *New Testament* image of Christ on the cross being offered a sponge dipped in vinegar is the focus of this article. The author proposes, that in Gospel passages the offer of the sponge was a gesture of compassion. Yet during the medieval period this idea was rejected and the terms "vinegar, sponge gall" became synomomous with the idea that the Jewish people and their religious belief were depraved in nature These images cropped up in the literature, paintings and Passion Plays of that time period. The figure of the person offering Christ the sponge was presented in a grotesque manner, often possessing a filthy, hairy and/or dark complexion and was clearly identified as a Jew, even though the Gospels of John and Matthew indicate he was a Roman soldier. This helped bind the idea of evil to Jews in the minds of many uneducated Christians.

Katz, Jacob. *From Prejudice to Destruction: Anti-Semitism, 1700-1933.* **Cambridge: Harvard University Press, 1982, 392 pp.**
Katz maintains, that the Christian tradition of anti-*Judentum* was decisive in the perpetuating anti-Semitism in the twentieth century. He contends that it was Christianity that was responsible for the "pariah" status of the Jews prior to their

emancipation in the eighteenth century, and it was this negative image, which later influenced secular images of the Jew.

Kaufman, Philip S. *The Beloved Disciple: Witness Against Anti-Semitism.* Collegeville, MN.: Liturgical Press, 1991, 71 pp.
This short text maintains that the primary source of Christian anti-Semitism is the allegation that the Jews murdered Christ. The author contends, that the Gospel of John is less accusatory of the Jews than that of Mark or Matthew. He also asserts, that the disciple John used the term "Jews" in relation to the death of Jesus to identify Jewish authorities and not the general population of Jews.

Klein, Charlotte. *Anti-Judaism in Christian Theology.* Philadelphia: Fortress Press, 1978, 188 pp.
A Roman Catholic nun converted from Judaism, the author, theorizes that anti-Semitism in Hitler's Germany was fostered by an anti-Judaism found in both Protestant and Catholic theology. She supports her argument with numerous citations from the *New Testament*, including passages conveying Jewish guilt in the death of Jesus, as well as its condemnation of the legalistic piety of the Scribes and Pharisees, which culminated with their rejection of Jesus as the Christ.

Koltun-Fromm, Naomi. "Psalm 22's Christological Interpretive Tradition in Light of Christian Anti-Jewish Polemic." Journal of Early Christian Studies (1998), Volume 6 Issue 1, pp. 37-57.
The contention is made that early Christian writers have used Psalm 22 and the imagery of "pierced hands and feet" as a foreshadowing of Christ's experience on the cross. Thus the psalm served as one basis for anti-Jewish polemics.

Kosmala, Hans and Robert Smith. *The Jews in the ChristianWorlld* S.C.M, 1942, 173 pp.
This volume claims to address the difficult questions that surround Christianity's "Jewish problem." The authors propose, that due to the Jews belief that they are "God's chosen people" there was bound to be conflict between Synagogue and Church. They also argue, that while Christianity is not "the author of Jewish exclusivity" the church did everything in her power to "widen the gap by acting contrary to God's command to love thy neighbor."

Krow-Lucal, Martha G. " Marginalizing History: Observations on the Origins of the Inquisition in Fifteenth Century Spain by B. Netanyahu." Judaism (Winter 1997), Volume 46 Issue 1, pp. 47-63.
The author focuses upon B. Netanyahu's book about the Spanish Inquisition. Krow-Lucal reviews the origins of the Inquisition and the forced conversion of Jews. Additionally, although Krow-Lucal credits Netanyahu with tremendous research, she feels that some of his conclusions are too simplistic.

Langmuir, Gavin I. *History, Religion, and Anti-Semitism.* Berkeley: University

of California Press, 1990, 380 pp.
The author proposes, that the history of anti-Semitism should be read primarily as the history of Western religiosity, rather than the history of Western religion. Langmuir draws a distinction between religion and religiosity; religion is defined as a social phenomenon, while religiosity refers to the mind-set of the individual. The author makes use of the disciplines of anthropology, psychology, and sociology to study the function of the religious mind. He discusses the methodological problems in the historiography of religion that arose in the course of his research of anti-Semitism in medieval Europe. In one of his more controversial insights, Langmuir draws a parallel between Paul's speculation concerning Jewish disbelief in *Romans* and Nazi speculations concerning Jewish biology. Throughout his work, the author contends that the origin of anti-Semitism and its relationship to Christianity is the touchstone regarding the adequacy of any explanatory scheme.

___. *Toward a Definition of Anti-Semitism.* **Berkeley: University of California Press, 1990, 417 pp.**
This collection of essays presented by the author examines anti-Semitic ideas from the fourth through thirteenth centuries and studies how those ideas have evolved over time. Langmuir distinguishes between irrational anti-Semitism which often has its basis in fabrication or fantasy, and anti-Jewish hatred founded on theological differences. For example, 'some Jews brought about the Crucifixion; all Jews are responsible for it'.

Lazare, Bernard. *Anti-Semitism: Its History and Causes.* **Robert Wistrich (Introduction). University of Nebraska Press, 1995, 200 pp.**
Originally published in France in 1894 with the Dreyfus Affair fresh in the public's mind, Lazare set out to determine the historical causes of anti-Semitism. He begins by considering what might possibly be present in the Jewish character to trigger such hostility and then looks to the nations in which Jews resided to examine the types of hatred and intolerance that were practiced against Jews. Through his study, Lazare concludes that anti-Semitism was based upon fear of the unknown and/or stranger, as well as society's need for a scapegoat in times of stress.

Levenson, John D. "Is There a Counterpart in the Hebrew Bible to New Testament Anti-Semitism?" Journal of Ecumenical Studies (Spring 1985), Volume 22 Issue 2, pp. 242-260.
This article makes the point that the *New Testament* provides the origins for demonizing the Jews. The author contends, that it creates a dualism between the "outdated' world of the Jews and the new "true" religion of Christianity. Levenson shows that Christianity's promotion of itself as new and surpassing Judaism was not new. The author insists, that the Jews engaged in the same sort of activity when they insisted that their faith was superior to that of the Canaanite religion. They justified their claims by misrepresenting the pagan belief and portraying the Amakelites as "evil." Levenson does state that other traditions within the Jewish faith did serve to temper the level of hostility directed toward the Canaanites.

Lieu, Judith M. "History and Theology in Christian Views of Judaism." *The Jews Among Pagans and Christians: In the Roman Empire.* **Eds. Judith Lieu et al. London: Routledge, 1992, pp. 79-96.**
Lieu asserts, that Christianity's portrayal of Judaism at the end of the first century as passive has become an accepted part of Jewish "history" and lends support to Christianity's claim, that God had rejected the Jews and doomed them to suffer. In reality Christian writers of the time felt threatened by the appeal and strength of Judaism and therefore looked for ways to undercut its attraction. Lieu claims, that "Judaizing" Christians were the real targets of writers like John Chrysostom, who denigrated Jewish religious traditions.

Limor, Ora and Gedaliahu Guy Stroumsa, eds. *Contra Iudaeos: Ancient and Medieval Polemics Between Christians and Jews.* **Tuebingen: J.C.B. Mohr, 1996, 290 pp.**
This volume contains some of the papers that were presented at the Tenth World Congress of Jewish Studies held in Jerusalem in 1989. The subjects covered in this collection study the Polemics between Christians and Jews, the Spanish Inquisition, the problems surrounding the *Conversos* and Christian theology in relation to the Jews. The following titles provide an idea of the contents; "From Anti-Judaism to Anti-Semitism in Early Christianity" and "Justin Martyr's *Dailogus cum Tryphone Iudaeo* and the Development of Christian Anti-Judaism."

Lipton, Sara. *Images of Intolerance: The Representation of Jews in the Bible.* **Berkeley: University of California Press, 1999, 241 pp.**
By using the illuminated Bible that was designed in 1225 for the King of France, Lipton investigates representations of Jews' economic activities. She also examines the depiction of Jewish scriptures in relation to Christian learning, the alleged associations of Jews with heretics and other malefactors in Christian society, and their position in Christian eschatology.

Littell, Franklin H. *Historical Atlas of Christianity.* **New York and London: Continuum Publishing Group, 2001, 440 pp.**
The *Historical Atlas* builds upon an earlier volume, *The Atlas History of Christianity,* published twenty-five years ago. In the current book, the author notes the impact the Holocaust, a crime perpetrated by baptized Christians, has had upon the teachings of Christianity. Littell maintains, that many churches have failed to honestly contend with their complicity in the murder of European Jews. This volume is the first "church history" to identify the Holocaust as the origin of a major credibility crisis in Christian history.

Livingston, Sigmund. *Must Men Hate?* **New York: Harper Books, 1944, 344 pp.**
The author argues that anti-Semitism is the result of ignorance or misinformation about the Jews, which the Gentile world has continued to disseminate over the centuries. Livingston exposes the many canards about Jews ranging from attitudes

which existed in the Roman Empire to the medieval blood accusations, and through witchcraft mania, which was closely linked with the hatred and fear of Jews. The author concludes his study of anti-Semitism with the observation that the dislike of the Jews has been caused largely by the fact that the mindset of the present is often nourished by the teachings of the past.

Lowe, Sanford. "What Jesus Did and did Not Say: A New Scholarly Portrait Reveals the Roots of Anti-Semitism." Moment (April 30, 1994), Volume 19 Issue 2, pp. 40-46.
This article reports on the work of a group of *New Testament* scholars known as the "Jesus Seminar." These men have been trying to formulate a consensus about what may or may not be the true activities and words of Jesus Christ. The scholars contend, that many of the anti-Jewish statements attributed to Jesus can be rejected and that anti-Semitism did not originate with Jesus, rather its roots are found in the early church. The findings may greatly influence future readings of the *New Testament* and Jewish-Christian relations.

Ludemann, Gerd. *The Unholy in the Holy Scripture: The Dark Side of the Bible.* Westminister John Knox Press, 1997, 144 pp.
The author notes the "unholy" elements present within the Scriptures. These include the passages that denigrate the Jews and Judaism. Ludemann questions how or why people can continue their commitment to Christianity in light of this darker side to the Bible.

Maccoby, Hyam. "Anti-Judaism and anti-Semitism." European Judaism (Spring 1985), Volume 18 Issue 2, pp. 27-30.
The author ties the anti-Judaism present in the words of Paul's teachings with anti-Semitism. Maccoby points to the portrayal of Jews as instruments of the devil, Satan's agents on earth, and murders of Christ as proof of passages from Paul's writings that contain elements of anti-Semitic stereotyping.

____. *A Pariah People: The Anthropology of Anti-Semitism.* London: Constable Publishing Co., 1996, 236 pp.
The theory put forth by Max Weber, that the Jews were a pariah people, is faulty according to Maccoby, because it echoes the anti-Semitic notion that the Jews were responsible for their alienated status in Gentile society due to their own self-segregation. In making the comparison between the Christian treatment of Jews as pariahs, and anthropological studies of primitive societies, Maccoby finds that in societies where human sacrifice (Jesus) has been practiced, a member of the community (the Jews) must be chosen to slay the victim.

____. *Judas Iscariot and the Myth of Jewish Evil.* New York: The Free Press, 1992, 213 pp.
Myths, Maccoby claims, have such immense ideological power that when they are continually reinforced through cultural and religious traditions, they have a

profound and concrete influence on our lives. Maccoby proposes, that this was true of the myth surrounding Judas Iscariot, whose betrayal of Jesus has been linked to Jews in many Christian renderings. Maccoby finds much of the roots of anti-Semitism in the Western world in this canard, and discusses how this myth, passed down through the centuries, has played a central role in modern anti-Semitism.

_____. **"Who Was Judas Iscariot?" Jewish Quarterly (Summer 1991), Volume 38 Issue 2, pp. 8-13.**
According to Maccoby, the "Judas myth", has greatly influenced the development of Christian anti-Semitism. Judas's image as a betrayer and dark figure is found in the Gospel stories. Though Paul does not relate the story in his scriptural passages the anti-Jewish commentary found in his writings, combined with the story of Judas, helped justify accusations that Jews had "rejected, murdered and betrayed Christ." Later, the Passion Plays provided further assistance in convincing Christians that Jews were to be despised. The idea of Judas's treachery has persisted through the centuries and has become entrenched in modern anti-Semitic attitudes. The author insists, that no matter what the Gospels report it is quite possible that Judas never betrayed Christ, rather he remained a loyal follower of Jesus.

Manuel, Frank E. *The Broken Staff: Judaism Through Christian Eyes.* **Cambridge: Harvard University Press, 1992, 363 pp.**
Manuel describes the manner in which early Christian Hebraists reconstructed Jewish tracts for purposes of shedding light on Christianity, and thus laid the basis for centuries of Christian scholars to redefine Judaism. Judaism, however, was neither lauded as a religion or a field of scholarly study. Rather, in the age of the Inquisition and thereafter, Judaism held the attraction of the forbidden. Church fathers in the fifteenth and sixteenth centuries held that even the study of Judaism would imperil the soul.

Mason, David R. "A Christian Alternative to (Christian) Racism and Anti-Semtitsm." Journal of Ecumenical Studies (Spring 2001), Volume 37 Issue 2, pp. 151-161.
While admitting that the *New Testament* Gospels and 2000 years of Christian anti-Judaism contributed in part to the Holocaust, Mason continues to argue, that these abuses are the result of human failings and that true Christian principles reject racism and anti-Semitism. The author contends, that Christian principles are not triumphalist, or exclusivist. Rather they promote "freedom, justice and good will for all." Mason encourages all Christians to adopt these authentic values and renounce the "demons of anti-Semitism and racism."

Matheson, Peter Clarkson. "Luther and Hitler: A Controversy Reviewed." Journal of Ecumenical Studies (1988), pp. 445.
The argument is proffered that while Martin Luther's writings contained ideas that appealed to National Socialism, and that German Christians were able to use

Luther's works to help justify support for the Nazi regime, any attempt to establish a causal relationship between Hitler and Luther are certain to fail. The author, however, insists that discussion about these points will encourage useful dialogue among Protestants, Catholics and Jews.

McCarthy, Brian Rice. "Reforming the Church's Self-Understanding: The Role of Historical-Critical Studies." Journal of Ecumenical Studies (Spring 1987), Volume 24 Issue 2, pp. 232-253.
In McCarthy's opinion the Christian Churchs' need to respond to the criticisms leveled at them and revise their doctrines and sacred texts. McCarthy asserts, that the Gospels were not written to update or rectify sacred text, but rather because Christianity needed to provide a justification for its claim of superiority over Judaism and the *Old Testament*. The Christian Church encouraged anti-Jewish attitudes by insisting that the Jews had rejected Jesus message. Christianity broke from Judaism by claiming it held the one and only path to salvation and in the process helped create hostility toward the Jews.

McCollister, Betty."Jesus and Caiaphas: The Indelible Libel Against the Jews." Humanist (July-August 1993), Volume 93 Issue 4, pp. 37-40.
Christian anti-Semitism, McCollister insists, is based upon the fictitious claim, that Jews were responsible for the death of Jesus Christ. In support of her contention, the author points out the inconsistencies and problems presented in the Crucifixion story. She also maintains that, until these falsehoods are corrected Christianity lacks moral credibility.

Michael, Robert. "Christian Theology and the Holocaust." Midstream (April 1984), Volume 30 Issue 4, pp. 6-9.
According to Michael, Christian theology is the source of much of the negative mythology that has been used to denigrate Jews over the years. The author makes the case that Christianity also bears responsibility for the Nazis anti-Semitic beliefs.

Mitchell, Nigel B. "Works Righteousness and the Synagogue of Satan: Rethinkiing Christian Caricatures of First Century Judaism." Gesher (November 1996), Volume 1 Issue 5, 7 pp.
Mitchell focuses on the inaccurate portrayals of first century Jews in the *New Testament* by examining some scholarly works that have studied the issue as well as the conclusions that have been drawn from these works. The author agrees with those, who contend that the writers of the Gospels did depict some Jews as Christ-killers, but he denies that the *New Testament* was ever intended as a condemnation of "Judaism or all Jews."

Morais, Vamberto. *A Short History of Anti-Semitism.* Norton Publishers, 1976, 300 pp.
The author presents the history of anti-Jewish prejudice from the ancient Egyptian, Greek, and Roman eras to medieval Christian anti-*Judentum*. Morais then examines

its development into modern anti-Semitism, culminating in the Nazi era.

Netanyahu, B. (Benzion). *The Origins of the Inquisition in Fifteenth Century Spain.* **New York: Random House, 1995, 1384 pp.**
According to the author, the Inquisition in Spain in 1480, which sought to root out *Conversos*, or converted Jews who were allegedly secretly practicing Judaism, had less to do with Christian zealotry than it did with a racial theory, which regarded the *Marranos* Jewishness as an ineradicable contaminant. In postulating that the Inquisition was motivated more by racial considerations than Christian doctrine, Netanyahu views the Spanish persecution of the Jews as foreshadowing later developments in Nazi Germany.

Nibley, Hugh. "Christian Envy of the Temple." The Jewish Quarterly Review (1959-1960), Volume 50, pp. 229-240.
Nibley proposes that Christianity has never been able to settle for the "spiritual Temple or forget the old one (Solomon's Temple)." Christianity reveled in the Jews loss of the Temple and worried that if it were ever reestablished Jews would prove a formidable force. By rebuilding the Temple doubt would be cast on Jesus as "Messiah." Evidence of this is seen in the reluctance of Christian leaders to discuss the issue. Despite this reluctance, the Temple has never lost its power to stir men's hearts and emotions. According to Nibley, for Christians the emotion it stirs is suppressed envy and fear.

Nicholls, William. *Anti-Semitism: A History of Hate.* **Northvale: Jason Aronson, 1997, 532 pp.**
Anti-Semitism, Nicholls claims, is integral to Christianity and he contends that the religion would disintegrate without it. He perceives contemporary anti-Semitism as continuous with the Christian past. He also contends, that the Holocaust is the result of the Nazi secularization of centuries of accumulated Christian hatred toward Jews. The author states, that Christian teaching is primarily responsible for anti-Semitism.

Oberman, Heiko Augustinus. *The Roots of anti-Semitism in the Age of Renaissance and Reformation.* **New York: Fortress Press, 1984, 163 pp.**
The author's primary thesis is that the era of the Renaissance and Reformation did not lay the roots for anti-Semitism, but rather served as a bridge upon which the old medieval tradition of anti-Jewish bigotry was transferred to the modern era. The author effectively rejects the notion that the path to toleration led directly from the Renaissance to the Enlightenment. Oberman argues that Martin Luther, and the convert and anti-Jewish bigot Johannes Pffefferkorn were representative of the age, and that humanists, such as Erasmus of Rotterdam and Johannes Reuchlin who opposed him, nevertheless, shared Pfferfferkorn's sense of the danger of the Jew and Judaism. The author concludes, that Martin Luther's anti-Judaism became the plaything of modern anti-Semitism.

Olson, Stanley. "Does Anything Justify Anti-Judaism? The Evidence of Christian Judaism." *Approaches to Ancient Judaism.* **New Series, Volume 13, Ed. Jacob Nuesner. Atlanta: Scholars Press, 1998, pp. 169-209.**
Olson focuses upon an examination of the first centuries of Christianity. He asserts, that the first century Church accepted the Jewish Law as well as Christian Judaism (those who believed in Christ and followed Jewish law). The author states, that it was not until Gentiles entered the Church that the Jewish Law and Christian Judaism were rejected. He contends that interpreters of Paul's Epistles were mistaken in their belief that Paul preferred Gentile Christians to Jewish followers of Christ. Olson maintains, that by rejecting Jewish Law we reject God. Furthermore, attempts to remove Jesus from his Jewish roots are flawed for they disregard historical fact. According to Olson, the anti-Jewish attitudes, mistakenly adopted by Christianity, have helped promote anti-Semitism and the murder of six million Jews.

Olster, David Michael. *Roman Defeat, Christian Response, and the Literary Construction of the Jew.* **Philadelphia: University of Pennsylvania Press, 1994, 224 pp.**
According to Olster, during the seventh century as the Roman empire continued to collapse, church leaders needed a way to convince fearful Christians that God was still committed to caring for them and that they would survive this time of uncertainty. They accomplished this, in part, by presenting the Jew as more unfortunate than Christians and by making them the "scapegoat" for any problems that Christians suffered. The Jews refusal to accept Christ was a sin and made them the enemy of Christianity and God. Thus Christians could feel reassured by viewing themselves as "superior and better off than the Jewish community."

Ostling, Richard N. "Why Was Christ Crucified?" Time (April 4, 1994), Volume 143 Issue 14, pp. 72-73.
This article examines the theories Father Raymond Brown has put forward about the Crucifixion of Christ in his multi-volume, *The Death of the Messiah.* Ostling discusses the theories of scholars who agree and disagree with Brown's study, as well as the implications that subject has on Jewish and Christian dialogue.

Overman, J. Andrew. *Matthew's Gospel and Formative Judaism: The Social World of the Mathean Community.* **New York: Fortress Press, 1990, 174 pp.**
The assertion of this book is that Matthew's community was but one of many sects within first century Judaism. However, Matthew came to believe he was losing the battle for members in the Jewish population to traditional Judaism so he turned to the Gentile community. Overman claims, that from this conflict an "insider – outsider" mentality developed in the Matthean group.

Pagels, Elaine H. *The Origin of Satan.* **New York: Random House, 1996, 214 pp.**
Pagel traces the origin of the concept of the Devil from the *Old Testament* to the

New Testament. She relates how the writers of the four Gospels condemned as creatures of Satan those Jews who refused to worship Jesus as the Messiah. Writing during and just after the Jewish war against Rome, the evangelists invoked Satan in order to portray their Jewish enemies as God's enemy.

Pawlikowski, John. "Developments in the Liturgy of Holy Week." Common Ground: http://www.jcrelations.net/articl1/pawlikowski.htm
Pawlikowski insists, that all Christians must commit to the positive vision of *Nostra Aetate* by working to strengthen Jewish-Christian relations. One way of doing this is to focus upon and change Holy Week services. The author notes the difficulties encountered when trying to rid Holy Week Liturgy of negative Jewish imagery and suggests that one method is to look at the common bonds Jews and Christians share. He also contends, that, the Jewish historian Ellis Rivkin appropriately felt the emphasis of Holy Week should be shifted from the question of "Who crucified Jesus?" to "What crucified Jesus?"

Pederson, Sigfred, ed. *New Readings in John: Literary Theological Perspectives Essays from the Scandinavian Conference on the Fourth Gospel in Aarhus 1997.* Sheffield Academic Press, Limited, 1999, 289 pp.
Scandinavian scholars provide new studies about the problems related to the Fourth Gospel. This collection addresses a variety of theological issues, including the claim of anti-Judaism in the Gospel, specifically that present in John 8.

Perkins, Pheme. "If Jerusalem Stood: The Destruction of Jerusalem and Christian Anti-Semitism." Biblical Interpretations (2000), Volume 8 Issue 1-2, pp. 194-204.
Perkins points out, that if the Jewish War of 66-70ce had not ended with the destruction of the Jewish Temple, Christian and Jewish history might appear very different. He insists that the war impacted Jewish identity, for it helped promote the idea that God had abandoned the Jews and doomed to them to suffer for their rejection of his son. Perkins claims that the most devastating result of the Jews' loss was the anti-Judaic attitudes that were incorporated into the Gospels and the hostility these texts continue to perpetrate among Christianity's followers. He also contends, that Christians and Jews might never have split apart if the moderate Jews had been able to stifle the uprising, and kept anti-Semitism from infecting the minds of Western societies.

Perry, Marvin and Frederick Max Schweitzer, eds. *Jewish-Christian Encounters over the Centuries: Symbiosis, Prejudice, Holocaust, Dialogue.* New York: Peter Lang, 1994, 440 pp.
Papers given at a New York conference sponsored by Baruch College, CUNY and Manhattan College in 1989 comprise the content of this text. Examples of papers include; Norman Beck's "The *New Testament* and the Teaching of Contempt", Robert Michael's "Anti-Semitism and the Church Fathers" and Teofilo F. Ruiz's "Jews, *Conversos* and the Inquisition of Spain." Other topics addressed in the

volume cover, the portrayal of Jews during the Reformation, The Vatican's response to the Holocaust, Christian thought in the post-Holocaust world and the efforts of Pope John Paul II to achieve reconciliation with the Jews.

Pinson, Koppel S., ed. *Essays on Anti-Semitism.* **New York: Conference on Jewish Relations, 1946, 269 pp.**
This volume consists of a collection of essays on the history of anti-Semitism beginning with its roots in medieval theory and practice. Salo W. Baron, who wrote the introduction, and Hannah Arendt and Waldemar Gurian, who contributed a searing essay on Martin Luther and the intolerant Protestant conception of the Christian state, are among the books contributors.

Poliakov, Leon. *The History of Anti-Semitism: From the Time of Christ to the Court Jews.* **New York: Schocken Books, 1974, 352 pp.**
Poliakov argues, that there are two explanations for anti-Semitism.The first is a supernatural one, whereby Christian hostility towards Jews is in accordance with the will of God. The second explanation is based on a variety of environmental and psychological causes. The book proceeds to examine the history of anti-Semitism in countries such as: England, France, Germany, Poland, and Russia.

Reid, Daniel G. "The Misunderstood Apostle." Christianity Today (July 16, 1990), Volume 34 Issue 10, pp. 25-27.
The author proposes, that the current theories being offered on Pauline Theology are far different than what has been offered in the past. No longer do scholars interpret Paul's words as a rebuke to Judaism, for having "perverted God's covenant with Moses." Currently a number of academics claim we have misunderstood Judaism and Paul's conclusions about the Jewish faith.

Richardson, Peter and David Granskou. *Anti-Judaism in Early Christianity: Paul and the Gospels.* **Wilfrid Laurier University Press, 1986, 240 pp.**
The result of a five-year study on anti-Semitism, this collection of essays attempts to understand what the *New Testament* really means to say about Jews and Judaism when examined and considered within the context of the time it was written.

Rohrbacher, Stefan. "The Charge of Deicide: An Anti-Jewish Motif in Medieval Christian Art." Journal of Medieval History (December 1991), Volume 17 Issue 4, PP. 297-321.
This article studies the depiction of the Jews as the murderers of Christ in pictures produced during the Middle Ages. The author shows that early images of the Passion portrayed the Jews as the murderers of Christ, but the imagery, though understandable, was subtle. According to Rohrbacher, as time passed more grotesque and graphic imagery was used to prove the Jews had betrayed, persecuted and killed Christ. The Passion Plays also contributed to the idea that Jews were evil and guilty of the worst treachery. These awful descriptions of Jews were extremely effective and convinced Christians that Jews and Judaism deserved to be despised.

Rousmaniere, John. *A Bridge to Dialogue: The Story of Jewish-Christian Relations.* **Mahwah and New York: Paulist Press, 1991, 149 pp.**
The author traces the evolution of the confrontation and rivalry of Rabbinic Judaism and early Christianity, from the "heritage of hate," that developed in the Patristic and Medieval Church, to the Nazi's "Final Solution."

Rousseau, Richard W., ed. *Christianity and Judaism: The Deepening Dialogue.* **Montrose: Ridge Row Press, 1983, 217 pp.**
Fifteen essays are included in this volume that deals with the connection between Christianity and Judaism, as the relationship has impacted upon the Holocaust. Included among the contributors are Michael Berenbaum, Eugene Borowitz, A. Roy Eckardt, Edward Flannery, and John T. Pawlikowski.

Rubenstien, Richard E and Michelle Brook. *When Jesus Became God – The Struggle to Define Christianity During the Last Days of Rome.* **New York: Harcourt Press, 2000, 288 pp.**
The author contends that, Church Councils of the fourth century, not the Gospels, determined that Christ was God. Rubenstien details the conflict that erupted between the two camps of Christians during the final days of the Roman Empire, and shows how eventually the Church concluded that Jesus was God, and that anyone who denied his divine nature was a heretic. The author discusses how this theological debate and solution affected Christian attitudes towards Jews and Judaism.

Ruether, Rosemary Radford. *Faith and Fratricide: The Theological Roots of Anti-Semitism.* **New York: Seabury Press, 1974, 303 pp.**
Ruether's basic thesis is that the character of anti-Judaic thinking in Christian tradition cannot be correctly evaluated until it is seen as "the left hand of Christology." *New Testament* writings maintain that, the Jew's rejection of the messianic claim of Jesus turned Judaism into an obsolete religion. According to Reuther, the authors of the *New Testament* and their successors in the patristic period insisted that the basic meaning of the Jewish Scriptures pointed to the coming of Jesus as the Christ. The Jews, in rejecting this interpretation of their sacred writings, confirmed the truth of another set of passages in the Scriptures which predict the apostasy of Israel. The author rejects the notion, that the clash between Christianity and Judaism centered upon the belief that Jesus was the Messiah. Rather, Ruether contends, the conflict arose because the Church erected a new "principle of salvation," whereby salvation was no longer found in any ritual or ethical observance found in the *Torah*, but solely through faith "in the messianic exegesis of the Church and the salvific role of Jesus as prophet-King-Son of man as predicted by the prophets." The Church claimed, that only a community accepting these beliefs could be God's true people.

Runes, Dagobert D. *Let My People Live: An Indictment.*   **New York: Philosophical Library, 1974, 74 pp.**

This slim volume is the highly emotional response of a Jew to Christian anti-Semitism. The author's thesis appears on an unnumbered page, titled "A Word to the Reader." It states: "The *New Testament* contains one-hundred-and-two references to the Jews of the most degrading, malevolent, and libelous kind, thereby creating in the minds and hearts of the Christian children and adults ineradicable hatred towards the Jewish people."

Russell, Jeffrey Burton. *Dissent and Order in the Middle Ages.* **Macmillan Library Reference, 1992, 200 pp.**
Russell provides an overview of the conflict between religious orthodoxy and heresy in the Middle Ages from the Council of Chalcedon (451 A.D.) through to the Protestant Reformation. The author places the debates between those who supported orthodoxy and those who championed dissent into the context of the time and concludes that without this tension Christianity might have died out. Russell's study sheds new light on the topic of how anti-Semitism originated and continued during the Middle Ages.

Rutgers, Leonard Victor. "Attitudes to Judaism in the Greco-Roman Period: Reflections on Feldman's *Jew and Gentile in the Ancient World."* **The Jewish Quarterly Review (January-April 1995), Volume 85 Issue 3-4, pp. 361-395.**
This text offers an analysis of Louis Feldman's works in writing about the relations between Jews and Christians in antiquity. Rutgers discusses the debate among scholars over how much interaction there was among Jews and non-Jews, as well as the conflicts that developed over religious issues. He recognizes Feldman's views as a welcome addition to the research already in place.

Sanders, E.P. *Paul, the Law and the Jewish People.* **Fortress Press, 1983, 227 pp.**
The author examines the problems surrounding Paul's attitude toward Jewish law and his relationship to the Jews. Sanders also addresses the role Paul played in the development of Christianity and examines his use of the scriptures.

Sanders, Jack T. *The Jews in Luke-Acts.* **Philadelphia: Fortress Press, 1987, 428 pp.**
Sanders endeavors to prove, that the author of the *Luke-Acts* was a Gentile Christian writer, who viewed Judaism as hopelessly lost to salvation and violently opposed to God's purpose. Luke, Sander's maintains, was a primary contributor to the later negative Christian images of Judaism. The author contends that Luke has so distorted the role of Jewish authorities in the death of Jesus, that one can read both Luke and *Acts,* and conclude that it was Jewish guards, led by Jewish leaders, who executed Jesus.

____. "The Parable of the Pounds and Lucan Anti-Semitism." **Theological Studies (December 1981), Volume 42 Issue 4. 12pp.**
By using Samuel Sandmel's book, *Anti-Semitism in the New Testament,* as a

starting point, Sanders is able to examine whether or not the Luke-Acts contain passages that are anti-Semitic. He pays special attention to interpreting the Parable of the Pounds and the Jews rejection of Jesus Christ as their Messiah and divine ruler.

Sandmel, Samuel. *Anti-Semitism in the New Testament.* **New York: Fortress Press, 1978, 168 pp.**
Throughout the Gospels Sandmel notes instances of *New Testament* anti-Semitism. His examples include Paul's attitude toward the Law, as well as a steady stream of hostility; sometimes subtle (Luke), and sometimes openly hostile (John).

Schaefer, Peter, Robert Goldenberg and Christine Hayes. *Judeophobia: Attitudes Towards Jews in the Ancient World.* **Cambridge, MA.: Harvard University Press, 1997, 306 pp.**
Several of the chapters in this book address the relationship between Christianity and anti-Semitism. For example; Gavin Langmuir discusses his ideas concerning Christianity's creation of an irrational prejudice through its anti-Semitic attitudes while Peter Schaefer points out, that it was from Egypt that hatred of the Jews was first transported to Syria-Palestine and then Rome. Schaefer contends that Christianity added new elements to the hostility and mistrust already directed toward the Jews. He also suggests, that Roman fears about a Jewish threat that might well instigate change were not so farfetched. Despite any problems between Christians and Jews, Christianity, which had its roots in Judaism, did alter Roman society.

Schiffman, Lawrence H. "At the Crossroads: The Jewish-Christian Schism." Jewish Christian Relations (2001), http://www.jcrelations.net. 8 pp.
Schiffman provides a brief historical account of the events that led to the separation of Judaism and Christianity. The author shows the development of Christianity and how it evolved from a sect within Judaism to become a distinct religious group with its own set of beliefs and practices. He also looks at the growth of animosity between the two faiths.

____. *Who was a Jew? Rabbinic and Halakhic Perspectives on the Jewish-Christian Schism.* **New York: KTAV, 1981, 131 pp.**
The intellectual basis for the split between Judaism and Christianity is examined by the author. It is often forgotten, that during the Roman occupation of Judea, Christianity began as a sect within Judaism. Schiffman points out, that the rabbis tolerated a wide range of diverse views within Judaism, including the messiahship of Jesus. With the ascendance of Gentile Christianity, which rejected *Halakah* (Jewish law), the rabbis no longer viewed Christianity as a denomination within Judaism.

Schussler-Fiorenza, Elizabeth. *Jesus and the Politics of Interpretation.* **New York: Continuum International Publishing Group, 2001, 176 pp.**

The book contends, that those who have written about Jesus over the centuries have, for the most part, portrayed him in their own image. This meant Christ was depicted as male, white and anti-Jewish. Currently, according to Schussler-Fiorenza, those engaged in writing about Jesus stress the need to be objective in researching the "historical" Jesus. Despite their claims, the author concludes they are still affected by their own interpretations and therefore Jesus tends to remain elitist, anti-Jewish and anti-feminist. Schussler-Fiorenza argues that, in order to overcome these deficiencies in the study of Jesus researchers must be subjected to a scholarly critique of the politics involved in interpreting Jesus.

Seiden, Morton Irving. *The Paradox of Hate: A Study in Ritual Murder.* **South Brunswick:** **Yoseloff Publishers, 1967, 258 pp.**
The author offers a psychological explanation for anti-Semitism. Seiden's title, however, is misleading inasmuch as it refers to the actual murder of Jews by Christians, and not the commonplace usage in which Jews were accused of engaging in ritual murder against Christians. The author argues that the Jew represents the primordial father, and more often symbolizes the "guilt through Original Sin", which Christians believe they inherited from Adam, the progenitor of mankind. This belief, contends Seiden, has led to Jews being held accountable for every misfortune which a Christian simultaneously holds himself responsible for. Seiden suggests, that anti-Semitism can be understood as emanating from a mixture of psychology and Christian theology.

Seif, Jeffrey. *Evolution of a Revolution: Ancient Christianity in its Judaistic, Hellenistic and Romanistic Expressions.* **University Press of America, 1994, 184 pp.**
This book traces and examines the Christian faith as a movement within Judaism through to the fourth century. The author studies how Christianity developed its anti-Jewish stance during the centuries in which it evolved into Roman Christianity.

Severus of Minorca Staff. *Severus of Minorca: Letter on the Conversion of the Jews.* **Scott Bradbury (Translator). Oxford: Oxford University Press, 1996, 154 pp.**
A translation and an introduction are provided for this important document that recounts the religious coercion Jews faced in late antiquity when forced to convert to Christianity. The *Letter*, an anti-Jewish writing, offers a depiction of Jewish-Christian relations and proposes reasons for the religious intolerance suffered by Jews in this Mediterranean town early in the fifth century.

Shapiro, James. *Oberammergau: The Troubling Story of the World's Most Famous Passion Play.* **New York: Pantheon Books, 2000, 238 pp.**
Shapiro discusses the history of the passion play, which began its performances in 1643 in a small town in Bavaria. Notorious for presenting Jews as 'Christ killers," and depicting them with demonic imagery, the play was a favorite of Adolf Hitler, who viewed it twice. Shapiro discusses the efforts of Jewish organizations, as well

as the efforts of the Catholic Church, following the Second Vatican Council in 1965, to change the anti-Jewish content of the play.

Sharmis, Michael and Arthur E. Zannoni. *Introduction to Jewish-Christian Relations.* **Paulist Press, 1991, 273 pp.**
The author suggests that this book is best suited for seminarians and college students. The essays included discuss various aspects of Jewish-Christian relations throughout history and the issues that have influenced the contact between the two faith communities. For example, Zannoni writes about Christianity's understanding of the *Old Testament* and the way in which Christians have tried to make Jewish interpretations of the scriptures irrelevant. Michael Cook's essay deals with the anti-Jewishness of the *New Testament* and calls upon Christians to make amends for the pain their prejudices have caused Jews. Michael Mc Garry's work offers a view of the Holocaust as "a tragedy of Christian history." John Pawlikowski's essay concerns Jesus as Jew. Though he defines Christ's differences with the Pharisees, he also points out the positive ties Jesus had to Judaism. Other essays target a variety of issues, that are important to the ongoing dialogue between Jews and Christians.

Shimoni, Gideon, ed. *The Holocaust in University Teaching.* **Oxford: Pergamon, 1991, 279 pp.**
This compilation of essays provides approaches and resources for teaching about the Holocaust in the university setting. Included are several pieces, which address the role that the Christian religion played in the Holocaust. Included are discussions about what theological issues have arisen from the Holocaust and what the responses to the Holocaust were by the Christian Churches.

Sigalov, Pavel. 'About Jewish Guilt in the Death of Jesus and This Theme in East Slavic Literature." *Jews and Slavs*, Volume 4. Eds. Wolf Moskovich et al. Jerusalem: Israel Academy of Sciences and Humanities; Hebrew University, Department of Russian and Slavic Studies, 1995, pp. 63-70.
This article makes the claim, that the charge of deicide made against the Jews makes no sense, since the Crucifixion through Biblical references is shown to be part of God's plan. Therefore, the involvement of the Sanhedrin in Christ's death was ordained by God, as part of his design for mankind's redemption. The author notes examples of Russian and Ukrainian literature that depict Jewish guilt for the murder of Christ.

Siker, Jeffrey S. *Disinheriting the Jews: Abraham in Early Christian Controversy.* **Westminister John Knox Press, 1995, 296 pp.**
The texts from Paul to Justin Martyr are examined in this study of how early Christian writers portrayed the figure of Abraham to Christian communities. Siker maintains, that early Christians retreated from the image of Abraham as the father of both Jews and Gentiles and adopted a view of a Christian Abraham who "abandoned and disinherited the Jews." The author not only provides an analysis of

Abraham's place in early Christianity, but also gives insight into how Christianity moved away from Judaism and how scriptures were reinterpreted to validate the new religious doctrines of Christianity.

Simon, Marcel. *Verus Israel: A Study of the Relations Between Christians and Jews in the Roman Empire (135-425).* **Oxford: Oxford University Press, 1986, 533 pp.**
This is the English translation of a text first published in 1948. The author takes issue with the contention of other scholars that once Jews rejected Christianity the two faith communities had little interaction as they developed alongside one another. Simon asserts, that the Jews' continued efforts to increase their membership and influence after the first century led to inevitable conflicts with Christianity. Polemics were a part of the rivalry that both sides used, but Christianity finally gained the upper hand and anti-Semitism became a by-product of the enmity that followed.

Singer, David G. "Has God Truly Abrogated the Mosaic Covenant? American Catholic Attitudes toward Judaism as Reflected in Catholic Thought, 1945-1977." Jewish Social Studies (Summer-Fall 1985), Volume 47 Issue 3-4, pp. 243-254.
Singer identifies the two tracks of thought about Jews that have developed in Catholic thought, and acknowledges the problems for Jewish-Christian dialogue that arise from these two ideas. Catholics traditionally believed that, with the coming of Jesus, Christianity moved beyond Mosaic Law and that eventually Jews would accept Jesus as the messiah and chose to convert to Christianity. The revision of this line of reasoning, however, holds, that Jesus was a devout Jew and that Christianity has benefited, and still has more to gain from Judaism. The author notes that despite attempts to revise Catholic ideas concerning Jews and the acceptance by most Christians that their religion played a role in promoting anti-Semitism, some traditionalists are troubled by revisionist claims and remain unconvinced that there is a link between the Church and anti-Jewish attitudes.

Skarsaune, Oskar. *In the Shadow of the Temple: Jewish Influences on Early Christianity.* **Inter Varsity Press, 2002, 480 pp.**
Skarsaune provides an analysis and view of the interaction and arguments that took place between Judaism and Christianity in the first centuries after Jesus' Death. He shows the influence of Judaism upon the practices and doctrines of the new religion. He insists, that despite the fact that there were points of conflict that erupted between Jews and Christians, the two faiths should be regarded as older and younger siblings, rather than as enemies. In his view, the perception of a decisive "parting of the ways" has distorted the correct understanding of the relationship during Christianity's earliest years.

Skoog, Ake. "The Jews, the Church and the Passion of Christ." Immanuel (Summer 1987), Issue 21, pp. 89-98.

The author notes the difficulties for Christians in dealing with the role of the Jews in the Crucifixion based upon *New Testament* accounts. Additionally, Christian scholars find it hard to tie the Gospels and Church teachings to anti-Semitism. The author proposes a new way of reading scriptural passages relating to the death of Jesus. He suggests Christ can be viewed as a symbol for the oppressed, and that he was executed for political, not theological, reasons. This allows for the acceptance of a Jewish role in the Crucifixion, while Christians continue to affirm that God, himself, called the Jews.

Snyder, Robert W. "A Voice Against the Flames." America (9/17/2001), Volume 185 Issue 7, pp. 15-17.
Catholic jurist Johannes Reuchlin is the focus of this article. Although Ruechlin showed distaste for Jews, he argued that disputes with them should be handled intellectually, not violently. The jurist also fought against the burning of Jewish books contending, that Christians should learn from these works in that the books provided proof of Christian Faith. His *Recommendation of 1511*, which is viewed today as a "treatise against anti-Semitism, remained controversial for a decade and Reuchlin's writings were condemned by Pope Leo X.

Stanley, David M. "Judaism and Christianity." Thought (September 1962), Volume 37 Issue 146, pp. 330-347.
The "facets of Judaism", which played an important role in shaping the Christian Church are highlighted by Stanley in this article. He attempts to show how Jesus' doctrines, which were presented as a "flowering" of the *Old Testament* religion, became blended with the Pauline doctrine that implies Christianity's superiority to Judaism. Stanley demonstrates through *Old* and *New Testament* passages how the two were tied together so that when the Gentiles identified themselves with Christ then became "true descendants" of the promises made to Abraham and the Jewish people.

Stevens, George H. "The Theology of Anti-Semitism." Christianity Today (April 27, 1962), Volume 6 Issue 15, pp. 17-20.
This text provides a discussion about the reasons offered for anti-Semitism. In all cases the Jews are regarded as different from other people. Stevens insists that scholars must search deeper for the origins of anti-Semitism. The author looks at the use of Jews as "scapegoats" by Christianity prior to and throughout the Middle Ages and before. He insists anti-Semitism is a "theological phenomenon." Christians attempting to evade culpability for the rejection of God in the Garden of Eden, transferred guilt to their scapegoat, the Jews.

Stone, Carole. "Anti-Semitism in the Miracle Tales of the Virgin." Medieval Encounters (November 1999), Volume 5 Issue 3, pp. 365-376.
Stone examines the tales Christians told about Jews during medieval times to reinforce their sense of unity. By creating fantasies about Jews, casting them as the "other" and portraying them in anti-Semitic ways, Christians helped ensure the

survival of their religion.

Taylor, Miriam S. *Anti-Judaism and Early Christian Identity: A Critique of the Scholarly Consensus.* **Leiden: Brill Publishing, 1994, 207 pp.**
Negative references to Jews and Judaism during the second and third centuries, according to Taylor, were products of Christianity's need to challenge Jewish theology, in the face of its claim to universal "triumphalism", and exclusivity. The author argues, that Christianity's antagonism towards Judaism was rooted in "theological ideas rather than as a response to contemporary Jews in the context of an ongoing conflict, and its anti-Judaism became essential to the system of meanings embodied in the symbols which make up the religion properly." In addition to its value for those engaged in studies of the early church, the book also examines Christianity's responsibility for the development of modern anti-Semitism.

Trachtenberg, Joshua. *The Devil and the Jews: Medieval Conceptions of the Jew and its Relation to Modern Anti-Semitism.* **New Haven: Yale University Press, 1943, 279 pp.**
This classic account investigates the manner in which Jews before the Enlightenment were identified with the Anti-Christ, the devil, magicians, sorcery, heresy, and other inveterate enemies of Christianity. Trachtenberg concludes that the "diabolization" of the Jews has its psychological origins in the Middle Ages, and continues to exist in a transmuted form in the present age.

Van Buren, Paul M. *According to the Scriptures: The Origins of the Gospel and of the Church's Old Testament.* **William B Eerdmans Publishing Company, 1998, 151 pp.**
Van Buren insists that it is time for Christianity to reevaluate the role of the *Old Testament* in religious belief. He maintains that the church can claim the *Old Testament* as its own, without challenging the claim of Jews to the sacred Scriptures. The author also concludes, that the Scriptures can debunk several of the myths that have developed about Christianity, such as; Paul was the real inventor of Christianity, or Christianity is less credible if it acknowledges and relies upon its Jewish origins.

Van Paassen, Pierre. *Why Jesus Died.* **New York: Dial Press, 1949, 283 pp.**
According to the author, the events surrounding the death of Jesus have long occupied the minds of Christians. Van Paassen contends that many reject the view that the Jews are responsible for Christ's Crucifixion. Although the author is not as careful about his use of the "facts" as he should be, he does put forward a case that relieves the Jews of responsibility for Jesus' execution.

Voyles, Richard J. "Teaching About Christian Anti-Semitism." **Emory Studies on the Holocaust (1988), Volume 2, pp. 163-180.**
Three Christian theological ideas are presented for examination by the author, who

claims these theories have led to anti-Semitism; the division of the *Old and New Testaments,* the perception of Jew as Christ-killer, and the Jew as a sinner. Voyles insists, that in the aftermath of the Holocaust Christians must renounce anti-Jewish traditions and give affirmation to Judaism so that the historical teaching of contempt can be overcome. The author notes, that Christianity has moved in this direction, but has more to do in order to atone for the past.

Waagenaar, Sam. *The Popes Jews.* **LaSalle: Open Court Publishing Co., 1974, 487 pp.**
Anti-Semitism was not a twentieth century invention, Waagenaar argues, it was a papal and Catholic Italian clerical tradition since at least the fifth century A.D. This book is an overall indictment of the papacy and its attitude toward Jews over the centuries. The author also contends that the number of Italian Jews saved during the Holocaust had little to do with the efforts of the Vatican.

Walker, Daniel. *The First Hundred Years Ad 1-100: Failures and Successes of Christianity's Beginning: The Jesus Movement, Christian Anti-Semitism, Christian Sexism.* **Universe Incorporated; 2001, pp. 279.**
This volume provides a history of the growth of Christianity during the first century. It also addresses the development of anti-Semitism by the followers of Jesus and how this hostility resulted in centuries of discord between Christians and Jews and the growth of sexism in Christianity

Washington, Harold C. "The Lord's Mercy Endures Forever: Toward a Post-Shoah Reading of Grace in the Hebrew Scriptures." Interpretation (April 2000), Volume 54 Issue 2, pp. 135-145.
The author suggests a Biblical framework within which resolution can be reached between Jews and Christians, given the effort by Christians to reject anti-Semitism and repent for past harm done to the Jews. Washington cites *Exodus* 34:6-7, which talks of Divine forgiveness and God's blessings upon all humanity, while Jews retain their position as bearers of "mutual blessings" for differing people and their religions.

Watson, John. *Jesus and the Jews: the Pharisaic Tradition in John.* **University of Georgia Press, 1995, 176 pp.**
In this book Watson argues that a Jewish oral tradition known as "S" is a significant source for the Gospel of John. Watson explores the legal and social circumstance in which the Gospel was written and holds, that whether or not John was a Jew he was "actively hostile toward Jewish religious traditions." Watson maintains that "S" was a Pharisaic account that sought to undermine Jesus' claim to be the Messiah, while still crediting him with the ability to heal and work miracles. The author insists, that John took up this text and re-fashioned it to support his anti-Jewish attitude. Watson's theory links secular and religious law to the narrative of Jesus and places theology in the context of history.

Wilken, Robert L. *John Chrysostom and the Jews: Rhetoric and Reality in the Late Fourth Century.* **Berkeley, Los Angeles: University of California Press, 1983, 207 pp.**
Wilkens shows, that following the Jewish revolt in the first and second centuries, Jewish communities in their homeland and in the *Diaspora* which remained strong in their commitment to Judaism, also remained attractive to non-Jews. Chrysostom's smears and malicious attacks against Judaism reflected his awareness that if Judaismwere allowed to continue to appear as a self-confident religious community, it would belie Christianity's claim to be the true Israel. It could also show, that the Jews had not severed their covenant with God. Thus Chrysostom's anti-Judaism, according to Wilken, was predicated on his refusal to take Judaism seriously, and his desire to keep from calling into question the truth of the Christian faith.

Williamson, Paul. **"Abraham, Israel and the Church."** **The Evangelical Quarterly (April 2000), Volume 72 Issue 2, pp. 99-118.**
In Williamson's theory, the Jews and Israel are regarded as a national entity while Christianity is the international manifestation of God's promise to Abraham. The Apostle Paul goes so far as to suggest that in fact Christianity is the climax of that promise. The author claims, that the *Old Testament* foreshadowed the *New* just as the national community of Israel anticipated the international community of Christianity. He suggests that both books of the Bible "complement each other's witness to salvation history."

Wilson, Marvin. **"A History of Contempt: Anti-Semitism and the Church and How they Grew."** **Christianity Today (October 7, 1988), Volume 32 Issue 14, pp. 60-65.**
This article covers two thousand years of the "teaching of contempt" that Christians directed toward Jews. Wilson contends that the Holocaust "did not occur in a vacuum", but rather was the culmination of anti-Jewish feelings long promoted by Christianity. The author suggests that the Holocaust happened because the church had forgotten its "Jewish roots."

Wilson, Stephen G. *Related Strangers: Jews and Christians, 70-170 C.E.* **Minneapolis: Fortress Press, 1995, 416 pp.**
The author challenges those historians who date the separation of Christianity from Judaism to the rupture, which followed the destruction of the Temple in 70C.E. Wilson contends, that is was not Bar Kochba's Revolt (132-35), and the failure of Christians to join the revolt against Rome which precipitated the parting of the ways, but the teachings of Melito, the second century Christian theologian. According to Wilson, it was Melito's teaching, with his consistently anti-Jewish interpretation of the Passover and his charge of deicide, which pointed the way to the hostility between the early Christians and the Jews.

Wistrich, Robert Solomon. **"Martin Luther and the Jews."** **Jewish Quarterly**

(Fall 1983-Winter 1984), Volume 31 Issue 1, pp. 37-40.
According to Wistrich, Martin Luther's intense anti-Judaism had its origins in the Gospels, especially the teachings of Paul. In studying Martin Luther's ideas in relation to the Jews, Wistrich, highlights the view of Heiko Obermann that Luther's anti-Judaism must be viewed in the context of his fight to renew the church and the Christian flock, and must be countered. Thus the psalm served as one basis for anti-Judaism.

Wolfe, Robert. *Christianity in Perspective.* New York: Memory Books, 1987, 329 pp.
The claim made by Wolfe, is that Christianity will never put aside anti-Semitism until it drops the practice of the Eucharist. Wolfe supports his theory by examining the origins of Christianity and pointing out its reliance upon the influence of Judaism and other religions. He maintains, that the Eucharistic ritual is premised upon the idea of Jesus' divine nature and serves to justify "the pretense of eating the Jew." Wolfe asserts, that this symbolic destruction of the Jews grew out of Christianity's need to reinforce itself by sacrificing the Jews and that the way in which the Eucharist brutalizes the Jews helped set the stage for the persecutions that followed, including the Holocaust.

_____. *Dark Star.* New York; Memory Books, 1984, 266 pp.
Wolfe emphasizes the role of the Jews in history. He provides details concerning their contributions to society. The author also presents an overview of the origins of anti-Semitism and discusses how Christian and non-Christian Gentiles have been conditioned to think about Jews by anti-Semitism.

Zeitlin, Solomon. *Who Crucified Jesus?* New York; Harper, 1943, 240 pp.
The conclusion reached by Zeitlin in this study is that the Jews and their leaders should be absolved of any responsibility for the death of Jesus. The author's exhaustive research leads him to identify a group of Gentile political leaders who conspired with Pontius Pilate to rid themselves of a man (Jesus) they considered a danger to their power.

Zukier, Henri. "The Essential "Other" and the Jew: From Anti-Semitism to Genocide." Social Research (Winter 1996), Volume 63 Issue 4, pp. 1110-115.
Zukier maintains that it is in the context of its struggle with the Jews that Christianity has found a way to define itself and therefore Jews have been cast as the classic "other." The church's teaching of a "universalistic doctrine" has taught followers of Christ to think in terms of all of humanity rather than in segments of the population. Because of this approach, Jews could be cast as "anti-human." In western civilization the Jew has remained the easiest and most available object for derision and exclusion.

2

From Anti-Judentum to Anti-Semitism

Implicit in the emancipation of the Jews, which began in France during the French Revolution and spread to other European countries in the nineteenth century, was the belief that the Jews would dissolve their collective identity and assimilate within Christian society. Most Jews, however, maintained their group identity. There were exceptions such as those who converted to Christianity or rejected their Jewish ancestry for involvement with causes on the Left of the political spectrum. In Germany, the majority of Jews continued to identify themselves by religion. Thus many of their enemies contended that by maintaining their corporate identity the Jews had betrayed the conditions of emancipation. Indeed, given the fact that centuries of Christian negative stereotyping of Jews had not disappeared, it is unsurprising that the existence of a thriving and vibrant Jewish community in much of Europe brought about a negative reaction.

The cliché "old wine in new bottles" is appropriate in describing the emergence of the new type of prejudice towards Jews in the nineteenth century. Unlike the older Christian anti-Judentum, which linked Jews with the diabolic, the new form of Jew-hatred substituted secular categories for religious stereotypes. Drawing on a crude interpretation of Darwinism, Jews were now defined as a racial group bent on world

domination. Instead of grouping Jews as followers of Satan, they were now accused of conspiring to rule over the world. First published in 1903, the Czarist forgery known as the *Protocols of the Elders of Zion* purported to describe a meeting of rabbis plotting a strategy, which would engulf the civilized world by conflict, from which the Jews would emerge triumpha
nt by participating on both sides of the expected struggle. In light of the accusations against Jews found in the *Protocols* it is little wonder that the later Nazi canard, that Jews were behind both international finance and the Bolshevik Revolution, although seemingly a contradiction, made perfect sense. From Henry Ford to Adolf Hitler, the belief was that Jews were conspiring to destroy Christian civilization and that only by taking strong measures against the Jews could the impending Jewish triumph be prevented.

Fear and hatred of Jews was placed within the context of the racial science that dominated much of European thought in the late nineteenth century. Indeed, it was a member of the German Reichstag, Wilhelm Marr, who made the claim in 1879 that the danger to Gentile Europe came not from the Jewish religion, but from the Jewish race. Marr used the term anti-Semitism to distinguish between the old type of anti-Jewish hatred, based on religion, and the new form of prejudice based on race. Marr's anti-Semitism was reinforced by the publication of Houston Stewart Chamberlain's work, *The Foundations of the Nineteenth Century (*1899), which argued that the history of humankind was one of struggle between the Aryan race and the Semites. The Jewish Semites, Chamberlain charged, were the enemies of the Aryan race and threatened Aryan superiority. Although historically the Aryan race had been successful in defeating the Semites on the battlefield, the argument maintained that in one area they had suffered a resounding defeat. *Volkisch* or racial anti-Semites pointed out that although physically superior to the Semites, the Aryan race had been conquered by the Semitic spirit in the form of Christianity.

Christianity was viewed as a Semitic import, which had weakened the fabric of the Aryan race by virtue of introducing moral commandments, which protected the weak from the strong. In Germany, distortions of the works of the German philosopher Frederick Nietzsche were invoked to make the claim that the nation required a superman who would restore the true natural order of things, whereby, the strong ruled over the weak. This natural order would function without the recourse to mercy or compassion preached in the Judeo-Christian tradition. Christianity was viewed by many of these racial thinkers, especially in Germany, as a form of Judaism for the Gentiles, and they were determined to break the hold of both Jews and Judaism on the Aryan race.

No European anti-Semite synthesized these Aryan racist themes more than did the German composer Richard Wagner. For many, his operas invoked a pre-Christian German religion, wherein the Jews, disguised as disfigured characters, are portrayed as the enemy. In his opera *Parsifal*, Wagner combined the imagery of race with Aryan Christianity, when he invoked the silver chalice, which Jesus drank from during the Last Supper. Only now, the imagery substituted the wine for blood and Wagner's Knights were sworn to protect the chalice, which contained the blood of race. Wagner's Ring operas, as well as *Parsifal*, were among Hitler's favorites. Hitler was inspired by Richard Wagner's works and to show his admiration for the operas he promoted the Wagner festival in Bayreuth. It is not an exaggeration to say that the composer was the muse of the Third Reich.

German mainstream Christians were not part of the efforts of *Völkisch* anti-Semites to create an Aryan form of Christianity and an Aryan Jesus Christ, even though both the Catholic Church and the Protestant denominations in Germany continued to perpetuate their own anti-Semitic attitudes. Early on the more liberal Protestant churches had anticipated that emancipation would lead to the mass conversion of German Jews to Christianity, but when this failed to materialize they continued to espouse the traditional forms of anti-*Judentum*. Therefore, on the eve of the Nazi seizure of power in 1933, German Jews could look for little help from the established Christian churches against the mounting anti-Semitic campaign directed towards them by the new Hitler government.

The books listed in this chapter include works that deal with the period from the Enlightenment to1932, the year before the Nazi seizure of power. The volumes focus on the subtle evolution from Christian anti-*Judentum* to *Völkisch* or racist anti-Semitism which, during the Third Reich, promoted the idea of an Aryan Jesus Christ, and a Christianity void of any Jewish symbols or traditions.

Abraham, Gary A. *Max Weber and the Jewish Question: A Study in the Social Outlook of his Sociology.* **Urbana: University of Illinois Press, 1992, 319 pp.**
Abraham has written a study of Weber's views on Jews and Judaism. The author contends, that Weber was a nationalist who, though tolerant of German Catholics, ethnic Poles, and Jews, asserted that they were all guests in Germany, and because of this status, were outcasts who clung together to survive. This belief was especially true of Jews, who possessed a pariah status throughout their history. Weber, according to Abraham, found the Jewish desire to maintain their group identity intolerable.

Abrahamson, Henry Maurice. "A Ready Hatred: Depictions of the Jewish Woman in Medieval Anti-Semitic Art and Caricature." American Academy for Jewish Research: Proceedings (1996), Volume 62, pp. 1-18.
The intertwined relations between misogyny and theological anti-Semitism as they affected the representation of Jews in medieval art and caricature are the focus of this article. During this period there were three major themes depicted: the Jewish woman as the mutilator of Jesus, the portrayal of the Synagogue as a blind and

unfaithful female figure and/or whore, and the bestial woman. Eventually the portrayal of Jews and Judaism as women declined, but the author notes that it remains unclear why this change occurred.

Abulafia, Anna Sapir *Christians and Jews in Dispute: Disputational Literature and the Rise of Anti-Judaism in the West.* **Brookfield, Vermont: Variorum, Ashgate Publishing Company, 1998, 310 pp.**
According to Abulafia, the "role of reason" is a striking aspect of the conversion process in medieval Christianity. The author notes, that as the "literature of debate" grew between Christian and Jew, the approach of rational argument proved less convincing. Most of the eighteen articles included in this volume deal with the literature of religious debate, and focus on the way in which Christianity attempted to link the emphasis on rational argument to the growth of anti-Judaism. The author insists, that the debate literature was defensive in nature, and widened the gap between Christians and those they regarded as non-believers.

____. *Religious Violence Between Christians ands Jews: Medieval Roots, Modern Perspectives.* **Palgrave Global Publishing, 2001, 205 pp.**
From medieval to modern times, the author examines the history of dispute between Christians and Jews, in order to bring about a better understanding of the relationship. She provides some new perspectives in the field by using documents made available through the newly opened Soviet archives.

Adler, H.G. *The Jews in Germany: From the Enlightenment to National Socialism.* **London: University of Notre Dame Press, 1969, 162 pp**.
This book is an indictment of the indifference shown by humanists and liberals (including churchmen) to the rise of anti-Semitism in pre-Hitler Germany. For the most part, liberals believed that assimilation was the best response to anti-Semitism. The book traces the response of European liberals to Jewish emancipation, which is best summarized in a speech made by Clermont-Tonnere in the French Revolutionary Assembly. In his speech he demanded that France "refuse everything to the Jews as a nation, yet grant Jews everything as individuals."

Alexander, Philip S. "The Origins of Religious and Racial Anti-Semitism and the Jewish Response" The Jewish Enigma Series: An Enduring People, 1992, pp. 169-195.
Alexander writes about the development of anti-Semitism. He dates the origins of modern anti-Semitic attitudes to pre-Christian times. Yet, he does not exonerate Christianity in promoting anti-Semitism. Rather he examines the early Christian belief that it had replaced Judaism in God's favor, focuses on the branding of Jews as murders of Christ, studies the medieval Christian view of Jews as "ritual murderers and devils", and finally looks at the anti-Semitic themes that were repeated d··ring the Protestant Reformation. The author notes the decline of

religious fervor that accompanied the Enlightenment. He also highlights the change to more modern forms of anti-Semitism during the Industrial Revolution. Alexander claims, that the Jewish responses to anti-Jewish attitudes included assimilation, conversion, the *Haskalah* and Reform movements, Jewish nationalism, revolutionary socialism and for many Jews the decision to leave Europe.

Altmann, Berthold. *Studies in Medieval German Jewish History*. New York: American Academy for Jewish Research, 1940, 94 pp.
The author asserts, that as late as the eleventh century Jews were free, respected and privileged in Western Europe. However, their freedoms were severely curtailed by the thirteenth century, and they had no rights left by the fourteenth century. Altmann argues, that the cause for the change in the Jews' circumstances arose from the medieval town's growing autonomy and struggle for power. The citizens of the town needed to expand their territory and jurisdictional control. The Jews property rights hampered their efforts. The author asserts, that the people in these towns justified their attacks upon Jews through Christianity's negative teachings. Robbing the Jews of their property and rights was acceptable because they were "evil" and the "murderers of Christ." Those in the Jewish community were forced to trade away their privileges in exchange for protection.

Arendt, Hannah. *The Origins of Totalitarianism, Pt. 1: Anti-Semitism.* New York: Harcourt Brace Jovanovich, 1973, 527 pp.
In this text, Arendt puts forth a controversial theory about the rise of anti-Semitism in nineteenth century Europe. She concludes her study with an analysis of the institutions, organization, and operation of totalitarian movements and governments. Arendt places most of her emphasis on examining Nazi Germany and Stalinist Russia.

Armstrong, Karen. *Holy War: The Crusades and Their Impact on Today's World.* London: Macmillan, 1988, 452 pp.
Armstrong's examination of the Crusade's highlights several important points. She proposes, that the Crusades, like other Holy Wars was a part of the pattern of aggression and violence that often emerged when one religion felt insecure and threatened by another. She contends, that this Holy War concept is inherent in the Biblical tradition of monotheistic religions. The author notes, that despite the disapproval of the official church, Crusaders persecuted the Jews and depicted both Jews and Muslims as demons. Armstrong ties the Crusades to the conflicts in the Middle East today, and to the anti-Semitism that has developed in the Islamic world. This book has been published under the same title in a revised edition (New York: Doubleday, 1991, 628 pp.)

Arnold, Ages. "Prelude to the Holocaust." Jewish Exponent (March 21, 1996), Volume 199 Issue 12, pp. 9

This article explores the research that has recently been done on the documentation and record of the Catholic Church during the Inquisition. The author regards the Inquisition as a prelude to the murder of six million Jews during the Holocaust. Arnold maintains, that while the Nazis' policies against the Jews took twelve horrible years to unfold, the Catholic Church targeted Jews and others for over four hundred years during the Inquisition.

Aschheim, Steven E. *Brothers and Strangers: The East European Jew in German and German Jewish Consciousness, 1800- 1923.* **University of Wisconsin Press, 1999,364 pp.**
The history of the development of German Jewish attitudes and stereotypical images about Eastern European Jews are traced in this book. Ascheim demonstrates the ways in which the historic rupture between Eastern and Western Jewry evolved as a function of modernism and its imperatives.

Bach, Hans Israel. *The German Jew: A Synthesis of Judaism and Western Civilization 1730-1930.* **Oxford: Oxford University Press, 1984, 255 pp.**
This text includes an introduction, which details the existence of Jews during the Middle Ages. It also deals specifically with the Catholic, and later the Protestant, Churches' attitude toward the Jewish people and Judaism. The author explores the struggle for Jewish Emancipation, and then offers a more in depth approach to the study of Jews living in Germany from 1730-1930. Bach covers the rise of political and other modern forms of anti-Semitism, and remarks on the response of Christian Churches to the growing incidence of German anti-Semitism.

Bacharach, Walter Z., Chaya Galai, Translator. *Anti-Jewish Prejudices in German- Catholic Sermons.* **Edwin Mellen Press, 1993, 204 pp.**
Bacharach examines German-Catholic sermons for evidence of anti-Jewish invective. His book includes chapters that analyze the ways in which sermons helped form the image of Jews as inhuman, and as the anti-Christ. The author also studies how these images, used in preaching, were developed over the centuries, and the influence that these sermons had in producing an atmosphere in which the Holocaust could take place.

Baldwin, Neil. *Henry Ford and the Jews: The Mass Production of Hate.* **Public Affairs Press, 2001, 416 pp.**
Readers of this book are reminded that Henry Ford, often hailed as an exemplary American entrepreneur, was also a bigot. Ford's hatred of the Jews prompted him to sponsor such notable anti-Semites as Father Coughlin and Reverend Gerald K. Smith. Ford was also responsible for disseminating the scurrilous *Protocols of the Elders of Zion*, which accused the Jews of conspiring to gain control of all countries.

Behre, Patricia E. "Raphael Levy: A Criminal in the Mouths of the People." Religion (January 1993), Volume 23 Issue 1, pp. 19-44.
An examination is provided of a 1670 criminal case that took place in France, wherein a Jewish peddler was accused of kidnapping a Christian child for the purpose of "ritual murder." Behre shows how broad the segment of Christians was, who willingly came forward to accuse the peddler, despite the lack of any true evidence. The author makes the argument that religion and religious imagery played a key role in inciting the prejudice of non-Jews against all Jews, guilty or innocent.

Bein, Alex. "Modern Anti-Semitism and the Meaning of the Jewish Question." Vjh. Zeitgesch (October 1958), Volume 6 Issue 4, pp. 340-360.
The article proposes that Hitler did not invent the idea of a "Final Solution" for Jews, rather he put into practice views that had been expressed and defended in the nineteenth century by authors such as Marr, Gobineau, Chamberlain and Drumont. These writers advanced the "scientific" image of Jews as a racial group that could not change and were as a source of contamination for non-Jews. Given the fact that Jews were inherently unable to change, the only way to deal with their presence was to eradicate them.

_____. *The Jewish Question: Biography of a World Problem.* New York: Herzl Press, 1990, 784 pp.
Christianity's influence in the development of anti-Semitism, the formation of the ghettos, anti-Jewish legislation, pogroms, persecution of the Jews, and Martin Luther's anti-Jewish writings are just a few of the topics covered as Bein traces the origins and developments of the so-called "Jewish Question " in Europe. The author examines how this "problem" resulted in the growth of modern forms of anti-Semitism in the nineteenth and twentieth centuries. Bein also studies the various reactions Jews have had to anti-Jewish attacks and their responses to the different phases of Hitler's anti-Jewish policy and the Holocaust.

Bereswill, Mechthild and Leonie Wagner. "Public or Private: Anti-Semitism and Politics in the Federation of German Women's Associations." Journal of Genocide Research (June 1999), Volume 1 Issue 2, pp. 157-168.
The authors present a detailed review of the 1915-1916 conflict that erupted between two factions within the Federation of German Women's Organization. According to the authors, disagreement between The General German Women's Association and the Jewish Women's League was more than a problem over personalities. Rather the anti-Jewish feelings expressed by the Women's Association were based on Christianity's tradition of anti-Judaism. The non-Jewish women's groups believed the Jewish Women's League had a disruptive effect on the unity of German women.

Berger, David. *From Crusades to Blood Libels to Expulsions: Some New*

Approaches to Medieval Anti-Semitism. **Annual Lecture of the Victor J. Selmanowitz Chair of Jewish History (2). New York: Touro College Graduate School of Jewish Studies, 1997, 29pp.**
In this essay, Berger examines the theories that Jeremy Cohen, Gavin Languor and Israel Yuval have proposed, in their efforts to explain why during the eleventh and twelfth centuries the attitudes of Western European Christians hardened toward the Jews. Berger studies the areas of agreement and disagreement among the three writers whose work he has chosen to present.

Bering, Diets. *The Stigma of Names: Anti-Semitism in German Daily Life, 1812-1933.* **Ann Arbor: University of Michigan Press, 1992, 345 pp.**
Until the early nineteenth century, most Jews in Central Europe did not have surnames, but were known to one another by their given names and by the names of their paternal ancestors. Bering demonstrates how the German population was able to identify Jews by virtue of name changes. As a consequence German Jews, who sought to change their names for purposes of assimilation, often found themselves objects of anti-Semitic slander by a prejudiced population that despised them and refused to accept them.

Blobaum, Robert. "The Politics of Anti-Semitism in Fin-de-Siecle Warsaw." Journal of Modern History (June 2001), Volume 73 Issue 2, pp. 275-307.
The article details the development of political anti-Semitism and ties it to the rise of radical nationalism, as well as to the dislocation that was felt with the onset of a capitalist economy in Central and Eastern Europe. These political and socioeconomic changes prompted a Christian boycott of Jewish owned shops in Warsaw in 1912. The author discusses the intended and unintended consequences of this boycott, and the role of the Catholic Church hierarchy in promoting it.

Blumenthal, W. Michael. *The Invisible Wall: Germans and Jews, a Personal Exploration.* **Washington D.C.: Counterpoint Books, 1998, 444 pp.**
The author, the former Secretary of the Treasury under President Jimmy Carter, and a refugee from Nazi Germany, recreates the history of Germany over the past several centuries from the perspective of his German-Jewish ancestors. He concludes, that there is little in German history to prove that a majority of the German people would have condoned the mass murder of the Jews.

Borchmeyer, Dieter, Stewart Spencer, trans. *Richard Wagner: Theory and Theatre* **New York: Oxford University Press, 1991, 444 pp.**
This study of the intellectual sources of Wagner's dramatic and poetic ideas, especially the inspiration that he drew from the Bible, does not significantly increase our understanding of the composer's political ideas. Despite the lack of new information, the author is defensive about the subject of Wagner's anti-Semitism.

Boyer, John W. *Culture and Political Crisis in Vienna: Christian Socialism in Power, 1897-1918.* **Chicago: University of Chicago Press, 1997, 702 pp.**
Boyer studies the Christian Socialist movement after Carl Lueger's rise to power in Vienna in 1897. The groups' opportunistic use of anti-Semitism and demagoguery to gain and retain power made them an insidious influence in Austrian politics. Boyer uses archival sources to show how these conservative politicians marginalized the Jews, along with other components of Austrian society.

Bronner, Stephen Eric. *A Rumor About the Jews: Reflections on Anti-Semitism and the Protocols of the Learned Elders of Zion.* **New York: St. Martin's Press. 2000, 160 pp.**
The Protocols of the Learned Elders of Zion, an infamous Czarist police forgery, is examined by Bronner. *The Protocols* was purported to have recorded the text of a secret plan formulated by the Jews to enslave Christian civilization. The author views the tract as the secular counterpart to the Christian belief, that Jews were the followers of the devil. Instead of belonging to the minions of Satan, the Jews of the modern age were cast as agents of progress. In explaining the willingness of personalities, such as Henry Ford, Ezra Pound and Adolf Hitler, to accept the veracity of *The Protocols*, Bronner argues that the forgery drew its credibility from a fear of democratic progress and modernity that was also infused with the paranoid fantasies of religious myth.

Brunner, Constantin. *The Tyranny of Hate: The Roots of Anti-Semitism.* **New York, and Lampeter: Edwin Mellen Press, 1992, 208 pp.**
Brunner examines the hatred of Jews through a psychological approach. The author deals with both the religious and secular prejudices that, over time, were perpetrated by the Germans against the Jews.

Canepa, Andrew M. "Pius X and the Jews: A Reappraisal." Church History (1992), Volume 61 Issue 3, 14 pp.
Pius X, in Canepa's opinion has either been neglected, or has received some unfair condemnation. While Canepa quickly admits that the pope's record in connection with the Jews is "less than exemplary", he claims that when viewed in a fuller context, Pius's episodes of anti-Jewish activity are hardly enough to accuse him of being hostile toward the Jewish people. In support of this contention, the author attempts to demonstrate that throughout his religious career, Pius viewed Jews in a positive manner. He had warm relationships with members of the Jewish community, defended the Jews from violence and was committed to ending a twenty year long anti-Semitic campaign that had been started by earlier clerics.

Cano Perez, Maria Jose. "Anti-Semitism in the Hispanic-Hebrew Tradition: Its Reflections in the Medieval Jewish Chronicles." *Europe at the Close of the 20th Century: International Symposium Christianity-Judaism-Islam.* **Fedor Gal,**

Jitka Pusova. Prague: European Culture Club, 1994, pp. 53-69.
By studying the medieval Hebrew chronicles that recount the existence of Jews in Spain, the author helps the reader to understand how Jews viewed the anti-Semitic conditions they experienced at the hands of their Spanish neighbors. According to Cano Perez, Christianity played a role in perpetuating the intolerance leveled at Jews. Due to religious and social ignorance, Jews became the victims of forced conversions, blood libel accusations, and attacks on their communities.

Carlebach, Elisheva. *Divided Souls: Converts from Judaism in Germany, 1500-1750.* Yale University Press, 2001, 336 pp.
The author focuses upon Jewish converts to Christianity in Germany, from the sixteenth through the mid-eighteenth century. He examines the place of converts in Jewish history and Christian society, and contends they played an important role in helping to shape the image of Jews (both negative and positive) for Christians. Carlebach looks at the converts' futile search for community in both groups. He maintains that Christians regarded Jewish converts as "baptized, but not truly converted." The author also discusses the terrible legacy these converts faced in Germany.

Chazan, Robert. *European Jewry and the First Crusade.* University of California Press, 1996, 380 pp.
Chazan's book describes the Christian Crusade of 1096 and the belief of the Crusaders that they were to " massacre or forcibly convert Jews" in the communities they passed through on the way to Jerusalem. The author attempts to help the reader understand the actions and thoughts of both the persecuted Jews and their Christians attackers during this period.

Cheyette, Bryan H. "The Other Self: Anglo-Jewish Fiction and the Representation of Jews in Engalnd 1875-1905." *The Making of Modern Anglo-Jewry.* ed. David Cesarini. Oxford: Blackwell, 1990, pp. 97-111.
This chapter of Cesarini's text examines the ideas of English writers who were intent on solving the "Jewish Question" in England by insisting upon total assimilation. Cheyette notes that these writers in an effort to make Jews acceptable for English society, attempted to revise the traditional stereotypes of Jews, many of which had been produced by Christianity. One of the English writers studied (Julia Frankau) saw Christianity as the "only way to overcome Jewish distinctiveness." Cheyette shows that ultimately the goal to totally assimilate the Jews into English society proved unattainable.

Chism, Christine. "The Siege of Jerusalem: Liquidating Assets." The Journal of Medieval and Early Modern Studies (Spring 1998), Volume 28 Issue 2, pp. 309-340.
A poem written in an English monastery, in the late fourteenth century, is the focus

of this article. Chism contends the poem "The Siege of Jerusalem" was written to lessen the concerns Christians had about the Crusades. The author suggests, that it may have been produced after a defeat suffered by Crusaders in 1396. Chism recounts the contradicting themes of the poem. On one hand the poet calls for the destruction of Jews as a revenge for the death of Jesus, while at the same time he insists that Jews, enslaved and exploited, could help Christians to unite spiritually and physically.

Claman, Harry. *Jewish Images In Christian Art: Art as the Mirror of the Jewish-Christian Conflict, 200-1250 CE.* **Mercer University Press, 2000, 212 pp.**
This survey of one thousand years of Christian art ties the theology of Christianity to the negative attitudes Europeans held toward Jews and Judaism. Claman demonstrates the ways in which the Church used derogatory depictions of Jews in art as tools for effective education and control of the Christian laity.

Clark, Christopher M. *The Politics of Conversion: Missionary Protestantism and the Jews in Prussia, 1728-1941.* **New York and Oxford: Oxford University Press, 1995, 340 pp.**
This is an examination of the efforts of Pietist Protestants to convert Jews in Prussia during the two centuries preceding the Holocaust. Clark points out, that in most cases, missionaries misunderstood Judaism. Many German Jews converted during the period, but very few were baptized because they had been swayed by the message of Christian supremacy. Clark concludes by calling the pietist missionary "an anti-Semite who loves Jews."

Cohen, Jeremy. *Living Letters of the Law: Ideas of the Jew in Medieval Christianity.* **University of California Press, 1999, 461 pp.**
The volume investigates the way in which medieval Christian theologians, from St. Augustine to Thomas Aquinas, fashioned the image of the "Jew" in society. Cohen examines Augustine's development of the doctrine of the "Jewish witness", which made the Jews survival an important element for a well-ordered Christian world. By tracing the medieval construction of imagery for Jews, and its importance to Christianity as a whole, Cohen provides insight into the history of anti-Semitism, and also to the role Jews played in Western intellectual history.

Cohen, Mark R. *Under Crescent and Cross: the Jews in the Middle Ages.* **Princeton, NJ: Princeton University Press, 1994, 280 pp.**
Cohen maintains, that during the medieval period Jews experienced greater serenity living in lands under Islamic control than in countries dominated by Christians. He points out that in both Islamic and Christian regimes Jews were regarded as outsiders who were taxed and regulated separately from the "native" populations. Yet, Cohen shows, that Jews had increased opportunity in Muslim lands. They could enter government service and join in mercantile partnerships. The author also

recounts the increase in anti-Semitism in Christian countries that took place during the thirteenth century when the *Talmud* was condemned and burned, and Jews were expelled from areas.

Cohen, Naomi W. "Anti-Semitism in the Gilded Age: The Jewish View." Jewish Social Studies (1979), Volume 41 Issue 3-4, pp. 187-210.
Though many have attributed anti-Semitism to social competition, agrarian radicalism, economic stereotypes, and ignorance, the writings of American Jews who were reporting in the Jewish newspapers of the late nineteenth century laid the blame for prejudice in America on the teachings of Christianity, minister's sermons, and the actions of Christians.

Cohn, Norman. *Warrant for Genocide: The Myth of the Jewish World Conspiracy and the Protocols of the Elders.* **London: Eyre & Spottiswoode, 1967. 303pp. Chico: Scholars Press, 1981, 285 pp.**
The author views the infamous *Protocols* as the modern adaptation of the Christian belief that Jews were the children of the Devil, and as such, they were a mysterious and uncanny people possessed of sinister power. Since the second century, Jews had been accused of killing Christian children (in ritual murders), torturing the consecrated wafer, and poisoning wells. *The Protocols* disseminated a more modern myth that contended Jews planned to dominate the globe through their control of political parties, banks, the press and public opinion. Although proven to be a hoax in a 1935 trial in Berne, Switzerland, the *Protocols*, nevertheless, continued to be accepted and was sold in large numbers. Cohn claims, that in one year in Germany, 120,000 copies of the forgery were sold. The author maintains, that belief in *The Protocols* helped convince seventeen million Germans to vote for the Nazis in 1933.

Conway, John S. "Protestant Missions to the Jews 1810-1980:Ecclesiastical Imperialism or Theological Aberration?" Holocaust and Genocide Studies (1986), Volume 1 Issue 1, pp. 127-146.
The author contends, that in the past Protestant missions to the Jews were based on the idea that Christianity was superior to Judaism and therefore the Jews needed help to accept conversion. Conway claims that with the Holocaust, and the Jews demonstration of their ability to survive against all odds, most Christians have recognized that missionary theories must be replaced by a feeling of mutual respect for the Jews.

Corrigan, Kathleen. "The Jewish Satyr in the Nineteenth Century Psalters." *Hellenic and Jewish Arts: Interaction, Tradition and Renewal.* **Asher Ovadiah. Editor. Tel Aviv: Ramot-Tel Aviv University, 1998, pp. 351-368.**
This portion of the book recounts the efforts of Byzantine Psalter artists to create Jewish images that were threatening to Christianity. They used the figure of

Selenius, a mythical dog, who embodied anti-religious and depraved values. Corrigan asserts, that this anti-Semitic imagery was intended to reinforce the negative attitude that the Christian laity felt toward Jews, and was tied to Psalm 21, which reads, "Many dogs have compassed me; the assembly of evildoers has beset round me."

Coudert, Allison P. "Seventeenth Century Christian Hebraists: Philosemites or Anti-Semites?" *Judaeo-Christian Intellectual Culture in the Seventeenth Century: A Celebration of the Library of Narcissus Marsh (1638-1713).* **Eds. Allison P. Coudert et al. Dodrecht: Kluwer Academic Publishers, 1999, pp. 43-69.**

Coudert maintains, that it is appropriate to use the term anti-Semitism, rather than anti-Judaism prior to the nineteenth century, because Christianity's hostility toward Jews included an element of ethnic hatred. Yet the term "philo-Semite" presents Coudert with problems. Its use, in her estimation, is incorrect. She asserts, that most supposed Christian "philo-Semites" did not really consider Jews unless they were potential converts. The author examines the views of a group of seventeenth century Lutheran thinkers, who she insists, were unable, for the most part, to reject the stereotypes of Jews as evil and agents of Satan. Those who did show sympathy or compassion for Jews did so only for Jews who seemed willing to convert.

Cutler, Allan Harris and Helen Elmquist Cutler. *The Jew as Ally of the Muslim: Medieval Roots of Anti-Semitism.* **South Bend, IN.: University of Notre Dame Press, 1986, 577 pp.**

The Cutlers contend that the rise of anti-Semitism that occurred in western Europe after 1000 C. E., was due to the idea that Jews could be dangerous allies of the Muslims. The authors propose, that when studying this time period one cannot separate the association of Christian and Jew from the relationship of Christianity to Islam. In making their case, the Cutlers analyze the anti-Jewish and anti-Islamic polemical writings of the period, and tie the Spanish Inquisition and the numerous attempts at forced conversions in the late Middle Ages to Christianity's fears about the rise of the Islamic religion.

Dalin, David G. "Popes and Jews; Truths and Falsehoods in the History of Jewish-Catholic Relations." The Weekly Standard (February 26, 2001), Volume 7 Issue 8, pp. 36-39.

The author is critical of David Kertzer's book, *The Popes Against the Jews*. He claims that Kertzer has missed the philo-Semitic tradition of papal support for the Jews in the fourteenth century, and that a succession of popes beginning in the twelfth century repudiated the accusations of "ritual murder" that were made against Jews. Dalin also contends, that during times of persecution several popes defended the Jewish community. According to Dalin, Kertzer's study of the popes is extremely one-sided in its approach. Therefore, the author considers *The Popes*

*Against the Jew*s to be a source of falsehoods.

Davies, Alan. Trewartha. *Infected Christianity: A Study of Modern Racism.* **Kingston, Ont.: McGill-Queen University Press, 1988, 160 pp.**
This volume proposes that the rise of scientific racism and the development of the Aryan myth were influenced by Christianity. The author notes the elements of Christianity that appear in the work of Chamberlain, the way in which Stoecker, a Lutheran theologian, helped open the door for the later cooperation between the German Protestant Churches and the Nazis, and the attempt to create a "Germanic Christ." Davies maintains, that in France Drumont succeeded in portraying Jews as enemies of both Christianity and the state.

Davis, Robert Gorham. "Passion at Oberammergau." Commentary, 1963, Volume 29 Issue 3, pp. 198-205.
Davis claims, that over 400,000 people travel to Oberammergau, Bavaria for the Passion Play that depicts the trial and death of Christ. The author declares, that the play portrays Jews as perfidious murderers. He notes, that the play has not undergone major revisions since 1860 and the changes made then were instituted by monks, who felt no compunction to reject the anti-Semitic characterizations. Davis proposes, that the portrayal of Jews as evil in Christian Passion Plays helped lay the foundation for acceptance of Nazi anti-Semitism. He focuses upon the reluctance, in recent years, of local citizens to discuss or deal with the anti-Semitic elements of the play. The author contends, that events such as these make it easier for anti-Semites to continue their harassment of the Jews.

Dobroszychi, Lucjan, ed. *Image Before My Eyes: A Photographic History of Jewish Life in Poland Before the Holocaust.* **New York: Schoken Press, 1977, 269 pp**.
Two hundred black and white photographs document Jewish life in Poland from 1864 to the time leading up to the Holocaust. They depict social change, wars, pogroms, modernization, and the political turmoil that shaped Jewish life in Poland before World War Two. Also explored are developments such as Hasidism, Jewish life in Warsaw, education, Zionism, and the cinema.

Driver, Tom F. "The Play that Carries a Plague." Christian Century (September 7, 1960), Volume 77 Issue 36, pp. 1016-1017.
In this review of the *Oberammergua Passion Play,* Driver contends that the dramatization is historically inaccurate, promotes a misunderstanding of the Gospels and is anti-Semitic in its interpretation. He concludes, that the play can only prove harmful to the relationship that has been developing between Jews and Christians and questions why the Catholic Church has conferred its blessing upon the production.

Duffy, Michael F. and Willard Mittelman. "Nietzsche's Attitude Toward the Jews." Journal of the History of Ideas (1988), Volume 49, pp. 301-317.
The authors address Nietzsche's ideas concerning Judaism, his respect for Jews and his opposition to anti-Semitism. The authors note the distinctions Nietzsche made between the Jewish religious practices of the *Old Testament*, Judaism as it existed during the beginnings of Christianity, and modern Judaism. They contend, that Nietzsche's focus on the Jews provided him with a basis upon which to develop his ideas concerning what he regarded as a necessary reassessment of principles in order to transform humanity's values.

Dundes, Alan, ed. *The Blood Libel Legend: A Casebook in Anti-Semitic Folklore.* University of Wisconsin Press, 1994, 400 pp.
In this compilation of essays, Dundes lays the guilt for the development of the blood libel accusations at Christianity's door. His study concludes, that folklore has a large impact upon thought and history. Thus the charges of ritual murder made against Jews laid the foundations for the development of more virulent forms of anti-Jewish feelings. Dundes asserts, that the basis for the false accusations arose out of Christianity's misunderstanding of the Passover feast. He notes, that while many might consider the blood libel accusations as resulting from the less attractive aspects of Christianity's psychological underpinnings, Jews view them as anti-Semitic and regard them as another point of conflict between themselves and Christians. The case studies provided by the author give a full picture of the complexities that surrounded the blood libel accusations.

Edwards, John. "The *Conversos*: A Theological Approach." Bulletin of Hispanic Studies (1985), Volume 62, pp. 39-49.
Edwards studies the Spanish Inquisition and contends, that while many scholars accept the idea that most Jewish converts did so under pressure, or because they saw the advantages of becoming Christian, the truth is that there were Jews who chose to be baptized out of true religious convictions. Also, according to the author, there were Catholics who acted out of a desire to help others by spreading their faith. Those who ignore this are likened to the intolerant perpetrators of the Inquisition.

____. "The Debate About the Origins of the Spanish Inquisition." Al-Masaq (1999), Volume 11, pp. 1-13.
This article reviews the debate that surrounds the question about whether or not the *Conversos* were genuine Christians or crypto-Jews. The author discusses the fact that it is a mistake to examine these people as a monolithic group. They were not uniformly Jewish or Christian. He asserts, that in order to understand the Inquisition one must look at experiences elsewhere in Europe and accept the fact that in fifteenth century Spain, people were confused about issues concerning faith and identity.

____. *Religion and Society in Spain*. **Aldershot, Hants: Variorum, 1996, 350 pp.**
The articles within this volume that deal with Christian anti-Semitism include; "The *Conversos:* A Theological Approach", "Why the Spanish Inquisition?", "Religious Faith and Doubt in late Medieval Spain", "The Popes, The Inquisition and Jewish Converts in Spain", "Jewish Testimony to the Spanish Inquisition", and "The Trial of an Inquisitor." There is also a chapter that addresses the origins of the "purity of blood" statutes in Spain.

____. **"Was the Spanish Inquisition Truthful?" Jewish Quarterly Review (January-April 1997), Volume 87 Issue 3-4, pp. 351-366.**
Edwards reviews Netanyahu and Roth's books about the Spanish Inquisition as it affected the Jews, and finds that, contrary to the assertions of both writers, the veracity of Inquisition records has long been debated by scholars. According to Edwards, despite the work put forth by these authors the nature of the *converso* in Spain is still unclear. He contends, while many Jews converted because of pressure from the Catholic Church and the attacks mounted against them in 1391, there were Jews who converted due to true religious convictions.

Efron, John. *Defenders of the Race: Jewish Doctors and Race Science in Fin-de-Siecle Europe.* **New Haven: Yale University Press, 1994, 225 pp.**
The author examines the participation of Jewish lay scholars and physicians/ scientists in the science of race in the period from 1880 to 1914. Efron's focus is England and Germany. He discusses how Jews of both of these countries engaged in the sciences helped define the Jewish people as a race. The author contends, that the idea of the Jewish race shaping the Jewish self-image was from the start a poisoned idea, inasmuch as it allowed anti-Semites to juxtapose the Aryan race against that of the Jews. This racial definition provided the groundwork for the Nazi contention that both races could not inhabit the same landscape without conflict.

Eidelberg, Sholmo. *Jews and the Crusaders: The Hebrew Chronicles of the First and Second Crusades.* **KTAV Publishing House, 1996, 186 pp.**
Eidelberg notes, that the Jews of Christian Europe were the first victims of the Crusaders. This text provides a first hand account of the Jews experiences at the hands of their Christian attackers. The author, having translated the memoirs of some Jews, shows their refusal to abandon Judaism even when threatened with violence and death.

Elbogen, Ismar. *A Century of Jewish Life.* **Philadelphia: Jewish Publications Society of America, 1944, 814 pp.**
This book studies the one hundred years that elapsed after the Jews began to be emancipated from the European ghettos. Elbogen provides an accounting of the movements and persons who affected Jews over this time period. He claims, that anti-Semitism looms large in his study because it occupies a vast portion of Jewish

history. He explores the impact that the Christian Churches had upon anti-Jewish attitudes. Some of the names and incidents specifically recounted in his study include; Father Rohling's charges against the *Talmud*, which even after proven false continued to influence people's opinions about the Jews; Christian accusations of ritual murder; and the Dreyfus Affair. Also included is the publication, *The Protocols of the Elders of Zion,* which charged the Jews with conspiring to take over the world and destroy Christian civilization. The author concludes, that Christianity's enmity towards the Jewish people underpinned the harm done to Jews.

Endelman, Todd M. *Jewish Apostasy in the Modern World.* New York: Holmes and Meier, 1987, 350 pp.
The author insists, that in the aftermath of the Enlightenment Christian attempts to convert Jews constantly plagued the relationship between the two groups. Jews, according to Endelman, considered these efforts as one more aspect of a long held hostility displayed toward them, while Christians saw their missionary work as "helpful and caring." In order to support his thesis, the author details Christianity's mission to the Jews as it unfolded in, among other locations, Germany, England and Russia. He also studies the responses these activities evoked.

Erspamer, Peter R. *The Elusiveness of Tolerance: The Jewish Question from Lessing to the Napoleonic Wars.* Chapel Hill: The University of North Carolina Press. 1997, 189 pp.
Erspamer considers the toleration debate in Germany from the publication of Gotthold Ephraim Lessing's *Nathan the Wise* (1779) to the Napoleonic era. Although German Jewry in the eighteenth century was a highly fragmented and heterogeneous group, the religious prejudices of the Middle Ages merged with the developing racial anti-Semitism of such German theorists as Ernst Moritz Arnt, to reinforce the popular myth of Jewish ethnic homogeneity. The author illuminates the escalation of the anti-Jewish feelings among German Romantics, such as Achim von Arnim and Johann Fichte, after Napoleon's wars of liberation and emancipation.

Evitt, Regula Meyer. "Anti-Judaism and the Medieval Prophet Plays: Exegetical Contexts for the *"Ordines Prophetarum."* Dissertation – University of Virginia (1992), 317 pp.
The author examines passages of the liturgical prophet plays and asserts that the earliest plays were intended to provide support for strengthening the faith of Christians. Evitt demonstrates, that during the thirteenth century a growing attempt to convert Jews to Christianity was underway, and this in turn affected the ways in which Jews were depicted in the prophet processions.

Fabre-Vassas, Claudine. *The Singular Beast: Jews, Christians, and the Pig.* Carol Volk (Translator). Columbia University Press, 1999, 416 pp.

According to the author, the differing practices and myths concerning the pig helped define the disparity between European Christians and Jews during the Middle Ages. Fabre-Vassas recounts the various taboos, rituals and myths associated with pigs. The author notes folklore that asserted the Jews craved the flesh of Christian children because they were deprived of pork, or that the Jews refused to eat pork because Jewish children had been turned into swine. Through tales like these, the pig was symbolically linked to Jews.

Falk, Gerhard, and Martin Luther. *Jew in Christian Theology: Martin Luther's Anti-Jewish VOM Schem Hamphoras, Previously Unpublished in English and Other Milestones in Church Doctrine Concerning Judaism.* **Jefferson: McFarland & Company Incorporated Publishers, 1992, 304 pp.**
This study reviews the earliest Christian writings concerning the Jews, and shows how Christian synods and influential theologians, like Martin Luther, legitimized and perpetuated hatred of Jews. Additionally, the author reviews current attempts to establish an ongoing dialogue between Christians and Jews.

Felsenstein, Frank. "Jews and Devils: Anti-Semitic Stereotypes of Late Medieval and Renaissance England." Literature and Theology (March 1990), Volume 4 Issue 1, pp. 15-28.
Though Jews were expelled from England in 1290, and only were readmitted in 1655, the author maintains that the English retained their caricatures of Jews due to Christian hostilities. Portrayals of Jews as usurers, agents of the devil, ritual murderers, and the murderers of Christ, who were constantly scheming to tear down Christianity persisted due to the efforts of Church leaders. The author also claims that, misunderstandings about the religious practices of the Jews reinforced the hostility Christians continued to feel toward Jews and Judaism.

Field, Geoffrey G. *Evangelist of Race: The Germanic Vision of Houston Stewart Chamberlain.* **New York: Columbia University Press, 1981, 565 pp.**
This intellectual biography of the author of *The Foundations of the Nineteenth Century* (1899) traces the sources of Chamberlain's thought within the context of his time. Field, using both published and unpublished writings, shows how Chamberlain brought his opinions about history, religion, science art, and politics, to bear on his pro-Aryan and anti-Semitic racist thought.

Fisher, Eugene Joseph. "Anti-Semitism and Christianity: Theories and Revisions of Theories." *Persistent Prejudice: Perspectives on Anti-Semitism.* **Eds., Herbert Hirsch and Jack Spiro. Fairfax, VA.: George Mason University Press, 1988, pp. 11-30.**
The author presents the views of several scholars in this examination of the links between Christianity and anti-Semitism. Special focus is given to the influence of the *New Testament* on hostility towards the Jews. Fisher also surveys the thirteenth

century, in which he claims Christianity's anti-Jewish fervor escalated. In light of this, the author claims this period as a major turning point in the relationship between Jews and Christians. Furthermore, he analyzes the Reformation's impact on Christianity's treatment of the Jews. Fisher points out, that it is often difficult for scholars to treat these subjects objectively, and notes the disagreements that arise from theories about these issues.

Fleischer, Roland. "Looking for Clues: Baptists and Jews in Southeastern Europe Before the Holocaust: The Jewish Baptist Missionary, Moses Richter." Baptist Quarterly (1999), Volume 38 Issue 3, pp. 139-142.
Moses Richter was a Jewish Baptist preacher, who worked with the Jews of Romania during the 1930s. According to Fleischer, Richter explained the importance of valuing Christian principle over the push for nationalism. Richter maintained, that it was a Christian's duty to treat Jews with compassion and kindness instead of hatred.

Foa, Anna. *The Jews of Europe After the Black Death.* **Andre Glover, Translator. Berkeley: University of California Press, 2000, 276 pp.**
Foa's study surveys the relationship between Jews and Christians from the fourteenth century to the twentieth century. The author argues, that following the Black Death of 1348 a new belief about Jews permeated the Christian world. Whereas in earlier centuries the Church judged Jews as living in error of a true understanding of scripture and sought to convert them, the new view held, that "the Jews possessed an intrinsic evil that could not be canceled, even by baptism." Thus the natural corruption of Jews contaminated the Christian world. Foa argues, that this centuries-old concept of inherent contamination lies at the very origin of anti-Jewish polemics. The author links anti-Judaism (the theological hatred of the Jews by the Christian world) with the racial anti-Semitism that led to the Holocaust.

Frankel, Jonathan. *The Damascus Affair: Ritual Murder, Politics, and the Jews in 1840.* **Cambridge: Cambridge University Press, 1997, 491 pp.**
The author argues, that the real consequence of the Damascus affair, in which Jews were falsely accused of the "ritual murder" of an Italian monk and his servant, was the backlash Jews suffered. According to Frankel, the suffering the Jews endured after this charge forged the first modern sense of solidarity among Europe's Jewish community.

____."Ritual Murder in the Modern Era: The Damascus Affair of 1840." Jewish Social Studies (January 31, 1997), Volume 3 Issue 2, pp. 1-9.
Frankel focuses on the facts surrounding the 1840 ritual murder case in Damascus and the long-term significance of "blood libel" charges for modern Jewish history. Ritual murder cases involved the claim that Jews murdered Christians as part of their religious practice. The author discusses the fact that charges of ritual murder,

though seemingly absurd, were still made in the nineteenth century, in part, as a backlash against modernity. These charges against Jews also supported rising nationalism in European countries.

Friedman, Jerome. "Sebastian Munster, The Jewish Mission and Protestant Anti-Semitism." *Archiv fur Reformationsgechichte* **(1979), Volume 70, pp. 238-259.**
The author argues, that the fact that Sebastiasn Munster has rarely been referred to demonstrates his unpopularity during the Reformation, which was marked by increasing anti-Semitism. Friedman examines Munster's writings, which include a missionary tract that encourages tolerance and compassion for the Jews, instead of the hostility that was historically shown to them by Christians. Munster's interest in the Jews and Judaism cost him any opportunity to maintain a respected theological legacy.

Gay, Peter. *Freud, Jews, and Other Germans: Masters and Victims in Modernist Culture.* **New York: Oxford University Press, 1978, 289 pp.**
German anti-Semitism on the eve of the Nazi seizure of power in 1933, according to the author, was partly a protest against modernity. Jews were viewed as personifying the world's evils; urbanization and its depersonalization, materialism, social rebelliousness, and cultural nihilism. Gay points out, that this perception was belied by the facts. Jews, for example, were not as numerous and preponderant in the avant-garde as has frequently been claimed. Additionally, their role as the 'disruptive stranger' was vastly exaggerated. Gay further argues, that there was no peculiarly Jewish element in modernism, nor was there a presumed Jewish proclivity for experimentation in the arts or innovation in literature.

Gilitz, Davids M. *Secrecy and Deceit: The Religion of the Crypto-Jews.* **Ilan Stavans (Introduction). University of New Mexico Press, 2002, 692 pp.**
Gilitz studies the crypto-Jewish culture and its traditions in Spain, Portugal and the New World colonies. He contends, that this group of Jews was forced to convert to Christianity and needed to develop a covert way of maintaining coveted traditions of Jewish theology, while seeming to adhere to the tenets of Christianity. Out of this determination to preserve their heritage under duress, the religion that evolved had its own peculiarities.

Gilman, Sander L. *Jewish Self-Hatred: Anti-Semitism and the Hidden Language of the Jews.* **Baltimore: Johns Hopkins University Press, 1986, 461 pp.**
This is primarily a study of Jewish anti-Semitism in literature from medieval times to modern times. The author examines Jewish self -hatred in Central Europe, and how Jews' self-definition, which was molded by outside cultural perceptions, confronted the perennial charge of being linguistic outsiders, and of possessing a secret conspiratorial language. Gilman explores the literature of medieval Jewish

converts, the writings of Martin Luther, and Enlightenment *maskilim,* among others.

____. *The Jew's Body.* **New York: Routledge, 1991, 303 pp.**
The text, a collection of essays, focuses upon the Christian theological passages that aided in shaping the anti-Semitic stereotypes by insisting that there are physical "differences" that mark Jews as Jews. These ideas helped modern anti-Semitism develop. According to Gilman, Freud viewed them as the source of Jewish self-hatred. The author maintains, that these negative religious views were secularized and used in the "science" of race.

____. **"Nietzsche, Heine, and the Otherness of the Jews." Studies in Nietzsche and the Judeo-Christian Tradition, University of North Carolina Press, 1985, pp. 206-225.**
Gilman argues, that Nietzsche was an "anti-anti-Semite" and not as some have suggested, a philo-Semite. Though Nietzsche regarded Jews as a strong and pure race, he blamed Jews for passing on to Christianity a set of values that he viewed negatively. The author asserts, that since Nietzsche was a minister's son these values were an instrumental part of his upbringing and he despised any trace of them that he detected in himself, or others. Additionally, Nietzsche took a great interest in Heinrich Heine because his ideas, though they predated Nietzsche's, were very similar in content.

____. **"R.G. Collingwood and the Religious Sources of Nazism." Journal of the American Academy of Religion (1986), Volume 54 Issue 1, pp. 111-128.**
Focusing upon the writings of R.G. Collingwood, the author, attempts to clarify how religious beliefs helped lay the foundations for Nazism. Collingwood maintained, that western civilization had laid itself open to the threat of "neo-pagan systems of thought". He argued, that even while Christians insisted they had a deep morality, they had actually abandoned Christian values in favor of liberalism. Gilman contends, that Collingwood's theories are an important part of the ongoing discourse about the role religion can play in modern society.

Glassman, Bernard. *Protean Prejudice: Anti-Semitism in England's Age of Reason.* **University of South Florida (UPA), 1998, 256 pp.**
The author argues, that despite scientific advances made during the "Age of Reason", prejudice persisted and the religious teachings that had promoted "contempt for the Jews" remained influential among Englishmen. The author's use of original source materials provides evidence that some of the most prominent English thinkers, during the Enlightenment period, retained the age-old anti-Jewish ideology taught by Christian Churches. Furthermore, ethnic, racial, and national factors also played a role in casting Jews as "the other".

Glick, Leonard B. *Abraham's Heirs: Jews and Christians in Medieval Europe.*

Syracuse: Syracuse University Press, 1999, 323 pp.
Glick suggests, that the history of medieval Ashkenazic Jewry can be best understood by focusing on the distinctiveness of the Jew in medieval society. Drawing on Christian documents, the author demonstrates the ways in which medieval Jews were regarded by Christian society. His account, delivered in great detail, describes how the complex relationship between Jews and Christians evolved.

Glouberman, Emmanuel. "Vasilli Rosanov: The Anti-Semitism of a Russian Judeophile." Jewish Social Studies (1976), Volume 38 Issue 2, pp.117-144.
Vasilli Rosanov, a prolific author of books and sometimes contributor to the Russian daily *Novoe Vremia,* was a strong voice in support of traditionalism and Christian idealism during the late nineteenth and early twentieth century. Rosanov's attitude toward the Jews and Judaism was contradictory. On one hand he respected Jewish beliefs and solidarity, yet he also attacked them and displayed virulent anti-Semitic feelings.

Goodrick-Clarke, Nicholas. *Hitler's Priestess: Savitri Devi, the Hindu-Aryan Myth, and Neo-Nazism.* **New York: New York University Press, 1998, 280 pp.**
The author states that the writings of the French-born Greek national Savitri Devi (Maximiami Portas) articulated a synthesis of paganism, Hinduism, anti-Semitism, and Hitler-worship. Portas hated Jews, and the Christian religion that she believed Jews had inspired. Taken together, the author argues, that Portas's ideas form the core ideology of Nazism, as well as the heart of the later Green and New Age movements. In making the argument that Nazism was influenced by pagan ideas, such as those espoused by Portas, Goodrick-Clark ignores its roots in the history of the Christian church.

Gregg, Joan Young. *Devils, Women, and Jews: Reflections of the Other in Medieval Sermon Stories.* **Albany: State University of New York Press, 1997, 275 pp.**
The documents of misogynist and anti-Semitic Christian medieval sermons are used to study tales about devils, women, and the Jews. Christianity through preaching and art portrayed the devil as an outcast from heaven, and the source of evil in the world. The Jews, regarded as treacherous dissidents, were linked with the devil. Gregg insists, that this and other negative images and stereotypes of the Jews have persisted through the centuries and are still found among people today.

Gutman, Robert W. *Richard Wagner: The Man, His Mind, and His Music.* **New York: Harcourt Brace, 1990, 492 pp.**
Gutman highlights the direct influence of Wagner's anti-Semitism upon the policies of Adolf Hitler. The author focuses on Wagner's most Christian of operas, *Parisfal,* which Gutman contends is a proto-Nazi work, wherein the figure of Kundry is a

Jewish character marked by inferior blood. The Knights of the Grail, guarding the chalice containing the blood of Christ are made analogous, by the author, to the SS guarding the purity of the Aryan race.

Haastrup, Ulla. "Representations of Jews in Danish Medieval Art." *Danish Jewish Art*. Ed. Miriam Gelfer-Jorgenson. Copenhagen: Rhodos, 1999, pp. 111-167.
Haastrup concentrates upon the imagery of Jews in Danish medieval churches. From the eleventh century through the beginnings of the Protestant Reformation these depictions of Jews in the paintings and altarpieces reflect attitudes ranging from neutrality to hatred. The article provides a historical background aimed at helping readers understand the changing portrayals of Jews that were promoted by the church, in the context of the times.

Hayes, Peter, ed. *Lessons and Legacies: The Meaning of the Holocaust in a Changing World*. Evanston, Il.: Northwestern University Press, 1991, 373 pp.
A conference held at Northwestern University in 1989 was the source of the papers presented in this volume. The topics that explore Christianity's relationship to anti-Semitism and the Holocaust are as follows; the comparison of Christianity's medieval anti-Semitism to the witchcraft craze and Nazi anti-Semitic policies, the Crusades, reactions to the Holocaust by Christians and others, the role of Righteous Gentiles, and the ways in which the Holocaust impacts the post-war world.

Healey, Robert M. "The Jew in Seventeenth Century Protestant Thought." Church History (March 1977), Volume 46 Issue 1, pp. 63-79.
The author presents an overview of the way in which seventeenth century Jews were regarded in the minds of Protestants. Healey demonstrates, that France, Spain and Portugal, during medieval times, treated Jews as greedy usurers deserving of contempt. The Jews were subjected to expulsion because of their refusal to convert to Christianity. In comparison, prior to the French Revolution the treatment of Jews in England and the Netherlands was less harsh. The reason for this more moderate approach to the Jews, included the need for laborers in the colonies of the New World, the necessity of increased monetary investments in overseas trade, and the conviction that Jews could be converted.

Helfand, Jonathan I. "Passports and Piety: Apostasy in Nineteenth Century France." Jewish History (Fall 1988), Volume 3 Issue 2, pp. 59-83.
The author asserts, that there was a considerable movement in France to convert non-Christians during the first half of the nineteenth century. The author contends, that these missionary efforts were especially directed toward Jews and he maintains, that once Jews were baptized they, in turn, became particularly active in trying to convince other Jews to become Christians. According to Helfand, the efforts of newly converted Jews in attempting to bring others to the Christian faith were

extremely controversial. Their activities caused a fair amount of concern in Jewish communities, and they were sometimes accused of participating in "forced conversions." Helfand reports, that as the authority of the Church weakened, the efforts to win over Christian followers also declined.

Hertzberg, Arthur. *The French Enlightenment and the Jews: The Origins of Modern Anti-Semitism.* **New York: Columbia University Press, 1968, 420 pp.**
According to this study, Jewish emancipation as well as the modern forms of anti-Semitism, had their origins in Enlightenment thought during the eighteenth-century in France.

Hoffmann, Stefan-Ludwig. "Brothers or Strangers? Jews and Freemasons in Nineteenth Century Germany." German History (2000), Volume 18 Issue 2, pp. 143-161.
The author uses a study of the Masonic Lodges from the end of the eighteenth century through 1914 to demonstrate, that even while the "universalist and inclusive rhetoric of the Enlightenment was being disseminated," there was a move toward exclusive and nationalist discourse. This reverted to, and built upon, the traditional anti-Semitism of Christianity. He contends, that this was done without any noticeable revision of language. Hoffmann asserts, that Masonic Lodges were expected to unify men and disregard social standing. However, religious Jews were not permitted entry and potential Jewish members were expected to become Christians. Therefore despite claims to the contrary, the number of Jewish Freemasons was relatively small.

Horowitz, Irving Louis. "Philo-Semitism and Anti-Semitism: Jewish Conspiracies and Totalitarian Sentiments." Midstream (May 1990), Volume 36 Issue 4, pp. 17-22.
Horowitz discusses the definitions of anti-Semitism and Philo-Semitism, and contends, that both originated from the same idea. That idea, according to the author, is that Jews are different and possess unearthly power. Christianity, to a large degree, helped initiate the mythology about the Jewish community. Horowitz notes, that while some philosemites, especially in the nineteenth century, sought to put an end to all religion by obliterating Judaism, others (like Christians) tried to convert Jews to their religious doctrines. The author maintains, that the State of Israel has put most anti-Semitism and philosemitism to rest. He proposes, that since Jews have gained their own homeland, both would be saviors and enemies have been forced to view Jews in a more human and less mystical light.

Hsia, R. Po-Chia and Hartmut Lehmann, eds. *In and Out of the Ghetto: Jewish-Gentile Relations in Late Medieval and Early Modern Germany.* **Cambridge: Cambridge University Press, 1995, 350 pp.**
Seventeen contributors discuss how popular myths about the Jews, stemming from

the medieval period, entered into the modern age. The general theme running through this collection of essays, is that the influence of the Enlightenment did not significantly improve the treatment of Jews. Otto Ulbricht's essay, for example, cites instances whereby torture in eighteenth century Germany was used to extract confessions of criminality from Jews.

Isser, Natalie. *Anti-Semitism During the French Second Empire.* **Peter Lang, 1991, 149 pp.**
The author attempts "to examine and define the peculiar characteristics of French anti-Semitism as it emerged in the nineteenth century." Isser contends that especially during the years 1850-1870 a conservative religious nationalist attitude took hold in France and that became the focus for anti-Semitism in France. The Catholic Church and the French government, embroiled in a number of disagreements, used the Jews as a political weapon in their arguments. The Church noted the government's support for many of the same liberal ideologies that were identified with Jews. The Church hierarchy blamed Jews for promoting modernism and secularism and claimed Jews undermined morality and the social order. The French government used the Jews to attack the evils of the papacy. Though most scholars note that the Second Empire, for the most part, demonstrated good relations between Christians and Jews, Isser maintains, the anti-Semitism that was promoted conditioned French citizens for the racist rhetoric Drumont would later circulate.

Jackson, Deirdre. *Marian Anti-Semitism in Medieval Life and Legend: A Study Based on Alfonso X's "Cantigas de Santa Maria."* **Canada: University of Victoria, 1997, 138 pp.**
Each of the three miracle stories reviewed present the image of a Jewish male, who when confronted by the image of the Virgin and Child reacted strongly. According to legend, those Jews who view the image positively are accepted into Christianity, while those who react negatively are brought great suffering. The stories, in the author's opinion, demonstrate the concern that Christians felt over the fact that Jews and Muslims refused to be affected by religious imagery, and rejected the influence that such images had on Christians. The tales also served to reinforce the Christian belief in the special influence and power placed in the Virgin Mother of Christ.

Jappinen, Ilona. "Was Nietzsche Anti-Semitic?" Encyclia (1991), Volume 68, pp. 133-154.
Jappinen suggests, that in order to understand the seemingly chaotic attitudes that Nietzsche held toward Jews the reader must separate them into the separate arenas of his thought processes. The author concludes, that to identify Nietzsche as an anti-Semite is too simple. He insists, that while Nietzache never really overcame the prejudices against Judaism that were part of his upbringing in a society that was primarily Christian, he did disassociate himself from contemporary anti-Semitism.

He disliked the social and cultural influence anti-Semitic attitudes had on society and claimed that Christianity had both continued and corrupted Judaism. Yet, Nietzsche also praised some aspects of the Jewish tradition.

Jastrow, Morris Jr. "The Jewish Question in Its Recent Aspects." International Journal of Ethics (July 1896), Volume 6 Issue 4, pp. 457-479.
This article, written over one hundred years ago, presents problems facing the Jewish population externally and internally. The author contends, that the external problems for Jews appeared as Christianity evolved and took on its own identity. Religious conflict developed between the two groups. This religious conflict, according to Jastrow, has been replaced by more modern anti-Semitic ideologies. One aspect of this hatred holds that Jews and non-Jews should not mix so that racial purity can be preserved. The author contends, that notions of racial purity and national traits are "scientific myths" that must be rejected. Internally the struggle for Jews, in Jastrow's view, centers on maintaining their identity and their relation to Judaism. The author offers no clear answers for Jews, but suggests that assimilation does not mean Jews must surrender their character or their religious convictions.

Jeansonne, Glen, Foreword by Leo P. Ribuffo. *Gerald K. Smith: Minister of Hate.* Louisiana State University Press, 1997, 284 pp.
Smith, according to Jeansonne, had the ability to leave his audiences awestruck even though he was a notorious bigot. This full-length biography traces his entire tempestuous career. Smith ran for president three times, and his publication *The Cross and Flag* helped him disseminate his anti-Semitic rhetoric among Protestant Americans. His hate speech contributed to the atmosphere of anti-Jewish feelings in America. Smith died in 1976.

Johnson, Paul. *A History of the Jews.* London; Weidenfeld and Nicolson, 1987, 643 pp.
Though this volume encompasses a broad study of Jewish history, there are chapters that deal specifically with the anti-Semitism of Christianity. For example, the author addresses how anti-Semitism developed through its early years and evolved during the Middle Ages with the Crusades and the Inquisiton. The author also notes the influence Christianity's anti-Semitism has had on the modern period.

Jordan, William Chester. "The Erosion of the Stereotype of the Last Tormentor of Christ." Jewish Quarterly Review (July-October 1990), Volume 81 Issue 1-2, pp. 13-44.
The author states, that the portrayal of Christ's last tormentor as a man offering Jesus a sponge dipped in vinegar while dying on the cross, became a primary way to depict Jews during the Middle Ages. Christian artists competed with one another to find ways to show the "sponge-bearer" in the most grotesque and hideous manners.

In the wake of the reformist movements of the late fifteenth century the evil depiction of Jews in paintings and within the Passion Plays declined. However, this did not mean that anti-Jewish attitudes lessened, rather in some ways they became more intense and increasingly cruel.

Katz, Jacob. *The Darker Side of Genius*. Waltham: Brandeis University Press, 1986, 158 pp.
This is among the first biographies to examine the basis for Wagner's anti-Semitism. Katz argues, that Wagner was obsessed with a deep-seated Judeophobia that was generated by his contacts with his Jewish mentors and competitors. The author argues against tying the Nazi's emergence to Wagner's life and work. He further contends, that Wagner's music is untainted by his anti-Semitism, and that there is very little in Wagner's art that, without forced speculation, can be related to his racist views.

_____. *From Prejudice to Destruction: Anti-Semitism, 1700-1933*. Cambridge: Harvard University Press, 1980, 392 pp.
Katz provides us with a history of anti-Semitism dating from the Middle Ages through the period of Emancipation, and continues his study into the eighteenth, nineteenth, and twentieth centuries. The book culminates in Hitler's rise to power. In tracing the history of anti-Semitism in Germany, Austria, Hungary, and France, Katz argues, that it is not possible to account for modern anti-Semitism in purely Christian terms. Rather, Katz sees modern anti-Semitism as a response to emancipation and cultural assimilation.

Kelley, John. J. "Christian Strategy on Passion Plays." The Ecumenist (March-April 1986), Volume 24 Issue 3, pp. 38-44.
The article addresses the efforts teams of Christians and Jews have made to revise the Oberammergau Passion Play, which contains elements that have been deemed offensive to Jews. Attempts to make changes in the text of the play have met with opposition from conservatives who feel their traditions havebeen unfairly attacked. The author provides some detail on the plan put forward by those affecting the revisions. Moreover he notes the areas of disagreement that still need to be resolved.

Kelly, Henry Ansgar. "Inquisition and the Prosecution of Heresy: Misconceptions and Abuses." Questia Media America, Incorporated (1988), http://www.questia.com, 16 pp.
Marking the one hundredth anniversary of H.C. Lea's, *A History of the Inquisition of the Middle Ages,* Kelly notes the mistakes that have been made by those studying the Catholic Church's prosecution of heresy. Kelly insists, that examinations have often provided misconceptions about the events of that time, and that in many instances the mistakes begin with the way in which "the term Inquisition is used."

The author asserts, that while many historians have endowed the word with "diabolical omniscience", or made it stand for a "central intelligence agency with its headquarters at the Vatican" , the truth is, "there was no centralized Inquisition during the Middle Ages."

Kertzer, David. *The Popes Against the Jews: The Vatican's Role in the Rise of Modern Anti-Semitism.* **Knopf; 2001, 368 pp.**
Through the use of newly released archives Kertzer contrsucts a formidable case in support of his conclusion that the Catholic Church has historically been complicit in creating and fostering Anti-Semitic attitudes. The author describes anti-Semitism and the dismal conduct of the papal states when dealing with Jews during the nineteenth century, the anti-Jewish mentality that persisted within the Church after the demise of the papal states, and the failure of popes to repudiate the superstitious myths that led to the continued persecution of Jews in the modern era.

Köhler, Joachim. *Wagner's Hitler: The Prophet and His Disciple.* **(Ronald Taylor, Translator) Cambridge: Polity Press. Malden: Blackwell Publishers, 2000, 378 pp.**
Wagner's influence, Kohler maintains, played an important role in shaping the cultural context in which Nazism developed. The author contends, that the legacy of the German Romantic Movement and the irrational, egocentric, nationalistic and intolerantly utopian features found in Wagner's operas influenced Hitler. The Fuhrer attempted to enact his megalomaniac, Wagnerian visions of ruling the world.

Kolatt, Israel. **"Jacob Talmon's Reflections on Jewish History." Jerusalem Quarterly (1986), Volume 39, pp. 113-125.**
According to Kolatt, Jacob Talmon opposed Christianity's "European centered view of the world and history", for it held that Christianity had surpassed Judaism in importance and relevance. Kolatt contends, that Talmon, though cognizant of the deeply held anti-Semitic attitudes of the nineteenth century, did not blame the hostility toward Jews on the traditionally held ideas of conservatives or nationalists. Rather, he contended, that "disappointed democrats" in their frustration had resorted to racism and the idea that the conflict between good and evil was based upon race. They rationalized, that the "Jews who had joined their left-wing universalist movements, had actually undermined their efforts and doomed their ideals to failure." Talmon, in Kolatt's view, saw the Jews salvation in liberal democracy, for their attempts at universalism had led to tragedy.

Kornberg, Jaques. **"Vienna, the 1890's: Jews in the Eyes of Their Defenders." Central European History (1995), Volume 28 Issue 2, pp. 153-173.**
Kornberg examines the activities and attitudes of the *Abwehrverein*, which was founded in Austria in 1891. The organization fought the growing waves of political anti-Semitism for their agenda of liberalism, rather than for the Jews. They also

published a brochure "Anti-Semitism from a Catholic Standpoint Condemned as a Sin", which lent support for the Jews through theological arguments that stressed the ultimate good that Judaism provided for Christianity.

Kulka, Otto Dov. "Critique of Judaism in European Thought: On the Historical Meaning of Modern Anti-Semitism." Jerusalem Quarterly (Fall 1989), Volume 52, pp. 126-144.
This article reviews the thoughts of Shmuel Ettinger about the origins of modern anti-Semitism. Kulka writes, that Ettinger believed anti-Jewish ideology in modern Europe sprang from society's need to re-examine itself as it encountered the crisis resulting from rapid change. The author contends, that Ettinger understood that there were two trains of thought upon which society's social and political anti-Semitic attitudes were manifested. The first was borne out by the response of anti-Christians, who viewed Judaism as the basis for the failings of Christian society, while the other type developed within conservative ranks, who connected Jews and Judaism to modernity.

Labovitz, Annette. *Anti-Semitism-From Time Immemorial.* Miami: Central Agency for Jewish Education, 1990, 63 pp.
The subjects included in this curriculum concern the study of anti-Semitism from its beginnings to through the present era. The test is meant for the use of high school students and adult education classes. Some of the aspects covered are; anti-Semitism in pagan writings, the anti-Judaism of early Christianity and Medieval Spain, the anti-Jewish rhetoric of Martin Luther, the Jews experience in Polish-Russia, the blood-libel accusations, the Holocaust and anti-Semitism in the post-World War II era.

Lang, Berel. *Act and Idea in Nazi Genocide.* Chicago: University of Chicago Press, 1990, 258 pp.
The author concludes, that the path leading to the Holocaust can be found in many of the ideas of the eighteenth century Enlightenment. He argues that Kant's ideas of individualism and universalism contributed to later Nazi ideology.

Langmuir, Gavin. *Toward a Definition of Anti-Semitism.* Berkeley: University of California Press, 1990, 417 pp.
This study focuses upon the development of Judeophobia in the Middle Ages, when a concrete, definable anti-Semitism first appeared. Jews became the target of hostility in northern Europe, in the twelfth and thirteenth centuries and the hostility displayed, according to Langmuir, was identical to Nazi anti-Semitism.

Lazare, Bernard. *Anti-Semitism: Its History and Causes.* Lincoln: University of Nebraska Press, 1995, 200 pp.
First published in 1894, at the time of the Dreyfus Affair in France, this classic

work concludes that anti-Semitism is fundamentally based upon society's fear of the stranger and need for a scapegoat. Lazare's study of anti-Jewish prejudice includes an exploration of the ethnic, nationalist, religious, economic, and social dimensions of anti-Semitism, as it has evolved throughout European history.

Leopold, David. "The Hegelian Anti-Semitism of Bruno Bauer." History of European Ideas (1999), Volume 25 Issue 4, pp. 179-206.
Despite being an atheist, Bruno Bauer, according to Leopold, preferred Christianity's modern religious tradition to that of the Jews. He agreed with Christianity that the Jews were largely responsible for their own difficulties. Bauer criticized the Jews for their separatist ways and declared that they deserved no pity or compassion. Ultimately, he accepted that race provided a basis for identifying Jews.

Lerner, David Levine. "The Enduring Legend of the Jewish Pope." Judaism (Spring 1991), Volume 40 Issue 2, pp. 148-170.
The legend of the Jewish Pope, which is related in several Hebrew manuscripts, tells (with some differences depending upon the source) of a Jewish boy who was kidnapped, forcibly converted, became a priest, and eventually was elected pope. The story ends with a meeting between the boy who was kidnapped (now pope) and his real father. Ultimately, the boy (pope) rejects Christianity and returns to Judaism, or in some of the versions is made a martyr for Judaism. Despite some variations in the tale, Lerner contends, that the message remains the same. The story portrays the Jewish worldview of the Middle Ages, and clearly demonstrates that Jews refused to compromise their beliefs and accept Christianity, even when threatened by forced conversions and martyrdom. The author claims the legend shows the societal split between Christians and Jews and asserts, that it remains, and will remain in place.

Levin, David J.   *Richard Wagner, Fritz Lang, and the Nibelunger: The Dramaturgy of Disavowal.* Princeton: Princeton University Press, 1998, 207 pp.
Levin discusses Wagner's use of Jewish stereotypes in his stage works. According to the author, Wagner used his operas as a platform for demonstrating what was, and was not, "German". The composer's imagery of the Jews depicted what he regarded as a threat to German character. Levin also explores how Germans have dealt with the mythology disseminated through Wagner' works since World War II, and the horrors of the Third Reich.

Lindemann, Albert S.   *Anti-Semitism Before the Holocaust.*   Reading: Addison-Wesley, 2000, 160 pp.
Included in this survey of anti-Semitism from ancient times to the Nazi Holocaust, are an examination of Russia, the United States, Poland, England, Germany, South

Africa and Holland. Based on his earlier work, *Esau's Tears* (1997), this book is particularly valuable in assessing the anti-Semitic writers and politicians of the La Belle epoch. Included in this survey of influential anti-Semitic spokesmen are Wilhelm Marr, Heinrich von Treischke, Adolph Stoecker, Houston Stewart Chamberlain, Richard Wagner and Austria's Karl Lueger. Lindemann argues that an ever-virulent anti-Semitic ideology was embedded in much of the German intellectual class at the turn of the twentieth century.

____. *Esau's Tears: Modern Anti-Semitism and the Rise of the Jews.* **Cambridge: Cambridge University Press, 1997, 568 pp.**
The title of the book suggests an analogy between the Biblical narrative of Jacob (the Jewish people) and Esau (the Gentiles), and the evolution of anti-Semitism. Lindemann contends, that anti-Semitism is not based on total fantasy, but rests on some realistic component of truth. The author reminds us that in the Biblical account, "Jacob did rob his brother Esau of his birthright, and that Esau's tears were, therefore, understandable." The author concludes, that "Jacob-Israel's" sometimes improper actions had something quite tangible to do with producing Esau's enmity, and thus the enmity of the Gentile world.

Lipton, Sara. *In the Bible Moralisee.* **Berkely: University of California Press, 1999, 241 pp.**
According to Lipton, a changing medieval society in which the qualities labeled as Jewish, as well as the traditional use of Jews as "scapegoats" gave rise to the condemnation of the Jews so-called 'sins." The author demonstrates the "visual vendetta" against the Jews through the use of a thirteenth century illuminated Bible produced for the King of France. In its pages are contained depictions of Jews as heretics engaged in carnality and perfidy. Lipton insists these ideas about Jews were rampant among Christians of the era.

Liptzin, Salomon. *Germany's Stepchildren.* **Philadelphia: The Jewish Publications Society of America, 1944, 298 pp.**
Germany's anti-Jewish attitudes, according to the author, are the result of religious and economic influences. He contends, that even when Jews had undergone conversion to Christianity they were not truly accepted as German citizens. Liptzin traces the various stages that Jews, living in Germany, experienced in their efforts to be recognized as full citizens. He contends, that they have come to realize that their attempts are in vain. Germans continue to view them as outsiders, who threaten the social and economic well being of the German nation.

Low, Alfred D. *Jews in the Eyes of the Germans: From Enlightenment to Imperial Germany.* **Philadelphia: Institute for the Study of Human Issues, 1979, 509 pp.**
Low studies the century and a half, which covers an era of the most radical change

in the lives and thoughts of Germans and Jews. By doing so he attempts to discover how Jews were viewed by German politicians, thinkers, and creative writers.

Lowry, Martin J.C. "Humanism and Anti-Semitism in Renaissance Venice: The Strange Story of "Décor Puellarum." La Bibliofilia (1985), Volume 87 Issue 1, pp. 39-54.
To make his case, the author uses an analysis of a "work of secular piety" that was written in 1471 in Venice. Traced to a Carthusian monastery, this text contains extremely potent anti-Semitic comments. According to Lowry, shows that Christian Elite proponents of humanism residing in Venice were not as liberal as has been suggested. Anti-Semitism was prevalent in this circle of Venetian society.

Luther, Martin. "Letter to George Spalatin, Wittenberg, 1514." Modern History Source Book, 1998, http://www.fordham.edu, 3 pp.
In this letter defending Johannes Reuchlin, who had been condemned by the Catholic pope, Luther points to the Jews to demonstrate where the papacy's energies against heresy should be directed. He comments 'the Jews will always curse and blaspheme God." Luther also refers to them as "incorrigible."

_____. "The Jews and Their Lies, 1543" Modern History Source Book, 1998, http://www.fordham.edu, 77 pp.
In this essay, Luther again demonstrates the depth of his anti-Semitic attitudes. Luther had expected the Jews to convert, and when they failed to do so he turned against them. In this piece he refers to them as "miserable and accursed", and insists that Jesus compared the Jews to a "brood of vipers." He also cautions Christians to "be on guard against the Jews."

Manilla, Morton. "Wagner in the History of Anti-Semitism." Midstream (February 1986), Volume 32 Issue 2, pp. 43-46.
Manilla examines the continuous thread of anti-Jewish attitudes from early Christianity, through to the Enlightenment thinkers and on to Wagner. Just as Christianity insisted it had supplanted Judaism as the true religious faith, Wagner created his own folklore around the Germans who were, in his view, the new "chosen people."

Manuel, Frank E.   _The Broken Staff: Judaism Through Christian Eyes._ Cambridge: Harvard University Press, 1992, 363 pp.
According to Manuel, in their attacks on Christianity, in particular, and religious superstition, in general, the illuminati of the Enlightenment, such as Voltaire and Diderot, desacralized ancient Jewish history and religion to the point that it no longer was of any utility for Christians. In so doing, eighteenth century Enlightenment intellectuals left a legacy of anti-Jewish rhetoric and stereotyping that contributed to the growth of modern anti-Semitism.

Marissen, Michael and Johann Sebastian Bach. *Lutheranism, Anti-Judaism and Bach's St. John's Passion: With an Annotated Literal Translation of the Libretto.* **Cambridge: Oxford University Press, 1998, 128 pp.**
The author contends, that Bach's *St. John's Passion*, though a masterpiece, has become controversial due to the anti-Judaic content it took from the Gospel. While other scholars tend to overlook the link, Marissen directly confronts the feelings of Bach toward Judaism, and relates them to the theology of Lutheranism. The author maintains, however, that even though hostility toward the Jews seems evident in the work, this was not Bach's primary intent.

Markish, Shimon Pered8sovich. *Erasmus and the Jews.* **Anthony Olcott, Translator, Chicago: University of Chicago Press, 1986, 216 pp.**
The argument is made by Markish, that those who claim Erasmus was anti-Semitic are wrong. Erasmus was not an anti-Semite in the way in which his contemporary Martin Luther was. Rather he was anti-Jewish in the tradition of the Church. The author contends Erasmus' use of "anti-Jewish invectives were polemical devices or, at worst incidental lapses…" While Markish presents an interesting thesis, few scholars share his conclusions, and some find fault with his reasoning.

Martinez, Ayaso and Jose Ramon. "Tolerance and Intolerance in the Christian Kingdoms of Medieval Spain: The Case of the Jews." Europe at the Close of the 20th Century: An International Symposium Christianity-Judaism-Islam (May 1994), pp. 93-114.
The point is made that there was no real "golden age of coexistence" between Jews and non-Jews in the Christian medieval kingdoms of Spain. The truth is that earlier in the medieval period Jews were tolerated due to economic interests and concerns. However, this did not last and in the fourteenth and fifteenth centuries the Jews were rendered defenseless and suffered restrictions. Growing nationalist fervor prompted forced conversions. Over time racial prejudice was tied to the practice of religion. The Inquisition and the expulsion of Jews from Spain followed.

Marx, Karl. *A World Without Jews.* **New York: Philosophical Library, 51 pp.**
Originally published in 1843, these anti-Semitic references of Marx were made in conjunction with his over-all indictment of religions. Nevertheless, Marx's views about Jews were perverted by the Nazis and the Soviet Union for their own ends.

Mayo, Louise A. *The Ambivalent Image: Nineteenth Century America's Perception of the Jew.* **Fairleigh Dickinson University Press, 1988, 225 pp.**
Mayo explores the contradictory images of Jews in the nineteenth century. She examines religious and secular press, and literature in order to provide a clearer picture of why Jews have been, at one time or another, reviled or respected during the last century.

Mellinkoff, Ruth. *The Devil at Isenheim: Reflections of Popular Belief in Gruenewald's Altarpiece.* **Berkeley, CA.: University of California Press, 1988, 109 pp.**
This article provides an analysis of the nine painted panels produced by Matthias Gruenewald, that form the altarpiece at Isenheim. Jews are vilified in the paintings. For example, a chamberpot bears Hebrew letters. This serves to symbolize the decay of the "Old or Jewish Law". The author pinpoints additional derogatory imagery and contends, that during the Middle Ages Christian art was filled with negative portrayals of Jews.

Michael, Robert. "Luther, Luther Scholars and the Jews." Encounter (Fall 1985), Volume 46 Issue 4, pp. 339-356.
The author takes issue with Luther scholars who try to defend the theologian's anti-Semitic rhetoric. He insists, that their efforts to cast Luther's statements in a less controversial light ignore the reality. According to Michael, Luther's condemnations of the Jews were very much akin to the anti-Semitism later expressed by the Nazis. Michael contends, that Luther's insistence that the Jews were evil and should be cast out of Germany laid a strong foundation for the anti-Jewish hostility expressed by many German Lutherans during the Nazi regime.

Minerbi, Sergio I. *The Vatican and Zionism: Conflict in the Holy Land, 1895-1925.* **Oxford University Press, 1990, 253 pp.**
This volume describes the nature of the relationship between the Vatican and Zionists in the late nineteenth and early twentieth century. Minerbi concludes, that the Catholic Church opposed Zionism on the grounds that the Holy Lands should not be placed in the hands of the Jews. The author claims, that political, religious, and theological issues were brought together in forming the Vatican's position on Jewish settlement in the Holy Land. Pope Pius X explained to Theodore Herzl in a 1904 meeting, that support for Zionism was not possible.

Nepaulsingh, Colbert I. *Apples of Gold in Filigrees of Silver: Jewish Writing in the Eye of the Spanish Inquisition.* **New York: Holmes and Meier, 1995, 149 pp.**
During the Spanish Inquisition Jews forced to convert to Christianity wrote "*Converso* literature", which, according to the author, sent message to Jews that were incomprehensible to non-Jewish readers. Nepaulsingh insists, that these texts have stumped interpreters for years precisely because Christians understood them in a way that was often directly opposite to the way in which the Jewish writers meant them to be read. Thus, the gulf between Christian and Jew was clearly demonstrated by the "*Converso* literature."

Niewyk, Donald L. *The Jews in Weimar Germany.* **Baton Rouge: Louisiana State University Press, 1980, 229 pp.**
This work is an overview of the place of Jews in the Weimar Republic. The author

discusses the role Jews played in the economic and political life of the Republic (although weak on the religious and cultural component of Jewish life), as well as the manner in which they attempted to defend themselves against anti-Semitism. Niewyk refutes the charge that Jews passively accepted the Nazis' ascent to power, and concludes that there was little that the Jews could have done to save themselves. According to the author, even if they had been perfectly united, scrupulously free from unpatriotic affiliations, and ready to a man to put money and brains to work against the Nazi foe, it would not have altered the outcome in any significant way.

No Author or Editor Listed. *The "Other" as Threat: Demonization and Anti-Semitism: Papers Presented for Discussion at the International Conference.* **Jerusalem: Vidal Sassoon International Center for the Study of Anti-Semitism, Hebrew University, 1995, 651 pp.**
Although this text was "not for publication", there are a number of papers available that were submitted for the conference. The topics addressed include; "Why is the Jew Dirty?" especially in depictions of Christian folklore, the role of Christian anti-Semitism in antiquity, and the hostility of certain Christian scholars, who reacted unfavorably to the idea that Christianity contained Jewish elements. There is also a chapter that addresses the controversy surrounding *The Protocols of the Elders of Zion.*

Oberman, Heiko Augustinus. "Discovery of Hebrew and Discrimination Against the Jews: The *Veritas Hebraica* as Double-Edged Sword in Renaissance and Reformation." *Germania Illustrata: Essays on Early Modern Germany Presented to Gerald Strauss.* **Eds. Andrew C. Fix and Susan C. Karrant-Nunn. Kirksville, MO.: Sixteenth Century Journal Publishers, 1992, pp. 19-34.**
Oberman contends, that mendicant friars began to study the Hebrew language and the writings recorded in that tongue during the early years of the Renaissance in an effort to gain a better understanding of the Scriptures. However, despite these efforts of Renaissance humanists to study the ancient word and text, Hebrew never garnered the respect afforded to Latin and Greek. This denial of Hebrew importance, according to the author, was due to Christianity's hostility toward the Jews and Judaism. Oberman notes, that while the study of Hebrew should have lessened anti-Jewish feeling, it actually was used by the friars to intensify their anti-Jewish rhetoric.

_____. **Designed by Rosemary Ellis.** *The Impact of the Reformation.* **Eerdmans, William B. Publishing Company, 1994, 263 pp.**
In this examination of the Reformation period the author, in thee chapters, pays special attention to the hostility toward Jews, and its escalation. The three chapters include; "Three Sixteenth Century Attitudes Towards Jews: Reuchlin, Erasmus and Luther", "The Stubborn Jews: Timing the Escalation of Anti-Semitism in Late

Medieval Europe", and "Reuchlin and the Jews: Obstacles on the Path to Emancipation."

____. "The Stubborn Jews: Timing the Escalation of Anti-Semitism in Late Medieval Europe." Leo Baeck Institute Yearbook (1989), Volume 34, pp. xi-xxv.
According to Oberman, the attitude of Christians toward Jews evolved during the Middle Ages. The change came about as Christianity, which had long regarded the Jews as being "blind" to the recognition that Christ was the Messiah, began to see their refusal to convert as "stubbornness." From that point on Jews were viewed as a threat that needed to be driven from Christian society. The ghettos were instituted as a means to separate the Jews from others. This image of the Jews as "outsiders" who were unfit and therefore unwelcome in civilized society has persisted through modern times. Oberman notes, that the mendicant friars, Pope Paul IV and Martin Luther, among others played a role in promoting the segregation of the Jews.

Ocker, Christopher. "Ritual Murder and the Subjectivity of Christ: A Choice in Medieval Christianity." Harvard Theological Review (April 1998), http:// findarticles.com, 40 pp.
The author studies the ways in which libels against the Jews, especially ritual murder, were utilized and emotionally regarded by Christians during the Medieval era. Ocker concludes, that these slanders were so effective when disseminated, and were met with such approval by the Christian laity, that even when Church officials tried to curtail the negative reactions toward Jews, Christian communities continued to persecute the Jews.

Olster, David Michael. *Roman Defeat, Christian Response, and the Literary Construction of the Jew.* Philadelphia: University of Pennsylvania Press, 1994, 203 pp.
Olster examines the response of Byzantine writers to military defeat at the hands of the Muslims. He analyzes a series of dialogues between Christians and "caricatured Jews" that were written in the seventh century. Olster contends, that these dialogues offer views of Byzantine social and psychological reaction to defeat, not a record of the Judeo-Christian debate.

Paris, Erna. *The End of Days: A Story of Tolerance, Tyranny, and the Expulsion of the Jews From Spain.* Prometheus Books, 1995, 327pp.
The author presents an overview of the events and patterns that led up to the expulsion of Jews from Spain in 1492. Paris argues, that circumstances in the late-medieval period prompted the Catholic Church of Spain to resurrect older anti-Semitic views of church and state, and that Isabella and Ferdinand recognized the benefit of cooperating with the church because the Inquisition served as a centralizing force for Spain.

Parkes, James William. *Anti-Semitism.* **Chicago: Quadrangle Books, 1963, 192 pp.**
Written by a Church of England cleric, this text surveys the history of anti-Semitism including chapters addressing the issues of Jews as "political scapegoats" in the period between 1879-1914, and the *Protocols of the Elders of Zion.* Parkes attributes anti-Semitism as much to the teaching of the Christian Churches, as he does to the adoption of the psychological pattern of the "authoritarian personality" as developed by Theodore Adorno and others.

____. *Jewish Problem in the Modern World.* **London and New York: Oxford University Press, 1946, 242 pp.**
First published in England in 1939, Parkes attempts to understand the causes of anti-Semitism. Towards the end of his work, he includes chapters on the following subjects; the unique religious and historical experience of the Jews, their emancipation in the nineteenth century, their status between wars, the catastrophe in Germany, the Jewish presence in Palestine, the problem of contemporary anti-Semitism, and the responsibility of non-Jews in combating this menace to democracy.

Pasachoff, Naomi E. and Robert J. Littman. *Jewish History in 100 Nutshells.* **Northvale, New Jersey: Jason Aronson, 1995, 343 pp.**
Pasachoff reviews one hundred specific topics in Jewish history; including entries concerning Christianity and anti-Semitism, the *Marranos*, the Inquisition, Martin Luther and the Jews, blood libel cases, pogroms, *The Protocols of the Elders of Zion,* and the "Final Solution."

Pauley, Bruce E. *From Prejudice to Persecution: A History of Austrian Anti-Semitism.* **Chapel Hill: University of North Carolina Press, 1992, 426 pp.**
This book traces the process by which indigenous Austrian anti-Semitism became the Nazi variety. Anti-Semitism was stronger in Austria then elsewhere in Central and Western Europe, thus Austrian Jews were extremely vulnerable to the anit-Jewish and violence promoted by the Third Reich.

Peters, Edward. *Inquisition.* **New York: Free Press, 1988, 362 pp.**
The author provides a history of the Inquisition. He recounts the Christian anti-Semitism that was prevalent during the Middle Ages. Peters also examines the ways in which Christian tribunals operated during the Inquisition in their efforts to prosecute the *"Conversos"* in Spain, Portugal and the New World.

Pinson, Koppel S. *Essays on Anti-Semitism.* **New York: The Conference on Jewish Relations: 1946, 269 pp.**
The fourteen essays included in this volume discuss a broad array of the aspects of anti-Semitism. In many of the works the author notes the role of Christianity in

cementing anti-Jewish biases. Whether anti-Semitism was motivated socially, economically, or racially, the editor insists that Christianity's influence cannot be overlooked in any full discussion of the topic.

Poliakov, Leon. *The Aryan Myth: A History of Racist and Nationalist Ideas in Europe.* **New York: Basic Books, 1974, 388 pp.**
Poliakov contends, that as part of their critique of the Judeo-Christian tradition, eighteenth century European racialists questioned the genealogical teachings of the Church (that all men are descended from a common father) and, in so doing, rejected the Mosaic tradition. Toward the end of the eighteenth century, philologists were promoting the theory of a congenitally superior Aryan race, which originated not in the ancient Near East but in India. By 1900, writes Poliakov, the Aryan myth had become a scientific axiom accepted by the leading minds of Europe.

____. *The History of Anti-Semitism: Vol.3, From Voltaire to Wagner.* **New York: Vanguard Press, 1977, 582 pp.**
This third volume in a four-volume history of anti-Semitism deals with the period of the Enlightenment and early industrialization. Poliakov repeats the argument made in his earlier books that modern anti-Semitism is linked to the belief of many European writers in a superior Aryan race that was juxtaposed against the inferior Jewish race. To support his thesis, Poliakov quotes heavily from many original sources: laws, edicts, letters, literary works, etc.

Pope Benedict XIV. "Encyclical on Jews and Christians Living in the Same Space, 1751." Jewish Virtual Library, http://www,us-israel.org, 2002, 5 pp.
According to Pope Benedict, Christians in Poland had reason during 1751 to be concerned about Jewish influences. The pope's encyclical directed Christians to be aware of the negative impact that Jews would have when living in the same spaces as Christians. Although he warned Christians not to be incited to violence against the Jews in their midst, he did give permission to expel Jews from Christian communities.

Pope Innocent III. "Letter on the Jews, 1199." Internet Medieval Source Book, http://www.fordham.edu, 1996, 1 pp.
This short letter, written by Pope Innocent for distribution to Catholic congregations, commanded that no violence be used in attempts trying to convert Jews to Christianity. The pope further ordered that when Jews were celebrating their festivals no harm was to be done to them, nor were their activities to be "disturbed." Innocent continued by warning Christians not to deface Jewish cemeteries, or extort money from Jews desiring protection.

Ragins, Sandford. *Jewish Responses to Anti-Semitism in Germany, 1870-1914: A Study of Ideas.* **Cincinnati: Hebrew Union College Press, 1980, 226 pp.**

Traced in this works are; how the hatred of Jews in Germany was transformed, following their Emancipation in 1871, into scientific and political anti-Semitism, and how the Jewish community responded to its newly attained rights. The author contends, that the radical Zionist movement in Germany mirrored external forms of German nationalism, but Ragins concludes, the radical Zionist perspective also constituted an unprecedented, anti-liberal defection from the new emancipation ideology.

Ravid, Benjamin. "On the Spanish Expulsion of 1492." The Jewish Advocate (March 27, 1992), Volume 182 Issue 13, pp. 11.
The author proclaims, that the Jews expulsion from Spain in 1492 was a major trauma, and contends that the events leading up to forcing the Jews out began about a century beforehand. Ravid recounts, that in the fourteenth century Jews were told they could either convert to Christianity or face death. This pressure was increased throughout succeeding decades. When some Jews converted, it was feared that these newly baptized Christians might backslide if they were in contact with Jews, who remained steadfast in their commitment to Judaism. With this in mind, it was deemed necessary to protect the new converts by ridding Spain of all remnants of Jewish influence.

Reinharz, Jehuda. *Fatherland or Promised Land: The Dilemma of the German Jew: 1893-1914.*Ann Arbor: University of Michigan Press, 1975, 328 pp.
Reinharz examines the responses to anti-Semitism of two major German Jewish organizations. First, the Central Union of German Citizens of Jewish Faith, which stressed loyalty and Jewish assimilation, and then the Zionist Federation of Germany, which stressed Zionism as a means of strengthening Jewish identity and pride.

_____ and Walter Schatzberg, eds. *The Jewish Response to German Culture: From the Enlightenment to the Second World War.* Hanover: University Press of New England for Clark University, 1985, 1986, 362 pp.
The book consists of a collection of seventeen essays, which trace the past two centuries of German-Jewish history, from the promise of the Enlightenment to the Holocaust. Included is a perceptive essay by Steven Aschheim on "the origins and the function of the Judaization-myth from Wagner to Hitler.' Among the other contributors in the volume are; Kurt Duvall with an essay about the Nazi sponsored and directed Jewish cultural centers that tried to maintain links with German civilization, and Jacob Katz and Shulamit Volkov, who discuss the limits of Jewish assimilation into German society. The book's unifying theme is that from the start German-Jewish symbiosis was a fragile, one-sided, and doomed arrangement.

Reuchlin, Johannes and Peter Worstman (Editor). *Recommendation Whether to Confiscate, Destroy and Burn All Jewish Books: A Classic Treatise Against*

Anti-Semitism. **Paulist Press; 2000, pp. 90.**
The contention is made that Johanne Reuchlin's legal opinion of 1510, maintaining that books necessary to the Jewish faith should not be destroyed, did not halt the anti-Semitic attitudes developing among Protestants during the Reformation. It did, however, prevent the elimination of Judaism in Europe and opened the way for a better understanding of Judaism.

Reynolds, Jan. *Inheritance: The History of Israel and Christianity Unvieled.* **New York: Shapolsky, 1989, 498 pp.**
The author uses his own personal experiences in the ghettos and concentration camps to provide a more effective and meaningful way in which to present a history of the Jews from Biblical times to the Holocaust. Reynolds proposes that anti-Semitism, which is a Christian creation, has remained a constant through the centuries. He reviews the Crusades, the Inquisition and other persecutions of the Jews over time, and contends that these outbreaks of violent anti-Jewish feeling were often triggered by periods of crisis.

Robertson, Ritchie. *The Jewish Question in German Literature, 1749-1939.* **Oxford: Oxford University Press, 1999, 544 pp.**
From the first pleas for Jewish emancipation during the Enlightenment to the eve of the Holocaust, this literary study examines the uneasy position of the Jews in Germany and Austria.

Rose, Paul Lawrence. *German Question/Jewish Question: Revolutionary Anti-Semitism from Kant to Wagner.* **New Jersey: Princeton University Press, 1992, 411 pp.**
The works of Immanuel Kant and Johann Fichte, Rose argues, promoted modern forms of anti-Semitism in Germany. For both Kant and Fichte, the Jews exemplified a degraded moral existence, which threatened the decency of the German people. Rose contends, that this type of moral anti-Semitism was almost entirely the work of radical or revolutionary thinkers. In addition, in examining the works of Martin Luther and other theologians of his time, Rose finds an unbroken chain of anti-Semitic feeling between theologically derived and secular (racial) anti-Jewish prejudice, which culminated in the distinction made by the Nazis between *Deutschtum* and *Judentum.*

____. *Wagner: Race and Revolution.* **New Haven: Yale University Press. 1992, 246 pp.**
Rose places Wagner's racism and anti-Semitism within the context of the Young German Revolutionists who were obsessed with ethnicity, and the later *Völkisch* nationalists of the Bismarckian age. The author states, that despite his ideological meandering between liberalism, socialism, and monarchism, Wagner's politics were always guided by an abiding anti-Semitism.

Rosenberg, Stuart Eugene. *Secrets of the Jews.* **Oakville, Ont.: Mosaic Press, 1994, 197 pp.**
Rosenberg examines a broad spectrum of the anti-Semitic attitudes that have existed throughout recorded history. He discusses the ancient pagan anti-Jewish beliefs and pays particular attention to the long-term role Christianity has played in disseminating hostility toward the Jews. He studies the myths about Jews that were created by the early Christian Church, the growth of anti-Judaism through the Middle Ages and the types of modern anti-Semitism that evolved from Christianity's anti-Jewish propaganda. The author reviews the anti-Semitism of Marx and the Soviet Union. He also refutes the idea that Jews are cowardly and powerless. Additionally, Rosenberg draws attention to the Arabs and their use of the Jewish stereotypes, which were put forward in *The Protocols of the Elders of Zion.*

Roth, Cecil. *The History of the Jews of Italy.* **Philadelphia: The Jewish Publication Society of America, 1946, 575 pp.**
This book traces the lives of the Jews in Italy. The portrait painted about the relationship between the popes and the Jewish community is less than flattering. The author recounts the anti-Jewish preachings of the clerics within the Dominican order, as well as that of the Jesuits and Franciscans. Dr. Roth details the religious, economic, and social factors that contributed to shaping the Jews lifestyle in Italy, and presents a clearer understanding of the Catholic Church's attitude toward the Jewish community.

Roth, Norman. *Jews, Visigoths and Muslims in Medieval Spain: Cooperation and Conflict.* **Leiden: E.J. Brill, 1994, 367 pp.**
The author examines the conversion of Visigoths to Catholicism in 587, and notes, that the influence of Byzantine Christianity upon the Visigoths resulted in extreme degrees of anti-Semitism among Visogothic Christian Spaniards. Roth claims, that during this era the Eastern Church took a much tougher stance against the Jews than the Roman Church. The Jews of Visigoth Spain faced more virulent anti-Semitic measures than Jews anywhere else in medieval Europe. Forced conversions, polemics, and anti-Jewish legislation were the order of the day for Jews. Roth notes, that interestingly enough, these virulent anti-Jewish policies did not continue and later in Christian Spain a policy of cooperation with the Jews was put in place. The author also looks at how the Jews fared in Muslim Spain and in Muslim and Christian Spain. He contends Jews did fairly well under Muslim rule.

Rubin, Alexis, P., ed. *Scattered among the Nations: Documents Affecting Jewish History.* **Toronto: Wall and Emerson, 1993, 350 pp.**
One hundred and seventeen documents dealing with Jewish-Christian relations through history are supplied in this text and each is accompanied by a short explanation. Rubin contends, that most of the documents contain very anti-Jewish

sentiments. The book is divided into six primary sections which cover; the origins of Christian anti-Judaism, the Middle Ages, ritual murder and other accusations, Jewish emancipation, repression and the development of more modern anti-Semitism, the challenges that Jews faced from Communism, Zionism and Nazism, and the post-Holocaust experience.

Rubin, Miri. *Gentile Tales: The Narrative Assault on Late Medieval Jews.* **New Haven: Yale University Press, 1999, 257 pp.**
This book recounts the creation and growth of a principal anti-Jewish story from the Middle Ages and details the violence that it bred. In this tale the Jews were accused of desecrating the Eucharist, which for Christians is the manifestation of Christ's body. Rubin shows how widespread such stories were in Europe during the medieval era. The author contends, that no matter how outrageous the tale, there were educated men even within the priesthood,who believed the lies. These clerics used these stories to justify inciting violence against the Jews.

Rubin, Theodore Isaac. *Anti-Semitism – A Disease of the Mind: A Psychiatrist Explores the Psychodynamics of a Symbol Sickness.* **New York: Continuum, 1990, 146 pp.**
The author studies the elements of Christianity that emphasize the predisposition to make the Jews an object of "symbol sickness." Rubin notes the stages and effects that are part of the psychology of a symbol sickness. These include envy, alienation from feelings, and dehumanization. According to the author, due to its envy of Jews and Judaism, Christianity posed Jews as the devil and regarded continued Jewish existence as an insult. Rubin also examines the psychological basis of Hitler's hatred of Jews, and the factors that contribute to Jewish self-hatred.

Rudin, James A. "How the Po׳   Systematically Fanned the Flames of Hatred: They Demonized, They Denigrated and, as David Kertzer Sets Out to Prove, They Sowed the Seeds for the Shoah." Forward (October 26, 2001), Volume 105 Issue 31, 364, pp. B5.
The author uses this review of David Kertzer's book, *The Popes Against the Jews* to show how credible he finds the argument that the Vatican and Christianity played a major role in helping to develop the modern components of anti-Semitism. Rudin follows the trail Kertzer lays in forming his case. He addresses the actions of various popes toward the Jews and, like Kertzer, rejects the idea that there is any real difference between what is deemed "Christian anti-Judaism" and the Anti-Semitic attitudes that eventually culminated in the Holocaust and the murder of six million Jews.

Sachar, Howard Morley. *The Course of Modern Jewish History,* **Revised .ed. New York: Vintage Books, 1990, 891 pp.**
Though this text of modern Jewish history addresses a broader range of events and

ideas than the tie between Christianity and anti-Semitism, the author does deal with this subject matter. He emphasizes the interaction between Jews and the Catholics. Moreover, he examines the relationships of Jews to Christian and Eastern Orthodox Churches during each period, and within the borders of each country.

Santaniello, Weaver. *Nietzsche, God, and the Jews: His Critique of Judeo-Christianity in Relation to the Nazi Myth.* **Albany: State University of New York Press, 1994, 214 pp.**
Nietzsche's writings were used as an anti-Jewish propaganda tool by the Nazis, thus the question is asked; was Nietzsche an anti-Semite? The author contends, that Nietzsche was not an anti-Semite, but rather was an "anti" anti-Semite. Nietzsche's use of the term Jew was often a code word for Christian. Although Nietzsche was positively disposed towards the Ancient Hebrews, he was profoundly opposed to priestly Judaism, and the prophetic tradition, which is precisely the strand of Judaism from which Christianity came, and is the only element of Judaism that anti-Semites could view positively. Santaniello argues, that Nietzsche's alienation from German Christian culture arose in part from a series of personally disappointing, experiences and tragic losses. The author also relates the story in which Nietzsche's sister became allied with members of the Nazi party through the Wagner circle led by Cosima Wagner, Richard's widow. Santaniello connects these facts to the Nazi misappropriation of Nietzsche's ideas. The author maintains, the Nazi's clearly and knowingly misinterpreted many of Nietzsche's ideas, especially his hatred of anti-Semitism, in order to benefit their own ideological purposes.

Schorsch, Ismar. *From Text to Context: The Turn to History in Modern Judaism.* **Hanover, NH.: University Press of New England, for Brandeis University Press, 1994, 403 pp.**
This collection of essays focuses upon the significance of Christian anti-Jewish feeling in the development of German hatred of the Jews, and its eventual conclusion in the horrific policies of Hitler. Though Christianity is one link in the chain leading to the Holocaust, it is not the only one. The work of Salo W. Baron's is also examined, as is his claim, that there is far more to Jewish history and tradition than suffering and anti-Semitism.

____. *Jewish Reactions to German Anti-Semitism, 1870-1914.* **New York: Columbia University Press, 1972, 291 pp.**
Based on the author's doctoral dissertation, this work examines the responses of German Jews to anti-Semitism. At first German Jews believed that their Christian friends would refute anti-Semitism, but when this failed to happen, and anti-Semitism increased, many Jews overcame their reservations about self-defense and formed the Central Union of German Citizens of the Jewish Faith in 1893. The organization defended Jews against libel and growing political agitation. The Union maintained, that they could simultaneously be both good Germans and good Jews.

Segel, Binjamin W, and Richard S. Levy, ed. *A Lie and a Libel: The History of the Protocols of the Elders of Zion.* **Lincoln: University of Nebraska Press, 1995, 148 pp.**
This English translation of Segel's book is of historical value, inasmuch as it was first published in Germany in 1926 at the height of the *Protocols of the Elders of Zion's* popularity. Although Segel exposed the work as a forgery, its plot was, nevertheless, adopted as the official ideology of the Nazis, and disseminated throughout the United States by industrialist Henry Ford.

Shapiro, James. *Oberammergau: The Troubling Story of the World's Most Famous Passion Play.* **Knopf Publishing Group: 2000, 238 pp.**
This book provides a portrait of the German village where the Passion Play has been given since the tradition began in 1634. Shapiro notes the problems associated with the play and the efforts that have been made to defend, or correct, some of the hostility toward Jews that is evident in the drama. By studying the play, he presents a broader view of the complexities surrounding attempts to eradicate any remaining Christian anti-Semitism.

Shell, Marc. "*Marranos* **(Pigs) or, From Coexistence to Toleration." Critical Inquiry (Winter 1991), Volume 17 Issue 2, pp. 306-335.**
Shell examines the contrast in the treatment of Jews between Muslim Spain where religious tolerance was the practice, and Christian Spain in 1449 when the "purity of blood" laws were put into place and Christianity's doctrine proclaiming "all men to be brothers" was transformed into "only my brothers are men." When this revised doctrine took hold, men who differed from Christians could justifiably be treated as less than human. The author studies the philosophy of religious tolerance that was espoused by men like Locke during the seventeenth century. He also insists that anti-Semitism was not, as some have proposed, a result of Jewish "particularism" that was held over from Judaism and infected Christianity's "universalism." Rather, Shell contends, that Judaism encouraged tolerance, while Christianity, despite its claim to be tolerant, has turned to violence when the "Other" is regarded as a threat and an animal unworthy of humane treatment.

Singerman, Robert. *Spanish and Portuguese Jewry: A Classified Bibliography.* **Westport, CT.: Greenwood Press, 1993, 720 pp.**
This bibliography contains over five thousand items, including books, articles, dissertations, and theses. The issues of anti-Semitism and Christianity are part of chapters dealing with the expulsion of the *Conversos*, the Spanish riots of 1391, blood libel accusations, blood purity statutes, and controversies between Jews and Christians.

Smith, David Charles. "Protestant Anti-Judaism in the German Emancipation Era." Jewish Social Studies (1974), Volume 36 Issue 3-4, pp. 203-19.

Smith contends that three attitudes emerged in Protestant Germany that helped prepare Germans to accept the persecution of the Jews during the Third Reich. First, a conservative Christian view emerged during the nineteenth century, which portrayed Jews as a danger to the divine order. Second, the traditional view of Jews as blasphemers of Christianity remained intact, and third, Judaism was purported to have nothing in common with Christianity and was deemed unrepentant for rejecting Christ. Thus Judaism was regarded as a threat to Christianity and to all Germans. This idea of the Jew as a danger helped lay a basis for justifying the extermination of European Jewry during the Holocaust.

Smith, Helmut W. *Butcher's Tale: Murder and Anti-Semitism in a German Town.* Norton, W.W. and Company, Incorporated, 2002, 288 pp.
The unfounded accusation of ritual murder against Jews during 1900 in Germany, is the focus of Smith's work. Violent riots erupted over the charge that Jews had murdered a young Christian boy as a part of their religious practice. Smith places the accusation, and the violence that followed, under a microscope for study. He concludes that what happened in Konig, Germany shows a process in which different forces came together to make "latent anti-Semitism visible." He examines the religious, social and class factors that figured into this event and proposes that the towns-peoples' violence against Jewish neighbors was in effect a form of "ritual murder."

____. *Protestants, Catholics and Jews in Germany, 1800-1914.* Berg Publishers; 2001, 336 pp.
During the nineteenth century the divisions that existed between German Protestants, Catholics and Jews were broken down and redrawn as circumstances warranted it. The author examines these changing relationships and the ways in which these groups coexisted with one another and affected each other. His work stresses not only conflict, but also cooperation among these religious groups. Smith's study is an effort to create a new approach to the study of religion.

Sorkin, David Jan. *The Berlin Haskalah and German Religious Thought: Orphans of Knowledge.* Vallentine, Mitchell Press, 2000, 191 pp.
A revised theory about the eighteenth century's so-called "Jewish Enlightenment" is proposed by Sorkin. The author contends, that in the past the Jewish community has been considered out of context. In order to truly understand what was happening within, and to, the Jewish community, Sorkin maintains one must examine the other developments taking place in both the Catholic and Protestant faith communities during the same period.

____. *The Transformation of German Jewry, 1780-1840.* New York: Oxford University Press, 1987, 255 pp.
The emancipation of German Jews was marked by the dramatic transformation from

feudal status to absorption into the most extreme manifestations of Western society. The author examines the encounter of German Jews with modern culture, and their consequent cultural productivity.

Stone, Gregory B. "Ramon Llull vs. Petrus Alfonsi: Postmodern Liberalism and the Six Liberal Arts." Medieval Encounters (March 1997), Volume 3 Issue 1, pp. 70-93.
Stone contrasts the attitudes about non-Christian religions held by two medieval thinkers. The work of Ramon Llull, a Spanish postmodernist, is placed alongside the writings of Petrus Alfonsi, who was an Enlightenment thinker and Spanish convert. Through his study, Stone concludes, that it was Alfonsi who began the more modern anti-Semitic practices. He proposes that Alfonsi identified Judaism as the "religion of grammar, vernacular and history" and claimed Jews accepted the *Old Testament* literally. Christianity, on the other hand was a religion of logic and therefore more appropriate for the changing world. According to Stone, Alfonsi believed and wrote that Jews had consciously chosen to kill Christ, knowing full well that he was God. They intentionally opposed Christ.

Stow, Kenneth R. *Alienated Minority: The Jews of Medieval Latin Europe.* Cambridge: Harvard University Press, 1994, 346 pp.
The author's study of the Jewish community during what he terms as "Medieval Latin Europe" begins in the fifth century, when Pope Gregory I put forward restrictive policies under which the Jews were forced to live. Stow argues that the Church and State crafted a legal position for Jews that became progressively harsher as time passed. Ultimately the Jews were regarded as a danger to society as a whole, and therefore had to be kept under control.

Stroll, Mary. *The Jewish Pope: Ideology and Politics in the Papal Schism of 1130.* Leiden: E.J. Brill, 1987, 205 pp.
This volume by Stroll studies the schism that occurred between Anacletus II, whose family had converted from Judaism to Christianity and Innocent II. Many have argued that the conflict between the two played itself out only through ideological arguments. Innocent II represented this difference in ideologies. Stroll concludes, however, that the struggle was fought on a political level rather than in disagreements over beliefs. In Stroll's estimation, Innocent and his supporters used Anacletus's Jewish heritage against him. She contends, that after the First Crusade the depiction of Jews as usurers was widely accepted. Innocent was able to tie this image to the banking activities of Anacletus's family and successfully used anti-Semitic prejudice to discredit his rival.

Tal, Uriel. *Christians and Jews in Germany: Religion, Politics, and Ideology in the Second Reich, 1870-1914.* Ithaca and London: Cornell University Press, 1975, 359 pp.

Tal links the growing ranks of anti-Christian, anti-democratic, anti-Semitic tendencies in the Second Reich to the totalitarian ideology of the Third Reich. The author argues, that the natural alliance between liberal Protestants and Jews had a fatal flaw. According to Tal, liberal Protestantism, although opposed to anti-Semitism, pressed for the full assimilation of the Jews into the Christian culture of Germany. When it became clear that the Jews were resisting their loss of identity, liberal Protestants supported the nationalism that contributed to Jewish oppression.

Taylor, Simon. *Prelude to Genocide: Nazi Ideology and the Struggle for Power.* **New York: St. Martin's Press, 1985, 228 pp.**
The ideology of the National Socialists during the fourteen years prior to Hitler's accession to power is the author's focus. Taylor argues, that the Nazis depicted their assault against the Jews as a life and death struggle between German and Jew. The party successfully conveyed this message by using political rituals and celebrations that imitated Christian myth and symbolism. The Nazis, concludes the author, were successful in convincing followers that only through the annihilation of the Jews could Germany attain "its promised golden age of harmony and prosperity."

Terry, Michael, ed. *Reader's Guide to Judaism.* **Chicago: Fitzroy Dearborn Publishers, 2000, 718 pp.**
This resource provides information about a broad array of books and articles, which address Jewish Studies. The volume lists entries, which are alphabetically organized. Some of the entries that deal with Christianity and its connection to anti-Semitism and the Holocaust include; "Anti-Judaism in Late Antiquity and the Middle Ages", "The Crusades, the Inquisition, Jewish-Christian Relations in the Context of Apologetics", "Polemics and Current Dialogue",and "Responses to the Holocaust: Christian."

Timmer, David E. "Biblical Exegesis and the Jewish-Christian Controversy in the Early Twelfth Century." Church History (1989), Volume 58 Issue 3, 13 pp.
Timmer argues, that during the twelfth century Catholic Church leaders took more notice of Jewish disputation over Christian exegesis of the *Old Testament,* whereas in the century before there was little note taken of any challenge mounted by Jewish Biblical scholars. The author contends, that the reason for the change in the Churche'sresponse by the church, was that the Jews were better positioned in northern European countries, economically and culturally during the twelfth century and so they were perceived to be more of a threat to Christianity.

Traverso, Enzo. *The Jews and Germany: From the Judeo-German Symbiosis to the Memory of Auschwitz.* **Lincoln: University of Nebraska Press, 1995, 215 pp.**
Influenced by the works of Hannah Arendt, the author contends, that the Jews attempt to integrate themselves into both German and Austrian society before the Nazi seizure of power was doomed to fail. They could never escape their "pariah

status" based, in part, on the perception that they were "parvenus." The volume also includes an excellent discussion of the historiography of the Holocaust.

Van Rahden, Till. "Beyond Ambivalence: Variations of Catholic Anti-Semitism in Turn of the Century Baltimore." American Jewish History **(1994), Volume 82 Issue 1-4, pp. 7-43.**
Rahden studies the way in which Baltimore's Catholic weeklies depicted Jews. From the years 1890-1924, the imagery used in the Catholic Diocesan press to portray Jews was highly anti-Semitic. Language metaphors and themes helped shape the Catholic laity's concept of Jews and Judaism. The role that the Catholic Church played in formulating the relationship between Jews and non-Jews, outside the Catholic faith, is also explored.

Viereck, Peter. *Meta-Politics: The Roots of the Nazi Mind.* **New York: Knopf, 1941, 385 pp.**
Certain elements of the Nazi philosophy are rooted, according to Viereck, in German romantic poetry, music (Wagner), and social thought. From these sources Viereck traces elements of Nazism, such as the emphasis on irrationalism and hysteria, and the belief in a German mission to direct the course of world history.

Vital, David. *A People Apart: The Jews in Europe.* **New York: Oxford University Press, 2001, 944 pp.**
Covering European Jewish history from 1789 to 1939, Vital's book, makes the argument that regardless of the efforts of Jews to assimilate, or even become apostates, they were regarded as aliens in the nations of their birth. This was especially true in Germany where both traditional anti-Jewish attitudes and the newer racial anti-Semitism worked against Jewish assimilation. Vital concludes, that the prejudices that have characterized Europe's two thousand year history were simply too strong for Jews to withstand. The author recounts the political problems that engulfed the Jews of Europe, from the French Revolution until the Holocaust.

Wagner, Gottfried. *Twilight of the Wagners: The Unveiling of a Family's Legacy.* **New York: St. Martin's Press, 1999, 303 pp.**
The author, the great -grandson of Richard Wagner, is critical of his family legacy and has written a memoir about their relationship with Adolf Hitler. Wagner contends, that no one took Richard Wagner's polemics more to heart than Hitler, and that the Nazi leader was an inescapable presence on the Wagner estate. The book serves to remind us of the connection between Wagner and Hitler. The author calls for greater understanding between Germans and Holocaust survivors.

Walfish, Barry, ed. "The Frank Talmadge Memorial Volume, Part II." Jewish History **(1992), Volume 6 Issue 1-2.**
The articles in this special issue address anti-Semitism from the fifteenth through

the eighteenth centuries. Some of the subjects covered include; Kenneth Richard Stowe's discussion of " The Papacy and the Jews: The Catholic Reformation and Beyond", Mark Meyerson's study of "Aragonese and Catalan Jewish converts at the time of Expulsion", and Anita W. Novinsky's work detailing "Padre Antonio Vieira, the Inquisition, and the Jews. Other articles deal with various aspects of the Spanish Inquisition, the *Conversos*, attempts to convert the Jews to Christianity, expulsions from Christian countries, and legislation that was passed to regulate Jews living in Christian countries.

Wein, Berel. *Herald of Destiny*: *The Story of the Jews in the Medieval Era, 750-1650.* Brooklyn, NY.: Shaar Press, 1993, 333 pp.
Written by an Orthodox Rabbi, this story of the Jews existence during the medieval period covers a broad base of subjects. However, Wein notes that an integral part of this story deals with the "calamities" that befell the Jews, and with the fact that many of these tragedies were the result of Christianity's hostility toward Judaism and Jews. He addresses the Crusades, the Inquisition, the expulsion of Jews from Spain, Luther's anti-Semitic writings penned during the Reformation, and the role the Church played in the sixteenth and seventeenth century persecution of Jews in Poland.

Weiner, Marc A. *Richard Wagner and the Anti-Semitic Imagination*. Lincoln: University of Nebraska Press, 1995, 439 pp.
Weiner argues, that Wagner adopted medieval, European anti-Semitic folklore, which connected Jews with malodorous emanations and noxious stenches, and used them to depict evil characters in his operas. Although he never mentioned the word "Jew" in his operas, Wagner used subtle and effective ways to demonstrate negative images of Jews. Employing other superstitions, which identified Jews with devilry, Wagner utilized stereotypical appearances such as goat feet to associate the Niebelungen with the Jews. Mime and Alberich in the Ring cycle, and Beckmesser in *Die Meistersinger* are all examples of Wagner portraying Jews with negative physical characteristics. Similarly, Wagner was concerned about degenerative human nature, and used the characters of Hagen and Siegfried in *The Ring* cycle to demonstrate the danger of racial mixing (Hagen) as juxtaposed to the purity of race (Siegfried).

Weiss, John. *The Ideology of Death: Why the Holocaust Happened in Germany*. Chicago: I.R. Dee Publishers, 1996, 427 pp.
In this survey of anti-Semitism in German history, Weiss finds that it grew rapidly during the Napoleonic era and became a forceful ideology in the 1870s. By the 1890s anti-Semitism gained the dedicated support of the generation that brought Hitler to power. Drawing upon early notions of Jewish responsibility for Jesus' Crucifixion, the author argues that the demonic image of the Jew was fixed in the Middle Ages.

Willebrands, Johannes. "The Church Facing Modern Anti-Semitism." Christian Jewish Relations (Spring 1989), Volume 22 Issue 1, pp. 5-17.
The author examines the Catholic Church's attitude toward anti-Semitism from 1840 to the present time. He asserts, that the church has, with a few exceptions, constantly rejected modern anti-Semitic constructions. Willebrands presents evidence in which clerics, church hierarchy, and popes have condemned these prejudices against Jews. The author notes instances in which the Church was responsible for Jewish suffering, but he insists, that any anti-Jewish feeling was not theologically based.

Wistrich, Robert S. *Anti-Semitism: The Longest Hatred*. New York: Pantheon Books, 1992, 341 pp.
This general history of anti-Semitism traces anti-Jewish hatred from its roots in the pagan world, through centuries of the Christian teaching of contempt, to the Enlightenment, when Voltaire and Rousseau ridiculed Jews as inherently perverse. Wistrich provides a country-by-country survey as he attempts to show how anti-Semitism has appeared in the past, and how it manifests itself in its current state.

____. *Demonizing the Other: Anti-Semitism, Racism, and Xenophobia*. Amsterdam: Harwood Academic, 1999, 329 pp.
Wistrich seeks to explain how and why society fabricates images of others as an enemy or demon. The author uses a cross-cultural approach, and brings together all disciplines of the social sciences. He pays close attention to the imagery of the Jew as the "other", which is viewed as an enemy to be destroyed, and to the portrayal of Jews as "demons" in society. The broad base of opinions offered by the scholars who have penned essays for this book provides a measure of insight into what is regarded as commonplace prejudice and what should be designated as the more virulent and unique forms of stereotyping.

Wood, Diana. *Christianity and Judaism: Papers Read at the 1991 Summer Meeting and the 1992 Winter Meeting of the Ecclesiastical History Society*. Boydell and Brewer, Incorporated, 1998, 493 pp.
Both Jewish and Christian scholars have contributed to the thirty-two essays collected for this book. The writings address a wide array of topics that cover several centuries of Jewish-Christian relations, and pay particular attention to discovering why this relationship has remained so strained for so long. Some of the subjects included are; "The Faith of Christians and Hostility to Jews", Anti-Semitism and the Birth of Europe", "Desecration of the Host: The Birth of an Accusation", "Why the Spanish Inquisition?", "Catholic Anti-Judaism in Reformation Germany", "The Bishops and the Jews" and "The Roman Catholic Church and Genocide in Croatia 1941-1945."

Wright, Stephen King. *The Vengeance of Our Lord: Medieval Dramatizations of*

the Destruction of Jerusalem. **Toronto: Pontifical Institute of Mediaeval Studies, 1989, 233 pp.**
This book explores the medieval tradition of Passion Plays that focused upon the siege and destruction of Jerusalem in 70CE. These plays were extremely popular with audiences in Spain, Germany, Italy, France and England from the fourteenth through the sixteenth centuries. Wright provides an explanation for how these dramatizations began, and presents details about the anti-Jewish stereotypes that were employed by the Christians, who put on these plays. Many of the plots included the charge of deicide and the theory that the Jews received punishment from God because they rejected Christ.

Yerushalmi, Yosef Hayim. *Freud's Moses: Judaism Terminable and Interminable.* **New Have: Yale University Press, 1991, 159 pp.**
Freud's *Moses and Monotheism*, according to the author, attempted to understand the meaning of Jewishness under the Nazi threat. Yerushalmi insists, that Freud believed that anti-Semitism was prevalent among Christians, in par, because they were unaware of the attitude in themselves. Freud recognized the connection between Christianity and anti-Semitism. This, despite his own feelings of being separate and different from his Christian patients, he consciously continued to treat Christians and other Gentiles so that he could protect psychoanalysis from being targeted and destroyed as a "Jewish Science.

Yovel, Yirmiyahu. "Sublimity and Resentment: Hegel, Nietzsche, and the Jews." Jewish Social Studies (July 31, 1997), Volume 3 Issue 3, pp. 1-13.
Yovel discusses the ways in which the philosophers Hegel and Nietzsche dealt with the "Jewish Question" in their work. Both men undertook the task of presenting a philosophical understanding of the modern world, and each displayed mixed ideas about where the Jews fit into the world. Hegel, presenting his ideas in the early nineteenth century, held strong anti-Jewish feelings that were rooted in Christianity. Though he came to recognize that Judaism had some value, and he supported Jewish emancipation politically, his philosophical view remained centered on Christianity. The Jews, however, were central to Nietzsche's plan to promote a "revolution in values" that would root out the corruption of Christianity. Neitzsche, working to combat the decadence of the modern world as it was developing in the latter half of the nineteenth century, was not pro-Jewish from the standpoint of liberalism. Rather, he defended the Jews as the catalyst for his new Europe and believed their education and experience made them strong and stable enough to play a dominant role in changing humanity.

3

The Moral and Religious Response to the Nazi Persecution and Genocide of the Jews

Following their seizure of power in 1933, the Nazis attempted to transform the German churches by removing all vestiges of Jewish roots and influences. Lutheran clergy, supportive of the Nazis, willingly supported the elimination of the Hebrew scripture as a source of revelation and cleansed the churches of "Rabbi" Paul's Jewish influences on Christianity. Subsequent to the July 1933 church elections, the radical wing of the Lutheran church endorsed the creation of "Positive Christianity," whereby Jesus was purported to be of Aryan stock, and Christian doctrine was synthesized with Nazi racial anti-Semitism. When the so-called German Christian movement expelled baptized Jews from the churches and purged ministers of Jewish ancestry from their pulpits, there was a reaction by the rival conservative "Confessing Church." Pastors, such as Martin Niemoller, Otto Dibelius, and Dietrich Bonhoeffer, challenged the banishment of converts from the churches, even as they continued to maintain their traditional Lutheran antipathy towards the Jews. Thus, as the persecution of Jews in Germany intensified through the decade of the 1930s, most pastors in the Confessing Churches refrained from speaking out on their behalf. In September 1939, on the eve of World War II, it was too late to mount an effective challenge against National Socialism. By that time the anti-Nazi pastors, such as Martin Niemoller, were already being held in concentration Camps, or too intimidated by Hitler's regime to protest its policies.

The Concordat signed by the Catholic Church and German government in 1933 had little meaning. The Nazis almost immediately violated the provisions of the pact. Following Pope Pius XI's issuance of the encyclical *With Burning Anxiety* in 1937, which condemned the Nazi treatment of the church, the government retaliated by arresting monks and nuns and falsely charged them with crimes that ranged from financial malfeasance to sexual aberrations. Hundreds of Catholic priests and nuns were sent to concentration camps with the objective of intimidating and silencing the Catholic prelates in Germany. Nazi terror tactics, however, did not prevent the Catholic hierarchy, as well as Protestant clergy, from joining in a successful protest against the Nazi Euthanasia Program, which was introduced at the onset of the war in 1939.

On the eve of his death in 1939, Pius XI had prepared a draft of an encyclical that would have condemned anti-Semitism. It was never published. Despite the efforts of Pius XI, the more typical response of the Catholic Church in Germany to the Nazi persecution of the Jews was silence. This was due, in part, to the fact that the Nazi effort to neutralize the Catholic Church coincided with the German governments escalation of violence against the Jews. Some Catholics feared that the situation would further deteriorate if they spoke out on behalf of the Jews. But the silence was also due to deeply ingrained anti-Jewish feelings held by many German Catholics, as exemplified by the church sanctioned *Oberammergau* Passion play, which depicted Jews as Christ-killers. Additionally, the general lack of compassion displayed by Catholic prelates towards the deteriorating situation of the Jew encouraged German Catholics to avoid taking action on behalf of the Jews.

Following the death of Pius XI in 1939, Cardinal Eugenio Pacelli ascended to the Throne of Peter and took the name Pope Pius XII. The new pope's tenure (1939-1958) was marked by controversy with regard to his response to the Nazi extermination of the Jews. Much of the criticism directed towards Pius XII emanates from his failure to publicly voice moral outrage against the Nazi's plans to murder European Jews. It is clear that relatively early on he received news about Nazi death camps, such as Auschwitz, where Jews were being gassed on a daily basis and yet, for fear of retaliation against Catholics, he did little to respond. There is, however, another side to examine on this issue. When the matter of the Jews did not threaten the interests of the Catholic Church, the papacy was active on their behalf. Indeed, Israeli diplomat and historian Pinchas

Lapide credits the Vatican with saving the lives of more than 800,000 Jews from the Nazis. Monasteries and convents opened their doors to hide Jews, however, historians continue to question whether this sanctuary resulted from the individual acts of courageous Catholic clerics, or from "signals" given by the pope, that such risks would not be opposed by the Vatican.

The papacy's record during the Holocaust has been further tarnished by information about its involvement in aiding leading Nazis, such as Adolf Eichmann and Josef Mengele, to escape to South America at the end of the war. It remains to be resolved whether the same "signals" that gave permission for Catholic clergy to hide Jews during the Holocaust were similarly given in behalf of fleeing Nazi war criminals.

The deportation of Jews from ghettos to the death camps also tested the belief of observing Jews. The overall religious response on the part of Jews to the Holocaust was varied. Many Jews lost their faith in the camps, whereas, others affirmed their belief in the face of death. In places such as Auschwitz, God-fearing Jews viewed their precarious condition as a divine test in their long history of persecution Historians have recorded acts of religious martyrdom (*Kiddush HaShem*), whereby, religious Jews insisted on maintaining Jewish ritual observance even if it meant immediate death. Responses, ranged from fasting on the Day of Atonement, to the *shofar* audaciously being blown in Treblinka, to the construction of a mini Succah in Mauthausen, and to adhering to the religious requirement of praying three times a day. All were characteristic responses of many Orthodox Jews held prisoner in the Nazis death camps.

The Nazis, while exterminating approximately six million Jews, murdered many rabbis and their students. Indeed, the flower of Jewish Orthodoxy perished in the Holocaust. In recent years, however, a small number of scholars have uncovered a controversial aspect of this tragedy. Despite the apparent Nazi danger, many heads of *yeshivas* (Talmudic academies) urged their students to remain in Europe even when they had opportunities to emigrate to the United States and other parts of the world. Once the Nazi onslaught against the Jews intensified, however, many of these heads of *yeshivas* fled to the United States, leaving their students behind. Many of those students eventually perished in the death camps. Additionally, recent scholarship has charged that the rescue attempts of Orthodox Jewish organizations in the United States primarily focused on efforts to rescue their fellow observant Jews.

Aarons, Mark, John Loftus, *Unholy Trinity*, St. Martins Press, 1997, 392 pp.
Aarons and Loftus explore the links between the Vatican, the British, and American intelligence agencies in the post war era. The authors contend, that these three entities conspired to help Nazi war criminals escape punishment for

WWII atrocities. The story they relate is complex and controversial.

Abramsky, Chimen, Maciej Jachimczyk, and Antony Polonsky, eds. *The Jews in Poland.* Oxford: Blackwell Publishers, 1986, 264 pp.
This book is a compilation of essays presented at the International Conference on Polish-Jewish Studies held at Oxford in 1984. It deals with the subject of Polish-Jewish relations, as well as Polish anti-Semitism.

Adler, Jacques. "The French Churches and the Jewish Question: July 1940-March 1941." Australian Journal of Politics and History (September 2000), Volume 46 Issue 3, pp. 357-378.
The author suggests a number of reasons why the French Catholic Church failed to speak out against the race laws that were introduced in France after the military defeat of 1940. Though the Catholic Church in France had rejected racism and anti-Semitism prior to the war, the Church hierarchy believed that under the new French government Catholicism might regain rights that had been taken away during the governance of the Republic, and well return to its former level of prominence in society. Because of its "silence" while fifty-thousand Jews were deported to death camps, the author concludes, that the Church relinquished any claim to moral integrity.

Akin, James. "How Pius XII Protected Jews." This Rock (February 1997), pp. 12-17.
In defense of Pius XII, Akins reports on the pope's statements, which condemned Nazi policies both before and during World War II. He also recounts Pius's efforts to save the lives of as many Jews as possible during the Holocaust.

Allen, John L. Jr. "Pope of Infallibility Set for Beatification." National Catholic Reporter (September 1, 2000), http://www.natcath.com/NCR.
The controversy surrounding the Vatican's decision to beatify Pope Pius IX is the focus of this article. According to the author, the statements of Pope John Paul II, renouncing anti-Semitism are deeply undercut by his beatification of a pope, who in 1858 used his power and influence to kidnap a Jewish boy (Edgaro Mortara) and bring him up as Catholic. Allen notes other troubling aspects of Pius IX's reign as pope; for instance he opposed the human rights standards of his own time. Additionally, the Catholic Church through Pius's *Syllabus of Errors* (1864) stood at the forefront of those who fought liberalism and modern culture, and in 1870 Pius IX issued the declaration of "papal infallibility." Allen contends, that few popes have been designated saints. He questions the wisdom of adding Pius IX to that list, especially since it might well reopen old wounds and hinder the dialogue that has been developing between Jews and Catholics.

Almog, Schmuel. *The Jewish Point: Jews as Seen by Themselves and by*

Others. **Tel-Aviv: Sifriat Poalim, 2002, 227 pp.**
This volume contains a collection of essays that deal with anti-Semitism, both Christian and modern, as well as the Holocaust. Examples include; "Neo-Pagan Reactions to the Jewish Roots of Christianity", The Other as Threat", "On Christian and Nazi Anti-Semitism", and the "Impact of the Holocaust on the Study of Anti-Semitism".

Altmann, Berthold. *Studies in Medieval German Jewish History*. New York: American Academy for Jewish Research, 1940, 94 pp.
Altmann asserts, that as late as the eleventh century Jews were free, respected and privileged in Western Europe. However, their freedoms were severely curtailed by the thirteenth century, and they had no rights left by the fourteenth century. He argues, that this was the result of the medieval townspeople's growing autonomy, and the struggle to retain power locally. The citizens of the town needed to expand their territory and jurisdictional control, and the Jews property rights hampered their efforts. The author contends, that the people in these towns justified their attacks upon Jews through Christianity's negative teachings. Robbing the Jews of their property and rights was acceptable because they were "evil" and "murderers of Christ." The Jews were coerced into giving up privileges in exchange for protection.

Alvarez, David and Robert A. Graham, S. J. *Nothing Sacred: Nazi Espionage Against the Vatican 1939-1945*. London: Frank Cass, 1997, 190 pp.
This article details the efforts of the Nazi government to establish a network of agents that could report on the activities of the Vatican during World War II. Despite Hitler's diplomatic overtures to the Vatican, he remained suspicious of the Catholic Church and its influence among Catholics throughout the world. The Nazi's attempts to spy upon the pope met with limited success.

Ancel, Jean. "The Christian Regimes of Romania and the Jews 1940-1942." Holocaust and Genocide Studies (Spring 1993), Volume 7 Issue 1, pp. 14-29.
The author points out, that the fascist regimes of Romania considered themselves Christians. They employed traditional Christian stereotypes as the justification for their anti-Jewish policies. Ancel notes, that many Catholic priests were among the supporters of violent anti-Semitism, and the hierarchy of the Christian Churches helped validate anti-Semitic propaganda through theology. Despite this level of support for the fascists by Church prelates, the author contends, that there were attempts by the Christian Churches to stop the deportation of Jews from Romania. However, he also admits that the Romanian government was more influenced by the war effort and national interests than by the Church's protests. Thus virulent anti-Semitic policies continued.

Arbesmann, Rudolph. "German Catholic Bishops Protest." Thought (December 1945), Volume 20 Issue 79, pp. 751-761.
Using letters written to Hitler's government from Germany's Catholic Bishops, as evidence, the author contends, that Germany's prelates took an active role in resisting the Nazis. The letters challenged Hitler's decision to exterminate those he deemed "unworthy of life." Arbesmann maintains, that the letters were meant to include anyone targeted by the Nazis for death.

Arendt, Hannah. *"The Deputy*: Guilt by Silence?" Amor Mundi: Explorations in the Faith and Thought of Hannah Arendt. Ed. James W. Bernauer. Boston: Martinus Nijhoff Publishers, 1980, pp. 51-58.
The author concurs with the controversial views of Rolf Hochuth as stated in his play *The Deputy*. Hochuth was critical of Pope Pius XII' silence about the Holocaust. Moreover, the playwright faults the pope for failing to take a strong moral stance and openly oppose Hitler's policies. The article also examines the political and traditional anti-Semitic issues that affected the Vatican's actions during World War II.

Article. "New Data Tells How Catholic Nuns Saved Jewish Children in Wartime Poland: One of Our Finest Hours." Polish American Journal (July 1, 1997), pp 3.
According to this article, the Christians in Poland were not "bystanders" during the Holocaust. The full story of how Christians helped save Jews is now coming to light. The article specifically takes note of the efforts of Catholic nuns who were members of the Sisters of the Holy Family of Nazareth. These women risked death in order to shelter Jewish children from the Nazis. This group of nuns and others "wrote a glorious page in the history of Catholic Poland."

Athans, Mary Christine. *The Coughlin-Fahey Connection: Father Charles E. Coughlin, Father Denis Fahey, C. S.Sp., and Religious Anti-Semitism in the United States, 1938-1954.* New York: Peter Lang, 1991, 265 pp.
The author argues, that Coughlin's anti-Semitism coincided with the beginning of his close relationship with Father Fahey in 1938. Two weeks after *Kristallnacht* (November 9-10, 1938), Father Coughlin began to publicize the *Protocols of the Elders of Zion* and justified the Nazi persecution of the Jews as a defense mechanism against Communism. Athans contends, that Fahey provided Coughlin with a theological framework for his anti-Jewish crusade, which enabled him to attract millions of Americans to his cause.

____. "A New Perspective on Father Charles E. Coughlin." Church History (1987), Volume 56 Issue 2, 18 pp.
This article provides a concise rendition of the thesis Athans used in her 1991 book about Father Coughlin. The author lays out her evidence and concludes,

that much of what Coughlin used as the foundation for his anti-Semitic campaign originated with the ideas of Father Denis Fahey.

Bacharach, Zvi (Walter). "From Jewish Emancipation to Genocide: Another Reflection on Germany's "*Sonderweg.*"   Bar-Ilan Studies in History (1991), Volume 3, pp. 113-121.
The ethical component of "*Sonderweg*", according to the author, is overlooked in the argument made by many German historians when addressing the treatment of the Jews in Germany.   The author points out, that the German people were Christians as well as citizens. Therefore, in Bacharach's opinion Christianity's role in promoting anti-Jewish attitudes among Germans cannot be ignored. This is especially true when studying their ability to move from a mostly religious anti-Semitic stance to acceptance of the criminal acts committed against the Jews during the Holocaust.

Baerwald, Friederich. "Catholic Resistance in Nazi Germany."Thought (June, 1945), Volume 20 Issue 77, pp. 217-235.
The author discusses the role that German Catholics played in resisting Nazi fascism. He insists this can "no longer be put off, because some elements of society are distorting and suppressing facts." Baerwald contends, that two groups are trying to libel the Catholic Church in Germany; anti-Catholics and anti-Germans. He counters claims that German Catholics did nothing to oppose Hitler. He shows that they too were targeted by the Nazis and recounts the efforts that some Catholics made to fight the Nazis and to help Jews.

Balling, Adailbert Ludwig and Reinhard Abein. *Martyr of Brotherly Love: Father Engelmar Unzeitig and the Priest's Barrachs at Dachau.* Crossroad Publishing Company, 1992, 128 pp.
Father Unzeitig, only two years after his ordination, was arrested by the Gestapo and sent to Dachau for defending Jews in his sermons. While a prisoner in the camp, he served as a volunteer in the typhus ward. Father Unzeitig died just weeks before liberating armies arrived at the camp. This biography was originally published in Germany in 1985.

Bankier, David, ed. *Probing the Depths of German Anti-Semitism: German Society and the Persecution of the Jews, 1933-1941.* Berghahn Books, 1999, 585 pp.
The papers in this book were presented at a conference in Israel that was convened to address the charges made by Daniel Goldhagen in his book *Hiltler's Willing Executioners.* The papers are divided by topic. Several of these sections address the role of the Christian Churches in promoting anti-Semitic beliefs, as well as the Church's response to the Holocaust.

Baranowski, Shelley. *The Confessing Church, Conservative Elites and the Nazi State.* **Lewiston NY: Edwin Mellen Press, 1986, 185 pp.**
This book shows the weak record of conservative opposition to the Nazi regime. It also details the attitude of the Confessing Church's attitude toward National Socialism, and toward the Nuremberg Laws in Germany. Baranowski notes the Protestant Churches' limited criticism concerning Nazi anti-Semitic policies. She also discusses the fact that many Protestant Church leaders agreed with the removal of Jews from public office and some went so far as to support the Nazi's call for German racial purity.

Barnett, Victoria. *Bystanders: Conscience and Complicity during the Holocaust. Conn***: Greenwood Publishing. 1999, 208 pp.**
Bystander behavior, the author contends, cannot be attributed to a single cause, such as anti-Semitism, but can only be understood within a complex framework of factors that shape human behavior individually, socially, and politically. The work draws upon the insights of historians, Holocaust survivors, and Christian and Jewish ethicists.

____. *For the Soul of the People: Protestant Protest against Hitler.* **Oxford and New York: Oxford University Press, 1998, 358 pp.**
Drawing on sixty interviews of Germans who were active in the Confessing Church, Barnett describes the moral confrontation between this group of Protestants and the Third Reich. In the process, the author illuminates the cultural, political and religious considerations responsible for the failure of a majority of German Protestants to resist National Socialism

____. "Guilt and Complexity." **Christian Century (October 10, 2001), Volume 118 Issue 27, pp. 26.**
Barnett examines the controversy surrounding the role that the Catholic Church and Pius XII played in the Holocaust. In reviewing some of the recent books that address this subject, Barnett concludes, that quite possibly no matter how much information is discovered the record on Pius XII will always remain complex and inconclusive. Ultimately, according to Barnett, the Vatican would appear both heroic and cowardly.

Bartoszewski, Wladyslaw. *The Warsaw Ghetto: A Christian's Testimony.* **Boston: Beacon, 1987, 117 pp.**
The author, a Polish Catholic and founder of the "Council for Aid to the Jews," describes how Poles risked their lives to help Jews. In attempting to show that Poles were not as indifferent to the plight of Jews as has been reported, Bartozewski recounts the organizations' work with both Jewish and Christian underground groups in helping Jews escape the Nazi terror. The council forged papers, provided food, and gave shelter.

Batzdorff, Susanne M. *Aunt Edith: The Jewish Heritage of a Catholic Saint.* **Springfield: Templegate Publishers, 1998, 237 pp.**
Batzdorff is a niece of Edith Stein; the controversial convert to the Catholic faith who was murdered at Auschwitz and was later made a saint by the Catholic Church. The purpose of the book is to honor Edith Stein's Jewish background, but the volume also includes the author's "own participation in the dialogue between Jews and Christians energized by her memories of Aunt Edith."

Bauer, Yehuda. "Christian Behavior During the Holocaust." Jewish Spectator (Fall 1978), Volume 43 Issue 3, pp. 17-21.
This is a criticism of the Vatican for its extremely cautious approach in confronting the Nazis and aiding the Jews during the Holocaust. Bauer insists, that there are few generalizations that hold true when studying the attitudes of Gentiles towards Jews during the Holocaust. However, he does accept the following; that countries opposed to Hitler were more inclined to help Jews, and that minority churches showed a greater regard for their Jewish members than larger religious institutions.

Baum, Rainer C. *The Holocaust and the German Elite: Genocide and National Suicide in Germany,* **1871-1945. Totowa: Rowman & Littlefield Press, 1981, 374 pp.**
Although a majority of the German people did not share the murderous anti-Semitism found within the higher echelons of the Nazi party, the author contends, that confusion about values was so prevalent during the Third Reich that the population remained passive in response to the ruthless policies of Hitler's henchmen.

Bein, Alex. *The Jewish Question: Biography of a World Problem.* **New York: Herzl Press, 1990, 784 pp.**
Christianity's influence on the development of anti-Semitism, the formation of the ghettos, anti-Jewish legislation programs, persecution of the Jews, and Martin Luther's anti-Jewish writings are just a few of the topics covered as Bein traces the origins and developments of the so-called "Jewish Question" in Europe. The author traces how early religious anti-Jewish attitudes helped facilitate the development of more modern forms of anti-Semitism in the nineteenth and twentieth centuries. Bein also studies the various reactions Jews have had to anti-Jewish attacks, and looks at Nazi Germany and the different phases of Hitler's anti-Jewish policy, as well as the Holocaust.

Bentley, Eric, ed. *The Storm over the Deputy: Essays and Articles About Hochuth's Explosive Drama.* **New York: Grove Press, 1964, 254 pp.**
Rolf Hochuth's drama, *The Deputy,* triggered an impassioned debate among Catholics and non-Catholics about Pope Pius XII's actions during the Holocaust.

Eric Bentley has compiled representative responses written about the subject. The essays he includes were written by, clerics, historians, philosophers, Catholics, and non-Catholics.

Bentley, James. *Martin Niemoller, 1892-1984.* **New York: Free Press, 1984, 253 pp.**
This book recounts the life of a founder of the Confessing Church, Martin Niemoller. Niemoller stood in opposition to the Nazis' efforts to control the Germany's churches. However, the famed cleric shared the same anti-Semitic sensibilities that many of the other leaders of the Confessing Church exhibited. It was not until the war was almost over that he repented his anti-Semitic attitudes. Bentley's work details Niemoller's opposition to the Nazis, in the form of his published pamphlets, sermons, and outspoken opposition to Hitler. His criticisms earned him imprisonment. Yet, Niemoller maintained his commitment to pacifism, and eventually concluded "the Jews in Germany were more like Christ than the Christians who persecuted them."

Berenbaum, Michael, ed. *Mosaic of Victims: Non-Jews Persecuted and Murdered by the Nazis.* **New York: New York University Press, 1990, 320 pp.**
The essays focus on the persecution of Gypsies, Russian Prisoners of War, homosexuals, Jehovah's Witnesses, Catholic activists, pacifists, and others. The volume is organized into sections dealing with the politics of extermination, forced labor, non-Jewish children, the position of German Catholics, and the Nazi programs for sterilization and euthanasia.

____and Abraham Joseph Peck, eds. *The Holocaust and History: The Known, the Unknown, the Disputed, and the Reexamined.* **Bloomington, Indiana: Indiana University Press, 1998, 836 pp.**
Included in this collection of articles dealing with the history of the Holocaust are pieces that address the reaction of the Catholic Church to the Holocaust, the German Christian Movement's "Ecclesiastical Final Solution", the use of Christian anti-Semitism in Nazi propaganda, the moral courage of rescuers, and post-Holocaust theologies.

Bergen, Doris L. "Collusion, Resistance, Silence: Protestants and the Holocaust." Dimensions (1998), Volume 12 Issue 2, pp. 31-36.
Bergen traces the role German Protestantism played in promoting European anti-Semitism. She begins her study in the sixteenth century, when Martin Luther made his vitriolic anti-Jewish statements, and continues her examination through to the Protestant leaders, who cooperated with those espousing racist ideology in the twentieth century. The author argues, that the anti-Semitic atmosphere, promoted by Christianity, helped to foster a climate in which

National Socialism and the Holocaust occurred. She also concludes, that anti-Semitic teachings prompted Christians to stand by passively while the Nazis exterminated Jews.

_____. "Germany is Our Mission – Christ is Our Strength: The Wermacht Chaplaincy and the German Christian Movement." Church History (1997), Volume 66 Issue 3, 15 pp.
The author insists, that the myth that German soldiers had nothing to do with the atrocities committed against the Jews has been shattered. As evidence, Bergen determines the role that Protestant and Catholic chaplains played in the crimes of the Nazi state, while ministering to the German troops placed under their spiritual care.

_____. " The Nazi Concept of *Volksdeutsche* and the Exacerbation of Anti-Semitism in Eastern Europe, 1939-1945." Journal of Contemporary History (October 1994), Volume 29 Issue 4, pp. 569-582.
The Nazi ideology of *Volksdeutsche* intensified anti-Semitism among the citizens of Eastern Europe. Hitler's racial policies were aimed at ridding Eastern Europe of Jews and replacing them with ethnic Germans. Though there was a measure of antagonism between the Church and the Nazis, some German religious leaders put aside their more traditional theologically based anti-Judaism and adopted the more virulent racial anti-Semitism promoted by Hitler.

_____. "Old Testament, New Hatreds: The Hebrew Bible and Anti-Semitism in Nazi Germany." *Sacred Text, Secular Times: The Hebrew Bible in the Modern World*. Leonard J. Greenspoon and Bryan F. LeBeau, eds. Omaha, NE.: Creighton University Press, 2000, pp. 35-46.
The author ties the traditional religious anti-Judaism of Christianity to the Nazis' use of racial anti-Semitism. Bergen supports her contention by showing the ways in which the Nazis employed Biblical allusions in their propaganda. This religious aspect of anti-Jewish feeling made racial hatred of the Jews all the more potent, for stereotyping the Jews with images like that of Judas was familiar to Germans, and therefore easy for them to understand.

_____. *Twisted Cross: The German Christian Movement in the Third Reich*. Chapel Hill: University of North Carolina Press, 1996, 341 pp.
The approximately six hundred thousand self-described "German Christians" were Protestants who sought to purge all Jewish elements from Christianity. Their efforts included attempts to purify the *Old Testament* and Jesus of Jewish traces. These "German Christians" also held key positions within the Protestant churches.

_____. and Johnathan Sperber. "Catholics, Protestants and Christian Anti-

Semitism in Nazi Germany." Central European History (1994), Volume. 27 Issue 3: pp. 329-48.

Most Catholics and Protestants held deep antipathies towards Jews during Hitler's twelve-year claim to power in Germany, yet the Nazi's were unable to persuade these groups to become part of the German Christian Church. Catholics were especially reluctant to give up their separate identity because it would eliminate their claim of superiority to other churches. The author contends, that the anti-Semitic feelings displayed by Catholic and Protestant churches helped promote the persecution of the Jews.

Berkovits, Eliezer. *With God in Hell: Judaism in the Ghettos and Death Camps.* New York: Sanhedrin Press, 1979, 166 pp.

Berkovits contends, that the response of observant Jews in the ghettos and the camps renders possible some inkling of the mystery of the Jewish faith, and offers examples of Jewish belief and observance during the Holocaust. He concludes, that "authentic Jews" armed with faith were better able to maintain self-respect in the camps than were "others," especially assimilated Jews.

Berkowicz, Jacek, Anna Kamienska and Szymon Datner, eds. *Under One Heaven: Poles and Jews.* Translator: William Brand. Warszawa: Wiez, 1998, 366 pp.

Though this volume contains a wide array of articles dealing with Jewish themes, several address the relationship of Christianity to anti-Semitism and the Holocaust. For example; "A Poor Christian looks at the Ghetto", "Did the Jews Crucify Jesus?", "The Jews as a Christian and Polish Problem", "Anti-Semitism and Religious Formation", "The Sin of Anti-Semitism" and a piece about the "The Jewish Children", which details the rescue of Jewish youth sheltered in a monastery.

Besancon, Alain. "The Second Silence of the Church." Midstream (1984), Volume 30 Issue1, pp 3-6.

The Catholic Church and the papacy have been charged, by many, with the crime of remaining silent during the Nazi atrocities of the Holocaust. Now Besancon claims they have repeated their moral failure by not speaking out against the crimes of Communism since 1964.

Besier, Gerhard. "Anti-Bolshevism and Anti-Semitism: The Catholic Church in Germany and Nationalist Socialist Ideology 1936-37." Journal of Ecclesiastical History (1992), Volume 43 Issue 3, pp. 447-56.

Both the Nazi government and Christianity both feared the threat of Communism. Supporters of National Socialism contended, that the Jews were closely tied to Bolshevism. Though the Catholic Church rejected the Nazi's racial anti-Semitism, the long held antipathy of Christianity toward those who practiced Judaism made it easier for them to support the Nazis in their efforts to fight Bolshevism.

Biberstein, Michael. "Open Letter to John Paul: Speak the Whole Truth about Christians and the Holocaust." National Catholic Reporter (October 23, 1998), http://www.natcath.com/NCR_online/archives/search.html.
As a member of Edith's Steins family, the author decided to publish a letter written to Pope John Paul by family members. This correspondence was sent prior to their trip to Rome for Stein's canonization ceremony in which the Catholic Church declared Edith a saint. The family sought to remind the pope of Edith's Jewish heritage. Moreover, she was raised as a Jew, and therefore was forced to counter the anti-Semitic propaganda of the Nazis and Christians. In fact, she continued to defend other Jews after she became a Catholic. They noted Stein's letter to Pius XI requesting an audience, so that she might speak to the pontiff about the plight of Jews. Stein lamented Pius's refusal to grant the request. Edith's family also took the opportunity to speak about their personal disappointment over the Vatican's statement *We Remember*. In their opinion, it provided a misleading picture of Christian efforts to help the Jews during the Holocaust. The letter complements John Paul for his efforts at reconciliation and asks that he keep in mind Edith Stein's pursuit of truth, so that the church might work toward the same goal.

Binchy, D.A. *Church and State in Fascist Italy*. New York: Oxford University Press, 1942, 774 pp.
Binchy studies the relationship between the Catholic Church and the Italian Fascist government of the 1930s. The author notes the "tragic error" of "clerico-Fascism." He presents a detailed examination of Mussolini and Pius XI and is critical of the Lateran Treaty and the Concordat. He does point out, that Pius XII did use his authority to stand up against the anti-Semitic laws of 1938.

Blet, Pierre, S.J. "The Myth in the Light of the Archives: The Recurring Accusations Against Pope Pius XII." Eternal World Television Network, 2002, http://www.ewtn, 9 pp.
Blet uses files from the archives of the Vatican to challenge those critics, who accuse Pope Pius XII of remaining impassive and silent while Jews died during the Holocaust. The author insists, that the charges are baseless and asserts, that those who continue to slander the pope do so without sufficient evidence.

____, Angelo Martini, and Burckhart Schneider. *The Holy See and the War in Europe, March 1939-August 1940*. London: Herder Publications Ltd., Cleveland and Washington: Corpus Books, 1968, 495 pp.
The volume contains Vatican documents regarding its response to the first years of World War II.

_____. *Pius XII and the Second World War: According to the Archives of the Vatican*. Lawrence Johnson, Translator. Mahwah: Paulist Press, 1999, 416 pp.

Based on the Vatican archives made available in 1964, Blet concludes that far from being "silent' in the face of the Nazi persecution of the Jews, Pius XII did much more privately than publicly to protect Jews and others threatened by the National Socialist regime. While this account refutes some evidence, it by no means provides final answers to the questions surrounding Pius.

Bliach, Roland."A Tale of Two Leaders: German Methodists and the Nazi State." Church history (June 2001), Volume 70 Issue 2, pp. 199-225.

The author shows how the Nazis, at a time when Hitler was still vulnerable, tried to use German religious institutions to help shape opinion about the Third Reich in foreign countries. Bliach details the cooperation, and the few points of opposition, that Methodist clerics demonstrated toward the Reich. The author concludes, that while many clerics in the post-war era have argued that they offered little resistance to the Nazis so that their churches would survive, they would be better served to ask themselves if their denominations have retained any moral integrity.

Block, Gay. *Rescuers: Portraits of Moral Courage in the Holocaust.* New York: Holmes & Meier, 1992, 255 pp.

This work presents forty-nine personal accounts of non-Jewish citizens in various European nations, who risked their lives to protect resident Jews from the Nazi horror.

Bowman, Steven Barrie. "Greek Jews and Christians During World War II." *Remembering for the Future: Working Papers and Addenda*. Volume 1-111, Oxford: Pergamon Press, 1989, pp. 215-222.

In this work the author contends, that there was no official anti-Semitism in Greece. He notes, that his assertion was formed through a review of the history of the Greek Orthodox Church's relations with the Jews. Greek Christians, raised in a culture that emphasized hospitality to strangers, attempted to give aid and protection to Jews during World War II. Their lack of anti-Jewish feelings in part stemmed from the Greek Church's rejection of the idea that Jews had to "remain as a visible sign of Christian superiority." Additionally, Greek Orthodoxy opposed forced conversions. The author provides details concerning the fate of Jews living in several areas of Greece and shows the efforts Greeks made to help Jews escape the Nazis.

Boyle, Stephen. "Pius XII and the Jews: Greatness Dishonored." Homiletic and Pastoral Review (April 1999), pp. 26-32.

Boyle defends the actions of Pope Pius XII during World War II. He points out, that after the war numerous Jewish communities commended Pius for his activities. The pope realized Hitler's predisposition toward terror and violence as early as 1933, and commented on the fact that Nazism was in direct opposition to Christianity. The author offers reasons for the Pope's "silence" about the persecution of Jews and insists that Pius's critics unfairly libel him.

Braham, Randolf "German Catholic Hierarchy and the Holocaust." Holocaust and Genocide Studies (Fall 1999), Volume 13 Issue 2, pp. 222-251.
The article examines the Vatican's 1998 statement, *"We Remember"* in the context of the Church's continued attempts to improve its relations with Jews. These attempts took a positive turn in 1965 when Vatican II issued *Nostra Aetate*. Braham notes the difficulties and criticisms that surround *We Remember*, but he also maintains that despite the statement's shortcomings the Church continues to pursue a path toward complete reconciliation with Jews.

____. *Studies on the Holocaust: Selected Writings*. Volume 2. New York: Rosenthal Institute for Holocaust Studies, City University of New York, 2001, 255 pp.
Braham's volume is a collection of previously published essays. Some of these relate to the issue of Christianity's influence upon anti-Semitism and the Holocaust. Included are; "The Christian Churches of Hungary and the Holocaust" and "Remembering and Forgetting; The Vatican, the German Catholic Hierarchy and the Holocaust." The subjects covered take account of the Vatican and the Catholic Church's activities through the years of 1919-2001, with special emphasis given to the countries occupied by the Nazis during World War II.

Brenner, Rachel Feldhay. *Writing as Resistance: Four Women Confronting the Holocaust: Edith Stein, Simone Weil, Anne Frank, Etty Hillesum*. University Park: Pennsylvania State University Press, 1997, 216 pp.
The author explores the manner in which these four women maintained their faith in humanity, despite the surrounding destruction that faced them. Of particular interest is Brenner's discussion of Edith Stein, born Jewish, who in 1933 was about to become a nun, and Simone Weil, who fled France and deportation in 1942.

Browning, Christopher. "Daniel Goldhagen's Willing Executioners." History and Memory (June 30,1996), Volume 8 Issue 1, pp. 88- 98.
Browning refutes Daniel Goldhagen's conclusions in *Hitler's Willing Executioners*. He contends, that Goldhagen's theories about what motivated ordinary Germans to participate in the Holocaust are mistaken. Browning suggests, that the idea of a "demonological German anti-Semitism" does not

provide an adequate explanation for those who participated in the murder of Jews. The author argues, that Goldhagen is guilty of viewing history through too narrow a lens. Browning insists the record concerning people's motivations is far more complex and needs to be studied within the broader contexts of the time.

Bukey, Evan Burr. *Hitler's Austria: Popular Sentiment in the Nazi Era 1938-1945.* **Chapel Hill; University of North Carolina Press, 2000, pp. 320.**
Bukey takes issue with the claims of the Austrian people, that they were not responsible for the atrocities that took place in their country during the Nazi era because they too were victims of the occupying German army. The author uncovers evidence that shows Austria was anti-Semitic prior to the German occupation, and that the Catholic Church in Austria was in part responsible for fostering anti-Semitic attitudes.

Burleigh, Michael. *The Third Reich: A New History.* **New York: Hill and Wang, 2000, 965 pp.**
In this important general history of the Third Reich, the author argues, that in the aftermath of the First World War, a pseudo-religious strain entered German politics. The rise of Hitler and the Nazis is viewed within the context of a people seeking a "savior" to deliver them from the chaos and revolution that followed the end of the Great War. In this atmosphere, Hitler focused upon the Jews as the source of all of Germany's problems much in the same manner that medieval Christians linked the Jews to Satan.

Buscher, Frank M. and Michael Phayer. "German Catholic Bishops and the Holocaust, 1940-1952." **German Studies Review (1998), Volume 11 Issue 3, pp. 463-485.**
According to Buscher and Phayer, Margarete Sommer, a Catholic social worker, gave reliable information about the deportations and mass murder of Jews to Catholic Bishops within Germany. Though some prelates wanted to come forward to speak to the issue, they were told to remain silent by Cardinal Bertram of Breslau. According to the author, both during and after the war Catholic Bishops failed to use their moral authority to speak out against the atrocities of the Nazis.

Cannistraro, Philip V. and Theodore P. Kovaleff. "Father Coughlin and Mussolini: Impossible Allies." **Journal of Church and State (Autumn 1971), Volume 13 Issue 3, pp. 427-445.**
The author documents the relationship between the Italian government led by Mussolini and Father Charles E. Coughlin, an American Catholic priest. Coughlin espoused extremist conservative policies and anti-Semitic propaganda on his radio program, which was heard across America during the 1930s and

early 40s. Connistraro details Mussolini's intentions to use Coughlin for propaganda value in the United States. He contends, that Coughlin misunderstood Italian politics and was in error when he assumed, that Mussolini was supportive of an anti-Jewish agenda. Ultimately, the Italian government saw Coughlin as more of a liability than help in shaping their image in the United States. According to the author, by 1942 the Vatican stepped in to effectively silence the "radio priest". Thus, any opportunity to use him ended.

Carrol, David. "What it Meant to be 'A Jew' in Vichy France: Xavier Vallat, State anti-Semitism, and the Question of Assimilation." SubStance (1998), Volume 27 Issue 3, pp. 36-55.
Carrol points out, that though there were differences between the Nazi "racist" and Vichy "state" forms of anti-Semitism, the Nazi's cannot be entirely blamed for the Vichy government's persecution of the Jews. Rather, French culture and politics emerged from long held Catholic and anti-republican traditions that were widely accepted. Given that history, The French citizenry offered little resistance to the government's adoption of anti-Semitic policies. The author examines the laws targeting French Jews in the 1940s that were introduced by French Commissioner General of Jewish Affairs, Xavier Vallat. While Vallat claimed French policies were a means for assimilating Jews into French society, in reality Jews faced increasing alienation due to these laws. Ultimately, the perceived differences in their anti-Semitic attitudes were irrelevant, and French policies assisted Nazis in committing atrocities against Jews.

Casey, Maurice. "Some Anti-Semitic Assumptions in the Theological Dictionary of the New Testament." Novum Testamentum (July 1999), Volume 41 Issue 3, pp. 280-291.
The *Theological Dictionary of the New Testament*, according to Casey is a "very dangerous book." Gerhard Kittel, the editor-in-chief, along with other scholars who were major contributors have been identified as Nazis. The volumes of *The Dictionary* were produced at a time in Germany when anti-Semitic attitudes prevailed. Casey insists, that individuals utilizing the dictionary should be made aware of their anti-Jewish bias. He asserts, that even those contributors who were not Nazis suffered from the anti-Semitic attitudes that pervaded the German Christian Churches of the era.

Cavnar, Cynthia. *Meet Edith Stein: From Cloister to Concentration Camp, A Carmelite Nun Confronts the Nazis.* Servant Publications, 2002, 158 pp.
This concise biographical account presents readers with a view of one of the most controversial saints of the twentieth century. Stein, a brilliant woman, converted from Judaism to the Catholic faith, and then entered an order of Carmelite Nuns. She was a victim of Nazi murder during the Holocaust.

Cesarini, David and Paul A. Levine. *Bystanders to the Holocaust: A Re-Evaluation.* **Frank Cass Publications, 2002, 280 pp.**
Nine papers delivered at a 1999 symposium held in Uppsala, Sweden study the responses and actions of a variety of so-called "bystanders" to the Holocaust. Among those studied are Jews living outside territories occupied by the Nazi's, neutral governments and agencies, ordinary German citizens, the governments and people of occupied countries, and most importantly the Allied governments.

Chadwick, Owen. *Britain and the Vatican During the Second World War.* **Cambridge: Cambridge University Press, 1987, 332 pp.**
This is an account of the Vatican's contacts with the British government on issues ranging from the abortive conspiracy against Hitler in the winter of 1939-40, to the British and American bombing policy in Italy. The author includes a chapter, "The Jew in 1942" in which Chadwick reconstructs how and when the Vatican discovered the truth about the "Final Solution." The book offers a new insight on the inner-workings of the Vatican during the war and presents Pius XII in a compassionate manner.

Cherry, Robert. " Holocaust Historiography: The Role of the Cold War." **Science and Society (1999-2000), Volume 63 Issue, pp. 459-477.**
Cherry takes issue with the portrayal of the Holocaust by those who have been concerned with America's Cold War political needs, rather than with accurate and fair historical writing. For example, the author contends that the Soviet Union's aid to the Jews is underreported, that the Catholic Church's actions to save Jewish children are focused upon while the anti-Semitic statements of Church leaders are largely ignored, that continued anti-Semitism in Poland is ignored, and finally that Raoul Wallenberg is mythologized because of political expediency.

Chesnoff, Richard Z. "Did a Wartime Pope Anticipate a Nazi Victory?" **U.S.News and World Report (November 15, 1999), Volume 127 Issue 19, pp. 44-48.**
The author states, that the Vatican's reasons for refusing to specifically condemn the Nazis, and the Pope's promotion of a compromise peace settlement during World War II may have been due to the belief of Church officials that Germany might defeat the Allied Forces. An examination of Argentina's newly released archives supports reports, that the Catholic Church aided German War Criminals who were trying to escape to Latin America as the war ended.

Claman, Henry N. *Jewish Images in the Christian Church: Art as the Mirror of the Jewish-Christian Conflict 200-1250ce.* **Mercer University Press; 2000, 212 pp.**
Claman explores the troubled relations between Jews and Christianity through

Christian art. The author notes, that while this art is aesthetically pleasing its purpose was to teach tenets of faith to the illiterate masses. Functioning as a tool for religious education, Christian art depicted Jews and Judaism in negative ways, and therefore, helped foster anti-Jewish sentiment among Christians.

Clark, Christopher. *The Politics of Conversion: Missionary Protestantism and the Jews in Prussia 1728-1942.* Clarendon Press, 1995, 340 pp.
The Protestant missionary efforts to convert Jews in Prussia are examined in this text. The author studies the conversion attempts in the context of events that took place between the years 1728-1942 with special emphasis on the nineteenth century. Clark notes, that the missionaries faced difficulties in trying to reconcile their tasks, which were "to defend Jews from anti-Semitism and to defend Christianity from the Jews." The author points out, that the missionaries "operated within, not against, the prevailing attitudes of discrimination against Jews." In order to present a comprehensive view of the missions this text integrates religion, politics, and culture. The book jacket tells the tale succinctly for it portrays a man with a millstone around his neck being baptized by a minister while another man waits to push the reluctant convert off a cliff. The motto that accompanies this chilling picture reads "In this way he will remain most faithful."

Controversy Section. "Pius XII and the Holocaust: Kevin Madigan and Critics." Commentary (January 2002), Volume 113 Issue 1, pp. 12-19.
This article provides a series of opinions offered that either criticize or agree with Kevin Madigan's article "What the Vatican Knew About the Holocaust and When" (October 2001). Madigan accuses Pope Pius XII of failing to act in defense of the Jews during the Holocaust. Doris Bergen, William Doino, Jr, Reverend Vincent A Lapomarda S.J., Michael Novak, and Ronald Rycchlak, are among those offering their views of Madigan's work. In addition, the article includes Madigan's response to his critics.

Conway, John S. "The Churches, the Slovak State and the Jews, 1939-1945." Slavonic and East European Review (1974), Volume 52 Issue 126, pp. 85-112.
By examining German Foreign Office records, Conway describes the resistance of Vatican and Slovak churchmen to the deportation of Slovak Jews. Once the Nazi's occupied Slovakia in 1944, however, all efforts to delay the deportations stopped.

____. "The Founding of the State of Israel and the Response of the Christian Churches." Kirchliche Zeitgeschichte (1999), Volume 12 Issue 2, pp. 459-472.
The author shows, that when the State of Israel was founded the Vatican was

more concerned with their rights to the Holy Sites, than with the Jews need for a place of refuge. Therefore, it took the Catholic Church four decades to recognize the State of Israel. This recognition came as the result of the Catholic Church's acceptance that it had been a source of anti-Jewish attitudes and that it held common bonds with Judaism. The response of Protestant Churches in the United States to the Zionist cause has been more varied. Some Protestant communities were concerned with the need for Jewish safety and survival, and welcomed an Israeli State. Others were more worried about the needs of the Palestinians, and opposed the Jews return to the Middle East.

____. *The Nazi Persecution of the Churches, 1933-1945.* **London: Weidenfeld and Nicolson, 1968.**
Conway's study elucidates the methods by which the Nazis were able to impose their totalitarian rule on the Christian Churches.

____. **"Protestant Missions to the Jews, 1810-1980: Ecclesiastical Imperialism or Theological Aberration." Holocaust and Genocide Studies (1986), Volume 1 Issue 1, pp. 127-146.**
The article examines the attitudes of nineteenth century missionaries towards Jews. Conway claims the missionaries believed, that when exposed to a more "progressive" religion, the Jews would want to convert. These missionaries opposed persecution of Jews, yet failed to realize that their goals of conversion helped increase anti-Semitic feelings among Christians. Mission societies contested the Nazis anti-Jewish policies, but were ignored by the German Protestant Church, and were rendered obsolete in 1941 when the Protestant Church gave way to the Nazis. In the aftermath of the war most Christian Churches began to work toward increased dialogue with Jews, rather than engaging in efforts to convert them.

Coppa, Frank J. *Controversial Concordats: The Vatican's Relations with Napoleon, Mussolini, and Hitler.* **Washington D.C.: Catholic University of America Press, 1999, 245 pp.**
The author surveys the relationship of the Roman Catholic Church with three dictatorial figures, including Hitler. Coppa concludes, that the papacy influenced the general course of international relations and modern history from the era of the French Revolution to the age of the dictators and World War II.

____. **"The Hidden Encyclical of Pius XI Against Racism and Anti-Semitism Uncovered – One Again." Catholic Historical Review (January 1998), Volume 84 Issue 1, pp. 63-73.**
The author examines the history behind Pope Pius XI's unpublished encyclical *Humanis Generis Unitas.* Written in 1938, the document denounced anti-Semitism and racism. The author discusses Father John La Farge's role in

producing the encyclical, the illness and death of Pius XI, and the decision by his successor Pope Pius XII to withhold publication of the document. Coppa refers to the insights of authors Robert A. Hecht, Georges Passelecq, and Bernard Suchecky in trying to uncover why the encyclical was not published and whether or not its publication would have helped or hurt the Jews.

Cornwell, John. *Hitler's Pope: The Secret History of Pius XII.* **New York: Viking, 2000, 430 pp.**
According to Cornwell, during his tenure in Germany through the decade of the 1930s, Cardinal Eugenio Pacelli did not view the plight of the Jews with a sense of urgency. Rather he remained influenced by the conviction that there was a link between Jews and the Bolshevik plot to destroy Christendom. Viewing the Hitler regime as a bastion against the spread of Communism, the future Pius XII did not seriously protest the escalating persecution of the Jews. Cornwell concludes, that Pius XII's lack of response to the Holocaust was governed more by a habitual fear and distrust of the Jews, than a strategy of silent diplomacy, or a commitment to neutrality in order to act as a broker between the warring nations.

Coughlin, F. *Father Coughlin His "Facts" and Arguments: How Father Coughlin Misquotes.* **New York: s. n., 1939, 64 pp. http://www.questia.com.**
This short text challenges the charges that Father Charles Coughlin, the famous "Radio Priest" of the 1930s, made against the Jews. Father Coughlin, an extreme anti-Semite, blamed the Jews for Communism and a host of other "evils". He also claimed Nazism was a "defense" against the Jews. The author of this sixty-four page refutation, accuses Father Coughlin of misquoting and manufacturing evidence in order to promote his anti-Semitic message.

Crane, Cynthia. *Divided Lives: The Untold Stories of Jewish-Christian Women in Nazi Germany.* **New York: St Martin's Press, 2000, 372 pp.**
The author has collected the stories of ten women, the offspring from Jewish-Christian marriages, whose families were persecuted under Hitler's Third Reich. These survivors were categorized as *Mischling* or "half breeds" under the Nuremberg Laws of 1935.

Cretzmeyer, Stacey. *Your Name Is Renee: Ruth's Story As A Hidden Child.* **Oxford and New York: Oxford University Press, 1999, 240 pp.**
The plight of Jews, who lived in unoccupied southern France during World War II, is documented through this biography of Ruth Hartz Kapp. At the age of four Kapp was given a new French identity and found refuge with a caring Catholic family. When she turned five, Kapp was placed in a convent in order to escape the Nazi roundup of Jews. Ruth was protected in the convent by the mother superior, who sheltered her and other Jewish children from raids by the German

police. Through this biography the author provides evidence of the strong resistance movement of Protestants and Catholics, who provided safe havens for Jews in their own homes or in nearby convents.

Curtiss, John S. *An Appraisal of The Protocols of Zion.* **New York: Columbia University Press, 1942, 118 pp.**
Published under the direction and sponsorship of a group of Christian historians, the book, written by John Curtiss, seeks to discredit the text, *The Protocols of the Elders of Zion* once and for all time. *The Protocols* have been used for decades to reinforce the image of Jews conspiring to take over the world and destroy Christian civilization. In his study, Dr. Curtiss applies strict rules of historical research to *The Protocols* and concludes that the evidence presented in its text is contradictory at every point. Additionally, many of the dates and facts recorded are unsupportable. Curtiss, also a Christian, points out that amazingly *The Protocols* have survived despite having been ridiculed and proved false numerous times.

Cymet, David. "Polish State Anti-Semitism as a Major Factor Leading to the Holocaust." Journal of Genocide Research (June 1999), Volume 1 Issue 2, pp. 169-213.
The author focuses upon what led up to and facilitated the "Final Solution" to the "Jewish Question" in Poland. He provides information about a pastoral letter published by the Catholic Church that demonstrates that the church in Poland supported the Polish government's policy to eliminate the Jews.

Davies, Alan and Marilyn F. Nefsky. *How Silent Were The Churches? Canadian Protestantism and the Jewish Plight During the Nazi Era.* **Ontario: Wilfrid Laurier University. 1998, 364 pp.**
Drawing upon letters, sermons and other documents, Davies presents a profile of Protestant attitudes toward the possibility of Jewish immigration to Canada during World War II, and explores anti-Semitism and pro-German sentiment in Canadian society. The author finds, that the resurgence of nativism among Protestants was a factor in restricting large number of Jewish immigrants from escaping the Nazis by entering Canada.

Davis, Douglas. "From Auschwitz to Sainthood: Does Edith Stein's Martyrdom Merit Sainthood, or is Her Canonization the Vatican's Holocaust Guilt?" Baltimore Jewish Times (October 16, 1998), Volume 243 Issue 7, pp.12.
Davis takes issue with the Catholic Church's decision to elevate Edith Stein to sainthood. In support of his argument, he briefly traces Stein's life and pays special attention to the fact that the Catholic Church, by refusing several of Stein's requests to be removed from territories occupied by the Germans,

ensured that she would be susceptible to the Nazi threat. The author also maintains, that Stein was not a martyr for the Catholic faith. She was executed by the Nazis because she was Jewish, not a nun.

Dawidowicz, Lucy S. *The War Against the Jews*. New York: Holt, Rinehart and Winston, 1975, 460 pp.
One of the earlier general histories of the Holocaust includes sections dealing with the response of religious Jews to the Nazis. Dawidowicz points out, that although the Nazis denied that the Jews were a religious group, they nevertheless, singled out observant Jews for sport and persecution. In addition, most synagogues were destroyed or desecrated and all functions pertaining to the observance of Judaism were prohibited, including worship, religious study and religious teaching. The author also reveals, that during the deportations from the Warsaw Ghetto to Auschwitz, pious Jews marched to the *Umschlagplatz* and into the waiting trains wrapped in their prayer shawls, reciting prayers and psalms, oblivious of the violence. Dawidowicz makes the argument that *Kiddush ha-shem* (martyrdom for the glorification and sanctification of the Name), reasserted its place in Jewish tradition.

Dedijer, Vladimir. Translated by Harvey L. Kendall. *The Yugoslav Auschwitz and the Vatican: The Croatian Massacre of the Serbs During World War II*. Amherst New York: Prometheus Books, 1992, 444 pp.
The author, a former Yugoslav ambassador to the UN, describes the Croatian fascists' program against the Serbs, and the Vatican's complicity in the "Final Solution". This account of the Catholic Church's role in the Jasenovac concentration camp includes details about the thousands of Jews and Serbs killed in the Croatian death camp, and how Catholic clerics, including Archbishop Stepinac, allowed and condoned the atrocities committed against the Jews.

Delzell, Charles, ed. *The Papacy and Totalitarianism Between the Two World Wars*. New York: John Wiley & Sons Publishers, 1974, 262 pp.
Seven essays consider the Vatican's relationship with Fascist dictatorships and its role in the Jewish question during World War II. The texts of relevant papal documents are included.

Dietrich, Donald J. *Catholic Citizens in the Third Reich: Psycho-Social Principles and Moral Reasons*. Brunswick: Transaction Press, 1988, 356 pp.
This volume examines the response of German Catholics to political and moral issues during the Weimar and Nazi periods. The author documents both Catholic accommodation and resistance to the totalitarianism and anti-Jewish policies of Hitler's regime.

____. **"Catholic Theologians in Hitler's Reich: Adaptation and Critique."** **Journal of Church and State (1987), Volume 29 Issue 1, pp. 19-45.**
In an effort to oppose liberalism and democracy, the Catholic Church opposed the Weimar Republic and gave early support to the National Socialist Party's ideology, which included anti-Semitism. Church prelates worked to assure the Nazis that Catholics were loyal German citizens. The Catholic hierarchy understood early on, that the Concordat of 1933 was a mistake. After 1935 they made no further effort to accommodate the Nazi Regime, although they continued to identify with Nazi maxims.

____. **"Introduction." Church History (June 2001), Volume 70 Issue 2, pp. 226-232.**
Diectrich's article is the opening piece for a group of essays appearing in this issue of *Church History*. These writings address the subject of how Christian denominations responded to the Third Reich's government. The author provides a brief overview of how different churches dealt with the "Jewish Question" prior to Hitler's regime, and what types of resistance to Nazism they engaged in, if they opposed the Reich at all.

____. **"Modern German Catholic Anti-Semitism." Face to Face (Winter 1985), Volume 12, pp. 4-10.**
The book points out the ongoing connections between the Catholic Church and Germany through the years 1870-1945. The author proposes, that the Catholic Center Party became intensely anti-Semitic when it tied Jews to those liberals within Germany who were antagonistic toward the Church. The Catholic Church, after 1879, reached an accord with the government and therefore its anti-Semitic rhetoric became less overt and intense. Yet the atmosphere in Germany concerning Jews remained hostile and opened the door to an acceptance of National Socialism. While the Church and the Catholic political party refused to give outright support to the Nazis, they did fail to mount a moral challenge to Hitler's policies against the Jews.

Dippel, John Van Houten. *Bound Upon a Wheel of Fire: Why So Many German Jews made the Tragic Decision to Remain in Nazi Germany.* **New York: Basic Books, 1996, 353 pp.**
Dippel attempts to discover why thousands of German Jews chose to remain in their homeland after Hitler came to power. The author's thesis, that Jews refused to leave Germany because of the deep emotional and psychological ties to their country, as well the fear of leaving their families, friends, homes and jobs for unknown destinations, is studied through the lives of six community leaders, including Leo Baeck, chief rabbi of Berlin.

Dipper, Christof. "The German Resistance and the Jews." Yad Vashem

Studies (1984), Volume 16, pp. 51-93.
By focusing on those who resisted the Nazis, the author shows that the Christian Churches, as well as politicians from the left and right of the spectrum, remained largely unconcerned over the violent activities perpetrated by the Reich against Jews. Statements regarding Nazi Jewish policies, taken from members within each of these groups, are presented and analyzed.

Dobkowski, Michael Nachin. "A Historical Survey of Anti-Semitism in America Prior to World War II." Persistent Prejudice: Perspectives on Anti-Semitism (1988), pp. 63-81.
This article examines a variety of factors that led to anti-Semitism in the United States both before and after World War II. Dobokski notes the influence that Christianity, and the negative Jewish stereotypes it developed, have had upon the American populace in the twentieth century.

Drinan, Robert F. "The Christian Response to the Holocaust." Annals of the American Academy of Political and Social Science (1980), Volume 450, pp. 179-189.
Ecumenical movements within Christian communities have developed due to Christianity's reexamination of its reaction to the Holocaust. Given that their efforts to stop the Nazi atrocities were almost non-existent, Christian denominations have begun to acknowledge their complicity in the extermination of European Jewry.

Duff, Michael. "Author Blames Vatican for the Holocaust." BBC News (January 15, 2002), Volume 20 Issue 28, 2 pp.
This article takes exception to the accusations made against the Vatican by Daniel Goldhagen in his recent New Republic article, "What Would Jesus Have Done?" (January 1, 2002). Duff contends, that Goldhagen's indictment of the Catholic Church for having provided the "intellectual stimulus for the Holocaust through centuries of anti-Semitism" is simplistic. In Duff's opinion, even though some of these accusations have been made by other authors, Goldhagen's charges against the Vatican and Pius XII rank "among the most savage yet."

Eckardt, Alice Lyons, ed. *Burning Memory: Time of Testing and Reckoning.* Oxford: Pergamon, 1993, 340 pp.
A compilation of papers, presented by a variety of authors, is included in this book. The papers were originally part of the sixteenth (1986) and eighteenth (1988) Annual Scholars Conference on the Holocaust. Some of the essays that specifically target the subject of Christianity and its influence on anti-Semitism and the Holocaust are; Alice Eckardt's piece about "The Pogrom of *Kristallnacht* in Christian Context", Franklin Littlell's ideas concerning "Reinhold Niebuhr's Christian Leadership in a Time of Testing", as well as

papers written about the Christian response to the Holocaust, the efforts of Righteous Gentiles to rescue Jews from the Nazis and the current state of relations between Christians and Jews in Poland and Germany.

Editorial. "The Massacred Jews." A Catholic Review of the Week (March 13, 1943), pp. 630.
The editorial recounts the message sent by the Catholic Church's Cardinal Hinsley, Archbishop of Westminster on March 1 of 1943 that detailed the terrible atrocities of the Nazis and the death of some five million Jews. He called for immediate aid for the survivors of the genocide. In light of the tragedy the Apostolic Nuncio of Romania offered to handle arrangements for transporting as many as seventy thousand Jewish refugees from Romania and Pius XII suggested they travel under the protection of the Papal flag. The editorial prompts all American Catholics to find ways to assist those in need.

Editorial. "Pius XII and the Jews." America (October 23,1999), Volume 181 Issue 12, pp. 3.
This editorial reviews the controversial questions that persist concerning the actions (or in-actions) of Pius XII during the Holocaust. The author suggests, that a joint commission of Catholic and Jewish scholars might be helpful in uncovering information about the pope's efforts on behalf of the Jews. He also proposes, that most likely they would discover that Pius was a good but flawed man trying to do his best when faced with horrendous circumstances.

Einhorn-Susulowska, Maria. "Psychological Problems of Polish Jews Who Used Aryan Documents." Polin: Studies in Polish Jewry (2000), Volume 13 pp. 104-111.
Polish Jews, who survived the Holocaust by using counterfeit documents, are the focus of this article. These Jews faced continued stress as they tried to maintain their false identities. This continued strain created psychological problems for many Jews. It was especially difficult for those who had not previously assimilated. Not only did they constantly fear discovery and arrest, but they also were forced to follow Catholic practices and ceremonies.

Eliach, Yaffa, ed. *Hasidic Tales of the Holocaust.* **Oxford: Oxford University Press, 1982, 266 pp.**
The book is a collection of eighty-nine stories told to the author by Hasidic survivors of the Nazi death camps. These ultra-Orthodox Jews faced calamity and death holding onto a strong faith in their religion. The book gives a voice to this community that is often overlooked in survivor accounts of the Holocaust.

Englemann, Bernt. *Germany Without Jews.* **New York and Toronto: Bantam, 1984, 380 pp.**

The author traces the history of anti-Semitism in Germany and concludes that the extermination of the Jews deprived the Germans of a people that had contributed enormously to Germany's cultural richness. Written before the recent unification of the two Germany's, the author compares Germany of the nineteenth and twentieth centuries with the post-World War II divided state, and finds a "cultural barrenness" that he attributes to the absence of Jews.

Ericksen, Robert P. *Theologians Under Hitler.* **New Haven: Yale University Press, 1985, 245 pp.**
The study deals with Gerhard Kittel, Paul Althaus, and Emmanuel Hirsch. Each was a Protestant theologian and university professor who supported Adolf Hitler and the Nazi Party. Erickson finds that his subjects (and others like them) supported the Nazis because they blamed the Weimar Republic for being the source of a modernity based on irrationalism (Nietzsche, Freud, etc.). This brought into question not only traditional values and social structures, but the very rationality upon which they believed religion was based. In addition they blamed the Weimar Republic for its support of a materialist-minded technology and its system of democratic pluralism that undermined faith. In Kittel's case, as a Professor of *New Testament* Theology at Tubingen during the Nazi years, he was regarded as an expert on Judaism. Thus after joining the Nazi party in 1933 he was able to make scholarly contributions to Nazi anti-Semitism.

_____ and Susannah Heschel. eds. *Betrayal: German Churches and the Holocaust.* **Minneapolis: Augsburg Fortress Press, 1999, 224 pp.**
This collection of articles examines why both Catholic and Protestant Christians in Germany reconciled their religious beliefs with National Socialism, and asks, how this accommodation and enthusiastic support facilitated the Holocaust. Other important questions regarding the relationship of German Christians to the Nazi regime are also explored. Contributors include, Shelly Baranowski, Kenneth C. Barnes, Doris Bergen, Micha Brumlik, Guenter Lewy, and Michael B. Lukens.

Falconi, Carlo. *The Silence of Pius XII.* **Boston: Little, Brown Publishers, 1970, 430 pp.**
Falconi rejects the suggestion that Pius XII was cowardly in his response to the Nazi regime, and accepts him as a man of deep piety and faith, who at the same time was morally corrupted by a lifetime of practicing Vatican diplomacy. Falconi advances a number of motives for the pope's alleged silence: his pessimistic analysis of the situation based on the psychological unreadiness of Catholics, especially in Germany, to respond to papal protest; the conviction that Communism would be strengthened by any weakening of the Nazis; the desire to guarantee the church's survival in Europe; to guarantee the church sufficient energy to exercise decisive influence on post-war reconstruction, and because of

his long professional training as a diplomat. Pius XII hoped that by adhering to a policy of strict neutrality between the combatants, the Holy See might be able to use its good offices to achieve a negotiated peace.

Falk, Avner. *A Psychoanalytical History of the Jews.* **Madison, NJ.: Fairleigh Dickinson University Press, 1996, 850 pp.**
The author psychoanalyzes events that mark the history of the Jews. This text includes discussions about Christianity's "demonization" of the Jews, the Crusades, disputations, pogroms and the Inquisition. Falk then turns to the more recent anti-Semitic attitudes spawned in the nineteenth and twentieth centuries and includes theories about Hitler, the Holocaust and responses to the Holocaust by non-victims.

Favez, Jean-Claude. *The Red Cross and the Holocaust.* **New York: Cambridge University Press, 1999, 353 pp.**
Although the Red Cross historically dealt with injured soldiers and prisoners of war, it was cautious and reticent in responding to the unique horrors faced by European Jewry, as civilian internees of a totalitarian state. The author attributes this to the Red Cross's fear, that by intervening on behalf of the Jews, its role as a neutral intermediary and moral guarantor would be jeopardized, and therefore their access to POWs would also be forfeited.

Fein, Helen. *Accounting for Genocide: National Responses and Jewish Victimization during the Holocaust.* **Chicago: University of Chicago Press, 1984, 468 pp.**
Fein suggests reasons to explain why the murder of Jews during the Holocaust was not more consistently applied across Europe. The author proposes, that the extent of anti-Semitism present in an area prior to the war had an effect, as did the extent of the Germans control of the region, and the size and ability of resistance movements to oppose the Nazis. Fein also discusses the Christian origins of anti-Jewish fervor and the failure of the Christian Churches, the Allies and neutral countries to prevent the persecution of the Jews before it began.

Feldkamp, Michael F. *Pius XII and Deutschland.* **Gottingen: Vandenoeck and Ruprecht, 2000, 236 pp.**
The author provides a study of Pius XII's relations with Germany prior to, during, and after the war. Feldkamp insists that the pope's "wartime silence" was due to Pius's "judgment that a public protest would not deter the Nazis, but would provoke even greater atrocities." In this work, Feldkamp relies on primary and secondary sources and sets out to refute the various negative claims that have recently been made about the pope.

Finzi, Roberto, Maud Jackson, Translator. *Anti-Semitism.* **Interlink**

Publishing Group, Incorporated, 1998, 128 pp.
Historian Robert Finzi examines the religious origins of anti-Semitism and explores how this anti-Jewish prejudice spilled over into secular society. The author notes, that for several centuries Jews have suffered hatred and persecution. He contends, that despite the Holocaust aspects of anti-Semitism still persist. This concise history points out the most significant ways in which anti-Jewish attitudes have been demonstrated and acted upon.

Fiore, Benjamin. "Vatican Holocaust Silence, Again." Polish American Journal (July 1, 1997), pp. 5.
Fiore counters James Carroll's accusation, that the Vatican, under the direction of Pope Pius XII, failed to speak out against Nazism and did little to protect the Jews. Fiore claims Carroll's criticism is superficial and biased. The author offers evidence designed to refute Carroll's claims.

Fischel, Jack and Sanford Pinsker. *The Churches' Response to the Holocaust.* Greenwood: Penkevill Publishing Co., 1986, 187 pp.
This collection of essays addressing aspects of Christianity's response to the Holocaust includes contributions from Samuel Abrahamsen, Shelley Baranowski, Donald Dietrich, Brian R. Dunn, Jack Fischel, Stephen MacDonald, Sister Mary Tinneman, and Robert W. Ross.

Fischer, Klaus P. *The History of an Obsession: German Judeophobia and the Holocaust.* New York: Continuum, 1998, 532 pp.
Fischer believes the term "Judeophobia", or the hatred of the Jews, is a more accurate term than anti-Semitism to describe the troubled course of German-Jewish relations in the thousand years that both groups lived side by side. Fischer argues, that Hitler sold the idea of a super race to a people who had been conditioned over centuries by Christianity to view Jews in an unfavorable position. This conditioning resulted in social and political discrimination, and later, under the Nazis, extermination.

____. *Nazi Germany: A New History.* New York: Continuum Press, 1995, 734 pp.
Despite the existence of authoritarian institutions in German history, Fischer contends, that Hitler and his party were *sui generis*, a force without a historical past. Had it not been for World War I, German society would probably have been able to make a stable adjustment to the challenges of modern industrial civilization.

Fleischer, Roland and Christopher Bentley, Translator. "Looking for Clues: Baptists and Jews in Southeastern Europe Before the Holocaust: The Jewish Baptist Missionary, Moses Richter." Baptist Quarterly (1999),

Volume 38 Issue 3, pp. 139-142.
Jews were drawn to the lectures delivered by Baptist missionaries, who worked with Romanian Jews during the 1930s, because they offered a respite from the anti-Semitic rhetoric of the times. Baptist ministers, like the convert Moses Richter, emphasized the importance of Christian ideology over nationalist attitudes and prompted their congregants to treat Jews kindly instead of with hatred.

Frankel, Jonathan. "Ritual Murder in the Modern Era: The Damascus Affair of 1840." Jewish Social Studies (January 31, 1997), Volume 3 Issue 2, pp. 1-9.
The author focuses on the facts surrounding the 1840 ritual murder case in Damascus and the long-term significance of "blood libel" charges for modern Jewish history. Ritual murder cases involved the claim that Jews murdered Christians as part of their religious practice. The author discusses the fact that charges of ritual murder, though seemingly absurd, were still made in the nineteenth century, in part as a backlash against modernity. These charges against Jews also supported rising nationalism in European countries.

Freilich, Rabbi Samuel, and Irving Greenberg, (ed.). *The Coldest Winter: The Holocaust Memoirs of Rabbi Samuel Freilich.* **New York: Holocaust Publications, 1988, 90 pp.**
In his memoir of the Holocaust, Rabbi Freilich relates the story of his survival in the midst of mass annihilation. He describes his loss of hope as well as an "indictment of God" out of extraordinary religious integrity. Rabbi Freilich maintained his faith, but this did not prevent him from protesting "God's abandonment of the Jews". After the war, Rabbi Freilich resumed his rabbinate, established a network of schools to assist Jewish orphans, and played a key role in the resettlement of Europe's surviving Jewish population.

Fremont, Helen. *After Long Silence: A Memoir.* **Delacorte Press, 2000, 368 pp.**
As an adult, the author discovered that though she had been raised Catholic her parents were not only Jewish, but were also survivors of the Holocaust. Fremont's mother, having suffered the horrors of virulent anti-Semitism, decided that she would raise her children as Catholics so that they would never have to face the bigotry directed toward Jews and Judaism. The author's journey to reconnect with her heritage provides a remarkable and enlightening story about her personal life and the dangers encompassed in religious and secular anti-Semitism.

Friedland, Ellen. "*Kristallnacht* **Speaker Emphasizes Role Of Christianity in Holocaust." New Jersey Jewish Times (November 16, 2000), Volume 54**

Issue 46, pp. 11-12.
Martin Niemoller's wife, Sibylle Sarah Niemoller spoke to a group on the anniversary of *Kristallnacht*, "The Night of Broken Glass." Mrs. Niemoller's husband was organizer and leader of The Confessing Church of Germany during Hitler's regime. Mrs. Niemoller emphasized the role that Christianity played in promoting the anti-Semitic attitudes of German citizens. She contends, that these attitudes helped make the Holocaust possible. She also insists, that the Catholic Church bears an especially heavy burden because it was aware of the genocide and did not attempt to end it.

Friedlander, Henry. *The Origins of Nazi Genocide: From Euthanasia to the Final Solution.* Chapel Hill: University of North Carolina Press, 1995, 421 pp.
According to Friedlander, the killing operations used against the handicapped in the Nazi's Euthanasia Program that was implemented at the start of World War II, connect with later extermination plans that were directed toward Jews and Gypsies. The Euthanasia Program, contends the author, contributed more than just the personnel for the Jew's extermination; it also provided the entire apparatus of subterfuge associated with the death camps.

Friedlander, Saul. *Kurt Gerstein: The Ambiguity of Good.* New York: Alfred Knopf, 1983, 247 pp.
Kurt Gerstein's story is told in this book. He was a devout Christian and anti-Nazi, who joined the SS, and then attempted to resist from within by alerting the churches in Germany, the Vatican, and the Allies about the mass murder of the Jews. The author deals with Gerstein's role as both resister and member of the murderous SS.

_____. *Nazi Germany and the Jews, Volume 1: The Years of Persecution, 1933-1939.* New York: Harper-Collins Publishers, 1997, 436 pp.
The author argues, that Hitler was driven by a fanatical hatred of Jews, which Friedlander labels "redemptive anti-Semitism," a term reminiscent of the Christian belief that the "end of days" would be preceded by the struggle between the followers of Christ and the anti-Christ. The author contends, that Hitler believed the restoration of racial purity required the destruction of the Jews. Friedlander asserts, that most Germans did not share Hitler's fanaticism, although anti-Semitism was endemic throughout Germany.

_____. *Pius XII and the Third Reich: A Documentation.* New York: Knopf Publishers, 1966, 238 pp.
This study consists of documents accompanied by brief notes that elucidate their historical setting. A large number of the documents come from the files of the Nazi Ministry of Foreign Affairs, and the rest from British and American

diplomatic papers, as well as from the Zionist Archives in Jerusalem. Absent from the volume, however, are documents from the Vatican archives that were released prior to the publication of the book. This important study, therefore, is based primarily on German diplomatic papers. The author concludes from the available sources that Pius XII, who had served as papal nuncio in Germany prior to becoming pope, had a predilection for Germany, which was not diminished by the nature of the Nazi regime. Additionally, Pius XII feared the Bolshevization of Europe and therefore was anxious not to weaken Germany by criticizing its wartime policies.

____. *When Memory Comes.* **New York: Farrar, Straus, & Giroux, 1979, 185 pp.**
A Holocaust historian's memoir, this book recounts the author's survival as a young boy during the Holocaust. After fleeing his native Czechoslovakia with his family and settling in France before World War II, his parents hid him in a Catholic seminary. Baptized, studying for the priesthood, when the war ended he discovered his true identity, and immigrated to Israel.

Friedman, Jonathan C. *The Lion and the Star: Gentile-Jewish Relations in Three Hessian Communities, 1919-1945* **Lexington: Kentucky University Press, 1998, 288 pp.**
The author addresses every day relations between German Jews and their Gentile neighbors in three German communities; Frankfurt am Main, Giessen and Geisenheim. Friedman describes the ways ordinary Germans helped to implement the Nazi's anti-Semitic program, and the impact everyday anti-Semitism had on the rise of Nazism. The author also explores whether or not Jewish integration into German society had been successful before the Third Reich denigrated the status of the Jews in Germany.

Friedman, Philip. "Was There an Other Germany During the Nazi Period?" *East European Jews in Two Worlds: Studies from the "YIVO Annuals."* **Ed., Deborah Dash Moore. Evanston IL.: Northwestern University Press, 1990, pp. 192-234.**
The focus of this text is to examine whether or not those who opposed the Nazis engaged in persecuting the Jews or treated them compassionately. The author contends, that there was no uniformity in the response of the Churches to Jewish suffering under the Nazi regime. He notes, that the Protestant Churches adopted the "Aryan Paragraph" in 1933, while Martin Niemoeller and the Confessing Church opposed anti-Semitic policies. Friedman asserts, that the Catholic Church's conflict with the Nazi's was more pronounced than that of the Protestant Church. The author also maintains, that both Christian Churches defended mixed couples in order to protect their authority over marriage. Yet, only a small number of clerics actively engaged in assisting the Jews escape

from the Nazis.

Friedrich, Otto. *The Kingdom of Auschwitz.* **New York: Harper Collins, 1994, 112 pp.**
This essay describes everyday life in Auschwitz and the human capacity for survival. It addresses the controversies surrounding the camp since the end of World War II, including the preservation of the site, as well as its significance for Christians.

Genizi, Haim. *American Apathy: The Plight of Christian Refugees From Nazism.* **Ramat-Gan, Israel: Bar –Ilan University, 1983, 411pp.**
Jews, Aryans and non-Aryan Christians were the victims of Nazi oppression and persecution and therefore sought ways to escape from Germany. Genizi's book details the efforts made by religious and secular agencies in offering assistance to Christian refugees fleeing from the Nazis. He concludes, that any attempts to help refugees were apathetic at best. The author documents the lack of concern, by agencies, and shows that there were no large-scale efforts made by Americans, in or out of government, to provide aid to those in need.

Gerlach, Wolfgang. *And the Witnesses Were Silent: The Confessing Church and the Persecution of the Jews.* **Lincoln: University of Nebraska Press, 2000, 304 pp.**
Gerlach argues, that anti-Jewish attitudes, long held by the leaders of the "Confessing Churches", resulted in their indifference to the unfolding persecution of the Jews in the Germany during the years prior to the outbreak of World War II. Although they risked their lives to aid Christian victims of the Nazis, and spoke out against the efforts of the Nazis to control the Churches, when it came to the matter of the persecution and later genocide of the Jews, the responses of the leaders of the Confessing Churches ranged from "tepid disquiet to avoidance". Gerlach's indictment helps us understand how the anti-Semitic policies of the Third Reich could evoke so little opposition.

Germar, Anders. "Exegesis, Postmodernism, and Auschwitz – On Human Dignity and the Ethics of Interpretations." Studia Theologica (1997), Volume 51 Issue 2, pp. 113-143.
The author uses the work of German theologian and Biblical scholar, Gerhard Kittell, to address the implications of postmodern ethics of interpretations on Biblical exegesis. Germar notes, that Kittell's theories, while not supportive of the plan to exterminate the Jews, did help lay a foundation for Nazi oppression and segregation of the Jewish population. Furthermore, the author contends, that scholars who shared Kittel's ideas were at work in countries besides Germany and this helped garner support for the Nazis policies. According to Germar, if Christianity adopts a new interpretation of man's dignity, it could well ensure

that there is no possibility of revisiting the type of atrocity that marked the Nazi era.

Gilbert, Martin. *The Holocaust: the History of the Jews of Europe During the Second World War.* **New York: Holt, Rinehart &Winston, 1985, 959 pp.**
This general history of the Holocaust is told from the perspective of hundreds of contemporary sources and documents, including the testimony of survivors and eyewitnesses. In dealing with the moral question of "resistance," Gilbert argues, "even passivity was a form of resistance."

Gilman, James. "R.G. Collingwood and the Religious Sources of Nazism." Journal of the American Academy of Religion (1986), Volume 54 Issue 1,. pp. 111-28.
Collingwood discusses the role of religion in a healthy society and contends that the Enlightenment's influence led to support for "liberal" ideas and correspondingly an attack on religion. This change promoted man's belief in, and worship of, his own power. Within this "liberal" framework came the foundations for Fascism, Nazism, and the Holocaust.

Gilmour, Peter. "A Pope in Limbo." U.S. Catholic (January 2000), Volume 65 Issue 1, pp. 6-10.
Noting the continuing arguments and questions that surround the actions of Pope Pius XII during the Holocaust, Gilmour directs readers to the book *La Popesa*, in which Paul Murphy recounts the recollections and insights of Mother Pascalina. Pascalina served as Pius XII's housekeeper and confidante for forty-one years.

Glass, James M. *Life Unworthy of Life: Racial Phobia and Mass Murder in Hitler's Germany.* **New York: Basic Books, 1997, 252 pp.**
Glass argues, that German society, particularly its professional classes, enthusiastically pursued genocide because of a culture-wide phobia against the Jews. This perception was reinforced by the state of biological and medical sciences in Germany, which promoted the objective of attaining a racially pure society.

Glick, David. "Reflections on the Holocaust." Pastoral Psychology (September 1995), Volume 44 Issue 1, pp. 13-29.
The author provides a personal reflection on the Holocaust and its impact upon the anti-Semitic teachings of Christianity, the relationship between Nazism and the Catholic Church, the uniqueness of the Holocaust, and its long term psychological affect upon Jews.

Goldhagen, Daniel Jonah. *Hitler's Willing Executioners: Ordinary Germans*

and the Holocaust. **New York: Knopf, 1996, 622 pp.**
The author's controversial thesis offers an interpretation of the Holocaust in which anti-Semitism is the sole motivating factor. Goldhagen argues, that the Holocaust was implemented with the full cooperation, understanding and approval of German citizens of all classes. He further contends, that "eliminationist" and "exterminationist" anti-Semitism was common among Germans before Hitler. The Holocaust became a "national project" for the German people when the Nazis legitimized the murder of the Jews. Reinforcing the theory that Christianity played a role in promoting widespread German anti-Semitism, the author observes that, " without a doubt, the definition of the moral order as a Christian one, with the Jews as its sworn enemies, has been the single most powerful cause in producing an endemic anti-Semitism.

_____. **"What Would Jesus Have Done?"** New Republic **(January 1, 2002), Volume 226 Issue 2, pp. 21-46.**
Goldhagen indicts both the Catholic Church and Pope Pius XII for their failure to confront the Nazis when faced with the evidence that the Germans were systematically annihilating the Jews during the Holocaust. The author highlights the efforts the church has made to sidestep the facts in the post-war era. Goldhagen references several books that cover this subject matter and picks up on James Carrol's assertion that Pius was anti-Semitic.

Goni, Uki. *Real Odessa*: *The Nazi Escape Operation to Peron's Argentina.* **Granta Books, 2002, 382 pp.**
Goni, an Argentine journalist, provides details about how Nazi war criminals were able to escape certain punishment in Germany after World War II by relocating in Argentina. Relying upon archival documents seen for the first time, the author is able to mount a convincing case that ties the Vatican, and the Catholic Church in Argentina, to this criminal activity. He also provides information that shows the operation had the enthusiastic support of Peron. The book's title, a take-off of a Fredrick Forsythe fictional novel, puts forth a compelling examination of the facts surrounding the Nazi's escape from Germany.

Gordon, Mary. "Saint Edith?" Tikkun **(March-April 1999), http://www.tikkun.org.**
This article reviews the conflict that has erupted between Catholics and Jews over the canonization of Edith Stein. In tracing Steins life and her choice to leave her Jewish faith behind and convert to Catholicism, the author notes that Stein's personal life choices are not the problem. Rather, what is debated is why she died and whether or not the Catholic Church, in making her a saint, is encouraging other Jews to follow her example and convert. While Christians maintain, that Stein died as a martyr for Christ, Jews insist she was targeted

because she was a Jew. Additionally, though Catholics contend they are not in the missionary business, many Jews still believe that the desire to win converts to Christianity lays at the heart of Catholic actions. Gordon believes it was a mistake to canonize Stein and asserts, that it reflects the "wishful revision of Europeans who have a stake in believing the Holocaust was something other than it was: the determination to obliterate the Jewish people." Gordon maintains, that the Catholic Church doesn't need more saints, but it does need to make amends for its sins against the Jews.

Gordon, Sarah. *Hitler, Germans and the "Jewish Question."* Princeton, NJ.: Princeton University Press, 1984, 412 pp.
The author studies the ways in which anti-Semitisms' influence on Germany helped Hitler attain power. Gordon examines the statistics of Nazi party members and uncovers their church affiliations. She also looks at local records to determine who resisted the Nazis' policies toward the Jews. The author includes information about whether or not Christian Churches tried to oppose the Nazis persecution of Jews.

Gottlieb, Roger S., ed. *Thinking the Unthinkable: Meanings of the Holocaust.* New York: Paulist Press, 1990, 446 pp.
A compilation of articles and essays are found in this volume. Topics addressed include; the role of religion in creating the death camps, the indictment of the victims in order to evade responsibility, the ways in which the Holocaust impacted Christian theology, the responses of Christians and others to the murder of six million Jews, and the reasons why it is "imperative" that we never forget the horror of the "Final Solution."

Graham, Robert A. "Pius XII's Defense of the Jews and Others, 1944-45". Milwaukee, Wisconsin: Catholic League Publications, 1964, 36 pp.
Graham contends, that Rolf Hochuth's 1963 play, *The Deputy* marks the beginning of the debate surrounding the actions (or inactions) of Pius XII and the Catholic Church during the Holocaust. The author insists accusations that Pius did nothing to assist the Jews, or others, who were under attack by the Nazis, are false. Using documents from the Vatican archives, Graham recounts the diplomatic and private efforts that were made by the pope and the Catholic Church to help those who were targeted by Hitler's regime.

Greenberg, Gershon. "American Catholics During the Holocaust." Simon Wiesenthal Center Annual (1987), Volume 4, pp. 175-201.
The article notes, that there were some efforts made diplomatically to rescue Nazi victims during the Holocaust. The Catholic Church's failure to mount an organized attempt to help Jews, however, along with the Church's opinion that the Jews should not be allowed to re-establish a state in Palestine influenced

how Catholics responded to Nazi atrocities.

____. **"Wartime Orthodox Jewish Thought About the Holocaust: Christian Implications." Journal of Ecumenical Studies (Summer/Fall 1998), Volume 35 Issue 3-4, pp. 483-496.**
Greenberg looks at the ideas of wartime Orthodox Jewish thinkers, who did not accept the "monolithic view of the non-Jewish world as polluted". Instead these men spoke about Christianity in positive ways and regarded any association between Christians and Nazis as a "tragic fall toward paganism." In addition, they recognized that there are common values shared by both religious traditions.

Grobman, Alex. "Keeping the Rescuers in Historical Perspective." http://www.holocaust-trc.org/rescdoc.htm, 2002.
The efforts of Holocaust rescuers, according to Grobman, must be reported for the recognition of their good deeds. However, the author cautions that by concentrating upon the rescuers deeds there is a danger that the themes of "abandonment, passivity, and complicity..." will be distorted and set aside, while a more positive view of the Holocaust is placed before the public. The challenge is to keep the stories in perspective.

Gross, Jan T. *Neighbors: The Destruction of the Jewish Community in Jedwabne.* **Princeton: Princeton University Press, 2000, 261pp.**
This book details the murder of sixteen hundred Jews in the Polish town of Jedwabne on July 10, 1941. The pogrom, initiated by the town's Polish peasants, followed the Nazi invasion of the Soviet Union. The murders took place as German occupation forces looked on. According to Gross, the peasants were motivated primarily by traditional Christian hatred of Jews, but there also was an expectation that the peasants would confiscate the property of their Jewish victims.

Gushee, David P. *The Righteous Gentiles of the Holocaust: A Christian Interpretation.* **Minneapolis: Fortress Press, 1999, 258 pp.**
According to Gushee, the Holocaust should be recognized as a significantly influential event in the history of Christian faith and the Christian Church. The churches' collective failure to aid and rescue the Jews should lead Christians to self-examination and repentance. Gushee admits that Christians only rarely were empowered by their faith to help their Jewish neighbors, yet, he contends, that those few moral heroes who did rescue Jews during the Holocaust have qualities needed by the church today. The qualities of those few "Righteous Gentiles", who risked their own lives to help Jews, states the author, can teach us much "if we take the time to let their examples become ours."

Gutman, Yisrael, Judith Reinharz and Ezra Mendelsohn, eds. *Jews of Poland Between Two World Wars.* **University Press of New England, 1994, 544 pp.**
Twenty-seven essays are presented in this book that explores the history of Polish Jews during the interwar period. The scholars, representing a variety of countries, contend that despite the anti-Semitism displayed by both church and state, the Jewish community managed to retain their Yiddish culture and language.

Gutteridge, Richard. *The German Evangelical Church and the Jews, 1879-1950.* **New York: Harper, 1976, 374 pp.**
The study assesses the indifferent response of the German Evangelical Church to the Nazi persecution of all Jews, as well as its own non-Aryan members. Gutteridge argues, that Luther's doctrine of the "Two Kingdoms", in part, explains why even the few churchmen who challenged aspects of the Nazi Holocaust policy did not themselves reject the government's anti-Semitic presuppositions. The book includes chapters on "Christian anti-Semitism" in the period 1879-1933, as well as the Protestant reaction to the Jewish Boycott and Aryan Paragraph of 1933. Gutteridge also describes the response of the Protestant Churches to the Nuremberg Laws of 1935, the pogrom known as *Kristallnacht*, and the "Final Solution."

Hallie, Philip. *Lest Innocent Blood Be Shed: The Story of the Village of Le Chambon and How Goodness Happened There.* **New York: Harper Perennial, 1979, 304 pp.**
This book follows the story of the citizens and clergy living in a southern French town and their efforts to save thousands of Jews. In full view of the Vichy government, the townspeople established a network that hid Jews and moved them into safety in neutral countries.

Halter, Marek. *Stories of Deliverance: Speaking with Men and Women Who Rescued Jews from the Holocaust.* **Chicago: Open Court Publishers, 1997, 304 pp.**
Halter, a survivor of the Warsaw Ghetto, relates his conversations with Gentiles who rescued Jews during the Holocaust.

Hamann, Brigitte. *Hitler's Vienna: A Dictator's Apprenticeship.* **New York: Oxford University Press, 1999, 482 pp.**
The author finds that Hitler's claim in *Mein Kampf* that he became an anti-Semite when, "Once, when I was strolling through the inner city (Vienna), I suddenly encountered an apparition in a black caftan and black hair locks. Is this a Jew? Was my first thought," is belied by evidence that during Hitler's years in Vienna, he made the acquaintance, and formed close relations, with a number of

Jews. In fact, his best friend in the men's hostel that he lived in, Josef Neuman, was an Orthodox Jew. Hamann details Hitler's relationship with a number of other Jews, including one who invited him to his home to listen to chamber music. The author makes it clear that Hitler had seen Jews before he arrived in Vienna as well as in his hometown of Linz.

Handlin, Oscar. "Jewish Resistance to the Nazis." Commentary (November 1962), Volume 34, pp. 398-406.
The author claims, that in their effort to absolve themselves of responsibility for the murder of millions of Jews in the Holocaust, Christians and others have stripped the Nazis of humanity and /or blamed the Jews for not assessing their situation realistically, and for not fighting back against Hitler and his followers. However, the author insists, that by "defaming the dead and their culture" in the effort to free themselves from guilt, Christians simply "complete the process of destruction begun by the Nazis." Not only does blaming the Jews for complicity in their own extermination continue the anti-Judiac traditions of Christianity, it also validates a lie. The lie is that all Jews went meekly to their deaths in the camps. The reality is that there were efforts to resist, but the odds against success were overwhelming. Handlin points out that not all Jews resisted the Nazi policies because Jews are not a homogenous group. Those who had the means, the opportunity, and the predisposition, did fight back. Ultimately, the author asserts, "we gain and learn nothing by blaming the victims for the catastrophe."

Hassing, Arne. "The Churches of Norway and the Jews, 1933-1943. Journal of Ecumenical Studies (Summer 1989), Volume 26 Issue 3, pp. 496-522.
Hassing claims, that although there were few signs of anti-Semitism in Norway prior to the Nazi takeover, the Norwegian Churches failed to issue an outright condemnation of anti-Jewish attitudes. The author reviews the failure of the leader of the Lutheran Church of Norway to oppose the Nazis anti-Semitic agenda. It was only with the first deportations of Jews from Norway that churches began to publicly issue their protest against the treatment of the Jews, but by that time it too late to make much of a difference.

Hausner, Gideon. *Justice in Jerusalem.* New York: Harper, 1966, 528 pp.
This classic history of the Eichmann trial, written by the Israeli prosecutor, concludes that Pius XII was guilty of silence and inaction in regard to voicing a protest in opposition to the Nazi genocide directed against the Jews.

Headden, Susan and Dana Hawkins. "A Vow of Silence." U.S. News and World Report (March 30, 1998), Volume. 124 Issue 12, pp. 34-38.
Headden provides details of the evidence that ties the Vatican to funds stolen from the Nazis' Jewish victims. While most states have pushed to open up the

banking records that would help locate the stolen funds, the Vatican has refused to allow investigators to have access to its archives and records. Mounting evidence suggests that the Reverend Krunoslav Draganovic, a Franciscan, was involved in helping war criminals escape from Europe to South America and that he handled some of the stolen money. Without the Vatican records, however, the picture remains incomplete.

Hecht, Ben. *Guide for the Bedeviled.* **New York: Scribner, 1944, 276 pp.**
Written by a newspaper reporter, Hollywood screenwriter, and Zionist activist, this book addresses anti-Semitism at the time when news of the Nazi extermination of the Jews permeated many sectors of American life. This highly personal account of the Hecht's love for America is juxtaposed with the problem of anti-Semitism, which he views as dangerous and threatening to American freedom.

Heinsohn, Gunnar. "What Makes the Holocaust a Uniquely Unique Genocide?" Journal of Genocide Research (2000), Volume 2 Issue 3, pp. 411-30.
The Nazi's attempt to exterminate the Jews, according to Heinsohn, was not the result of racial anti-Semitism. Rather it was an effort to weed out Jewish influence and to repudiate the commandment against killing. Hitler's plan for Germany depended upon *Lebensraum* (living space). In order to move into and take over the territories to the east of Germany, Hitler had to rid Germans of the idea that killing non-combatants was wrong. Therefore, he needed to do away with ties to Judeo-Christian ethics, and reeducate Germans by providing them a license to kill without fear of recrimination. Thus, it served his purpose "to make Jews the enemy."

Hellman, Peter. *When Courage was Stronger than Fear: Stories of Christians and the Jews They Saved from the Holocaust.* **California: Marlowe & Co., 1999, 320 pp.**
Hellman profiles five of over sixteen thousand persons from thirty-four countries that have been honored as "Righteous Among the Nations." This is the designation bestowed by *Yad Vashem*, Israel's National Holocaust Memorial, to honor Gentiles who actively saved Jews during the Holocaust. Those profiled include an Italian priest who hid a Jewish family in a vacated convent and a Polish woman who took in and raised an abandoned Jewish infant. The current volume is a revised edition of the author's 1980 book, *Avenue of the Righteous.*

Helmreich, Ernst Christian. *The German Churches Under Hitler: Background, Struggle, and Epilogue.* **Detroit: Wayne State University Press, 1979, 616 pp.**
This book traces the history of German Christianity from the aftermath of the

Reformation to the Nazi regime. In the process Helmreich details the struggle of the Churches to maintain control of their corporate existence in the face of the Nazi regime's successful efforts to achieve *"Gleichshaltung"*, which deemed it necessary to subdue and coordinate every other German institution. Helmreich describes the Churches' reaction to the Nazi persecution of the Jews, as well as the Jehovah Witnesses.

Herbstrith, Waltraud, Bernard Bonowitz, Translator. *Edith Stein: The Untold Story of the Philosopher and Mystic Who Lost Her Life in the Death Camps of Auschwitz.* **Ignatius Press; 1992, 207pp.**
Edith Stein, a Jewish woman, gained prominence as a German philosopher. Her conversion to Catholicism, decision to become a Carmelite nun, her death in the Nazi concentration camp of Auschwitz, and the Vatican's decision to beatify her make her a fascinating and controversial figure. This work, an effort to help us learn about and understand Edith Stein, is based upon Stein's own words, which were taken from diaries and letters. Also included are the reflections of Edith's acquaintances through oral histories and written testimonies. The biography, an affectionate study, gives a brief but intense glimpse into Stein's character, and leaves the door open for further in depth examinations.

Herczl, Moshe Y. *Christianity and the Holocaust of Hungarian Jewry.* **Translated by Joel Lerner. New York: New York University Press, 1993, 299 pp.**
The author argues, that the Catholic and Protestant Churches in Hungary supported the deportation of more than a half million Jews to Auschwitz in 1944. From the *Ausgleich* of 1867 to the first deportation, Hungarian churches emphasized the centrality of Christianity to Hungarian nationalism. Only when Nazi and Hungarian racial policies refused to discriminate between Jews and baptized Jews did church authorities voice opposition.

Herzog, Dagmar. "Theology of Betrayal: Betrayal; German Churches and the Holocaust." Tikkun (June 30, 2001), Volume 16 Issue 3, pp. 69-72.
A discussion is provided of the points made in essays from the book *Theology of Betrayal*. Herzog agrees, that Catholics and Protestants in Germany regarded Jews as too powerful and influential. Therefore, Christian theologians, even when opposed to National Socialism, persisted in seeing Jewish existence as somehow "intolerable."

Heschel, Susannah. "Nazifying Christian Theology: Walter Grundmann and the Institute for the Study of the Eradication of Jewish Influence on German Church Life." Church History (December 1994), Volume 63, Issue 4, pp. 587-605.
The author reviews the activities of the Institute that was created by the

Deutsche Christen movement in Eisenach during 1939. Walter Grundmann was appointed as the director of this Protestant Church group. In adhering to the racial ideology of H. S. Chamberlain, the Institute tried developing "an Aryan Christianity." Their intent was to rid Christianity of any Jewish elements and to show the world how degenerate Jews were. In the aftermath of the war, Grundmann and others in the Institute claimed they had only tried to defend Christianity, yet the evidence demonstrates they were far more involved in the Nazi's war activities than they admitted. Despite their assistance in the promotion of virulent anti-Semitism during the war, most of the Institute's members retained their church positions in post-war Germany.

Hilberg, Raul. *The Destruction of the European Jews.* Revised and definitive ed. 3v. New York: Homes & Meier, 1985, 1273 pp.
Hilberg has expanded and revised his classic 1961 study. There are many additions in the revised work, but little in the way of interpretive changes. Hilberg details the bureaucratic structure and means by which the Nazis implemented the "Final Solution" against the Jews, but remains unsparing in his critical portrayal of the passivity of the Jews in the face of the Nazi destructive process.

____. *Perpetrators, Victims, Bystanders of the Jewish Catastrophe, 1933-1945.* New York: Harper-Collins, 1992, 340 pp.
This collection of essays, by the dean of Holocaust studies, focuses on the perpetrators of the Holocaust, as well as the response of the victims and the inaction of the so-called bystanders.

Himmelfarb, Milton. "No Hitler, No Holocaust." Commentary (March 1984), Volume 77 Issue 3, pp. 37-43.
Himmelfarb insists, "that without Hitler there would have been no Holocaust." He contends, that Christian anti-Jewishness was an insufficient factor to cause the genocide and cannot be held responsible for the death of six million Jews. The author asserts, that Hitler was the necessary and determining element of the Holocaust. He points out, that not only was Hitler anti-Jewish, he was also anti-Christian.

Hochuth, Rolf. "The Vatican and the Jews." Society (1983), Volume 20 Issue 3, pp. 4-20.
As the author of the controversial play *The Deputy,* which vilified Pope Pius XII for his inaction during the Holocaust, Hochuth continues in this article to insist. "that Pius failed the world when it most needed a moral leader." The author contends the pope was an ambitious careerist, who ignored the facts concerning Nazi atrocities when they were presented to him. Therefore millions of Jews went to their deaths at the hands of the Nazis.

Hoffmann, Peter. "Roncalli in the Second World War: Peace Initiatives, Greek Famine and the Persecution of Jews." Journal of Ecclesiastical History (January 1989), Volume 40 Issue 1, pp. 74-99.
Monsignor Angelo Roncalli, in the author's opinion, acted to help those in need during World War II. Roncalli's efforts included procuring and helping to distribute immigration certificates and baptismal certificates to Jewish citizens in order to assist them in escaping the Nazis. Roncalli was later selected to be leader of the Roman Catholic Church as Pope Pius XXIII. Moreover, he claimed, that the Vatican supported his attempts to help the Jews, and tried to assist him whenever possible.

_____. *Stauffenberg: A Family History, 1905-1944.* Cambridge: Cambridge University Press, 1995, 424 pp.
The focus of the book centers on the military career of Claus, Count Stauffenberg and his fight to overthrow Hitler, which culminated in the failed assassination attempt of 20 July 1944. The book is also a family biography of the three Stauffenberg brothers, who are portrayed as men spurred to action by the mass murder of Jews. Their religious background, noble birth, and intellectual inclinations drove them to respond to the genocide in atonement for Germany's crimes.

Hogan, David John and David Aretha, eds. The Holocaust Chronicle. Lincolnwood, IL: Publication International, 2000, 765 pp.
This illustrated history of the Holocaust is arranged chronologically. Although it studies a broad array of those groups (political, religious and secular) that played roles in the Holocaust, it does examine issues that concern the anti-Jewish fervor that the Christian Churches helped promote during the interwar period. The editors also review the activities of the Christian Churches both during and after the extermination of six million Jews.

Hoover, Arlie J. *God, Britian, and Hitler in World War II: The View of the British Clergy, 1939-1945.* Westport, Conn: Greenwood Publishing, 1994, 168 pp.
Hoover contends, that while many Britons viewed German Fascism as repulsive, British clerics did not defend the war as a battle against the German "worship" of race, leader and state. Rather, recognizing that racial attitudes, such as anti-Semitism, were also found in British society, the clerics insisted that the war was proper because it protected their particular Christian religious culture.

Housden, Martyn. *Resistance and Conformity in the Third Reich.* London and New York: Routledge, 1997, 199 pp.
The author examines the main loci of German society that could have served as potential sources of opposition to the Nazi regime. The chapter on the German

churches, however, is particularly curious, inasmuch as the author omits mention of Christian anti-Semitism among the leaders of the Confessing Church, which opposed Hitler's policies towards baptized Jews.

Huberband, Shimon, 1909-1942. *Kiddush Hashem: Jewish Religious and Cultural Life in Poland During the Holocaust.* **Translated by David E. Fishman; Jeffrey S. Gurock and Robert Hirt, eds. (Heritage of Modern European Jewry, v.1) New York: KTAV; Yeshiva University Press, 1987, 474 pp.**
This account by Rabbi Huberband, who was deported from the Warsaw Ghetto and murdered in Auschwitz, is an eyewitness account of ghetto life between 1940-1942. Despite the hardship face by the author, Huberband maintained his devotion to the Jewish tradition of the *Torah.* The book is a vivid account of religious life in the ghetto in the face of impossible conditions.

Huneke, Douglas K. *The Moses of Rovno: The Stirring Story of Fritz Graebe, a German Christian Who Risked His Life to Lead Hundreds of Jews to Safety During the Holocaust.* **New York: Dodd, Mead, 1985, 208 pp.**
The little known story of Herman "Fritz" Graebe, a German construction engineer, is told in this account. Graebe worked on railway projects in German-occupied Ukraine from 1941 to 1944, and after witnessing the massacre of Polish and Soviet Jews was determined to protect those that he came into contact with. He accomplished his goal by taking Jews into his labor forces and providing them with false papers. Through this process he was able to save the lives of hundreds of Jews during the Holocaust. Graebe arranged for their disguise and proceeded to smuggle them to different cities.

James, Pierre. *Murderous Paradise: German Nationalism and the Holocaust.* **Westport, CT.: Greenwood Publishing Group; 2001, 216 pp.**
According to James, German redemptive anti-Semitism lay at the root of forming the type of attitudes that enabled Nazis to murder Jews. The author explains, that redemptive anti-Semitism links the demise of Jews to a deliverance from worldly problems. James traces the nationalist feelings that finally culminated in Hitler's plan to exterminate the Jews as they evolved from the fourteenth to the twentieth century.

Janzten, Kylr. "Propaganda, Perseverance, and Protest: Strategies for Clerical Survival Amid the German Church Struggle." Church History (June 2001), Volume 70 Issue 2, pp. 295-327.
The author contends, that scholars need to understand the diversity that existed within German churches on the local level. With that goal in mind, Jantzten conducted a comparative study of three different Protestant Church districts, between the years 1933-1945. The author concludes, that there existed

"sufficient freedom" for pastors, with a modicum of courage, to influence the course of his parishes' struggle against Nazi control. Additionally, women's groups, mayors, schoolteachers, and parish councils were also able to effect the overall church struggle in districts like Ravensburg, Nauen and Pirma.

Jeanrond, Werner G. "From Resistance to Liberation Theology: German Theologians and the Non-Resistance to the National Socialist Regime." The Journal of Modern History (December 1992), Volume 64 Issue Supplement: Resistance Against the Third Reich, pp. S187-S203.
Jeanrond explores the relationship between Christian theology and Christian resistance to the Third Reich. The author maintains, that not only did Christians lack the resistance theology needed to challenge the Nazis, they did not have the foundations necessary for constructing an opposition movement. Once they realized the dangers of Hitler's regime and moved to resist the Reich, it was too late to do so. Some contemporary theologians recognize the need to provide "an institutional platform" for Christians to utilize when "fighting oppressive political groups.' Men like Moltmann, Metz, and Sobrino challenge all Christians to actively participate in the political process so that the evils of the Nazis cannot be repeated.

Johnson, Douglas. "French Historians and the Holocaust." History Today (October 1996), Volume 46 Issue 10, pp. 2-4.
A book written by a French philosopher in 1945 attacked the State of Israel, and contended that the Holocaust never happened. Johnson maintains the book would have been ignored were it not for the support it received from a very popular Frenchman, the Abbe Pierre. Because of this support, Johnson questions whether a latent anti-Semitism persists among French Catholics. He notes, that there have always been those who try to deny the "accepted version of Hitler's Final Solution", and in this article he reviews that tradition as it has developed among men of religion and through advocates from both the left and right wings of politics.

Kahane, David. *Lvov Ghetto Diary.* Jerry Michalowicz, Translator. University of Massachusetts Press, 1990, 162 pp.
Rabbi Kahane, in this book covering the period of 1941 through 1944, condemns those Ukrainians, who helped the Nazis in exterminating Jews. In contrast, he commends the Uniate Catholic Church for its efforts to save his family from death. The author notes, that the Ukrainian Archbishop hid them in a nearby monastery and convent, and gave his family shelter from the Nazis, while over one hundred thousand Jews were murdered.

Kalib, Goldie. *The Last Selection: A Child's Journey through the Holocaust.* Amhearst: University of Massachusetts Press, 1991, 266 pp.

As a child survivor of Auschwitz and a death march, the author describes her pre-war life in Poland, her lost childhood, and the way in which Christian Poles hid her and her family for money. The book examines the complexities of Polish responses to the mass murder of the Jews.

Kaplan, Marion. *Between Dignity and Despair: Jewish Life in Nazi Germany.* **New York: Oxford University Press, 1998, 290 pp.**
The author examines the thoughts and feelings of Jewish men, women, and children as they coped with persecution in Nazi Germany. She focuses on the everyday lives of ordinary Jews and their struggle to survive, rather than on Nazi perpetrators and the responses of Jewish organizations.

Katz, Steven T. *The Holocaust in Historical Context. v.1* **New York: Oxford University Press, 1994, 702 pp.**
This is the first of a projected three-volume study on the Holocaust. Katz argues, "that the unprecedented nature of the Holocaust derived from Hitler's intention to rid the planet of its Jewish population..." In focusing on the uniqueness of the Holocaust, Katz compares the Nazi genocide with other examples of mass murder from ancient times to the present. He concludes, that in none of these historic examples was there the intention on the part of the perpetrators to systematically engage in genocide. The author also provides an excellent account of the relationship, rather than the likeness, of Christian anti-Judaism to Nazi anti-Semitism.

Kaufman, Jonathan. *A Hole in the Heart of the World: Being Jewish in Eastern Europe.* **Viking Penguin, 1996, 320 pp.**
Covering almost a century, the author traces the lives of four families before, during and after World War II to current times. Three of the four families are of Jewish heritage, and one is Catholic with some Jewish ancestry. All four managed to survive the hostility of secular and religious anti-Semites prior to the war, the Holocaust, and finally Communism. The author maintains, that now that the Soviet Union has lost its hold on Eastern Europe, Jews may be able to live peacefully in the region.

Keefe, Patricia M. "Popes Pius XI and Pius XII, the Catholic Church, and the Nazi Persecution of the Jews." **British Journal of Holocaust Education (Summer 1993), Volume 2 Issue 2, pp. 26-47.**
Keefe points out that in spite of the Concordat between the Catholic Church and Hitler Pius XI spoke out against Nazi racism, while Pius XII did not, even though he had evidence of the Holocaust. The author contends, that the Church's fear of Communism influenced its response to the murder of the Jews and that some within the Church connected Jews to the perceived Communist threat. Note is also taken of the traditional anti-Jewish attitude of the Church.

Kent, George O. "Pope Pius XII and Germany: Some Aspects of German-Vatican Relations 1933-1943." American Historical Review (October 1994), Volume 70 Issue 1, pp. 59-79.
Kent reports on the relations between the Vatican and the German government as seen through the eyes of German diplomats from 1933-1943. The author discusses the Concordat of 1933 as a diplomatic victory for Hitler and notes that the disputes between the Church and the Nazis began as soon as the Concordat was signed. According to the author, Pius XII had no illusions about National Socialism, but was caught between the evil of Hitler and the evil that a possible Communist victory might bring. The pope also was forced to try to pursue a just peace. Therefore, he could not fully endorse or antagonize either side.

Kertzer, David. *The Popes Against the Jews: The Vatican's Role in the Rise of Modern Anti-Semitism.* Knopf; 2001, 368 pp.
Through the use of newly released Vatican archival documents, Kertzer constructs a formidable case to support his conclusion that the Catholic Church has historically been responsible for the dismal treatment of the Jews. He traces this (in his opinion) abysmal record as it developed in the Papal States during the nineteenth century, through to the anti-Jewish mentality that persisted within the Church after the demise of the Papal States. He is highly critical of each pope's consistent failure to openly repudiate the superstitious myths that have resulted in the continued persecution of Jews in the modern era.

____. *The Unholy War: The Vatican's Role in the Rise of Modern Anti-Semitism.* New York: MacMillen Press, 2002,168 pp.
Once again, Kertzer puts forward evidence to substantiate his contention that the Vatican placed Jews in the most humiliating circumstances from the time of the defeat of Napoleon, through to the unification of Italy in 1870. He examines the revival of blood libel accusations, the indignity and horrific conditions of life in the ghetto, and the overall anti-Semitic attitude by Catholic clerics throughout Western Europe.

Kessler, Sidney H. "Fascism Under the Cross: The Case of Father Coughlin." Wiener Library Bulletin (1980), Volume 33 Issue 51-52, pp. 8-12.
Father Coughlin's radio program, his newspaper *Social Justice,* and his paramilitary units spewed anti-Semitism. Yet, the Catholic Church historically and did nothing to silence the priest. The silence of the Catholic Church in the face of Coughlin's virulent attacks upon Jews lends credence to the argument that the Church bears some guilt for the Holocaust.

King, Christine. *"Jehovah's Witnesses under Nazism." Mosaic of Victims: Non-Jews Persecuted and Murdered by the Nazis.* New York: New York

University Press, 1990, 320 pp. Berenbaum, Michael, ed.
King's essay outlines the refusal of the Jehovah's Witnesses to conform to the dictates of the Nazi regime in Germany, and the persecution they endured as a result.

____. *The Nazi State and the New Religions: Five Case Studies in Non-Conformity.* Edwin Mellen Press, 1990, 350 pp.
In this book King presents a study of five small religious sects that existed inside the Nazi regime. These sects; the Christian Scientists, the Mormons, the Seventh-Day Adventists, the New Apostolic Church and the Jehovah's Witness survived Nazi rule by various means. To date, however, only two of the religions have undertaken an examination of their behavior on behalf of the Jews during the Holocaust.

Kirschner, Robert, ed. *Rabbinic Responsa of the Holocaust Era.* New York: Schocken Publishing, 1985, 192 pp.
This volume is an anthology of the rabbinic responses to the various problems of observing *Halakha* (religious law) faced by Orthodox Jews under Nazi rule.

Klemperer, Victor. *I Will Bear Witness: A Diary of the Nazi Years, 1933-1941.* New York: Random House, 1999, 501 pp.
A convert to Christianity, Klemperer was, nevertheless, designated a Jew by the Nazis. The diary reports the steady deterioration of his life as well as that of the lives of all Jews of Germany. The chronicle is filled with insights in regard to German anti-Semitism, the support of his fellow Germans for Adolf Hitler, and acerbic comments about Jews and Zionists. Inadvertently, the diary refutes the thesis proffered by Daniel Jonah Goldhagen, that the Holocaust was a national project of the German people, inasmuch as Klemperer found many "good" Germans who displayed sympathy for his plight and for Jews in general.

Kochavi, Aryeh J. "The Catholic Church and Anti-Semitism in Poland Following World War II as Reflected in British Diplomatic Documents." Gal-Ed: On The History of the Jews in Poland (Israel 1989) Volume 11, pp. 116-128.
Documents from 1946 located in the British Foreign Office offer proof that the Polish government retained deeply anti-Semitic attitudes after the Second World War. The British faced difficulties in trying to balance their desire to improve the treatment of Jews in Poland with the need to persuade Polish leaders to help fight Communism.

Kofman, Sarah, Translated by Ann Smock. *Rue Ordener Rue Labat* Lincoln: University of Nebraska Press, 1994, 85 pp.
A distinguished French philosopher recounts how the police dragged her father,

the rabbi of a small synagogue, from the family home and deported him to Auschwitz in July 1942. Not long after her father's departure, Kofman and her mother took refuge in the apartment of a Christian woman on Rue Labat, where they remained until liberation.

Kren, George M. and Rodler F. Morris. "Race and Spiritually: Arthur Dinter's Theosophical Anti-Semitism." Holocaust and Genocide Studies (1991), Volume 6 Issue 3, pp 233-52.
The popular novel *The Sin Against Blood* (1918), written by Arthur Dinter, portrayed the Jews as evil. Dinter, a leading spokesman for the Nazi's in the 1920's, proposed the creation of a Germanic Christianity minus any Jewish influence. He was instrumental in helping to define the Jew in Nazi ideology, even though he was opposed to the idea of murdering Jews. Dinter was silenced when his own religious views conflicted with Hitler's ideas.

Krieg, Robert A. "Karl Adam, National Socialism, and Christian Tradition." Theological Studies (September 1999), Volume 60 Issue 3, pp. 432-457.
This article lays out the beliefs of Karl Adam, a German Catholic theologian. It explains why he felt that the Catholic Church could co-exist with the National Socialist regime. Adam believed that political independence, secularization, social pluralism and other modern ideologies were major threats to the Catholic Church. The theologian pointed out that the values Hitler promoted were in concert with those that would ensure a strong church. According to Krieg, Adam supported the idea that Germany should be reserved primarily for German Christians.

Krzesinski, Andrew J. *National Cultures, Nazism and the Church*. Boston: Bruce Humphries Incorporated, 1945, 128 pp.
Though the author agrees, that the Church has had a significant impact upon German culture, he insists, that this has no connection to Hitler and the Nazis. He contends, that the "religion of Christ" had nothing in common with Nazi ambitions, and therefore, was as much a target of Hitler as the Jews or anyone else. The author convicts Nazism as evil, " in defiance of God, deporting men like cattle to hidden concentration camps."

Kugelmass, Jack and Jonathan Boyarin, eds. *From a Ruined Garden: the Memorial Books of Polish Jewry*. New York: Schocken Books, 1983, 275 pp.
This is a distillation of more than one hundred memorial books written by survivors in Eastern Europe. The purpose for the books was to memorialize the Jews slain during World War II by the Germans and their helpers in Poland, Lithuania, Hungary, the Ukraine, and other lands. These *yizkor-bikher,* or memorial books, perform on paper what, in the Jewish religious tradition, used

to be done in stone.

Kulka, Otto Dov, and Paul Mendes-Flohr. *Judaism and Christianity Under the Impact of National Socialism, 1919-1945.* **Jerusalem: Historical Society of Israel and Zalman Shazar Center for Jewish History, 1987, 558 pp.**
The volume describes the state of Jewish-Christian social and theological relations both during the Weimar Republic and the Third Reich.

Kurek, Ewa, Ewa Kurek-Leslik and Jan Karski (Introduction). *Your Life is Worth Mine: Story Never Told Before of how Polish Nuns in World War II Saved Hundreds.* **Hippocrene Books Inc., 1995, 255 pp.**
This article provides details about the wartime efforts of Polish Christians, who gave aid to Jews trying to survive the Holocaust. These Righteous Gentiles, who's ranks included many Catholic nuns and priests, chose to provide assistance even though they had been warned by the Nazis that anyone discovered helping the Jews would be sentenced to death. The evidence presented is extracted from extensive interviews with nuns and the Jewish children who survived.

Kurth, James. "The Defamation of Pope Pius XII." Modern Age (Summer 2002), Volume 44 Issue 3, pp. 283, 5 pp.
In this review article the author takes issue with some of the recent books, which have, in his opinion, libeled Pope Pius XII. James contends, that the promotion of these books has little to do with the Holocaust and the pope's role during World War II. Rather these texts are an attempt by liberals and radicals to silence the Church so that it will not speak out on moral issues.

_____. "The Vatican's Foreign Policy." National Interest (1993), Volume 32, pp. 40-52.
Kurth looks at Catholic Church policies in connection with Communism. The author concludes, that the Vatican, from the days of the Russian Revolution to the fall of the Soviet Union, has viewed Communism as a major threat. This preoccupation with the threat of Communism has affected papal foreign policy and teachings on issues like the Holocaust, Christian Democratic parties, the United States, and events in Eastern Europe.

Kushner, Antony. "Ambivalence or Anti-Semitism? Christian Attitudes and Responses in Britain to the Crisis of European Jewry During the Second World War." Holocaust and Genocide Studies (1990), Volume 5 Issue 2, pp. 175-189.
Kushner asserts, that Christianity's view of Jews from the Middle Ages through World War II has been contradictory. On one hand Jews were rejected because of their role in Christ's death and their refusal to accept the "true" religion, yet at

the same time Jews were accepted because they were potential converts. The author contends, that the Catholic Church was especially hostile to Jews. He demonstrates with the use of government documents, newspaper articles and memoirs, that while the Church and Britons may have opposed Hitler's policies and felt some compassion for the plight of Jews, they still held an aversion to them.

Landau, Ron. *The Nazi Holocaust.* **Chicago: I.R. Dee Publishing Co., 1994, 356 pp.**
Among the questions raised by the author is; how was it possible for a supposedly civilized society such as Germany to produce such barbarity? Towards answering the moral, religious, and psychological queries posed by the Holocaust, Landau revisits some of the major Holocaust interpretations surrounding the Nazi genocide.

Lang, Berel. " 'Not Enough' Versus 'Plenty' Which did Pius XII Do?" **Judaism (Fall 2001), Volume 50 Issue 4, pp. 448-452.**
The point is made that those arguing one side or the other about whether or not Pius did or did not do enough to defend and protect Jews during World War II are not necessarily contradictory. According to Lang, Pius was faced with tough choices. While he did to some extent lend his assistance to the Jewish population, he balanced his actions with attempts to mitigate the threats Nazis were making. His obligation to protect the Catholic Church was in conflict with his moral duty to issue an outright condemnation of the Nazis. However, according to Lang, when faced with this dilemma he should have opted to put himself and the Vatican at risk, rather than allow the Nazis to proceed with their evil activities.

Lantner, Henry L. *What? Again Those Jews?* **Jerusalem: Gefen, 1997, 150 pp.**
The author contends, that the Christian Church has been the primary source for hatred of, and hostility towards, the Jews throughout history. Lantner's ideas and personal experiences with anti-Semitism are presented. He maintains, that he has encountered a variety of forms of anti-Semitic ideology while a member of the Polish military corps, and when stationed in Britain and South Africa during World War II.

Lapide, Pinchas E. *Three Popes and the Jews.* **New York: Hawthorne Books, 1967, 384 pp.**
Lapide, an Israeli diplomat and journalist, argues that under the direction of Pius XII the Catholic Church helped save over eight hundred thousand Jews. The author contends, that if the pope would have issued a strongly worded condemnation of the Nazi extermination of the Jews, the result would have been

disastrous for the Catholic Church.

Lapomarda, Vincent. "The Jesuits and the Holocaust." Journal of Church and State (Spring 1981), Volume 23 Issue 2, pp. 241-258.
Lapomarda, a member of the Society of Jesus, defends the Vatican's role in relation to the Jews. He insists, that the Jesuits prior to World War II eschewed anti-Semitism. In addition, the author notes the Jesuits were actively opposed to Nazi policies and worked to protect Jews whenever possible, thereby leaving themselves open to attacks by the Third Reich.

Laqueur, Walter. *The Terrible Secret: Suppression of the Truth about Hitler's Final Solution.* Boston: Little Brown. 1981, 262 pp.
Focusing on the eighteen months from June 1941 to the end of 1942, the author argues, "millions of people cannot be killed without participants in the murder and without witnesses." He argues, that news of the mass killing of Jews was not a systematic cover-up, but was simply played down. Laqueur accuses allied politicians, neutral countries, the Vatican and the Red Cross of knowing about the tragedy of the Holocaust. He maintains, they kept silent out of fear.

_____ and Judith Tydor Baumel, eds. *The Holocaust Encyclopedia.* Yale University Press, 2001, 765 pp.
The article offers comprehensive and in-depth coverage of issues concerning the Holocaust in brief. Of the three hundred entries included, about one hundred-sixteen range in length from one to fourteen pages. There are entries for each country that had a sizable Jewish community during the Holocaust. Thus the book presents a broad perspective about the Holocaust.

Lautmann, Rüdiger. *"Gay Prisoners in Concentration Camps as Compared with Jehovah's Witnesses and Political Prisoners." Mosaic of Victims.* Berenbaum, Michael, ed. New York: New York University Press, 1990, 320 pp.
By comparing the plight of homosexuals to that of the Jehovah's Witnesses and political prisoners in the concentration camps, the author argues that Nazi racial ideology and public attitudes placed homosexual men alongside the Jews at the bottom of the camp hierarchy.

Lawler, Justus G. *Popes and Politics: Reform, Resentment, and the Holocaust.* New York: Continuum International Publishing Group Inc., 2002, 256 pp.
There have been many books published in the last few years that strongly criticize the Vatican's response to the plight of Jews during World War II and the Holocaust. Lawler contends, that most of these works are flawed and he presents scholarly and well-reasoned arguments to support his criticisms. He

maintains that personal bias and presupposition provide the basis for many of the problems contained in these published works. Not content just to take issue with the work of other authors, Lawler also proposes principles for papal reform and its future renewal.

Lease, Gary. *Odd Fellows in Politics and Religion: Modernism, National Socialism, and German Judaism.* **Mouton de Gruyter, 1994, 325 pp.**
Lease studies the links between religion, politics, and modernism in Germany. He notes the accommodations attempted between the Christian Churches and the National Socialists, the problems both had with modernity, the eventual efforts of the Nazis to imbue a religious quality into their own ideology, and the negative ways in which Jews were affected.

Leschnitzer, Adolf. *Magic Background of Modern Anti-Semitism: An Analysis of the German-Jewish Relationship.* **New York: International Universities Press, 1956, 236 pp.**
The author states, that although German Jews considered themselves to be as nationalistic and patriotic as any other German, the reality was, that they were never accepted as legitimate citizens by other Germans. The only exception to this rejection of Jews was found within certain well-educated, socio-economic groups. Thus anti-Semitism, deeply entrenched within the historical, sociological and psychological parameters of German society, helped open the way for the Nazi regime.

Levi, Primo. *The Drowned and the Saved.* **New York: Random House, 1989, 170 pp.**
Levi wrote this final contemplation of the Holocaust before his suicide in 1987. His memoir of life in Auschwitz is a companion piece to *Survival in Auschwitz* (1958). In this volume, Levi discusses the moral collapse that occurred in Auschwitz and the unfortunate fallibility of human memory that allows such atrocities to recur.

____. *Moments of Reprieve.* **New Jersey: Summit Books, 1986, 144 pp.**
This book is composed of brief sketches based on the author's experiences in Auschwitz. Among the prisoners described by Levi are religious fanatics, and Orthodox Jews too gentle to steal even when starving.

____.*Survival in Auschwitz: The Nazi Assault on Humanity* (**If** *This Is a Man*). **New York: Simon & Schuster, 1996, 187 pp.**
This is Levi's classic memoir, which was first published in 1958. It records his ten months in Auschwitz where he observed and wrote, without rancor, about the systematic cruelty that abounded in the death camp and his miraculous survival.

Lewy, Guenter. *The Catholic Church and Nazi Germany.* **New York: Da-Capo Press Inc., 2000, 432 pp.**
Lewy describes the Catholic episcopate's support for German expansionist policies, and its failure to speak out about the persecution of the Jews. The author states, that the Church's mistakes were made because Catholics ascribed to some of the goals of National Socialism. He notes, that the church's "silence" was later due to its gradual entrapment by Nazi policies.

Liebster, Simone Arnold. *Facing the Lion: Memoirs of a Young Girl in Nazi Europe.* **New Orleans: Grammaton Press, 2000, 369 pp.**
In writing about the experiences and trials faced by Simone Arnold and her family, Liebster provides important information about the treatment of Jehovah's Witnesses living under Nazi rule. The Arnold family displayed courage by defying the Nazis despite the threat of punishment. The story of Simone's efforts to remain true to her faith in God, to resist the evils of National Socialism, and to restart her life after the war may give insight into what is required of people whose strength of character is challenged by the worst of circumstances.

Lifton, Robert Jay. *The Nazi Doctors: Medical Killing and the Psychology of Genocide.* **New York: Basic Books, 1986, 576 pp.**
The author attempts to explain the moral question of how some two hundred physicians, sworn to uphold the Hippocratic Oath, became murderers by engaging in medical experiments in camps such as Auschwitz. Lifton introduces the term "twinning" to explain his thesis, a term that has become controversial among those attempting to understand how healers became killers.

Linsay, Mark R. *Covenanted Solidarity: The Theological Basis of Karl Barth's Oppostion to Nazi Anti-Semitism and the Holocaust.* **Peter Lang Publishing Incorporated. 2001, 368 pp.**
Linsay, a history professor at the University of Western Australia, bases his book upon his earlier doctoral dissertation, as well as papers he has studied concerning the subject of the Swiss theologian, Karl Barth. The author examines Barth's life in an attempt to discredit the theory that Barth was indifferent to the plight of Jews during the Nazi regime. Linsay portrays Barth's activities in opposition to the Nazi's in the context of theology, church-state relations, German anti-Semitic attitudes, the evolution of the theologian's thinking, and his mixed feelings concerning biblical Israel.

Littell, Franklin H. "Amsterdam and its Absentees." Journal of Ecumenical Studies (1979), Volume 16 Issue 1, pp. 109-111.
Studies of the Holocaust and World War II have brought to light the lack of representation of the Jewish faith at the 1939 World Conference of Christian

Youth held in Amsterdam. Today the contributions Christianity has received from Judaism are more openly recognized at ecumenical gatherings.

____. *German Phoenix: Men and Movements in the Church in Germany, Volume 1.* **New York: Doubleday, 1960, 226 pp.**
This volume began a continuing examination by the author of the encounters between the National Socialist regime and the German Protestant Churches. The book provides a study of the nineteenth century influences that paved the way for the Nazi government as well as the events that determined the nature of the relationship between Hitler and the German Protestant congregations.

____ **and Zev Garber.** *German Phoenix: Men and Movements in the Church in Germany ,Volume 2.* **University Press of America, 1992, 242 pp.**
This is a reprint of the 1960 edition. It contains updated information about the type of actions and events that characterized the encounter between the Nazis and the Protestant Churches. There is also a new foreword written by Herbert Locke.

____. **" The Holocaust and the Christians." Journal of Church and State (1999), Volume 41 Issue 4, pp. 725-738.**
Using his memories of a Nazi rally held in Nuremberg, Littell notes the pseudo-spiritual elements of the National Socialist movement that drew in many twentieth century Christians who experienced feelings of alienation from their religious institutions. Littell maintains, that the basis for this alienation and the need for many Christians to seek a new source of spirituality were a result of the established church's failures to repent their wrongs. This failure dates as far back as about 325 A.D. when the Council of Nicea took place.

____ **and Hubert G. Locke, eds.** *The German Church Struggle and the Holocaust.* **Detroit: Wayne State University Press, 1974, 328 pp.**
The volume is a collection of papers read at the 1970 conference for the Wayne State University project on "The History of the Church Struggle and the Holocaust." The focus of the conference was to investigate the common theological and political roots of "idolatrous" patriotism and the Nazi hatred of the Jews. Contributors include: John Conway, Henry Friedlander, Franklin Littell, Wilhem Niemoeller, and Gorden Zahn.

Locke, Hubert G. and Marcia S. Littell, eds. *Holocaust and Church Struggle.* **University Press of America, 1996, 366 pp.**
The editors have collected and printed this group of essays in order to provide a comprehensive study of the Church and its relation to the Holocaust. The essays are divided into topic headings that include; Historical Observations; Philosophical Reflections; The Church Struggle; Education: Jewish-Christian

Relations; and Survivor Testimony.

____. *Remembrance and Recollection: Essays on the Centennial Year of Martin Niemoller and Reinhold Niebuhr and the Fiftieth Year of the Wannsee Conference.* **University Press of America, 2002, 138 pp.**
The essays presented in this volume show the importance of these two German clerics in leading the opposition to National Socialism within their churches. The scholars, who presented these papers at a 1992 conference dedicated to the German Church Struggle, show the determination of Niemoller and Niebuhr to resist the Nazi plan, organized during the Wannsee Conference, to exterminate the Jews.

Lookstein, Haskel. *Were We Our Brothers' Keepers? The Public Response of American Jews to the Holocaust.* **New York: Hartmore House, 1989, 287 pp.**
Written by a prominent American rabbi, the author of this text concludes that there was no lack of information in the United States, within the American Jewish community, in regard to the Nazi extermination campaign against the Jews. Through a reading of the Yiddish press as well as the Anglo-Jewish press for several U.S. cities, Lookstein finds, that the American Jewish community, given its small size (less than four percent of the population) could not have done much to help the Jews under Nazi control. However, they did much less than they could have.

Lowenthal, Larry. "Time to Clear the Air on Pius XII." The Jewish Advocate (November 11, 1999), Volume 189 Issue 45, pp. 17.
The debate surrounding the actions of Pope Pius XII during the Holocaust has raged for over thirty years. According to the author, the Vatican's decision to beatify Pius and John Cornwell's book, *Hitler's Pope,* have increased the level of argument about Pius. Lowenthal insists, that the differences of opinion concerning Pius' effort (or lack of effort) to save the Jews from the Nazis will not be resolved anytime soon. He suggests the ongoing debate will become more rancorous if the Catholic Church persists in its attempts to confer sainthood upon the controversial pope.

Loy, Rosetta. *First Words: A Childhood in Fascist Italy.* **New York: Henry Holt and Company, Incorporated, 2001, 192 pp.**
The author recounts growing up in Italy prior to and during World War II. The child of a well-to-do Catholic family, Loy recalls the treatment of the Jews. She insists, that the Vatican, as well as Italy's intellectuals and elite did little to help the Jews escape the Nazis murderous policies.

Madigan, Kevin. "What the Vatican Knew About the Holocaust, and When." Commentary (October 2001), Volume 112 Issue 3, pp. 43.

The case Madigan lays out supports the theory that the Vatican was informed as early as the Fall of 1941 about the massacre of Jews in Slovakia. Thereafter, the author contends there was a flow of correspondence and communiqués coming into the Vatican from prelates and laity that detailed the crimes of the Nazis. Information was given about the deportations and the murders of Jews under Germany's control. Having established his case, Madigan asks what the Church did or did not do in response to the evidence. He concludes, that the Vatican, under the direction of Pius XII, was not as forceful and active on behalf of the Jews as it should have been. The author claims, that Pius was not an anti-Semite or pro-Nazi as some have asserted, nor was he the "Righteous Gentile" that his defenders depict him as. Pius, in Madigan's view, was a diplomat conditioned to act with caution. The author states "The Jews needed a prophet, or at least a priest more alert to depravity and evil."

Magil, A.B. *The Real Father Coughlin*. New York: Worker's Library Publishers, 1939, 31 pp.
This pamphlet, published by a Communist organization, was issued in an attempt to bring to light the pro-German and anti-Semitic preaching of Father Coughlin. Coughlin, a Catholic priest, had a popular radio program that provided him with a public forum in which he could disseminate his prejudices to the public.

Mahler, Jonathan. "Vatican Paper Lauds Fascist, Igniting Furor." Forward (October 6, 1995), Issue 31, 048, pp. 1
This article examines the controversy ignited when a Vatican publication contained a piece defending Italy's fascist leader Benito Mussolini. The defense has created some resentment among Jews who suffered at the dictator's hand. Mahler notes, that the Pope's spokesperson has reassured the Jewish community that the publication's view does not always reflect the pope's. Yet Mahler warns that incidents like this threaten any progress that has been made to reconcile Jews and Christians, for it serves to highlight the divisions that still exist.

Manilla, Morton. "Wagner in the History of Anti-Semitism." Midstream (February 1986), Volume 32 Issue 2, pp. 43-46.
Manilla examines the continuous thread of anti-Jewish attitudes from early Christianity, through to the Enlightenment thinkers, and on to Wagner. Just as Christianity insisted it had supplanted Judaism as the true religious faith, Wagner created his own folklore around the Germans who were, in his view, the new "chosen people."

Marchione, Sister Margherita. *Consensus and Controversy: Defending Pope Pius XII*. New York: Paulist Press, 2002, 400 pp.
Marchione relies on first hand sources to reveal Pope Pius's efforts for peace

during World War II. The author tries to refute charges that Pius stood by and did nothing while the Nazis murdered six million Jews in the Holocaust.

____."New Volume by Sister Margherita due in the Fall: Continues Defense of Pope Pius XII and his Efforts to Save Jews in World War II." The Italian Voice (April 15, 1999), Volume 67 Issue 46, pp. 4
This excerpt from Sister Margherita's book makes the case that Pius XII acted wisely and properly during World War II. According to Marchione, Pius did confront and resist Hitler and also gave aid to the Jews. Furthermore, she claims that those who attack Pius do so out of ignorance of the facts, or because their personal agenda requires them to find ways to defame the Catholic Church.

____. *Pope Pius XII: Architect for Peace.* New York: Paulist Press, 2000, 345 pp.
According to Marchione, Pius XII saved many Jews and Christians through his diplomatic efforts during the war. She maintains, that his work for peace was not "aloof", rather it was an effort to limit "the horrors of war." The pope provided aid to the victims of war through humanitarian assistance.

____. *Yours Is a Precious Witness: Memoirs of Jews and Catholics in Wartime Italy.* Mahwah: Paulist Press, 1997, 258 pp.
On the fiftieth anniversary of World War II, the author contends that Catholics in Italy, who saved Jews from death during the Holocaust, firmly believed that they were doing so in consonance with the Pope's wishes. Marchione uses many oral histories to support her ideas and to present a more personal picture of Pius XII.

Matheson, Peter, ed. *The Third Reich and the Christian Churches.* Grand Rapids: Eerdmans, 1981, 111 pp.
The author, a church historian at Edinburgh, has translated sixty-eight documents illustrative of Nazi ecclesiastical policies, and the responses offered by the Roman Catholic Church, members of the Confessing Church, and the German Christian Church.

Maxwell, Elisabeth. "The Rescue of Jews in France and Belgium During the Holocaust." Journal of Holocaust Education (Summer-Fall 1998), Volume 7 Issue 1-2, pp. 1-18.
The author studies the rescue attempts made on behalf of Jews in Belgium and France during the Holocaust. Maxwell points out that in France, where there had been anti-Semitism, the position of French citizens changed once the Nazis violent policies toward the Jews were made public. The author asserts, that the rescue efforts of Jews in France were initiated by Church leaders, while in Belgium the attempts to assist Jews escaping the Nazis often came through

individual clerics. Maxwell notes that in both countries offers of help often were directed toward saving Jewish children. The author concludes, that these stories of rescue could well provide an important moral lesson in Christian education.

____. *Silence or Speaking Out.* **Southampton: University of South Hampton, 1991, 27 pp.**
Maxwell maintains, that the Christian world remained silent about the murder of the Jews because of the anti-Semitism that Christian Churches had implanted in men's minds for two centuries. The contempt towards Jews and Judaism that the Church promoted bred an indifference to the Jews suffering that made it easier for the Nazis to carry out the Holocaust. Maxwell insists, that in the aftermath of the genocide the Church must continue attempting to change its teachings about Jews.

McInerny, Ralph M. *Defamation of Pius XII.* St. Augustine's Press, 2000, 211 pp.
McInerny defends the actions of Pope Pius XII and the Catholic Church during the Holocaust. He insists, that the pope and the church have been unjustly vilified and that Pius saved the lives of many Jews during World War II. The author also claims, that the church's critics are guilty of harboring prejudice and hatred against the Catholic Church. In McInerny's opinion, this intolerance is remarkably similar to the type Hitler displayed toward the Jews.

Meyers, Odette. *Doors to Madame Marie.* Seattle: University of Washington Press, 1997, 463 pp.
Jewish born, Meyers describes how she survived in German-occupied France by posing as a Christian. Madame Marie Chotel, a Catholic consierge and seamstress, hid Odette and her mother while the Nazis searched for them. Chotel then made certain that the girl was placed in a safe haven so that she could continue to elude the Germans.

Michael, Robert. "Religious Anti-Semitism and the American Immigration Policy During the Holocaust." Australian Journal of Jewish Studies (1993), Volume 7 Issue 1, pp. 8-40.
In this article Michael states, that the anti-Jewish attitudes that developed through Christian theology have, throughout American history, impacted the citizenry's response to Jews. This was made especially clear by the way that America's government institutions, the press and the population at large addressed the needs of Jews who were trying to immigrate into the United States in the inter-war era. The President, the State Department, the newspapers and U.S, citizens were hostile to the idea of allowing Jews into the country. They continued their opposition, even when informed of the persecution the Jews were experiencing in Nazi Germany.

Michalczyk, John J., ed. *Resisters, Rescuers, and Refugees.* **New York: Sheed and Ward Publications, 1999, 352 pp.**
Michalczyk has gathered together essays that study the historical issues concerning Christian rescues of Jews during the Holocaust, the resistance of Nazi oppression, and the plight of refugees in the post-war world. The scholars featured in this text maintain that the Holocaust was not just a Jewish tragedy, but one of epic proportions for humanity as a whole. Their work attempts to help guide the actions of future generations.

____. **"Theological Myth, German Anti-Semitism and the Holocaust: The Case of Martin Niemoeller." Holocaust and Genocide Studies (1987), Volume 2 Issue 1, pp. 105-122.**
The author claims, that while many have declared Martin Niemoeller a hero for his opposition to National Socialism, he was in fact an anti-Semite. The author argues, that Christianity relies upon negative Jewish imagery for validation, and therefore, church leaders, like Niemoeller, failed to protest Nazi anti-Semitism. Michalczyk presents evidence that in a 1935 sermon Niemoeller condemned Nazism, but also compared Jews to Nazis and predicted that both would suffer for their rejection of the Christian faith.

Mishell, William W. *Kaddish for Kovno: Life and Death in a Lithuanian Ghetto, 1941-1945.* **Chicago: Chicago Review Press, 1999, 408 pp.**
The *Kaddish* is a prayer for the dead. The author documents in detail the creation and obliteration, by the Nazis, of the Kovno ghetto.

Modras, Ronald E. *The Catholic Church and Anti-Semitism: Poland, 1933-1939.* **Chur, Switzerland: Harwood Academic Publishers, 1994, 429 pp.**
Based on a persuasive mass of documentation drawn from Catholic newspapers and periodicals, as well as published authoritative pronouncements, Modras concludes, that the Polish Catholic Church must be held largely responsible for legitimizing hostility toward the Jews prior to World War II. The author also maintains, that " the Catholic clergy...were not innocent bystanders or passive observers of... the wave of anti-Semitism that encompassed Poland in the latter half of the 1930s."

____. **"The Catholic Press in Interwar Poland on the Jewish Question: Metaphor and the Developing Rhetoric of Exclusion." Eastern European Jewish Affairs (1994), Volume 24 Issue 1, pp. 49-70.**
Though the Catholic press in Poland condemned the vitriolic anti-Semitism of Nazi Germany during the interwar period, their use of buzzwords in connection with Jews helped foster Polish indifference to Jewish suffering. Describing Jews as "outsiders" and "threats", the Catholic press further marginalized Jews, so that Polish citizens felt no need to confront the Nazis persecution of Jews.

____. "Father Coughlin and the Jews: A Broadcast Remembered." *America* (March 11, 1989), Volume 160 Issue 9, pp. 219-223.
Modras examines and analyzes the radio broadcasts of Father Charles Coughlin from the years 1938-1942. The popular programs of the "radio priest" were filled with anti-Semitic rhetoric. The author details the Catholic Church's response to Coughlin's commentary. He also provides some reflections on the lessons to be learned from anti-Semitism and the Holocaust.

____. "The Inter-war Polish Catholic Press on the Jewish Question." *Annals of the American Academy of Political and Social Science* (1996), Issue 548, pp. 169-190.
This article examines the way in which the Catholic Press in inter-war Poland wrote about Jewish citizens. The press identified Jews as the primary promoters of modern, secular democracy. This Catholic press crusade against the Jews was designed to support the Vatican's claim, that a Jewish-Masonic conspiracy was in place to create a more secular and liberal Polish society.

Moore, James F. "A Spectrum of Views: Traditional Christian Responses to the Holocaust." *Journal of Ecumenical Studies* (1988), Volume 25 Issue 2, pp. 212-224.
Moore traces the theological responses Christians have traditionally expressed when confronted with the atrocities perpetrated by the Nazis against the Jews during World War II.

Morley, John F. *Vatican Diplomacy and the Jews During the Holocaust, 1939-1943.* New York: KTAV, 1980, 280 pp.
Morley's text was among the first critical studies of Pope Pius XII's response to the Holocaust. The author does not charge Pius XII with being anti-Semitic, but does accuse the pontiff of pursuing a policy of prudence in order to protect Church interests at the expense of the humanitarian needs when identified by the plight of the Jews.

National Association of Catholic Families. "Pius XII and the Jews – A Fact Sheet." Eternal Word Television Network, http://www.ewtn.com, 1999, 3 pp.
This "fact" sheet is a defense of Pius XII. It challenges those, who contend that the pope remained impassive, while the Jews were murdered, during the Holocaust. This text asserts, that Pius helped rescued close to nine hundred thousand Jews, and that he protested the Nazi persecution of European Jewry.

Nawyn, William E. *American Protestantism's Response to Germany's Jews and Refugees, 1933-1941.* Ann Arbor: UMI Reserve Press, 1980, 330 pp.
This is a study of the response of American Protestants to Germany's treatment

of the Jews in the 1930s, and to the refugee problem that arose from the Nazi persecutions. The author concludes, that except for the Quakers, American Protestants were only concerned with their European denominational brethren in regard to their treatment by the Nazis, and paid little attention to the suffering of the Jews.

Neuman, Isaac with Michael Palencia-Roth. *The Narrow Bridge: Beyond the Holocaust.* **Urbana and Chicago: University of Illinois Press, 2000, 202 pp.**
Neuman, a survivor of concentration camps and Auschwitz, and rabbi emeritus at Sinai Temple in Champaign, Illinois, describes the world of Polish Jewry before, and during, the Holocaust. He also tells how his religious faith sustained him through the most harrowing experiences in the Nazi camps.

Niewyk, Donald and Francis Nicosia. *The Columbia Guide to the Holocaust.* **Columbia University Press, 2000, 473pp.**
This book gives general readers the opportunity to briefly review, or delve more deeply into, the subject of the Holocaust. Divided into five parts the volume offers an overview of the atrocity, the problems and interpretations that surround the subject, people, places, terms and organizations connected to the Holocaust, and offers information about resources available for study.

O'Carroll, Father Michael. *Pius XII: Greatness Dishonored.* **Dublin: Franciscan Herald Press, 1980, 220 pp.**
The author mounts a defense of Pius XII, insisting that notables such as Pinchas Lapide, Golda Meir, and the Chief Rabbi of Rome all expressed gratitude to the pope for his efforts on behalf of the Jews during the Holocaust. O'Carroll uses correspondence, memoirs, and secondary sources to support his case.

____. "Saviour of the Jews." Eternal Word Television Network, http://www.ewtn.com, 1999, 4 pp.
This article, first published in February 1995 in *The Irish Family*, provides a more recent version of Father O'Carroll's defense of Pope Pius XII. The author briefly reviews the events that took place in regards to the Jews and to Pius's relationship with Hitler in the 1930s. He then recounts the efforts the pope made to protect the Jews from the Nazis.

Opdyke, Irene. *Into the Flames: The Story of a Righteous Gentile.* **San Bernardino: Borgo Press, 1992, 176 pp.**
Opdyke is a Polish Catholic woman who risked her life to protect her Jewish friends during the Holocaust. She hid twelve Jews in the basement of the villa, which housed the Gestapo officer for whom she worked.

Paldiel, Mordecai. *The Path of Righteousness: Gentile Rescuers of Jews*

During the Holocaust. **Hoboken: KTAV Publishing, 1993, 401 pp.**
This volume presents the stories of the Gentile rescuers of Jews, who resided in German-occupied Europe, during World War II. Each chapter reflects upon a different country. The author and his family were hidden by a French priest and smuggled into Switzerland.

_____. *Saving the Jews: Amazing Stories of Men and Women Who Defied the "Final Solution."* **Schreiber Publishing, Incorporated, 2000, 338 pp.**
The author contends, that while the stories of Jews being rescued by men like Oskar Shindler are well reported, there are a host of other "Righteous Gentiles" scattered across Europe, who when faced with the Nazis atrocities put themselves at risk to assist the Jews. His study includes some eighteen thousand non-Jewish men and women rescuers from a variety of countries. He also notes that a good number of these rescuers came from Christian backgrounds. Chapters devoted to Christians, who chose to live their faith include; "A Prince of the Church and Humanity"; "The Martyrdom of a Russian Nun in Paris"; "Clergy in Various Robes"; "A Personal Search Leads to the Discovery of Many Clergy Rescuers"; and "A Nun With a Broken Heart".

_____. *Sheltering the Jews: Stories of Holocaust Rescuers.* **Minneapolis, MN.: Fortress Press, 1996, 224 pp.**
At *Yad Vashem,* Paldiel has served thirteen years as the director of the department that addresses the "Righteous among the Nations." In this volume the author recounts some of the inspiring stories that note the efforts of individuals and groups (many of whom were Christians) to save the Jews from the Nazis. Paldiel maintains, that these were ordinary citizens, who when faced with an evil and murderous policy, risked there own lives for their neighbors. They exemplify the best and most moral of human beings. The author insists, that the horror of the *Shoah* should never be forgotten, nor should the heroism of those who put everything on the line to help the Jews.

Passelecq, Georges and Bernard Suchecky. *T****he Hidden Encyclical of Pius XI.* **Steven Rendall, Translator. New York: Harcourt Brace, 1997, 319 pp.**
The volume recounts the history of *Humani Generis Unitas,* the encyclical commissioned by Pius XI before his death in 1939. Drafted by Father John LaFarge, an American Jesuit priest, the encyclical would have denounced Nazi racism and anti-Semitism. Following the death of Pius XI, the encyclical was buried in a secret Vatican archive until the late 1960s when it was discovered by a Jesuit seminarian. Despite the denunciation of anti-Semitism, the "Hidden Encyclical" tell us much about the religious prejudices of the Vatican towards the Jews.

Patterson, Charles. *Anti-Semitism: The Road to the Holocaust and Beyond.*

New York: Walker & Company, 1982, 150 pp.
Anti-Semitism's history is traced from the Crusades and Inquisition to the twentieth century. An entire section is devoted to the development of Hitler's attitudes towards Jews, and the subsequent execution of his ideas by his followers during the Holocaust.

Perelman, Marc. "Catholics, Jews Unite to Attack Scholar's Creed: Goldhagen Stirring Ire With Article on Pius XII." Forward (January 18, 2002), Volume 105 Issue 31, pp. 376-377.
Jewish and Christian scholars have challenged Daniel Goldhagen's recent article about Pope Pius XII. Both sides have accused Mr. Goldhagen of allowing his anti-Catholic bias to color his work. Those criticizing the article agree that while there are accurate statements made by Goldhagen, he demonstrates an "ignorance of the Catholic Church's efforts at reform in the last few decades" and seems to have excluded some of the relevant documents needed for an adequate study of the topic.

Phayer, Michael. *Catholic Church and the Holocaust, 1930-1965.* Bloomington: Indiana University Press, 2000, 301 pp.
Phayer shows that, given Pius XII's ineffective leadership, Catholics acted ambiguously during the Holocaust. Some Catholics saved Jews, others helped the Nazis murder them, but the majority were simply bystanders.

_____. "The Catholic Resistance Circle in Berlin and German Catholic Bishops During the Holocaust." Holocaust and Genocide Studies (1993), Volume 7 Issue 2, pp. 216-229.
The Berlin Circle, a group of Catholics who resisted the Nazi's and worked to help Jews escape from Germany, is the focus of Phayer's article. Though these people successfully aided many Jews, they could not convince the entire Catholic Church to condemn Nazi anti-Semitism.

_____. *Protestant and Catholic Women in Nazi Germany.* Detroit: Wayne State University Press, 1990, 287 pp.
According to Phayer, prior to 1933, many Protestant women were supportive of National Socialism. At the same time, Catholic women remained less enthusiastic about Hitler because the Catholic League warned them about the anti-Christian nature of Nazi racism. The author argues, that the Concordat of 1933 limited the freedom of action of the Catholic League and other Catholic women's organizations. Phayer notes, that after 1935 both Catholic and Protestant women, for the most part, resisted National Socialism's social agenda.

_____. "Questions About Catholic Resistance." Church History (June 2001),

Volume 70 Issue 2, pp. 328-345.
This article poses a series of questions concerning the Catholic Church's resistance to the Nazi regime in Germany. Phayer offers reasons why the Church hierarchy chose to seek an accord with Hitler. He also suggests possible theories about why the Vatican failed to organize a strong opposition against National Socialism, once it became clear that Nazi ideology was evil. Despite the chance that the bishops' responses were premised on worthy intentions, Phayer maintains, that their reasoning was flawed, and it was far too late to resist the Nazis once the Church recognized its mistake.

_____ **and Eva Fleischner.** *Cries in the Night, Women Who Challenged the Holocaust.* **. Kansas City, Mo.: Sheed and Ward, 1997, 153 pp.**
The author relates the stories of seven Catholic women, who attempted to save Jews from the Nazis at the risk of their own lives. Phayer claims, that while the stories of these women does not explain why many other Catholics did nothing to assist the Jews, it does show that Catholic values and morality still existed in the hearts of some .

Pierard, Richard V., Robert D. Linder and Robert G. Clouse. "Fascism Steps Right This Way." Christianity Today (January 27, 1978), Volume 22 Issue 8, pp. 14-17.
With Helmut Thielicke's 1978 Christianity Today article, "Why the Holocaust?" in mind, the authors question how today's generation of American evangelicals would respond to a fascist takeover. Would they be anymore prepared to confront and resist social injustice than the German Churches were when Hitler rose to power?

Pogany, Eugene L. *In My Brother's Image: Twin Brother's Separated by Faith After the Holocaust.* **Penguin Books, 2001, 352 pp.**
This is the story of twin brothers born to Jewish parents in Hungary and raised as Catholics until World War II. During the war one brother was sent to a Nazi concentration camp, while the other was given shelter in an Italian monastery. The brother who survived the horrors of the camp renounced Catholicism after the war and returned to the Jewish faith. The other brother became a Catholic priest. The brothers grew apart due to their differing experiences during the war, and the choices they made after the war. The story shows the savageness of the Nazis, religious divisions, the emotional damage left in the wake of war, and the unbridgeable gulf created by family members who feel betrayed by each others choices.

Pois, Robert A. *National Socialism and the Religion of Nature.* **New York: St. Martin's Press, 1986, 190 pp.**
The author argues, that the National Socialist movement was a political religion

in which the ideas of Nazism conflicted with the Judeo-Christian tradition of Germany. Pois argues, that the Nazi quest for a religion of nature led to Auschwitz, and remains a dangerous forerunner of contemporary forms of nationalism.

Polen, Nehemia. *The Holy Fire: The Teaching of Rabbi Kalonymus Kalman Shapira, the Rebbe of the Warsaw Ghetto.* **New York: Jason Aronson, 1999, 232 pp.**
Through his subjects' writings, Rabbi Polen analyzes the social and spiritual anguish of war-besieged Warsaw, and the teaching of Eastern Europe's last Hasidic master. Pollen's research articulates Rabbi Shapira's realization that the "theological garment, however holy and true," is inadequate for understanding the atrocities which he confronted.

Polonsky, Antony. *M y Brother's Keeper?: Recent Polish Debates on the Holocaust.* **London and New York: Routledge Press, 1990, 242 pp.**
The volume consists of responses by Polish intellectuals to a 1987 article written in a Krakow-based Catholic weekly by Jan Blonski, a professor of Polish literature. The article called upon Poland to admit its moral guilt for the Holocaust and its indifference to the Jewish genocide. The book concludes with a transcript of discussions between Polish and Israeli scholars at a 1988 conference on Polish Jewry.

Pultzer, P.G.J. *The Rise of Political Anti-Semitism in Germany and Austria.* **John Wiley and Sons, Incorporated, 1964, 370 pp.**
The late nineteenth century, Pultzer maintains, gave rise to the modern form of political anti-Semitism in Germany. His study discusses the role that Christianity played in helping to forge hostility toward Jews into a coherent political ideology.

Ramati, Alexander. *The Assisi Underground: The Priests Who Rescued Jews.* **New York: Stein & Day Publishers, 1978, 181 pp.**
An Italian priest saved some three hundred Jews in Assisi. The author tells of how the priest dressed some of the Jews in the clothing of monks and nuns, found jobs for others, made false identity cards, and created an entire underground movement to save Jewish refugees.

Rausch, David Albert. *Building Bridges.* **Chicago: Moody, 1988, 251 pp.**
Rausch attempts to explain the doctrines and traditions of Judaism in order to provide Christians with a better understanding of the Jews and the Jewish faith. In an effort to combat the negative mythology that has been falsely applied to Jews, the author explores the history of the Jewish-Christian relationship and how Christianity helped put derogatory images of Jews in place. Rausch

recounts the hostility directed toward the Jews by the early church, the anti-Jewish stereotypes and attitudes promoted by Christians throughout the medieval era, Martin Luther's anti-Semitic rhetoric. He also follows the evolution of Christianity's anti-Judaism into the more modern nineteenth century expressions of anti-Semitism. Rausch ends his book with proposals on how Christians can further their dialogue with Jews, and hopefully reconcile the two faith communities.

Rebhun, Joseph M.D. *Leap To Life: Triumph Over Nazi Evil.* **New York: Ardor Scribendi, 2001, 226 pp.**
This is a story of survival in Russian and Nazi-occupied Poland. The author recounts his experiences while confined in the Przemysl Ghetto, and his eventual escape from a train bound for Auschwitz. The author survived the Holocaust because he was able to acquire an identity card that labeled him a Polish Catholic. After the war, Rebhun testified against some of the Nazis responsible for atrocities in the Przemysl Ghetto. The author devotes several pages to explaining why he never lost faith in God.

Redlich, Shimon. "Metropolitan Andrei Sheptyts'kyi, Ukrainians and Jews During and After the Holocaust." Holocaust and Genocide Studies (1990), Volume 5 Issue 1, pp. 39-51.
This article makes the case that it is necessary to examine the actions of Andrei Sheptyts'ski, head of the Ukrainian Uniate Church in Galicia, in a context broader than Ukrainian-Jewish relations. Sheptyts'ski displayed courage in his statements and deeds on behalf of Jews during the Holocaust. His heroism is especially evident when compared to the non-Jewish population of Europeans under Hitler's control, the Catholic Church Hierarchy, and other Ukranians.

Reese, William L. "Christianity and the Final Solution." Philosophical Forum (Fall 1984-Winter 1985), Volume 16 Issue 1-2, pp. 138-147.
The author insists, that Christian anti-Semitism provides an answer for several questions that arise because of the Holocaust. It explains why the Vatican did not act more forthrightly and openly to protect the Jews from the Nazis, why the government in Vichy France followed Hitler's orders with little or no resistance, and why the Allies failed to wipe out any of the railroad lines used to move Jews to the concentration camps. Reese demands, that Christians accept responsibility for the development of the anti-Semitic attitudes that led to the "Final Solution". He asserts, that this is an aspect that needs to be dealt with if we are ever to be done with the lessons to be learned from the Holocaust.

Riegner, Gerhart M. "From the Night of the Pogrom to the Final Solution: The Experiences and Lessons." Jewish-Christian Relations, http://www.jcrelations.net, 2002, 14 pp.

Riegner reviews the horrific events that occurred on *Kristallnacht* in November of 1938. He examines the policies of the Nazis that led up to the violence perpetrated against the Jews, and then moves forward to apprise readers of the cold fact that six million Jews lost their lives during the atrocity, known as the Holocaust. The author prompts readers to honor those who died in the *Shoah,* by adopting the ideas put forward in the *United Nations Universal Declaration of Human Rights*.

R.N.S. "French Catholics Repent Holocaust Silence." Christian Century October 22, 1997, Volume 114 Issue 29, 939-945 pp.
In a Paris suburb some fifty years after World War II ended, the Roman Catholic Church of France issued an apology for its failure to speak out against the persecution and murder of the Jews during the Holocaust. Archbishop de Berranger, speaking on behalf of French Catholics, acknowledged, "silence was the rule" for the church at a time when Catholics should have defended and protected the Nazi's victims. Jewish leaders called the apology " a major turning point" and felt it was a positive step in the ongoing attempt to improve Jewish–Christian relations.

Rohrlich, Ruby, ed. *Resisting the Holocaust.* Oxford and New York: Oxford University Press, 1998, 264 pp.
Rohrlich states in her introduction that the concept of "resistance' has been defined in many ways, ranging from armed conflict to any humane action by non-Jews towards Jews. Many of the essays in this volume focus on the role of women in resisting the Nazis. Brief descriptions are given that recount the heroic activities of Germaine Ribiere, "little Wanda" Teitelboim, Mala Zimetbaum. Rohrlich points out, that resistance was often collective, and in the case of the Danes, Bulgarians, and the Italians, the collectivity involved the majority of their populations. One essay, by Martin Cohen, contends that the image of the passive Jew being slaughtered by the Nazis owes much to the status of Jews as a small minority among an often, hostile Christian majority. Contributors include, Murray Baumgarten, Ami Neiberger, Eric Sterling, Nechama Tec, and others.

Rosenbaum, Irving J. *The Holocaust and the Halakah.* New York: KTAV, 1976, 177 pp.
The book surveys the efforts of the Jews of Eastern Europe to maintain the integrity of their religious lives during the years of Nazi terror. The work is based largely on rabbinic responses to issues pertaining to Jewish religious observance in Nazi-occupied Eastern Europe. The author deals with questions ranging from ritual observance, the maintenance of dietary laws, the commemoration of fast days, to questions of moral action. Rosenbaum provides evidence that under the most adverse circumstances, Orthodox Jews were able to

defy the Nazis by observing their faith, given the conditions they endured.

Ross, Robert W. *So It Was True: The American Protestant Press and the Nazi Persecution of the Jews.* **Minneapolis: University of Minnesota Press, 1980, 374 pp.**
This study of fifty-two American Protestant periodicals from 1933-1945 attempts to determine what was known about the Nazi persecution of the Jews and the Holocaust, in order to assess how this information was presented to its readership. Ross concludes, that this knowledge was readily available and that most Protestants did nothing to aid or protest the situation faced by Jews.

Roth, John K. and Carol Rittner, eds. *Pope Pius XII and the Holocaust.* **Leicester University Press, 2001, 256 pp.**
This volume includes a compilation of essays addressing Pope Pius XII's life, career, and actions during the Holocaust. The editors also survey the literature that has been published about this controversial figure in recent years. Topics include; "Ten Essential Themes Regarding Pius and the Holocaust"; "Pius: A Reappraisal"; "An Easy Target"; "Pius XII and the Rescue of the Jews"; "Ethical Questions about Papal Policy"; and "High Ideals and Innocuous Reaction: An American Protestant's Reflections on Pius XII and the Holocaust".

Rubenstein, Richard. "Holocaust and Holy War." **The Annals of the American Academy of Political and Social Sciences (1996), Volume 548, pp. 23-46.**
Rubenstein argues, that the Holocaust was a Holy War. Although the Nazi regime was hostile to Christianity, its supporters helped those who believed Christianity was the foundation for civilization. Additionally, they felt the best way to preserve and protect Christian ideology was to eliminate the Jews and defeat Communism. The author points out, that while the Holocaust represents a break from the standard ways in which outcasts have been treated, European history contains many instances of attempts to minimize the influence of those who were not part of Christendom's mainstream religious and cultural identity.

Ryan, Donna F. *The Holocaust & the Jews of Marseille.* **Urbana and Chicago: University of Illinois Press, 1996, 266 pp.**
Ryan contends, that the hierarchy of the Catholic Church in France took no public stand against Vichy's treatment of Jews before 1942. In 1940 and 1941, when church support was essential in Vichy, the French episcopacy raised no objections to government decrees, which attacked Jews politically, socially, and economically and deprived foreign Jews of their liberty. The reason, argues Ryan, was that "...the France Petain promised was simply too attractive to the church hierarchy to risk an open breach." Only the deportations of 1942 brought objections from some church leaders, and even those were accompanied by

expressions of "allegiance to Petain." Ryan, however, in an effort to be balanced, does not ignore the individual Catholic nuns and priests who hid Jews in their monasteries and convents, helped them obtain forged baptismal papers, and facilitated their escape to the border.

Ryan, J.S. "Australian Novelist's Perceptions of German Jewry and National Socialism." Australian Journal of Politics and History (1985), Volume 31 Issue 1, pp.138-46.
This article notes and examines the works of three Australian writers whose books examine the relationship between Christians and Jews, the shared burdens of guilt, and the concentration camps as a symbol of evil. The writers examined are David Martin, Geoffrey Taylor, and Patrick White.

Rychlak, Ronald. *Hitler, the War and the Pope*. North Andover: Genesis Publishing Company, 2000, 470 pp.
This book is a sympathetic portrait of Pope Pius XII in regard to his reactions to the Nazi genocide against the Jews. Rychlak examines the controversies surrounding Pius's actions during World War II and the Holocaust by exploring the Vatican's response to issues of religion, diplomacy and military tactics. Within this historical context the author attempts to defend Pius's decisions, once he was faced with the evidence of Hitler's barbaric treatment of the Jews.

Saltman, Avron. "Christian Writers on Jewish History." Bekhol Derakhekha Daehu (Winter 1999), Volume 8, pp. 29-50.
Saltman points out that although non-Jews have historically been ignorant of Jewish history, Christian writers have produced texts about the history of Jews. He examines the works put forth over the last one hundred and seventy years, and the fact that most of these works have been filled with negative stereotypes. The article highlights exceptions to this tradition, especially when they occurred in the twentieth century. For example, James Parks held Christianity complicit in the Holocaust and Malcolm Hay demonstrated that Christian anti-Judaism helped pave the way for the Holocaust, and also influenced the British government to close off Palestine to Jews attempting to escape the Nazis.

Sanchez, Jose M. *Pius XII and the Holocaust: Understanding Controversy*. Washington, D.C. Catholic University of America Press, 2002, 200 pp.
The author discusses Pope Pius's behavior during the Holocaust. He examines the arguments made by historians regarding the defense and criticism of the Pontiff's "silence" during the Holocaust. Sanchez explores Pius's personality and places it within the context of the institutional framework in which the pope operated.

____. "The Popes and Nazi Germany: The View From Madrid." Journal of

Church and State (Spring 1996), Volume 38 Issue 2, pp. 365-377.
Sanchez maintains, that the issues surrounding Pope Pius XII and his silence about the murder of Jews during the Holocaust remain unresolved. The author notes the inconsistencies of Pius XIIs' words and actions, and suggests, that perhaps his roles as pastor and diplomat explain away any contradictions. For example, while Pius the diplomat tried not to alienate Germany in hopes of using a strong Germany as a bulwark against Communism, Pius the pastor warned his flock to avoid being drawn into the evil influence of Hitler and the Nazis. According to Sanchez, the pope's success in both roles is still to be determined.

_____. **"The Search for the Historical Pius." America (February 18, 2002), http://pqasb.pqarchiver.com/americapress.**
The role of Pius XII during the Holocaust and the controversy the subject has created, is examined by Sanchez. The author claims, that the research that has been done is incomplete and that a deeper examination of the facts is needed in order to determine the nature of Pius's actions during the Holocaust.

Saunders, Father William. "Did Pius Remain Silent?" Eternal Word Television Network, http://www.ewtn.com, 1999, 4 pp.
Father Saunders reminds readers, in this defense of Pius XII, that they must view the pope's actions within the context of his times. He recounts Pius's efforts to protect anyone facing persecution by the Nazis. He also notes the commendations and gratitude Pius received from the Jewish community after the war. The author insists that those who condemn the pope today are guilty of slander.

Scaperlanda, Maria Ruiz, Susanne Batzdorff (Foreword), Michael Linssen (Preface). _Edith Stein: Saint Teresa Benedicta of the Cross._ Our Sunday Visitor Publishing Division, 2001, pp. 207.
This book offers a biographical account of Edith Stein. It recounts her struggle with faith, her conversion from Judaism to Catholicism, her death during the Holocaust, and the controversy surrounding the Catholic Church's decision to declare her a saint and martyr.

Scholder, Klaus. _The Churches and the Third Reich: Two Volumes._ Philadelphia: Fortress Press, 1988, 717 pp.
A comprehensive history of the Protestant and Catholic Churches in Nazi Germany is given in this volume. The author presents an account of the severe crisis faced by the German churches once Hitler's dictatorship was established, and clearly indicts the churches for failing to oppose the policies of National Socialism.

Schwarz, Jenö. *A Promise Redeemed.* **Fromm: Butler and Tanner, 1964, 264 pp.**
As a young rabbinical student in Hungary during 1944, Schwarz was sent to Auschwitz and Mautheusen where he was able to survive with help from his fellow prisoners and some German sympathizers. His book emphasizes the importance of religious faith in overcoming despair.

Section: Comment of the Week. "German Bishops and Anti-Semitism." America (July 17, 1943), pp. 393.
A report from Stockholm regarding all German Catholic Bishops is the focus of this commentary. The report notes, that all of the bishops signed a protest against any further extensions of the Nazi's anti-Semitic laws. According to the article, some Catholic prelates, including, Cardinal von Faulhaber, Bishop von Preysing, and Bishop von Galen were restricted in their movements as a result of the protest.

Section: Explorations and Responses. "Request to Historians From the International Catholic-Jewish Historical Commission." Journal of Ecumenical Studies (Summer/Fall 1999), Volume 36 Issue 3-4, pp. 487-488.
The article suggests, that the examination of the Vatican archives material on World War II by a joint commission of Catholic and Jewish historians may well lead to a better understanding of Pope Pius XII's role during the Holocaust. It may also improve relations between Catholics and Jews. The article also expresses the hope that the Vatican will make all documents accessible to the scholars, and invites historians who are not personally involved in the project to contribute any information they feel will help further the work.

Segev, Tom. *Soldiers of Evil.* **New York: McGraw-Hill Book Co., 1987, 240 pp.**
Segev argues, that those death camp commandants directly responsible for implementing the "Final Solution" were not ordinary individuals. Rather, they sought out their responsibilities and enjoyed the power that accompanied their authority.

Shapiro, Marc B. *Between The Yeshiva World and Modern Orthodoxy: The Life And Works Of Rabbi Jehiel Jacob Weinberg, 1884-1966.* **Oxford, England: Littman Library of Jewish Civilization, 1999, 283 pp.**
At the time of the Nazi "seizure of power" in 1933, Weinberg was one of Germany's leading Orthodox rabbis. Through this biography, Shapiro reveals that not all Jews felt that Hitler threatened them as a community. This included Rabbi Weinberg, who initially welcomed the Nazis and became an apologist for them. He played down the anti-Semitic nature of the regime and believed that both Hitler and Mussolini were in the forefront of the fight against atheism and

communism. Furthermore, he hoped the Nazis would restore traditional moral values in Germany.

Sheffi, Na'ama. "The Jewish Expulsion from Spain and the Rise of National Socialism on the Hebrew Stage." Jewish Social Studies (1999), Volume 5 Issue 3, pp. 82-103.
Sheffi examines the success of the play *The Marranos*, which was first seen in Tel Aviv in 1938. The play depicted the fifteenth century expulsion of Jews from the Iberian Peninsula. The author contends, that in the late 1930s contemporary stories about the way in which Nazis treated Jews failed to awaken the Jewish population, living in Tel Aviv, to the true nature of the persecution that was taking place in Europe. Instead Jews living outside the control of the Third Reich viewed the atrocities as a conflict between two groups of people, Jews and Germans. However, upon viewing *The Marranos,* a historical fiction that portrayed an earlier trauma, Jews were able to finally recognize the dimensions of the disaster that had befallen European Jewry.

Shriver, Donald W. "Bystanders: Conscience and Complicity During the Holocaust." Christian Century (August 2, 2000), http://www.christiancentury.org.
According to Shriver, Victoria Barnett and others are correct when they contend that the Nazis were successful in their efforts to systematically murder the Jews because citizens outside the party rank and file were prepared to aid the Nazis, or stand passively by, while the Jewish population was attacked.

Silver, Eric. *The Book of the Just: The Unsung Heroes Who Rescued Jews From Hitler.* New York: Grove-Weidenfeld Press, 1992, 175 pp.
Stories of Gentiles who saved Jews during the Holocaust are recounted. The author demonstrates, that there were people, who cared about those suffering from Nazi persecution, and who were not intimidated by the Nazi threat. In addition, the rescuers were willing to risk everything, including their lives, to save Jews.

Snoek, Johan M. *The Grey Book: A Collection of Protests Against Anti-Semitism and the Persecution of the Jews, Issued by Non-Roman Catholic Churches and Church Leaders during Hitler's Rule; Introduction. By Uriel Tal Atlantic Highlands: Humanities Press, 1971, 315 pp.*
This is a collection of protest actions initiated by various church groups and leaders in opposition to the Nazi's treatment of Jews. The source material clusters chronologically around the promulgation of the Nuremberg Laws in 1935, *Kristallnacht* in 1938, and the wartime extermination policies of the Nazi regime. The moderation of the protests and their relative ineffectiveness confirms the inability of the Protestant Churches to affect any relief for the Jews

in Nazi-occupied Europe. The organizational listing by country makes this volume an important reference tool for our understanding of Christian-Jewish relations during the Holocaust.

Spector, Shmuel and Geoffrey Wigoder. *Encyclopedia of Jewish Life Before and During the Holocaust.* **New York University Press, 2001, 1824 pp.**
Decades of bibliographical and archival research have gone into these three volumes that chronicle the stories of thousands of Jewish communities thriving prior to World War II. Using prose, maps and photographs the encyclopedia recreates and explores centuries of settlements, lifestyles and culture. All of this was irrevocably destroyed by war. The final fifty-six pages are devoted to the Holocaust.

Steiman, Lionel B. *Paths to Genocide: Anti-Semitism in Western History.* **New York: St. Martin's Press, 1998, 84 pp.**
The author surveys the history of anti-Semitism from its beginnings in early Christianity, through the Middle Ages, the Reformation, the Enlightenment, and during the Holocaust. Steiman shows how the inter-relationship between religion, science, and socioeconomic forces converged to bring about the Nazi genocide against the Jews.

Steinlauf Michael C. *Bondage to the Dead: Poland and the Memory of the Holocaust.* **Syracuse: Syracuse University Press, 1997, 189 pp.**
Steinlauf examines the complex political, historical, and psychological background, which has influenced the treatment of the Holocaust in post-War Poland. The author avoids generalizations and stereotypes in regard to the Polish response to the Holocaust. For example, he finds that some Catholic nationalists, who were not reticent about their anti-Jewish sentiments, nevertheless, helped to save Jews during the war.

Stiegmann-Gall, Richard. *"The Holy Reich": Religious Dimensions of Nazi Ideology, 1919-1945.* **Toronto: Dissertation; The University of Toronto, 1999, 432 pp.**
Through the use of archived materials and theories of ideology and secularization, the author examines the religious views held by leaders within the National Socialist movement. He asserts, that despite theories to the contrary many Nazis retained their Christian identity and felt the beliefs of the Nazi movement were an extension of their Christian ideology. These people did not feel that Nazism was replacing their religion. Rather they saw their actions as a defense of Christianity. They were improving upon their religion and revitalizing it with the concept of "positive Christianity." Germany was the new spiritual center of the world and Martin Luther provided an example of a religious hero who had the courage to take on the corruption of Rome in pursuit

of his goal to reform the Christian faith. Therefore, the Nazis could attack religious institutions and yet hold that they were not rejecting Christianity.

Stille, Alexander. *Benevolence and Betrayal: Five Italian Jewish Families Under Fascism.* **Penguin USA, 1993, 365 pp.**
Provided in this book is an examination of how Jews fared in fascist Italy during World War II. The author presents details about those "Righteous Gentiles", who were willing to risk their own safety in order to aid Jews. He contrasts these moral citizens with those, who turned their backs on the suffering. Stille also includes information concerning the role that Catholic clerics and the Vatican hierarchy played in helping Jews escape the Nazis.

Stoltzfus, Nathan. *Resistance of the Heart: Intermarriage and the Rosenstrasse Protest in Nazi Germany.* **New York: W.W. Norton and Co., 1996, 386 pp.**
This study describes the successful efforts of Christian women, who were protesting the deportation of their Jewish husbands. The Jewish spouses of these women were locked up by the Gestapo in the temporary collection center on Rosenstrasse in the old center of Berlin in early 1943.

Tal, Uriel and Miriam Shapira. *Political Theology and the Third Reich.* **Ed. Miriam Shapira. Tel-Aviv: Sifriat Poalim, Tel-Aviv University, 1991, 317 pp.**
The following topics are a partial listing of what is contained in this collection of articles; a study of the historical roots of the Holocaust in German religion, a look at Lutheran theology and the Third Reich, how Jews and Judaism were regarded by Lutheran theologians, and the status of Jews in law and religion after the Nazi "seizure of power."

Tec, Nechama. *Dry Tears: The Story of a Lost Childhood.* **New York: Wildcat Publishing Co., 1982, 216 pp.**
Tec recalls how a Gentile family saved her family from the Nazis.

___. *When Light Pierced the Darkness: Christians Rescue of Jews in Nazi-Occupied Poland.* **Oxford: Oxford University Press, 1986, 262 pp.**
The author interviewed Christian rescuers of Jews in Nazi-occupied Poland. She found that many of her subjects risked their lives without the prompting, or approval of the Catholic clergy.

Ten Boom, Corrie. *The Hiding Place.* **New York: Bantam, 1974, 219 pp.**
The book is the autobiography of a Christian who hid Jews in Holland during World War II. Arrested and imprisoned by the Nazis, she and her family were tortured, and most died. The author survived. Her experience stresses the power

of love and the necessity of rejecting hate.

Thielicke, Helmut. "Helmut Thielicke: Why the Holocaust?" Christianity Today (January 27, 1978), Volume. 22 Issue 8, pp. 8-14.
Thielicke proposes, that the main reason for the Holocaust was theological. He maintains, that a shift in values and belief resulted in viewing people for their functional worth, rather than as creatures who benefit from God's love and protection. The author also offers his opinion about whether or not the German people were aware of the Holocaust. He presents his reasons for believing they may have been unaware. Thielicke criticizes the "postwar denazification programs" as unfair and as the cause of animosity among German citizens.

Thomas, Theodore N. *Women Against Hitler: Christian Resistance in the Third Reich*. Westport, Conn.: Praeger, 1995, 166 pp.
Women of the "Confessing Church" and their role in the church struggle of Nazi Germany are the author's focus. One interesting aspect of the book examines those non-Aryan women members within the "Confessing Church" who took action on behalf of Jews.

Thornton, Larry. "The New Light: German Christians and Biblical Distortion During the Third Reich." Fides et Historia (1986), Volume 18 Issue 2, pp. 32-43.
The article focuses upon some of the clerics in the leadership of the Evangelical Church in Germany during the Nazi regime. To offer examples of his contention, that many Christian prelates cooperated with, rather than opposed the Nazis, the author studies the actions of specific individual clerics. He argues that Bishops Ludwig Mueller and Heinz Wiedermann found ways to justify the anti-Semitic policies of National Socialism in order to make the actions acceptable to their German Christian congregations.

Tobler, Douglas F. "Education, Moral Values, and Democracy: Lessons From the German Experience." Brigham Young University Studies (Spring 1988), Volume 28 Issue 2, pp. 47-63.
Tobler studies the history of Germany in the early twentieth century. He notes, that the education system failed to instill any moral values in students and gave a new respectability to anti-Semitic attitudes. He insists, that the Christian Churches seemed more intent on fighting modernity, and halting change than in combating moral indifference. Therefore, in a society that was uncommitted to ethical values, Hitler's plan to exterminate the Jews met with little opposition, and in many cases enthusiastic endorsement.

Todorov, Tzvetan. *The Fragility of Goodness: Why Bulgaria's Jews Survived the Holocaust.*? Arthur Denner, Translator. New Haven: Princeton

University Press, 2001, 190 pp.

According to Todorov, Bulgaria is not a heroic country, even though its Jewish population was not annihilated during the Holocaust. Rather, the author demonstrates, that fortunately for Bulgarian Jews the composition of government, including intellectuals and clerics of the Orthodox Church, worked to influence public opinion. The author claims, that had even one of the above groups promoted a different attitude the "fragile goodness found in Bulgaria" might well have been destroyed and thousands of the Jews would have died.

Toll, Nelly. *Behind the Secret Window: A Memoir of a Hidden Childhood During World War Two.* New York: Dial, 1993, 212 pp.

Toll, a survivor from Lvov who was hidden along with her mother by Christians, kept notes from the time the Germans entered the city in 1941 through to the Russian Liberation in July of 1944. Photographs of her watercolor paintings illustrate her life in hiding during the Holocaust.

Tschuy, Theo. Dangerous *Diplomacy: The Story of Carl Lutz, Rescuer of 62,000 Hungarian Jews. Grand* Rapids, Michigan: William. B. Eerdmans, 2000, 265 pp.

This is the first biography of Carl Lutz, Budapest's Swiss Consul, from 1942 to 1945. Lutz rescued sixty-two thousand Jews from deportation to the Nazi death camps. Motivated by his Christian convictions, Lutz risked his own life to save thousands of Hungarian Jews, and is recognized as a "Righteous Gentile" by *Yad Vashem.* According to the author, Lutz's actions show what Christians could accomplish when they followed the dictates of their religious values. Tschuy also claims, that without these stories it becomes harder to educate the next generation to oppose future genocide.

Valaik, J. David. "In the Days Before Ecumenism: American Catholics, Anti-Semitism and the Spanish Civil War." Journal of Church and State (Autumn 1971), Volume 13 Issue 3, pp. 465-477.

The author states, that in recent years the evolving dialogue of Jews and Christians shows promise for a positive relationship between the two communities. He contrasts this with the 1930's when Jews and Christians faced major divisions. Valaik asserts, that much of the hostility displayed between American Jews and Christians during that time resulted from disagreements over the Spanish Civil War. While Jews were anti-Fascist and mostly supported the Loyalist cause, many Catholics aligned themselves with Franco, who they viewed as the "scourge of Communism." Catholics were angered because they believed Jews controlled the press, and therefore the coverage of the war. American Catholics were told to put aside the secular press and read Catholic publications for their news. In some American cities Catholic priests accused evil Rabbis of supporting Communism. Father Charles Coughlin could be heard on the radio attacking the influence of "American Jewry" on the country. It was only with the United State's entry in to World War II that the conflict over the politics of the Spanish Civil War was put aside.

Van Biema, David, Emily Mitchell and Martin Penner. "The Pope and der Fuhrer." Time (September 20, 1999), Volume 154 Issue 12, pp. 61-63.
Van Bien and company criticize and refute the charges made by John Cornwell in his book, *Hitler's Pope.* The authors claim Cornwell has made assertions with inadequate evidence and has allowed his personal agenda to color his work.

VanHoek, Kees. *Pope Pius XII, Priest and Statesman.* New York: Philosophical Society, 1944, 106 pp.
This book attempts to provide a detailed portrait of Pope Pius's career as a priest, diplomat and leader of the Roman Catholic Church. Written prior to the end of the war, the author praises Pius's actions, both prior to, and during the conflict.

Voll, Fritz B. "Night of the Broken Glass (Reichskristallnacht)." Jewish Christian Relations, http://www.jcrelations.net, 2001.
Although Voll, a German Protestant, was eight years old in November of 1938, his recollections of *Kristallnacht* are very vivid and compelling. He discusses the things he was taught about Jews as a child, his work in later years with the Canadian Council of Christians and Jews, the guilt Christianity bears for centuries of persecuting the Jews and his hopes for improving Jewish-Christian relations in the future.

Warren, Donald. *Radio Priest: Charles Coughlin, The Father of Hate Radio* New York: Free Press, 1996, 376 pp.
In 1940 the Catholic Church finally acted to silence Father Charles Coughlin. Until that time, the "radio-priest" achieved international fame and popularity through his program. His incendiary speeches vilified President Franklin Delano Roosevelt, promoted Adolf Hitler to American audiences, and professed a coded anti-Semitism that blamed Jews for everything from the Depression to America's involvement in World War II.

Wasserstein, Bernard. *Britain and the Jews of Europe, 1939-1945.* Books Informational Incorporated, 1999, 352 pp.
Wasserstein's account of the abandonment of the Jews by the British government and religious institutions during the Holocaust is told in a scholarly manner. Though lacking histrionics, the author's study leaves the reader with little doubt that Britain failed to provide assistance to the Jews when they most needed it.

Webster, Ronald D.E. "German 'Non-Aryan' Clergymen and the Anguish of Exile After 1933." The Journal of Religious History (February 1998), Volume 22 Issue 1, pp. 83-103.
The article examines the interviews of a small group of non-Aryan Protestant German pastors, who were forced to flee from their homeland in an effort to escape the virulent anti-Semitic policies of the Nazi regime. The author notes the assistance of Germans, who gave aid to refugees, such as Bishop George Bell of Chichester, Dietrich Bonhoeffer and Martin Niemoeller. Additionally, the author studies the ways in which these interviews demonstrate the traumatic affects of the war and its influence upon the future of Christian–Jewish relations.

Weisbord, Robert G. and Wallace P. Sillanpoa. *Chief Rabbi, the Pope and the Holocaust: an Era in Vatican-Jewish Relations.* Transaction Publishers, 1991, 224 pp.
The authors examine the record of Pope Pius XII's efforts to aid the Jews during the Holocaust, in an effort to determine whether or not Chief Rabbi Zolli was justified in taking the baptismal name of Eugenio, when he converted to Catholicism in 1946. Zolli claimed that he took the name because the Pope had demonstrated his humanitarian goodness in helping the Jews during World War II.

Weiss, Gershon. *The Holocaust and Jewish Destiny: Jewish Heroism, Human Faith and Divine Providence.* Jerusalem: Targun Press. 1999, 240 pp.
This study, by a prominent rabbi, details the martyrdom of Orthodox Jews, during the Holocaust. The author argues, that found among Orthodox Jews, were those willing to sacrifice their lives (*Kiddush HaShem)* in the death camps rather than compromise their religious beliefs.

Weiss, John. *Ideology of Death: Why the Holocaust Happened in Germany.* Chicago: I.R. Dee Publishers, 1996, 427 pp.
In taking the "intentionalist" position that the "Final Solution" was not a "functionalist" response to the outbreak of World War, Weiss convincingly demonstrates that the plan to murder Europe's Jews was implicit from the start. He contends, that the Nazi ideology of racial hatred of the Jews was shared by millions of Germans and Austrians. The author's thesis was reached after examining the history of anti-Semitism in Germany. According to Weiss, Hitler's genocidal policies were shared by middle and upper class Germans. Weiss further argues, that German culture and society were different from other Western nations because the liberal ideas of the French Revolution never took root in Germany.

Wiesel, Elie. *The Night Trilogy: Night, Dawn, The Accident.* New York: Farrar, Straus & Giroux, 1987, 318 pp.

This trilogy, consisting of *Night (*1960), *Dawn* (1961), and *The Accident (1962),* is Wiesel's effort to address the fundamental questions about humanity, which were raised due to his experiences during the Holocaust. For example, in *Night,* Wiesel writes of his battle for survival and of his struggle with God for a way to understand the wanton cruelty he witnessed each day. Overall, the trilogy offers meditations on mankind's attraction to violence and on the temptation of self-destruction.

Wills, Gary. *Papal Sins: Structures of Deceit.* New York: Doubleday, 2000, 328 pp.
Wills criticism of the papacy includes sections where he accuses the church of evading responsibility for the death of Jews during the Holocaust, and avoiding sincere and adequate apologies ever since. The author charges, that even when the Vatican tries to tell the truth about Catholics and the Holocaust, it ends up resorting to historical distortions and evasions, rather than facing its sordid history.

Wistrich, Robert S. *Hitler and the Holocaust.* Random House Incorporated, 2001, 320 pp.
In this examination of Hitler and how he came to the idea of exterminating the Jews, Wistrich reminds readers about the Church's long history of promoting anti-Semitic attitudes through its teachings and actions. His chapter "Between Cross and Swastika" explores the controversial issues concerning the Church's legacy of hostility towards the Jews and its role in the Holocaust.

_____. *Hitler's Apocalypse: Jews and the Nazi Legacy.* New York: St. Martin's Press, 1986, 309 pp.
The author argues, that Hitler plunged the world into war in 1939 in order to realize the essential prerequisite for the dawn of a new Aryan millennium: The extermination of the Jews. Militants, in their opposition to the State of Israel, called for a Holy War to destroy the Jewish state, and thus continued Nazi anti-Semitism, after Hitler's death.

_____. "The Vatican and the Shoah." Modern Judaism (2001), Volume 21 Issue 2, pp. 83-107.
The Vatican and Pius XII do not fare well in this article. Wistrich regards the decision to maintain "silence" while the Nazis exterminated the Jews as morally inexcusable. He also takes issue with the Catholic Church's plans to canonize Pius, and views this effort as one more example of the Church's refusal to face the reality of its past sins against the Jews. He calls for the church to embrace the need to undertake sincere and lasting change in its attitude.

Wolff, Richard J. and Joerg Konrad Hoensch, eds. *Catholics, The State and*

the European Radical Right, 1919-1945. **Atlantic Research Publications; New York: Columbia University Press, 1987, 257 pp.**
This collection of articles examines the Catholic Church's attitudes toward Nazism and Fascism, and looks at how these attitudes affected the Church's reactions to the Holocaust, racial ideology and anti-Semitism. Featured are entries which include: Frank Coppa's "The Vatican and the Dictators: Between Diplomacy and Morality, Richard Wolff's "Italy: Catholics, the Clergy and Church Reactions to Fascism", and John Zeender's "Germany: The Catholic Church and the Nazi Regime."

Wollenberg, Jorg. *The German Public and the Persecution of Jews, 1933-1945: No One Participated, No One Knew.* **Atlantic Highlands: Humanities Press, 1996, 217 pp.**
Originally published in 1989, this collection includes fifteen contributions to a symposium sponsored by the city of Nuremberg. The goal of the symposium was to explore the reaction of German citizens towards the Jews during the Hitler years. Included were eyewitness accounts of seven Jews and non-Jews and eight essays by contributors. The volume adds to the debate raised by Daniel J. Goldhagen's contention, in *Hitler's Willing Executioners,* that the average German knew what was happening to the Jews during the Holocaust. In a series of accounts presented in this volume by those who lived in Germany during the Nazi years, and in the scholarly essays that follow, it becomes evident that the "whole system of robbery, persecution, and destruction of the Jews... was accepted by the majority of the population."

Wood, E. Thomas and Stanislaw M. Janowski. *How One Man Tried to Stop the Holocaust.* **John Wiley and Sons, 1995, 316 pp.**
This is the story of Jan Karski, a young, Polish Catholic, military officer, who acted as a courier during World War II. Karski carried information to the Polish government, which was exiled in London after the Nazis marched into Poland. As a courier he came into contact with the Polish and Jewish underground and was shown the horrors of the Warsaw Ghetto. Karski, a "Righteous Gentile" tried unsuccessfully to convince the Allied leaders of the atrocities taking place in Poland. He was declared a hero by the Israeli government after the war.

Woodward, Kenneth L. "In Defense of Pius XII." Newsweek (March 30, 1998), Volume 131 Issue 13, pp. 35-36.
Woodward argues, that those who blame Pius XII for failing to act against or speak out in condemnation of the Nazis are engaging in "revisionist" history. According to Woodward, the pope was active in defense of the Jews and did speak out about Nazi atrocities. The author insists Pius had to maintain a neutral stance during the war, and it is wrong to suggest the pope could have prevented the Holocaust.

Yahil, Leni. *The Holocaust: the Fate of European Jewry, 1932-1945.* **New York: Oxford University Press, 1990, 808 pp.**

In this full-length study of the Holocaust, Yahil, attempts to describe the Holocaust from the perspective of the victims. In this effort, the author provides the best available treatment of the Jewish communities varied responses to anti-Semitic legislation, propaganda, and terror. Yahil also notes that in conjuring up the Jew as the essence of corruption and the personification of evil, the Nazis were emulating their medieval religious counterparts. The author views racism in the twentieth century as superceding Christian anti-*Judentum* as the foundation for the hatred of Jews. As Yahil writes, " Considering the long-standing anti-Jewish tradition of the Christian churches...it was not difficult in the electrified atmosphere following World War II to portray Jews as the epitome of the forces that had brought about the defeat of the Second Reich. Many Germans felt a strong urge to punish the party that they had branded as responsible for the disaster."

Zahn, Gordon C. *German Catholics and Hitler's Wars: A Study in Social Control.* **New York: Sheed and Ward Publishers, 1962, 232 pp.**

By documenting the support of German Catholics for Hitler's wars, Zahn seriously weakens the claim that the Church was one of the pillars of resistance to the Nazi regime. According to Zahn, the records show conclusively that the Church fully and, at times, with enthusiasm supported the German war effort.

____. "Catholic Opposition to Hitler: The Perils of Ambiguity." Journal of Church and State (Autumn 1971), Volume 13 Issue 3, pp. 413-426.

Zahn examines the reason why the churches failed to mount resistance to the policies of National Socialism. He contends, that church leaders may have been reluctant to act because they feared that their flocks would not heed the call. The author maintains, that the Catholic Church failed to present its members with an unmistakable message to combat the evil. While it called for spiritual heroism, it also promoted loyalty to authority. Therefore, even though it is doubtful that a majority of German Catholics would have been morally courageous enough to openly oppose Hitler, they were never given a clear moral imperative to do so. Zahn presents two documented sermons that he contends demonstrate both the strength and weakness in the Church's effort to fight the Nazis

____. "Catholic Responses to the Holocaust." Thought (1981), Volume 56 Issue 221: pp. 153-162.

The author claims, that though the Catholic Church's response both in and outside of Germany was inadequate to say the least, the Vatican's silence was not just a result of theological anti-Semitism. Rather, church authorities were considering possible reprisals by the Third Reich. They feared that Catholic laity and clerics located in areas under Nazi control would be targeted. Zahn also contends, that, to date, little attention has been paid to the shelter and relocation efforts the Catholic Church undertook to help Jews safely escape from the Nazi's.

Zerner, Ruth. "Dietrich Bonhoeffer and the Jews: Thoughts and Actions, 1933-1945." Jewish Social Studies (1975), Volume 37 Issue 3-4, pp.235-50.
Bonhoeffer's early anti-Semitic attitudes present difficulties when viewed in the context of today's post-Holocaust Christian theology. Yet, it is important to remember that his prejudices toward Jews reflected the Protestant theology of his day. According to the author, Bonhoeffer eventually came to feel guilty about his intolerance and he renounced his anti-Semitism. Additionally, Bonhoeffer showed his courage by subsequently opposing the Nazi regime he had come to revile.

Ziegler, Herbert. *Nazi Germany's New Aristocracy: The SS Leadership, 1925-1939*. Princeton: Princeton University Press, 1989, 181 pp.
A quantitative study of the social backgrounds of the SS elite, organized by Ziegler, considers age, religion, class, education, and the occupational background of the SS recruits, in an attempt to understand the nature of the SS officer corps. The leadership of the SS, according to the author, was not simply a grouping of the racially elite. Rather it tended to be young, ambitious, and from all regions and classes in Germany.

Zuccotti, Susan. *Under His Very Windows: The Vatican and the Holocaust in Italy*. New Haven: Yale University Press, 2001, 464 pp.
Zuccotti traces the history of anti-Semitism in Italy and studies the role of the Vatican in promoting hostility toward Jews. She examines the policies of Pope Pius XI, who despite his "hidden encyclical" denouncing racism was publicly timid in the face of Fascism and Nazism. According to the author, early on Pius XII was told about the massacres on the eastern front, yet he failed to publicly condemn Nazism, or the persecution of the Jews. Additionally, he provided no refuge for Jews and appeared indifferent to their deportation from Rome during the Holocaust

Zuroff, Efraim: The Response of the Orthodox Jewry in the United States to the Holocaust: The Activities of the Vaad-Ha-Hartzala Rescue Committee, 1939-1945. Hoboken, New Jersey: KTAV, 2000, 316 pp.
This book records the history of the American Orthodox Jewry's relief and rescue efforts to save Jews from the Nazis. Originally focused on missing rabbis and yeshiva students in Lithuania, the organization broadened its scope to help any Jews threatened by Holocaust perpetrators.

4

Post World War II Responses to the Holocaust

The enormity of the Nazi war against the Jews, which resulted in approximately 6 million dead, was not fully realized until 1961. In that year millions of people were able to view, on television, the Israeli court trial of Adolf Eichmann, the Nazi official responsible for implementing the "Final Solution." Despite the fact that in May 1953 the Israeli Knesset established *Yad Vashem*, the Holocaust Martyr's and Heroes Remembrance Authority, and in 1956 a stage adaptation of *The Diary of Anne Frank* was premiered in several West German cities to great critical acclaim, it was not until the Eichmann Trial that the Nazi genocide, which in the mid-1950's came to be known as the Holocaust, stirred the popular imagination.

Within the religious community there was recognition among segments that the Holocaust was not an aberration and that centuries of Christianity's "teaching of contempt" towards Jews had predisposed Germans and other Europeans to act indifferently when faced with the persecution of their Jewish countrymen. In 1959, when Pope John XXIII declared that the phrase *pro perfidis Judaeis* ("Let us pray for the unbelieving Jew") be deleted from the Good Friday Service, a process was initiated by the Catholic Church to engage Jewish leaders in an ecumenical dialogue with the objective of finding means by which the church could eliminate negative teachings about Jews in the New Testament. Pope John XXIII's efforts, at the beginning of this dialogue, were quickly followed, in November of 1964, by the opening of the Second Vatican Council. Vatican II issued the historic document *Nostra Aetate* (October 28, 1965), a repudiation of the idea that Jewish people were "rejected, cursed or guilty of deicide." This document was followed with "Guidelines and Suggestions for Jewish-Catholic Relations" (1975), and "Notes on the Correct Way to Present Jews and Judaism in Preaching and Catechesis in the Roman Catholic Church" (1985).

Despite the efforts of both faiths, the course of ecumenical dialogue between Catholics and Jews has not always flowed smoothly. In 1984 when Carmelite nuns attempted to establish a convent in a vacant building that bordered the Auschwitz death camp, Jewish groups opposed the plan. This set off a bitter controversy between Poles and Jews that was not resolved until Pope John Paul II interceded. The relationship between the Catholic Church and the Jewish community was further tested when in 1998 Pope John Paul II pronounced Edith Stein, a Jewish intellectual who became a Carmelite nun and died in Auschwitz, a saint and a martyr for the Roman Catholic faith. The pope's action angered many Jewish groups who argued that Edith Stein was sent to Auschwitz because she was a Jew, not because she was a Catholic. Similarly, in 1998, Jewish and Serbian groups protested the action of Pope John Paul II when he beatified Alojzije Cardinal Stepinac, the Archbishop of Zagereb. Both Jews and Orthodox Serbs viewed Stepanic as a wartime sympathizer of the pro-Nazi Croation government that was responsible for murdering tens of thousands of Serbs, Jews and Gypsies.

Even with these setbacks, ecumenical dialogue continues. Early in 1998, the Catholic Church issued a document, *We Remember: A Reflection on the Shoah*, which acknowledged, that centuries of Christian prejudice toward the Jews resulted in the indifference and inaction of many Christians who were faced with Nazi atrocities against the Jews. The document, however, went on to absolve the Church from complicity in the Holocaust. Additionally, it gave credit to Pope Pius XII for saving the lives of several hundred thousand Jews, while skirting the issue of the Pius's silence about the "Final Solution " despite his knowledge of it.

The matter of Pius XII's "silence" during the Holocaust was dramatically brought to the world's attention in 1963 with the presentation of Rolf Hochuth's controversial play *The Deputy*. Hochuth depicted the pope as having chosen not to speak out against genocide even though he had been provided with direct evidence of the death camps and the Nazi plan to exterminate the Jews. The play's indictment of the pope's "silence" during the Holocaust spawned a debate that continues to the present. This ongoing argument led Jewish groups to protest Pope John Paul's II plan to elevate Pius XII to sainthood.

The books and articles listed in this chapter illustrate scholarly works that deal with the impact of the Holocaust upon Jewish-Christian relations and also examine how the *Shoah* has internally affected both faiths. Where appropriate, books and articles have been included that reflect the moral and philosophic dimensions of the Holocaust. The intent of these volumes is to help the reader comprehend how it was possible for a modern and enlightened German society to produce a mass movement that enticed an entire people to condone, if not remain indifferent to National Socialism's barbarous policies.

Abrams, Elliott. *Faith or Fear: How Jews Can Survive in a Christian America.* **New York: Free Press, 1997, 237 pp.**
The focus in this piece is upon the need for Jews to once again make Judaism a central part of their lives. The author notes, that even though mainline Christian Churches have rejected the "theology of contempt", there are many American Jews who still harbor suspicions and resentment against Christianity. The author contends, that anti-Semitism and the Holocaust have helped unite Jews in recent decades, but he warns that this will not be sufficient. Over time Jews and Christians will need to achieve mutual respect for one another's faiths. This will help Jews reinvigorate their religious roots (which can be practiced in various forms) and in turn, adherence to faith will provide a force to further unify Jews.

Agamben, Giorgio. *Remnants of Auschwitz: The Witness and the Archives.* **Daniel Helter, Translator. Zone Books, 2000, 176 pp.**
By closely examining the literature that Holocaust survivors have produced, Agamben, an Italian philosopher, is able to probe the ethical and philosophical aspects of the atrocity. He insists the Holocaust has raised questions that affect us on many levels, including religious doctrine and belief. The author also asserts " the survivors have borne witness to something impossible to bear witness to."

Alexander, Edward. "**Gore Vidal's Anti-Jewish Nationalism.**" **Society (March-April 1988), Volume 25 Issue 3, pp. 78-80.**
Alexander shows, that Gore Vidal's anti-Semitic rhetoric is based upon traditional Christian anti-Judaism, and the more modern forms of anti-Semitism. Because Jews have failed to support the causes he espouses, Vidal has accused them of being "Nazis." Alexander charges, that Vidal has also insisted Jews cannot be loyal and patriotic because of their dual allegiance to Israel and the country they reside in. Vidal's belief that Jews have corrupted America's language and literature is founded, states the author, on the anti-Semitic idea of

Jews as a malevolent influence on society.

____. *The Holocaust and the War of Ideas.* **New Brunswick: Transaction Publishers, 1994. 242 pp.**
The author surveys the historical, ideological, and literary disputes that inform writings on the Holocaust. Alexander argues, that the war of ideas over the Holocaust should be understood within the larger context of the efforts of both Jewish and non-Jewish "universalists". These "universalists" are determined to undermine Zionism as an idea, and to erode the moral legitimacy of Israel as a Jewish state. The author also contends, that there is a campaign to steal the Holocaust from its Jewish victims and to transform it into a "blurred, amorphous agony, an indeterminate part of man's inhumanity to man."

____. *The Resonance of Dust: Essays on Holocaust Literature and Jewish Fate.* **Columbus: Ohio State University Press, 1979, 256 pp.**
If God is just, how could the Holocaust have happened? And if God is so imagined, why pray to a deity powerless to prevent the Nazi's murder of more than a million children? Alexander examines these questions in essays that attempt to identify the problems of maintaining faith after Auschwitz.

Allen. Diogenes. "Acting Redemptively." Theology Today (October 1984), Volume 41 Issue 3, pp. 266-270.
The author outlines a Christian response to the Holocaust. He insists, that the Holocaust as an event did not end in the 1940s, for a "total event" only comes when a response has been made and acted upon. Though we cannot change the pain and suffering endured by those who suffered through the Holocaust, our response can change the meaning and significance of the atrocity. He notes, that Christians have adopted a defensive attitude, and feeling of resentment toward Jew, when their religious faith has been charged with helping to persecute the Jews. Allen insists, that these feelings only worsen the situation. The author suggests Jews must try to rise above their outrage over the Holocaust, so that Christians can try to examine their role in the atrocity in a less defensive way. He understands that this asks a lot of Jews, but he reminds them that there is much to be gained if a dispassionate and serious study is done about the Holocaust.

Allen, John Jr. "Three Bishops Say, "I'm Sorry." National Catholic Reporter (December 17, 1999), http.//www.natcath.com.
Within a period of a few weeks, three Catholic prelates in the United States issued separate apologies for the Catholic Church's role in promoting anti-Jewish feelings. Denver's Archbishop Charles Chaput, New York's Cardinal John O'Connor and Milwaukee's Archbishop Rembert Weakland, independent of one another, felt compelled to make public apologies in light of Pope John Paul's

call for a "church-wide examination of conscience" in preparation for the millennium. According to Allen, Weakland's comments were the most memorable.

Allswang, Bradley Benzion. *The Final Resolution: Combating Anti-Jewish Hostility.* **Jerusalem: Feldheim, 1989, 293 pp.**
The author brings an Orthodox Jewish theological view to the study of anti-Semitism. Allswang traces anti-Judaism in the ancient world and moves on to examine the attempts by Christianity to denigrate the Jews and Judaism. The author also reviews anti-Semitism in the Islamic world. Additionally, he looks at the modern evolution of violent anti-Jewish attitudes in Nazi Germany that were drawn, in part, from the Christian tradition. He asserts, that Jewish attempts to assimilate over the centuries have not lessened the instances of anti-Semitism among Christians and other Gentile groups. The author claims, the only way to combat the hatred of Jews is for Jews to return to their religious roots.

Amery, Jean. *At the Mind's Limits: Contemplations by a Survivor on Auschwitz and its Realities.* **Bloomington: Indiana University Press, 1980, 111 pp.**
Amery analyzes his Auschwitz experience in five essays that discuss the nature of Jewish identity, the need for a Jewish homeland, his own feelings of resentment, the "dark riddle" of the Nazi regime systematic cruelties, and the limits of the intellect in Auschwitz.

Amishai-Maisels, Ziva. "The Christological Symbolism of the Holocaust." Holocaust and Genocide Studies (1988), Volume 3 Issue 4, pp. 457-481.
This article studies the phenomena of depicting Holocaust victims as Christian symbols of suffering. The author examines the uses of Jesus' Crucifixion by both Jewish and Christian artists from the nineteenth century to modern times. He demonstrates the linkage between images of the Passion, with Jewish martyrdom in the post-Holocaust era and explores the way in which this imagery had developed among Christian and Jewish artists since World War II.

Anderson, Robert. "A Critique of the Vatican Statement on the Holocaust." Gesher (October 1998), Volume 2 Issue 1, 4 pp.
Anderson, a minister of The Uniting Church of Australia, appraises *We Remember,* the Vatican's statement about the Holocaust and finds it overly nuanced and lacking. The author contends that the Vatican leaves too much unexamined and unexplained. The information contained in *We Remember*, states the author, is too selective and though the Vatican expresses compassion and regret, its "sorrow over the tragedy" of the Holocaust seems insufficient.

Arendt, Hannah. *Eichmann in Jerusalem: A Report of the Banality of Evil.* **New York: Viking Publishers, 1963, 275 pp.**

This book about the Eichmann trial leaves readers with the conclusion that the Jews themselves contributed to their tragic fate. Arendt contends, the Jews neither availed themselves of opportunities to escape nor did they, with rare exceptions, offer resistance. Her use of the term "banality," in her reference to Eichmann, suggests that this "desk murderer" was merely a cog in the Nazi wheel that was responsible for the extermination the Jews of Europe. Eichmann is characterized as bureaucrat carrying out orders, not the personification of evil. The impression is that under similar circumstances, we would all be murderers.

Ariel, Yaakov. "The Faithful in Time of Trial." Journal of Religion and Society (2001), Volume 3, 8 pp.
The author claims that books about the Holocaust have been popular with evangelicals since about 1970. Evangelicals are particularly interested in the behavior of Christians, during that time of moral crisis. The author contends, that most evangelicals assert that those who refused to resist Hitler were not in fact Christians. They insist that any person who has truly been saved could not have acted immorally and assisted the Nazis. Evangelicals, therefore, focus their studies on the memoirs of those who acted with courage during that time and are worthy of the designation "Christian." Yaakov presents several examples of works that are popular within evangelical circles and concludes that these biographies serve several needs of evangelicals. They set standards for other Christians to aspire to, promote the Christian ideals of forgiveness, reconciliation and unity, portray Nazism and other evils as "alienation from God", show the Jews fulfilling part of God's plan for them with their return to Israel and give hope to evangelicals who long for the Messiah's return and the total fulfillment of God's promise.

Article. "A Pilgrim's Progress." Commonweal (April 7, 2000), Volume 127, pp. 5-8.
This article offers a positive opinion of Pope John Paul II's actions to promote better relations between Jews and Christians, by looking at the pope's visit to Israel and his admission and apology for the Catholic Church's past transgressions against Judaism.

Article. "Catholic–Jewish Statement on Conversion Draws Controversy." America (September 9, 2002), Volume 187 Issue 12, 2 pp.
The joint Catholic-Jewish statement, published on August 12 of this year, regarding campaigns that target Jews for conversion is reviewed in this article. Both Jews and Catholics repudiate attempts to convert Jews to Christianity. The article also addresses the criticisms that this rejection of conversion programs has drawn from other Christian faiths.

Article. "Pope and Jews Hold differing Views on Repentance." Jewish Bulletin (March 31, 2000) Volume 104 Issue 13, pp. 25 A.

The author contends, that there are "fundamental theological" differences between the way in which Christians and Jews view the same issues. Recognizing these different ideologies sheds light upon the reactions of the two faiths to the Pope's apology to the Jewish people. According to the author, Jews regard deeds, rather than words, as the crucial element in repentance. Given that fact the Pope's statement was not sufficient for forgiveness, and his actions in promoting the elevation of Pius XII to sainthood made his words of atonement seem all the more insincere to many Jews. Additionally, since those people who were hurt by Christianity, through the Inquisition and the Crusades, are no longer able to give their assent, no real forgiveness can ever take place.

Article."Statement on Holocaust Criticized for not Faulting Silence of Church Officials." National Catholic Reporter (March 27, 1998), http://www.natcath.com.
When the Vatican issued its statement concerning the Holocaust, *We Remember: A Reflection on the Shoah*, it expected that Jews would respond positively. However, the support the statement received from Jewish leaders was, at best, tepid. Those who have spoken out in response, have criticized the Vatican for stopping short of blaming Church leaders for not intervening to stop the atrocities and for attempting a defense of Pius XII. Jewish leaders admit that the Catholic Church has taken a positive step forward with this document, but insist it is a small one. Meanwhile, Church officials maintain, that criticisms are the result of misunderstandings of the text of *We Remember*. The article provides statements about the document that have been made by Jews and Christians.

Article." Vatican Urges Repentance for Sins of Omission." U.S. Catholic (May 1998), Volume 63 Issue 5, pp.9-10.
This article focuses upon the Vatican's statement about the Holocaust titled *We Remember*. Pope John Paul II's comments, which accompanied the release of the document, are cited. In the statement the Church asks for forgiveness for having failed to oppose the Nazis murderous policies against the Jews.

Article. "Weakland's Three Affirmations and Five Requests for Forgiveness." National Catholic Reporter (December 17, 1999), http://www.natcath.com.
Archbishop Rembert Weakland, of Milwaukee offered affirmations and requests for forgiveness in his talk before members of a Catholic/Jewish organization. His affirmations of wrongdoing included; acknowledgement that Catholics had acted toward Jews in a fashion contrary to God's law, that those actions harmed Jews, and that these anti-Jewish feelings contributed to persecution of the Jews and made the Holocaust possible. Weakland asked for forgiveness for harmful statements made about the Jews, that promoted the idea that God had abandoned the Jews, comments that made Jews seem less than human, any teaching and

preaching that may have helped cause the Holocaust and forgiveness for any Catholic in Milwaukee who had contributed to hostility toward Jews.

Auerbach, Jerold S. "Being Jewish in Public." First Things (June/July 1992), Issue 24, pp. 7-8.
The author contends, that he and other Jews living in America have clung to the idea of "separation of church and state" as a safeguard against the Christian majority, at whose hands they have suffered. By adhering to this principle they have submerged their own religious belief, hidden it away from public. As Auerbach has become a more religiously observant Jew, he has also begun to believe that insisting upon the separation of religion and the public sphere is a mistake. According to Auerbach, Jews must publicly distinguish themselves as Jews, despite the threat of a possible Christian backlash, or risk losing their identity.

Augustine, Cardinal Bea. "The Jewish People in the Divine Plan of Salvation." Thought (Spring 1966), Volume 41 Issue 160, pp. 9-32.
Cardinal Bea argues, that the Gospel texts of Sts. Peter, Paul and Stephen do not indict the entire Jewish race for the death of Christ. Rather if any guilt is to be placed, it rests upon the leaders of the Sanhedrin. Yet, the author points out, that even these leaders who participated in Christ's trial may be deemed innocent because it is possible they did not fully understand the divinity of Jesus. Therefore, the charge of deicide cannot be leveled at the Jewish race as a whole, or even most likely at their leaders.

Bacharach, Zvi (Walter). "Christianity and Judaism: Polemic or Dialogue?" Bar-Ilan Studies in History (1984), Volume 2, pp. 293-304.
Bacharach reviews the problems surrounding any future progress in Jewish-Christian relations. He examines the anti-Jewish stance of Christianity in the past and the more recent attempts by Christians to make amends through statements such as *Nostra Aetate* (1965). The author contends, that despite these efforts, the Church retains its anti-Semitic stance and has exchanged benevolence for persecution as a method for retaining its belief in its superiority. Bacharach insists, Christianity must change its theological approach to Judaism or there can never be successful dialogue and coexistence between Christians and Jews.

Bader-Saye, Scott. "Post-Holocaust Hermeneutics: Scripture, Sacrament, and the Jewish Body of Christ." Cross Currents (Winter 2000/2001), Volume 50 Issue 4, pp. 458-74.
The author argues, that though Christian Churches have repudiated the earlier Biblical interpretations that taught contempt for Jews, Christianity still produces followers who believe, through reading the bible, that their faith is superior to Judaism. He insists, that the very methodologies employed by Christianity to

weed out anti-Judaism have, in fact, reinforced it. Rather than focus on methods, Bader-Saye suggests, we focus attention on "who is doing the reading, the context, and for what purpose the readings are done.' He suggests, that the politics of Christendom in the past made anti-Jewish readings of the scripture beneficial, but as the church's political situation changes in the modern world we are presented with better opportunities to alter our reading practices. Therefore, Christians should adapt to the idea that the Eucharist must be placed within its original Jewish roots of a Passover

Banki, Judith H. "The Image of Jews in Christian Teaching." Journal of Ecumenical Studies (Summer 1984), Volume 21 Issue 3, pp. 437-451.
Banki demonstrates, that studies conducted by Jewish and Christian groups during the last few decades have unmistakably proved that Christian teachings about Jews and Judaism represent an "enduring source of anti-Semitism." With this understanding in place, progress has been made in establishing closer ties between Christians and Jews. However, there are still areas of concern and problems to be addressed. The author suggests, that these areas of concern be made priorities for Christian Churches to deal with.

Barnett, Victoria. "Guilt and Complexity." Christian Century (October 10, 2001), Volume 118 Issue 27, pp. 26-32.
Barnett looks at the recent books that have attempted to accuse or defend Pope Pius XII and the Catholic Church for the lack of opposition directed toward the Nazis during the Holocaust. She makes the case that some of the publications add important information to the debate surrounding the Church's actions, others do not. The author contends, that even if the Vatican opened archives fully it is possible the evidence would still be incomplete and complex. This is evident from the works of scholars, who have perused the documents of Protestant Churches, wherein they have discovered moments of "courage and cowardice, good intentions and indifference, and failure and success in rendering aid to Jewish victims of the Holocaust."

Barth, Marcus. "Salvation From the Jews?" Journal of Ecumenical Studies (Spring 1964), Volume 1 Issue 2, pp. 323-327.
This article addresses the Statement on the Jews issued from Vatican II. Though the author credits the Catholic Church with its attempt to condemn anti-Semitism, Barth notes, there have been problems in agreeing upon what will and will not be included in the statement. While some church officials welcome steps toward reconciliation with the Jewish community, others oppose accepting any guilt for promoting anti-Jewish sentiment over the centuries.

Bartoszewski, Wladyslaw. *The Convent at Auschwitz.* New York: George Braziller Publishers, 1991, 169 pp.

A detailed account is provided about the Carmelite convent controversy that ensued in 1984. The Polish Communist Government gave permission to Carmelite nuns to move into a building at a concentration camp for Polish political prisoners that was built by the Nazis in 1940, on the perimeter of Auschwitz. Jewish groups protested the plan. The author attempts to present both the Jewish and the Polish side of the conflict, and in the process presents the reader with the history of Jews residing on Polish soil from the tenth century to the present. Bartoszewski offers a strong overview of the broad theological issues involved in the conflict.

Batzdorff, S.M. " Catholics and Jews: Can We Bridge the Abyss?" America (March 11, 1989), Volume 160 Issue 9, pp. 223-223.
Edith Stein's niece notes the issues that divide Christians and Jews. She insists, that by working to understand one another's faith and culture the two groups can arrive at ways in which to peacefully live together.

Bauer, Yehuda. "Modern Anti-Semitism." Nes Ammim Lezingen: Gesprekken in Israel (1985) Volume 11 Issue 3, pp. 4-21.
Though Bauer's article deals with anti-Semitism, as it exists today in the West, the Arab world and the USSR, he insists, that all forms of anti-Semitism originated within the Christian tradition. Bauer contends, this is so even though some anti-Semites are also anti-Christian.

_____. *Rethinking the Holocaust.* New Haven: Yale University Press, 2001, 335 pp.
Bauer, a leading Holocaust historian, presents an insightful overview and reconsideration of the history of the Holocaust and its meaning. Controversial is the chapter," Theology or God the Surgeon," whereby the author rejects the position held by ultra-Orthodox Jews that the Holocaust was a result of God's punishment of His people because they had strayed from His law (Torah). In particular, Bauer is critical of the late Lubavitcher Rebbe, Menachem Mendel Schneersohn. The author contends the Rebbe's writings suggest "Hitler was sent from God," and that "the Holocaust was basically a good thing because God is good, and he must have ordained it to save many souls at the expense of their bodies."

Baum, Gregory. *The Jews and the Gospel: a Reexamination of the New Testament.* Westminister, Maryland: Newman Press, 1961, 288 pp.
This book, written by a Catholic priest, was intended to promote the dialogue between Jews and Christians. Father Baum recognizes the tensions that have existed between the two groups and notes the negative stereotypes concerning Jews that have gained credence among Christians over the centuries. He discusses some of the foundations for these derogatory images, and points out, that no theological base exists for any of them. The author hopes, that by highlight-

ing the scriptural passages that libel the Jews, and showing how they have been misinterpreted, he can help alter the thinking of Catholics toward Judaism and the Jewish people.

Bauman, Zygmunt. *Modernity and the Holocaust.* **Ithaca: Cornell University Press, 1989, 224 pp.**
The author argues, that among the conditions that made the Holocaust possible, the most decisive was modernity. Bauman disputes the tendency to reduce the Holocaust to an episode in Jewish history, or to regard it as a unique instance of social madness, one that cannot be repeated in the West because of the progressive triumph of modern civilization. Rather, contends Bauman, we must understand the Holocaust was deeply rooted in the very nature of modern society and in the central categories of modern social thought. The author rejects scholarship contending the Holocaust was powered by widespread and uncontrolled anti-Semitic hatred, and argues, that the extermination of European Jewry was the product of a calculated exercise of bureaucratic and technical rationality.

____. *Modernity and Ambivalence.* **Ithaca: Cornell University Press, 1991, 285 pp.**
Social engineering's promise, to some day deliver humankind from material enslavement, is viewed with skepticism by the author. Rather, Bauman argues, it is modernity, not barbarism that is responsible for genocide and other atrocities committed in this century. Modernity, states the author," aims at establishing universality, control and management, a well-ordered garden."

Baumann, Paul. "Catholicism and Anti-Semitism." Commonweal (February 9, 2002), Volume 128 Issue 3, pp. 8-9.
The article is critical of James Carroll for the accusations made against Pope Pius XII in the book *Constantine's Sword*, which examines the role of the pope and the Catholic Church in the Holocaust. Baumann discusses a recent meeting at the Interfaith Center at which novelist Mary Gordon appeared with James Carroll. Ms. Gordon, according to Baumann, spent the evening making numerous outrageous and slanderous remarks about Pius, Catholicism, and Pope John Paul II, in relation to Jews and Judaism. Baumann contends, though the Church's role before, during, and after the Holocaust is problematic, Gordon's caricatures of the popes and Catholic belief does little to promote dialogue and reconciliation.

Bayme, Steven. *Understanding Jewish History: Texts and Commentaries.* **Hoboken, N.J.: Ktav, in association with the American Jewish Committee, 1997, 443 pp.**
In order to make this volume more accessible to a general audience the author has included textual readings, discussion questions and bibliographies for each

section. Topics relating to the Christian influence on anti-Semitism include; "The Church and the Jews", "The Crusades and the Jews", "Jews and Christian Spain" and a chapter that emphasizes both the victims and those who stood by and watched as the Holocaust took place.

Beck, Norman. "Removing Anti-Jewish Polemic from Our Christian Lectionaries: A Proposal." Jewish Christian Relations (December 28, 2001), http://www.jcrelations.net/articl1/beck.htm, 15 pp.
In this article the author contends, that over the past few decades Christians have increasingly recognized the anti-Jewish polemic that are contained within *New Testament* texts. Beck lists the most offensive texts in each of the *New Testament* books. For example, the *Gospel According to Saint Matthew* contains eighty verses of defamatory anti-Jewish polemic many of which are utilized in the Catholic *Lectionary for Mass* during its three-year cycle. Beck makes a case for revising the Lectionary and extending it to a four-year cycle in which the use of Anti-Jewish texts could be avoided.

____ and Christopher M. Leighton. *Mature Christianity in the 21st Century: The Recognition and Repudiation of the Anti-Jewish Polemic of the New Testament.* Crossroad Publishing Company, 1994, 320 pp.
The authors insist, that while it is normal for new religions to try and separate themselves from their "parent " religion, the way in which Christianity has repudiated Judaism has helped promote the persecution of Jews through the generations. The authors identify the ways in which Christian doctrine has slandered and hurt the Jews. Now, in the opinions of Beck and Leighton, it is time for Christianity to rethink and revise its teachings about the Jews and Judaism, for this is the only path open to a truly "mature" religion.

Bemporad, Jack and Michael Shevack. *Our Age: The Historical New Era of Christian-Jewish Understanding.* New City Press, 1996, 96 pp.
According to the authors, *Nostra Aetate* was a breakthrough document that changed the dynamics of the Christian–Jewish relationship. In this concise text, they examine the developments that have taken place since the issuance of this significant document, and discuss the difficulties and positive actions that have affected the dialogue between Jews and Christians.

Berenbaum, Michael. "The Holocaust as Commandment." Perkins Journal (November 2, 1979), Volume 9 Issue 180, pp. 165-166.
In response to Arnold Wolf 's criticism that the Holocaust has become too central to Jewish identity, Berenbaum insists, the Holocaust raises serious theological issues, which cannot be put aside. He suggests, the Holocaust must be considered with care and that it occupies a place of importance that is equal to the Exodus.

sidered with care and that it occupies a place of importance that is equal to the Exodus.

_____.*The Vision of the Void: Theological Reflections on the Works of Elie Wiesel.* **Middletown: Wesleyan University Press, 1979, 220 pp.**
The subject of this volume is Elie Wiesel, the religious thinker, personal witness to and survivor of the Holocaust, a man, who confronted the abyss. Berenbaum writes, that for Wiesel there are no answers, only questions. In this important work, the author provides both Christians and Jews with a key to understanding Wiesel and the Holocaust

_____. **"Who Owns the Holocaust?" Moment (December 31, 2000), Volume 25, Issue 6, pp. 60.**
Over the last twenty-five years, according to Berenbaum, the public's level of consciousness about the Holocaust has been considerably heightened. He points out the number of television documentaries and books produced each year, the increasing attendance of classes about the Holocaust on college campuses and concludes "that in a world of moral relativism, the Holocaust has taken its place as an absolute." Berenbaum notes the continued efforts of the Catholic Church and other Christian institutions to address their role in promoting the anti-Jewish attitudes that eventually led to the Holocaust. However, Berenbaum recognizes why some Jewish leaders worry about what some might term "Holocaust fatigue" and that with this the story of the murder of six million Jews may lose its impact. Yet, Berenbaum insists, that we must continue to teach about the Holocaust and address the questions it raises for the sake of humankind.

Berger, David. "*Dominus Iesus* and the Jews." America (September 17, 2001), Volume 185 Issue 7, pp. 6-7.
The author studies the controversy surrounding the Vatican's document *Dominus Iesus*, which was released in September 2000. Jews take issue with the statement that God's saving grace is only available through Jesus and the Church. While the statement is made that "individual non-Jews" can attain this grace, the means by which this happens is vague and according to the Church's line of reasoning, non-Catholics seem less likely to be saved than Catholics. The framers of this document insist that they did not have Jews in mind when composing the piece, and in fact, that Jews were excluded because of their special covenant with God. Yet, in the opinion of some Jews this explanation seems hard to accept, given the language of the document. Berger asserts, that many of the criticisms of *Dominus Iesus* are unwarranted, but he also admits that at the heart of the statement there is an officially stated policy by the Church and the pope maintaining that a key purpose of interfaith dialogue is the desire to promote conversions. This, in Berger's eyes, makes continued dialogue between Catholics and Jews difficult and suspect.

Bergmann, Werner, ed. *Error Without Trial: Psychological Research on Anti-Semitism.* **Berlin: W. de Gruyter, 1988, 546 pp.**
This collection of articles and extracts from books covers a broad variety of subjects that analyze the reasons for anti-Semitism. It includes chapters that deal with the ways in which religion has contributed to anti-Semitic attitudes. This includes; "The Ambivalent Attitudes of Christians toward Jews, "Catechesis and Anti-Semitism", "A Cognitive Theory of Anti-Semitism in the Context of Religious Ideology", and a study conducted among Catholic high school students in Brussels that examined attitudes toward, and knowledge of Jews. A chapter on "Ethnic Identification (of Jews by name, appearance and speech)" and one concerning efforts to use education as a means for preventing anti-Semitism, are also of interest.

Bergmann, Martin S, and Milton E. Jucovy, eds. *Generations of the Holocaust.* **New York: Basic Books, 1981, 338 pp.**
This volume offers contributions by thirteen authors, all but one of whom are psychoanalysts. Each writer attempts to describe and interpret the trauma experienced by the children of Holocaust survivors and perpetrators. The studies persuasively argue that we tend to be more dependent upon our parents, husbands, wives and children than we care to acknowledge, or admit. The proverb quoted and rejected in Jeremiah 31:29-30, "The fathers have eaten sour grapes and the children's teeth are set on edge," seems to hold true in a majority of these cases.

Berkouwer, G.C. "Anti-Semitism: To the Gas Chambers Again?" Christianity Today (February 29, 1960), Volume 4 Issue 11, pp. 3-4.
Berkouwer calls attention to the fact that anti-Semitc attitudes and actions persist even after the Holocaust. He finds these new waves of hatred more disturbing, or at least as disturbing, as that displayed by the Nazis. The author feels this way because the anti-Jewish attitudes exist, despite the fact that the Holocaust demonstrates clearly just how evil intolerance and hatred can be.

Berkovits, Eliezer. "Judaism in the Post-Christian Era." Judaism (Winter 1966), Volume 15 Issue 1, pp. 74-84.
According to Berkovits, Christianity, due to its decline, has been forced to switch from the militant position it held, since the time of Constantine the Great, to a position promoting tolerance. One result of this change is Christianity's pursuit of friendlier relations with Jews and other religious groups. Despite the overtures made by Christians, however, Berkovits insists, Jews have no reason to overlook the oppression and violence they were subjected to by Christians and wish only to be left alo .e.

_____. *Faith After the Holocaust.* **New York: KTAV, 1973. 169 pp.**

The author deals with the philosophical challenges posed by the Holocaust for religious faith. The book depicts the vitality of the religious faith that enabled numerous Jews to retain their dignity and self-respect, amid a brutality unprecedented in the annals of history.

____. *With God in Hell.* **London, New York: Sanhedrin Press, 1979, 166 pp.**
This book is a sequel to the author's *Faith after Auschwitz* (1973). Berkovits rejects the one-sided approach of survivors, who claim the Holocaust has rendered obsolete the religious ideals of *Kiddush Ha-Shem* (This is the Sanctification of the Divine Name, even at the risk of life itself). The author argues, the very fact that the Nazis sought not merely the eradication of the Jewish people, but also Judaism itself provides added grounds for renewed commitment to the Jewish religious value system. Berkovits also deplores the long established Jewish tradition of non-resistance to evil. In his opinion, part of the blame for the compliance of the Jews with the Nazi authorities, which helped facilitate their examination, can be found within this tradition.

Bernards, Solomon S. "The Jewish-Christian Agenda." Theology Today (April 1984 - January 1985), Volume 41, pp. 271-279.
The question asked is whether "anti-Semitism is really inseparable from Christianity?" The author claims, it is, although he can understand why many Jews, given the history of Christian anti-Semitism, might think the two can never be pulled apart. He admits, that progress has been painfully slow, but also notes, improvements in the relationship between Christians and Jews are noticeable. Bernards recounts the tensions that have hindered the connections of Christians and Jews, and asserts, that since Vatican II events and publications have lessened that tension. He particularly emphasizes the role that books written by John Gager, Charlotte Klein and Rosemary Ruether have had on Jewish-Christian dialogue, and insists, that in order to move the discussion forward Christians must reconsider their origins and admit their responsibility for Jewish suffering.

Bernstein, Michael Andre. *Foregone Conclusions: Against Apocalyptic History.* **Los Angeles: University of California Press, 1994, 181 pp.**
This author argues, that the Holocaust was not inevitable, that the victims cannot be faulted for not knowing what was at the time unknowable and even unthinkable, and that "victimization" is not a permanent or necessary attribute of Jewish history, nor is it a legitimate rationale for organizing Jewish life after the *Shoah*. Bernstein further asserts, that "apocalyptic" history, dominated by the shadow of the Holocaust does justice neither to the past, nor to the present, because "it renders individual human creativity and freedom irrelevant and removes any significance from imagining alternative paths.

Besser, James D. "More Pain in Auschwitz." Baltimore Jewish Times (July 24, 1998), Volume 242 Issue 4, pp. 35.
Auschwitz death camp. He contends, that there are no easy answers to the problem. Besser understands that while there are Jews who insist the site should contain nothing but Jewish symbolism in order to preserve the sanctity and memory of those who were murdered at Auschwitz, there are others who accept the fact that total Jewish control of the area may not be possible and their best hope to preserve the site is to compromise while maintaining as much control over the camp as possible. In explaining the debate, Besser recounts the high level of Christian and secular anti-Semitism that has infected Poland for many years and the affect such anti-Jewish attitudes have had on the discussion.

Birnbaum, David. *God and Evil: A Jewish Perspective.* Hoboken: KTAV, 1989, 266 pp.
This book raises the question, "if God is good, then how can he allow evil to operate in the world?" (Birnbaum changes the question to fit the Holocaust). The author, however, is not concerned with how God can allow natural disasters where innocent people suffer and die, but with how God can allow evil beings to cause other blameless humans to suffer and die. Towards an explanation to this question, Birnbaum draws on the Kabalistic idea of *tsimtsum,* or the internal withdrawal of the infinite God to make room for finite creation. According to this idea, finite creation includes human freedom and thus the ever-present option to do evil, even enormous and monstrous evil like the Holocaust.

Blumenthal, David R. *Facing the Abusing God: A Theology of Protest.* Westminster: John Knox Press, 1993, 318 pp.
The author raises the question of God's responsibility in the Holocaust " by understanding and working from the experience of survivors of the Holocaust and child abuse." Through the interplay of Biblical texts, theology, psychotherapy, and survivor experiences, Blumnethal explores the disturbing image of God as an abusive parent. In the quest for religious healing, the author seeks to build bridges between survivors of the Holocaust and survivors of physical abuse.

Bodendorfer, Gerhard. "Excuse Instead of Confessions of Guilt?" Jewish-Christian Relations, http://www.jcrelations.net, 2002, 6 pp.
We Remember, the Vatican's statement regarding the *Shoah,* is the focus of this article. The author examines the document and concludes that the statement has rightfully left many Jews and Christians dissatisfied. Bodendorf notes the points within the final product that have prompted criticisms, and he also encourages the Catholic Church to take its self-examination further, in an effort to heal the wounds between Jews and Catholics.

Boonstra, Janrense, Hans Jansen and Joke Kniesmeijer. *Anti-Semitism: A History Portrayed.* **Translator, Jean Kramer-Updike. Gravenhage: SDU - Anne Frank Foundation, 1993, 131 pp.**
This short text provides a general overview of anti-Semitism. The authors discuss the influence Christianity and the Crusades had in the formation of the stereotypes and caricatures used to depict the Jews and Judaism. They also explore the connections of anti-Semitism to anti-Zionism and the Holocaust.

Borowitz, Eugene. " Anti-Semitism and the Christologies of Barth, Berkouwer, and Pannenberg." Dialogue (Spring 1997), Volume 15 Issue 2, pp. 38-42.
The author examines Rosemary Ruether's contention that ties Christology to anti-Semitism, as well as the possibility that despite contemporary, liberal "ethical concerns", Christian theologians wedded to the *New Testament* may well be carrying forward anti-Jewish attitudes. In order too analyze these ideas Borowitz studies the theologies of Barth, Berkouwer, and Pannenberg. He concludes, Ruether's assertions may need some revision for there are modern theologians who have found ways to diminish the ties between Christology and anti-Semitism.

Borowitz, Eugene B. *Renewing the Covenant: A Theology for the Postmodern Jew.* **Philadelphia: Jewish Publication Society, 1991, 310 pp.**
Borowitz, a theologian of liberal Judaism, presents an in-depth philosophical examination of the Covenant. The author discusses and scrutinizes ethical and moral issues involving the *kabala*, holistic theology, and more. The pre- and post-Holocaust problems of evil, and God's nature are given close attention.

Boys, Mary C. "Authenticity, Not Demonization: An Education for Paradox." Journal of Ecumenical Studies (Summer 1997), Volume 34 Issue 3, pp. 350-355.
The "paradox of teaching people to be committed Jews and Christians, and then telling Christians they must also recognize that other faiths have a claim to authenticity is examined." Boys argues, that sustained encounters with the "religious other" does not need to diminish our own faith, and we do not have to weaken our own belief system in order to understand and tolerate the religious traditions of others.

____. "Contending With God: Elie Wiesel and the Meaning of Faith." The NICM Journal for Jews and Christians in Higher Education (Spring 1978), Volume 3 Issue 2, pp. 69-74.
Boys notes, the perspective of faith and the vision of God that is portrayed in Elie Wiesel's writings. She maintains, Wiesel's work demonstrates that Judaism and Christianity are inseparable and proves that a respect for one another's be-

liefs and traditions should be central to the two faiths.

____. *Has God Only One Blessing? Judaism as a Source of Christian Self-Understanding.* **Paulist Press, 2000, 384 pp.**
In an effort to improve the ongoing dialogue between Christians and Jews, Boys offers suggestions for how Catholic liturgy can be revised in order to lessen the divide between the two religious groups. She also provides an examination of how Jews and Christians separated from one another. Boys attempts in this volume to bring together both practical and theoretical elements of the issues confronting Jews and Christians, who are intent on trying to improve their relationship.

____. *The Jewish-Christian Dialogue: One Woman's Experience.* **Paulist Press, 1997, 112 pp.**
The author contends, that by studying the traditions outside one's own faith we can gain a better understanding and appreciation for our own religious belief. Therefore, noting the prospect of greater contact between the various faith communities, Boys explores the challenges to our religious commitment that we might confront during this present focus on pluralism.

Bradlow, Frank R. "The Consequences of the Second World War for the Jews of the World." Jewish Affairs (September 1985), Volume 40 Issue 9, pp. 42-56.
When World War II ended, Bradlow contends, few people understood the enormous tragedy of the Holocaust, nor could they imagine the lasting affect it would have on Jews and non-Jews. The author examines the reactions of both Jews and non-Jews and highlights the fact that the Holocaust had some positive effects. For example, it prompted Christians to examine their consciences, which led to changes in the way that Christian theology and teaching dealt with the Jews and Judaism. Additionally, once the truth of the Holocaust became clear there was a decline in anti-Semitic attitudes within democratic countries.

Braham, Randolph L. "Remembering and Forgetting: The Vatican, The German Catholic Hierarchy, and the Holocaust." Holocaust and Genocide Studies (1999), Volume 13 Issue 2, pp. 222-251.
The 1998 Vatican pronouncement, *We Remember: A Reflection on the Shoah* is examined. Other statements made by Catholic episcopates, since the 1960s, regarding the anti-Jewish views of Catholics during the Holocaust are also assessed. The author concludes, though most of the Catholic Church's statements have helped alleviate some of the tensions between Catholics and Jews, there are still problems to be resolved.

____, **ed.** *The Vatican and the Holocaust.* **New York: Columbia University**

Press, 2000, 280 pp.
This volume contains essays responding to the Vatican's release of its long awaited statement on the Holocaust in March 1998. Titled *We Remember: Reflections on the Shoah*, the document reflects the Vatican's view of the long and turbulent history of Christians and Jews. Those contributing responses include; Franklin H. Littell, Hyam Maccoby, Reverend John F. Morley, and Rabbi James Rudin. These scholars take both sides of the argument surrounding the Catholic Church's role in anti-Semitism and the Holocaust.

Braiterman, Zachary. *God After Auschwitz: Tradition and Change in Post-Holocaust Jewish Thought.* Princeton: Princeton University Press, 1998, 208 pp.
The author contends, that the impact of technology-enhanced mass death in the twentieth century has profoundly affected the shape of future religious thought. Braiterman shows how key Jewish theologians faced the memory of Auschwitz, by rejecting traditional theodicy, and abandoning any attempt to justify and vindicate the relationship between God and catastrophic suffering. Braiterman terms this rejection "anti-theodicy" and bases his arguments on the writings of three particular theologians; Eliezer Berkovitz, Emil Fackenheim, and Richard L. Rubenstein.

____. "Hitler's Accomplice?: The Tragic Theology of Richard Rubenstein." Modern Judaism (1997), Volume 17 Issue 1, pp. 75-89.
This article challenges the hostile responses to Richard Rubenstein's theological reflections about the Holocaust, as they appeared in his 1966 book, *After Auschwitz*. In his work, Rubenstein proclaimed "the death of God", for in his mind any God who had "covenanted with Israel, and remained "active in its affairs" must have "willed the murder of six million Jews" and therefore possessed "tragic fatalities." While others have repudiated Rubenstein's ideas, Braiterman insists, that despite some problems with Rubenstein work, Richard remained a "loyal son of Israel", and was never a true "death of God theologian." According to Braiterman, Rubenstein's critics have misinterpreted his writings.

Breitbart, Sidney. "The Jewish and Christian Covenants and the Holocaust." Dor le Dor (Winter 1988), Volume 17 Issue 2, pp. 97-106.
The author examines the Jewish and Christian concepts of redemption. Breitbart argues, Christian doctrine, formulated by Paul, provided men freedom from the obligation to observe the law. This, according to the author, destroyed man's sense of responsibility for the well being of his fellowman, which opened the door for the Holocaust. The Holocaust ultimately "demonstrated the genocidal implications of Christian anti-Semitism." Additionally, Christianity's claim to have replaced the Jews as God's chosen people was undermined once the State

of Israel was created.

Brenner, Reeve Robert. *The Faith and Doubt of Holocaust Survivors.* **New York: Free Press, 1980, 266 pp.**
This study explores the changes in religious belief and practices undergone by Holocaust survivors as a result of their ordeal. Of the thousand survivors surveyed in this study, seven hundred and eight respondents reported few drastic changes in either their belief or practice. Brenner's finding that, "Holocaust survivors, as a collective, rather than gaining faith in God during the Holocaust, were losing faith in God by a full seventeen percent," (from fifty-five percent before the Holocaust to thirty-eight percent after) is especially relevant to the current debate on the theological significance of the Holocaust.

Brockway, Allan, and Paul Van Buren, et al. *The Theology of the Churches and the Jewish People: Statements by the World Council of Churches and its Member Churches.* **Geneva: World Council of Churches, 1988. 186 pp.**
The commentators document the way in which the Holocaust shocked church leaders into recognizing the depth of Christian anti-Semitism. They conclude, that it is urgent for churches to re-examine their theological beliefs regarding positions, such as the continuing validity of the covenant, the Christian use of Hebrew scriptures, the Jewishness of Jesus, and the theological implications of the *Shoah.*

Brookman, Terry. "The Holy Conversation: Toward a Jewish Theology of Dialogue." Journal of Ecumenical Studies (Spring 1995), Volume 32. Issue 2, pp. 207 225.
Brookman points out that much of the dialogue that has transpired between Jews and Christians has been the result of goodwill. From this point on, however, the author insists, that more divisive issues concerning core elements of belief must be tackled. For example, the Christian teaching that there is no road to salvation without acceptance of Christ is an aspect of faith that invites disagreement. Subjects such as these, in Brookman's opinion, will require much more than cordial relations.

Brooks, Roger, ed. *Unanswered Questions, Theological Views of Jewish-Catholic Relations.* **South Bend: University of Notre Dame Press, 1988, 224 pp.**
This text reprints papers delivered at a symposium held at the University of Notre Dame in 1985. The conference celebrated the twentieth anniversary of the issuing of *Nostra Aetate* (October 1965). The papers covered three areas of study; the impact of *Nostra Aetate*, the progress gained over twenty years of Jewish-Christian dialogue, and the future relationship between the two faith communities. The author contends, that although the language of *Nostra Aetate*

was "halting" in style and context, it did open the door to dialogue and reconciliation between Catholics and Jews. The book offers suggestions for improving Catholic /Jewish relations and provides notes on the proper ways in which Catholics and Jews can present each others theologies through preaching and teaching.

Brosseder, Johannes. "The Church and the Jews." Ecumenical Review (January 2000), Volume 52 Issue 1, pp. 123-126.
Brosseder notes, that the following issues were part of the study put forward by the Cologne Ecumenical Study Group while working on the relationship between Christians and Jews. The group emphasized the following aspects, the challenge of Christians to reject the belief God abandoned Israel, the need to consider the influence of Judaism upon Christianity, and the salvation offered by God in the *Old Testament.*

Brown, Michael Gary, ed. *Approaches to Anti-Semitism: Context and Curriculum.* New York: American Jewish Committee, 1994, 330 pp.
The papers that appear in this book are based upon work first presented at a 1991 conference. The conference, sponsored by the International Center for the University Teaching of Jewish Civilization, was concerned with educating people about anti-Semitism. Yehuda Bauer, Alan Davies, Robert Marrus, Paul Lawrence Rose, Frank Stern, and the author are among the scholars whose work is offered. Subjects include; the ability to teach about anti-Semitism in a Christian setting, the type of myths and negative stereotypes that Christianity tied to Jews and Judaism, and Christians presented from a Religious Studies perspective.

____. "On Crucifying the Jews." Judaism (Fall 1978), Volume 27 Issue 4, pp. 476-488.
The author is critical of Jewish writers, who use Christian myths and symbolism to portray the Holocaust. Brown worries, that the use of Christian symbols and mythology implies a rejection of Jewish tradition due to the competition that has always existed between Judaism and Christianity. Examples are given to support the author's contentions.

Brown, Michael. *Our Hands Are Stained With Blood: The Tragic Story of the "Church" and the Jewish People.* Shippensburg, Pa.: Destiny Image Publishers, 1992, 241 pp.
Written by a Jewish Christian, this volume traces the centuries long history of Christian persecution of the Jews. The author contends, Christians are almost completely unaware of the suffering Jews have undergone over the ages. Brown condemns the slanders that have been attached to the Jews and the hostility the lies have promoted. He encourages Christians to revise their ideas about Jews and to understand that in expressing hatred for the Jews they are following Sa-

tan, not God.

Brown, Robert McAfee. *Elie Wiesel: Messenger to All Humanity.* **Notre Dame: Notre Dame Press, 1983, 262 pp.**
The author is a Protestant theologian, who has arranged Elie Wiesel's writings as of the date of publication, and summarized them in chronological order as a continuing story. By placing Wiesel's work in order, McAfee has tried to show the transformation of the Holocaust scholar's thoughts by allowing readers to trace his utter despair in *Night,* and its evolution through to the redemptive spirit Wiesel displayed in *The Gates of the Forest.*

Brunett, Alexander J. " Crossing the Threshold of Catholic-Jewish Relations." Journal of Ecumenical Studies (Summer 1997), Volume 34 Issue 3, pp. 377-383.
Pope John Paul II's book, *Crossing the Threshold* provided the idea for this article. The pope's work included a chapter in which he discussed his ideas about Judaism and reminisced about childhood Jewish friends who died at the hands of the Nazis during the Holocaust. John Paul's vision of "crossing the threshold of hope" presented a challenge to the Catholic Church. It called for the repentance of crimes committed against the Jews. Brunett claims, Catholics have finally crossed the threshold by rejecting the church's teaching of contempt for Jews and by finally accepting that the Jews were not responsible for the death of Christ. Thus the way for dialogue between Catholics and Jews is open and can move forward.

Bukiet, Melvin Jules. *While the Messiah Tarries: Stories.* **New York: Harcourt Brace, 1995, 197 pp.**
Bukiet's collection includes nine fictional stories that describe not only the tensions between Polish anti-Semites and Jews, but also the complicated arithmetic by which Jewish trouble can be traced to "the destruction of the Temple and to a Messiah who tarries". Belief and dispersion, memory and theology, are the supporting planks upon which Bukiet's disturbing stories are based. The author places ordinary Jews in extraordinary circumstances, and then forces them to confront what Jewishness means in the post-Holocaust universe.

Burleigh, Michael. *Ethics and Extermination: Reflections on Nazi Genocide.* **New York: Cambridge University Press, 1997, 261 pp.**
Nazi racial policy, according to Burleigh, was not just anti-Semitic (though its principal victims were Jews); it was also an elaborate program for the complete "eugenic" transformation of Europe and it identified many categories of people as "unworthy of life." The volume addresses such topics as the response of Christian Churches to the Nazi's obsession with eugenics, the Euthanasia Program and the persecution of the Jews.

gram and the persecution of the Jews.

Cargas, Harry James. *Holocaust Scholars Write to the Vatican.* **Westport: Greenwood Publishing Group, 1998, 176 pp.**
The volume's thirteen essays, written by prominent Holocaust scholars and theologians, centers on the following question; If you were to speak to the pope, what would you ask him about the Holocaust? Cargas reminds us that the Holocaust was a Christian, as well as a Jewish tragedy, and that the Roman Catholic hierarchy has offered very little official discourse on the Church's role in the tragedy. The essays featured focus on this problem and offer suggestions on what the Church can do to revise its teachings and refute anti-Semitism.

____, ed. *Problems Unique to the Holocaust.* **Lexington: Kentucky University Press, 1999, 194 pp.**
Leading Holocaust scholars examine difficult moral and theological questions surrounding the destruction of European Jewry. For example; Was it legitimate to betray others to save yourself? If a group of Jews were hiding and a baby began to cry, was it morally permissible to smother the infant so that the others could survive? How guilty were the bystanders who witnessed what happened to the Jews and did nothing to aid the victims of persecution? Cargas also explores the role of the Christian Holocaust scholar, as well as how men's ethics have been affected by the atrocity that resulted in six million murdered Jews.

____. *Reflections of a Post-Auschwitz Christian.* **Detroit: Wayne State University Press, 1989, 159 pp.**
The issues and questions the Holocaust raises are considered in the seventeen essays the author has compiled. Cargas concludes, that Christian Churches must accept a major portion of the blame for the centuries of Jewish persecution that culminated in the Holocaust. Further, he criticizes the silence of many Christians during the Holocaust, including that of Pope Pius XII.

____. *Shadows of Auschwitz: A Christian Response to the Holocaust.* **New York: Crossroad, 1992, 182 pp.**
In an effort to show the Holocaust in its Christian context, Cargas notes, that Hitler and Himmler were never excommunicated from the Catholic Church, Pius XII never condemned the mass murder of Jews, the killers came from Christian families and had Christian educations, and many Christian dignitaries supported Hitler.

____, ed. *The Unnecessary Problem of Edith Stein: Studies in the Shoah .* **Lanham; London; and New York: University Press of America, 1994, 105 pp.**
This book consists of essays commenting upon the controversy surrounding

Edith Stein, the Jewish convert to Catholicism, who later became a Carmelite nun. Stein was also an accomplished philosopher, having served as assistant to Edmund Husserl. She wrote widely of her religious experiences and struggled to meld her Jewish background with her Christian faith. After the Nazis gained control of her native Germany, Edith was arrested, deported to Auschwitz, and killed there in 1942. The Roman Catholic Church considers her a martyr, and so she was beatified in 1987 as a prelude to canonization as a saint. Jewish groups, however, argue that Stein was murdered in Auschwitz due to her Jewish heritage, not because of her status as a Catholic. The issue of Edith Stein and the Carmelite convent has stirred controversy and strained the strength of Jewish-Catholic relations.

_____. *Voices from the Holocaust.* **Lexington: University Press of Kentucky, 1975, 221 pp.**
A collection of the author's interviews with prominent witnesses to the Holocaust is found in this volume. Those interviewed include Jewish survivors, as well as "Righteous Gentiles", who saved the Jews during WWII. The themes of birth and death run through each of the interviews. Among those interviewed are, Emil Fackenhiem, Elie Wiesel and Simon Wiesenthal.

_____, ed. *When God and Man Failed: Non-Jewish Views of the Holocaust.* **New York: Macmillan Publishers, 1981, 238 pp.**
Cargas's collection of poems, prayers, sermons, and essays by Christian members of the United States Holocaust Memorial Council, represents an attempt to come to grips with the historical and theological ramifications of the Holocaust for contemporary religion.

_____."World Literature and the Holocaust." **Christian Century (November 14, 1979), Volume 96 Issue 37, pp. 1125-1127.**
By offering a country-by-country survey of modern literature, Cargas proposes that the Holocaust has been the most noteworthy event in Christianity. The psychological trauma it caused continues to be a significant influence upon the work of contemporary authors.

Carlson, Paul R. *Christianity After Auschwitz: Evangelicals Encounter Judaism in the New Millennium.* **Xlibris Press, 2000, 460 pp.**
Anyone seeking a better rapport between Christians and Jews, according to the author, must address certain difficult issues. These topics include the Holocaust, anti-Semitism, Zionism, and revisionist historians. Carlson, a Presbyterian minister, explains that there is hope for improved relations between the two faiths if these subjects are openly and honestly discussed.

Carmichael, Joel. "The "PR" Symposium on Anti-Semitism: A Self-

Destruct." Midstream (December 1994), Volume 40 Issue 9, pp. 8-14.
Carmichael examines the contents of a 1994 symposium entitled "Anti-Semitism: Is There a Cure?" The author takes issue with the speakers because they dealt with anti-Semitism as it relates to ethnic slurs and ignored the mystical element of anti-Semitic attitudes. It is within the realm of mystical anti-Semitism that charges are made concerning the Jews acting as agents of the devil and as the murderers of Christ. Without a discussion of these issues, as well as the racial epithets, it is no surprise that the symposium fell short in its work. Carmichael calls upon the Christian Churches to revise their teachings so that Jews are presented as human beings and not inhuman devils.

Carroll, James. "The Silence." The New Yorker (April 7, 1997), Volume 73 Issue 7, pp. 52, 18 pp.
There are several issues addressed in this article. Mr. Carroll discusses the relationship of Pope John Paul II with the Jews, the Catholic Church's acquiescence in the Holocaust, and the attacks of Hans Kung upon the Catholic Church for its past sins and its system, which promoted those sins.

Carroll, Vincent and David Shiflett. *Christianity on Trial: Arguments Against Anti-Religious Bigotry.* Encounter books, 2001, 204 pp.
Carroll and Shiflett confront, in a straightforward manner, the tragic events caused by Christian bigotry throughout the centuries. They note the anti-Semitism that Christianity has long been guilty of. Yet, they challenge the idea that Christian belief has justified racism and encouraged genocide. The authors argue, that despite the mistakes made in the name of Christianity, the religion has helped inject morality into our social order and lessened brutality among men. They claim, anyone who overlooks these positives of Christianity use tunnel vision in their examination.

Cartus, F.E. "Vatican II and the Jews." Commentary (January 1965), Volume 39 Issue 1, pp. 19-29.
The document of Vatican II on the Jews, according to this article, reverses the negative ways in which Christians have long portrayed Jews. The statement condemns anti-Semitism and acknowledges Judaism as a valid religious faith.

Cesarani, David. "Holocaust Memorial Day in Britain: David Cesarani Reflects on the Past, Present and Future of Education about Genocide and Bigotry." History Today (February 2002).
The author recounts a moving visit to the graves of World War II soldiers and expresses doubt that despite the efforts to make Holocaust Memorial Day (HMD) relevant for non-Jews, it will never inspire people the way the commemorative events for soldiers of war do. Cesarani reviews the fierce debate and criticism that erupted as plans developed for the first Holocaust Memorial Day.

He cites the potential for conflicts over historical interpretations and the role that politics will play when planning Holocaust memorials. The author prompts professional historians, to act as experts, counselors, arbiters and advocates during the planning of an event that should "characterize the formation of public memory."

Charlesworth, James H, ed. *Jews and Christians: Exploring the Past, Present and Future.* **New York: Crossroad Publishers, 1990, 258 pp.**
The papers and discussions of scholars who met in Philadelphia in 1987 to debate issues of Christian-Jewish dialogue are contained in this book. The collection focuses on the beliefs, attitudes, and actions of Christians, as they have been and continue to be, directed towards Jews. The key concept of all the papers is "anti-Semitism", understood either as theological anti-Judaism, or socio-cultural anti-Jewishness.

____, Frank X. Blisard and Jerry L. Gorham, eds. *Overcoming Fear Between Christians and Jews.* **New York: Crossroad, 1993, 198 pp.**
The papers featured in this volume are based upon presentations given at a 1987 symposium that was held in Philadelphia. Each deals with a particular issue that hinders the dialogue between Christians and Jews. For example; Hugh Anderson examines "The Fantasy of Superiority: Rethinking our Universalist Claims", Alan Culpepper addresses "The Gospel of St. John as a Threat to Jewish-Christian Relations", and Eugene Joseph Fisher studies "Eighteen Months in Catholic-Jewish Relations."

Close, Brian E. *Judaism.* **London: Hodder and Stoughton, 1991, 127 pp.**
This volume is part of a series designed to help students understand the religions of the world. This particular text includes topics concerning Jewish-Christian relations prior to, and after, the Holocaust, anti-Semitism throughout the centuries (with particular attention paid to the nineteenth century), the church's efforts to purge itself of anti-Semitism since Vatican II, and post-Holocaust theology for Jews and Christians.

Cohen, Arthur A. *Arguments and Doctrines: A Reader of Jewish Thinking in the Aftermath of the Holocaust.* **New York: Harper & Row, 1970, 541 pp.**
Cohen, a major figure in Jewish theology, has assembled an anthology for the purpose of engaging the contributors in a dialogue in regard to "the search for meaning in Judaism, Jewish existence, and the Jewish people." The volume is divided into four parts; the first addressing "the foreground of Jewish existence," the second, "the renewal of theology," the third, "challenges to Jewish belief," and the fourth, "the expectation and the trust." Contributors include, Hannah Arendt, Nahum Glatzer, Will Herberg, Aharon Lichtenstein, Gershom G. Scholem, and others.

___. *The Tremendum: A Theological Interpretation of the Holocaust.* **New York: Crossroad, 1981, 110 pp.**
In the four chapters that comprise this book, the author attempts to redefine "God and his relations to the world and man." Cohen contends, that God is the source of all historical possibility, and that human beings exercising the freedom of choice God had given them made the possibility of the Holocaust a reality. That horrific choice brought "Jews to the borders of extinction". What remains unclear, is the author's response to the question "What should be said of a God whose possibilities include death camps?" Cohen concludes, God's involvement with evil is the fundamental theological problem posed by the Holocaust.

____. **David Stern and Paul Robert Mendes-Flohr.** *"An Arthur A. Cohen Reader: Selected Fiction and Writings on Judaism, Theology, Literature and Culture.* **Detroit: Wayne State Press, 1998, 573 pp.**
This series of essays have been previously published. Some of those included in the volume deal with Christianity, the Holocaust and anti-Semitism. Examples are; "The Holocaust and Christian Theology" and "Thinking the Tremendum: Some Theological Implications of the Death Camps."

Cohen, Naomi, ed. *Essential Papers on Jewish-Christian Relations in the United States: Image and Reality.* **London and New York: New York University Press, 1990, 377 pp.**
This is a compilation of fifteen articles on Jewish-Christian relations in America. It includes a section devoted to "The Holocaust."

Cohen, Richard. **"Pius XII: Not Vindicated." Commonweal (March 3, 2001), Volume 127 Issue 5, pp. 29-32.**
Cohen comments on the Vatican difficulty in portraying Pius XII as deserving of being regarded as "most holy." He cites the work of two authors, Michael Phayer and Susan Zucotti, and notes that their studies of Pius do not conform with the portrait the Catholic hierarchy has tried to present to the public. The question of Pius's failure to adequately assist the Jews during the Holocaust remains a difficult issue to overcome.

Cohn-Sherbok, Dan, ed. *Future of Jewish-Christian Relations.* **Edwin Mellen Press, 1999, 291 pp.**
The essays collected in this text are a mix of new works, and those previously presented at various conferences. The topics covered in these essays include responses to anti-Judaism and anti-Semitism, Jesus Christ and Auschwitz, the role of Paul in framing the debate between Christians and Jews, the role of Jesus in the dialogue between the two religious faiths and the future of Jewish-Christian relations.

____. *Holocaust Theology*. **New York: New York University Press, 2002, 400 pp.**
The author provides a sweeping survey of writings by Jewish and Christian intellectuals. These writers have concentrated their efforts on trying to understand such theological issues as; how God could have allowed the Holocaust to happen and how his "absence" during that atrocity has changed our religious beliefs. The list of essayists includes notables such as, Leo Baeck, Eugene Borowitz, Steven Katz, ,Primo Levi, John Pawlikowski, Rosemary Reuther and Elie Wiesel.

Conway, John S. "The Founding of the State of Israel and the Response of the Christian Churches." Kirchliche Zeitgeschichte (1999), Volume 12 Issue 2, pp. 459-47
Conway shows, that when the State of Israel was founded the Vatican was more concerned with the Catholic Church's rights to the Holy Sites than with the Jews need for a place of refuge. Therefore it took the Church four decades to recognize the State of Israel. This recognition came as the result of Catholicism's acceptance that it had been a source of anti-Jewish attitudes and that its doctrine held common bonds with Judaism. The response of Protestant Churches in the United States to the Zionist cause have been more varied. While some Protestant communities were concerned with the need for Jewish safety and survival and welcomed an Israeli State, others were more worried about the needs of the Palestinians and opposed the Jews return to the Middle East.

Conyers, A.J. "Teaching the Holocaust: The Role of Theology." Perspectives in Religious Studies (Summer 1981), Volume 8 Issue 2, pp. 128-142.
Theological questions, according to the author, concerning humanity and evil as well as good and evil must be dealt with if we are ever to adequately teach lessons about the Holocaust. In attempting his own study of these questions, Conyers examines the ideas put forward by theologians, such as Abraham Heschel, Richard Rubenstein,, Helmut Thielicke, and others.

Crocker III, H.W. "Liberal Lies and the War Against Religion." Human Events (February 4, 2002), Volume 58 Issue 5, pp. 14-15.
Crocker criticizes the historical accuracy of Daniel Goldhagen's accusations, which were made against the Catholic Church for its "silence and complicity" during the Holocaust in a recent *New Republic* article entitled "What Would Jesus Have Done?" The author makes the argument that Goldhagen's charges are "hysterical" and largely unconvincing. Crocker worries, that by printing such a piece in a mainstream magazine interfaith relations are weakened and anti-Christian prejudice is strengthened.

Cunningham, Philip A. *Proclaiming Shalom: Lectionary Introductions to*

Foster the Catholic and Jewish Relationship. **Liturgical Press, 1995, 139 pp.**
The author has compiled introductory remarks that can be used prior to reading *New Testament* passages at Christian services. Cunningham proposes, that placing these readings in the proper context can help promote a better understanding of Christianity's Jewish heritage and of Jewish traditions.

_____. *Sharing Shalom: A Process for Local Interfaith Between Christians and Jews.* **Paulist Press, 1998, 120 pp.**
Cunningham presents a six - session procedure designed to help Christians and Jews better understand one another's traditions and practices. Each session includes activities, short essays, and a closing prayer exercise.

_____. **A Story of Shalom: The Calling of Christians and Jews by a Covenanting God. Paulist Press, 2001, 106 pp.**
The author explains why Christians must rethink their story as it relates to Jews and Judaism. He recounts the past abuses that Jews have suffered due to Christian teaching and doctrine. Cunningham contends, that God has covenanted with both faiths.

Curtis, Michael, ed. *Anti-Semitism in the Contemporary World.* Boulder, CO.: Westview Press, 1986, 333 pp.
Though this text, comprised of papers presented at a 1983 conference at Rutgers University, deals with broader issues concerning anti-Semitism, there are a number of essays, which address the role of Christianity in developing anti-Semitic attitudes. Some included are, "The German Churches and the Jewish People Since 1945" presented by John S. Conway, and "New Testament Anti-Semitism" written by John Pawlikowski.

Daane, James. "The Anatomy of Anti-Semitism," Christianity Today (February 14, 1964), Volume 8 Issue 10, pp. 10-12.
The author claims, that Christian Churches have failed to convince their members that the Jews are not responsible for the death of Christ and that negative attitudes toward Jews should be rejected. He notes, there are historical facts tying Christ's Jewish disciple, Judas, to his betrayal, but contends, that Christians owe their chance for salvation to this betrayal, and so no anti-Jewish feelings should result from it. Daane asserts, that only through the renunciation of anti-Semitism do Christians prove their understanding of the Gospel.

Davies, Alan T. "Anti-Zionism, Anti-Semitism and the Christian Mind." Christian Century (August 19, 1970), Volume 87 Issue 33, pp. 987-989.
Davies recognizes the growing trend toward anti-Zionism among Christians and notes that they insist anti-Zionism has no connection to anti-Semitism. These Christians assert, they have no problem with Jews, but simply oppose the state

of Israel. Although some Jewish leaders believe, there is no relation between anti-Zionism and anti-Semitism, others remain unconvinced. The fact that there are Jews who are against a Jewish state does not lessen the concern. Many Jews worry that anti-Zionism can easily slip into anti-Semitic feelings. Given the lasting pain of the Holocaust, it is difficult for many Jews to separate one form of anti-Jewish feeling from another. Davies suggests that, to a degree, this is a matter of miscommunication that both sides must work to correct

____. *Anti-Semitism and the Christian Mind: The Crisis of Conscience after Auschwitz.* **New York: Herder & Herder, 1969, 192 pp.**
Davies argues, that any new Christian theology of Judaism must reject outright the patristic heritage of anti-Judaism rooted in *Romans* 9-11, and must acknowledge the independent validity of post-Biblical Judaism as a world religion.

____. **"The Jews in an Ecumenical Context: A Critique." Journal of Ecumenical Studies (1968), Volume 5, pp. 488-506.**
The author admits, Christianity contributed to anti-Semitic attitudes in the past and that even in the post-Holocaust era some Christian theologians find it difficult to move beyond feeling superior to Jews. Davies points out, that although the relationship between Christians and Jews has improved in recent years and both sides have embraced the ecumenical movement, Christian theologians have to a large extent failed to understand and appreciate Judaism on Jewish terms.

Davies, William David. *Christian Engagements with Judaism.* **Harrisburg, Pa.: Trinity Press International, 1999, 321 pp.**
The essays compiled in this book attempt to counter some of the negative charges made against Christianity in relation to its treatment of the Jews. In particular, the authors endeavor to present Paul's teachings in a more favorable light, as well as the fact that some Christians opposed the Nazis. Additionally, a chapter is devoted to refuting the accusations Joel Carmichael made in *The Satanizing of the Jews: Origin and Development of Mystical Anti-Semitism* (1992). Davies contends, that anti-Jewish attitudes existed prior to Christian hostility directed at the Jews and that the Jews suffered more horrific attacks once Christianity's power declined

Della Cava, Ralph. "Jews and Christians of Russia and the Ukraine Speak About Anti-Semitism: Notes From a Travel Journal, May-June 1995." Religion in Eastern Europe (February 1997), Volume 17 Issue 1, pp. 26-43.
Della Cava relates the information he gathered while traveling to Moscow, Kiev, Saint Petersburg, and Lvov. In each of these locations he spoke with Christians (Both Orthodox and Catholic) and Jews about anti-Semitism and other issues. From these conversations he discovered that Jews in the Ukraine still fear anti-Semitism, that anti-Semitism still deeply affects the Russian Orthodox Church

and targets Jewish converts, as well as Jews who are secular and those who remain adherents of Judaism.

Des Pres, Terence. *The Survivor: An Anatomy of Life in the Death Camps.* **New York: Oxford University Press, 1976, 218 pp.**
The author contends, "there is a concomitant impulse to ignore the Holocaust survivor himself, who appears to us as a painful reminder of the unspeakable events." In an effort to overcome this tendency, Des Pres uses survivor's testimonies as evidence of the horrors of Auschwitz, and to substantiate the conclusions made about man's nature, which Auschwitz has been used to support. Des Pres argues, that the structure of experience in extremity, as faced by the victims in the camps, constitutes an inversion of the values of Western civilization. This forces us to reevaluate the heroic ethic of our culture, which regards pain and suffering as ennobling.

Diamond, Malcolm L. "Catholicism in America: The Emerging Dialogue." **Judaism (Fall 1960), Volume 9 Issue 4, pp. 307-319.**
Diamond applauds the fact that the Catholic Church has, in the past few years, demonstrated a willingness to criticize its own teachings. He suggests, that some Catholic publications have taken the lead in promoting the idea that this self-examination continue. Furthermore, they support the attempts the Church has made to open conversation with the Jewish community. However, the author decries the fact that the Catholic Church, despite its efforts, still maintains it is the "one true faith." He does find this less threatening since the Catholic faith is not monolithic and therefore there are members willing to rethink the Church's traditional doctrine.

Dietrich, Donald J. *God and Humanity in Auschwitz: Jewish-Christian Relations and Sanctioned Murder.* **New Brunswick: Transaction Publishers, 1995, 355 pp.**
Dietrich, a Catholic theologian, discusses the historic role of anti-Semitism in Christian theology, as well as the Holocaust, as he examines the ongoing dialogue between Christians and Jews. The author contends, although religious anti-Semitism alone was not a sufficient condition for the Holocaust, it was a necessary one. He hopes that through discussion Jews and Christians can learn to work together in defense of human rights around the world, so that the atrocities of the twentieth century can never be repeated.

Ditmanson, Harold H. 'Christian Declarations on Anti-Semitism." Dialogue (Summer, 1967), Volume 6 Issue 3, pp. 168-175.
This article examines the factors that led to issuing important statements from

Christian Churches rejecting anti-Semitism and the notion of the Jews collective guilt for the death of Christ. According to the author, the death of six million Jews, the creation of the State of Israel, the movement toward a pluralistic society, and new Biblical research have all contributed to Christianity's desire for reconciliation and discussion with Jews. Ditmanson provides statements from a variety of Christian institutions that are meant to further Jewish-Christian relations.

Donovan, Gill. "Importance of Jewish Scriptures Examined." The National Catholic Reporter (December 21, 2001), http./www.natcath.com.
The author examines the Vatican's response to the charge that the *New Testament* condemns Jews. A document entitled "The Jewish People and Their Sacred Scriptures in the Christian Bible" contends, the vast majority of references to Jews in the *New Testament* are positive, the scriptures never claim that God rejected the Jews, and that the Gospels affirm God's intent to save Israel. According to the author, the Pontifical Biblical Commission, which released these findings intended to increase understanding of Biblical texts for Jews and Christians by placing the references to Jews in the proper context. They attribute the derogatory comments about Jews in the *New Testament* to a "handful of leaders who do not recognize Jesus as Messiah or to Jews who have violated God's law."

Drinan, Robert F. "The Christian Response to the Holocaust." Annals of the American Academy of Political and Social Science (1980), Volume 450, pp. 179-189.
Drinan describes the reaction of Christians to the horrors of the Holocaust as, for the most part, mild and belated. He contends, that the Church failed to act in a moral and decisive way to oppose the crimes the Nazis committed against the Jews. It is only recently that the Church has begun to understand the need to rethink its teachings about the Jews and to understand that it contributed to the atmosphere that made the Holocaust possible.

Dulles, Avery Robert, Commentaries by Leon Klenicki. *The Holocaust, Never to be Forgotten: Reflections on the Holy See's Document "We Remember."* **Paulist Press, 2001, 92 pp.**
This brief volume contains the full text of the Vatican's statement, *We Remember* issued in 1998 that deals with the Holocaust. It is accompanied by an explanatory address from Cardinal Edward Cassidy. The Vatican's statement acknowledges the need to request the Jews' forgiveness for Christian responsibility in the Holocaust. The book also contains two essays; one written by a Jewish theological scholar and the other by a Catholic theologian. These essays focus upon the ongoing dialogue between the two religious communities.

Dushaw, Amos Isaac. *Anti-Semitism: The Voice of Folly and Fanaticism.* **Brooklyn, N.Y.: Tolerance Press, 1943, 116 pp.**
The author examines the Jews contributions to Christianity and surveys the reasons why Christians should work together with the Jewish community to end all forms and expressions of anti-Semitism and racial intolerance. Dushaw supports the development of a Jewish homeland in Palestine.

Eckardt, Alice Lyons. "Post-Holocaust Theology: A Journey Out of the Kingdom of Night." Holocaust and Genocide Studies (1986), Volume 1 Issue 2, pp. 229-240.
Christian 'triumphalism", according to Eckardt, has to end. She declares that it is no longer acceptable for Christians to regard Jews, or others refusing to accept Christ, as inferior. If the myth of Christian superiority continues, then Christians must try to justify the murder of six million Jews.

Eckardt, Roy A. "Anti-Semitism is the Heart." Theology Today (April 1984 /January 1985), Volume 41, pp. 301-308.
Christianity's role in the Holocaust, Eckardt insists, is evident even though some still insist it is not. The Christian Church has traditionally demonized the Jews and asserted their superiority over Judaism. This belief, according to Eckardt, " spelled doom for Jews." The author claims, Christianity has no ability or right to try and revise its ideas concerning Judaism because for so long it tried to eradicate the religion of Jews. He also asserts, that for over forty years Israel has been forced to defend its very existence and that this demonstrates that the plan of anti-Semites has been to "put the Jews always on trial." Eckardt emphasizes his belief that Christian anti-Semitism still exists in the form of "anti-Israelism." The author calls anti-Semites the "devil's chosen people." Additionally, he contends that the fact that Christian Churches do not fully dedicate their energy to ridding the world of anti-Semitism "is more than sad. It is a reflection of moral bankruptcy."

____. "Christians and Jews: Along a Theological Frontier." Encounter (Spring 1979), Volume 40 Issue 2, pp. 89-127.
The author argues, that the Holocaust has become a substitute for Judaism. He warns that the Holocaust, used by secular Jews as their primary cause, has been infused with too much significance. The author insists, that the Jewish people must put the Holocaust into perspective and reaffirm that Judaism is far more than just a single tragic event.

____. *Christianity and the Children of Israel.* **New York: King's Crown Press, 1948, 223 pp.**
Eckardt maintains, that Christian liberalism has failed to understand or confront the question of anti-Semitism. He theorizes, that by rejecting the Jewish people

through anti-Semitism Christians are, in effect, rejecting God since the Jews are his chosen people. The author proposes a "Theology for the Jewish Question" that challenges Christians to break away from their prideful natures and seek repentance for their anti-Semitic words and actions. Only then will the Christian community, in Eckardt's view end their rebellion against God.

_____. *For Righteousness' Sake: Contemporary Moral Philosophies.* Bloomington: Indiana University Press, 1987, 365 pp.
Both Judaism and Christianity, Eckardt argues, are essentially tied to certain specific historical events, without which they simply would not be what they are. For Eckardt, the historic event that is decisive for both faiths is the Holocaust. It is the engine that drives, in the author's view, the relationship between the religions. The worst possible thing that a Jew or a Christian can do, Eckardt insists, is to proceed in a post-Holocaust world as if nothing had happened. The author contends, that the Christian teaching of contempt for Judaism prepared the ground for the "Final Solution."

_____. "Is There a Way Out of the Christian Crime? The Philosophic Question of the Holocaust." Holocaust and Genocide Studies (1986), Volume 1 Issue 1, pp. 121-126.
In the context of the Holocaust, Eckardt binds together the relationship between Christian anti-Judaism and Christian anti-Semitism. The author accuses Christian theologians of continuing to preach about the Resurrection in a way that condemns Jews who refuse to accept Christ as their Savior. Eckardt insists, that only when Christians own up to their responsibility for the suffering of the Jewish people will they be able to find a solution to their theological problems concerning Judaism and Jews. He questions the moral credibility of Christianity and expresses hope that Christians will be able to accept those who do not, and will not, recognize the Resurrection.

_____. *Jews and Christians: The Contemporary Meeting.* Bloomington: Indiana University Press, 1986, 177 pp.
In this text the author proposes ways in which Christians can reevaluate Judaism in the post-Holocaust world. Eckardt argues, that the Holocaust has had the same impact on this generation of Jews that the Crucifixion of Jesus had upon the first disciples. Thus, Christians should understand why Jews react to the Holocaust, and Christians, as they do.

_____. "Recent Literature on Christian-Jewish Relations." The Journal of the American Academy of Religion (1980/81), Volume 49 Issue 1, pp. 99-111.
This article provides a comprehensive, but concise, listing of publications dealing with the relationship between Christians and Jews. Eckardt divides the list-

ing by subject so that readers can easily identify the books that will be of most interest to them. The author includes topics dealing with theological questions, Christian anti-Semitism, the Holocaust, Christian self-criticism, and the State of Israel.

____. "The Shadow of the Death Camps." Theology Today (October1977), Volume 34, Issue 3, pp. 286-290.
The author surveys the thoughts of many scholars who are dealing with the impact of the Holocaust on Christianity and on the world. Eckardt examines the answers provided by scholars who are concerned with how we should view God, Christian morality and theology, and the politics and security of the State of Israel in a post-Holocaust society. He closes by citing Paul Van Buren's warning, that unless more Christians begin to recognize the legality of Judaism, and stop shutting out the horror of Auschwitz, any reconsideration of theology and morality are pointless.

____. *Your People, My People: The Meeting of Christians and Jews.* New York: Quadrangle/The New York Times Book Co. 1974, 275 pp.
The primary argument made by the author is that the Christian Church is guilty of causing the suffering of Jews over the centuries, and more particularly, responsible for having helped lay the groundwork for the rise of the Nazi party in Germany. The images of the Jews as the cursed of God, members of a deicide race, and agents of the Devil, were all part of the Church's teachings, which were later brutally transformed by the Nazis.

____ and Alice Lyons Eckardt. "The Contents of Jewish Education and Its Responsibility Within the Jewish-Christian Encounter." *Jewish Education and Learning: Published in Honour of Dr. David Patterson.* Eds. Glenda Abramson and Tudor Parfitt. Chur: Harwood Academic Publishers, 1994, pp. 175-194.
The Eckardts address subjects about Jewish education that relate to the Christian-Jewish dialogue. The authors discuss the Jewish demand for justice and respect and how that is countered by the ways in which Christians attempt to sidestep any responsibility for anti-Semitism and the Holocaust. According to the Eckardts, Christianity's occasional acceptance of some guilt for past actions against the Jews is simply offered as a token response to Jews calling for honesty and deference. The Eckardts insist, that the subject of Christian "triumphalism" must be dealt with if the concerns of Jews are ever to be assuaged. They contend, that Jesus' teachings were not anti-Jewish and argue that Christian theology must come to terms with the Holocaust and the State of Israel.

____. Long Night's Journey Into Day: Life and Faith After the Holocaust. Detroit: Wayne State University Press, 1982, 206 pp.

In an effort to address the difficulties of the theological impact of the Holocaust, the Eckardts view the *Shoah* as a crucial confrontation for Christian theology, whereby the critical issue is how Christians view Jewish survival; with regret or thanksgiving. The Eckardts maintain that it is critical for Christians to recognize the existence of anti-Semitism in the *New Testament.*

___. *Long Night's Journey Into Day: A Revised Perspective On The Holocaust*. **Detroit: Wayne State University Press, 1988, 277 pp.**
In this revised edition of their 1982 book, Roy and Alice Eckardt take up Jewish evaluations of Christian culture, as a basis for thinking through what post-Holocaust Christianity should be like. The authors contend, that the Holocaust was the outcome of the traditional Christian "teaching of contempt" for Jews and Judaism, and the idea that Christianity was superior to, and/or superceded Judaism in God's plan for humanity. The Eckardts insist, that Christianity must reject any vestige of "supersessionism" as inappropriate in the light of the Holocaust. Only then can men " pass beyond the horrors of the kingdom of night into the kingdom of day."

____. **"Studying the Holocaust's Impact Today: Some Dilemmas of Language and Method." Judaism (Spring 1978), Volume 27 Issue 2, pp. 222-232.**
The Eckardts discuss the difficulties connected with studying the Holocaust. The word "Holocaust", according to the authors, fails to adequately describe the intentional and systematic massacre of Jews. The authors also examine the possibility that the Holocaust will be seen as an aberration and thus will be ignored as a stepping-stone to increase our understanding of the dangers of intolerance.

Eckstein, Jerome. "The Holocaust's Impact on Christian Theology." Midstream (1978), Volume 24 Issue 1, pp. 62-66.
Eckstein reviews several post-Holocaust works in an effort to explore the need for a reassessment of Christian theology in the aftermath of the Holocaust. Each of these works, in varying degrees, prompts Christians to atone for anti-Semitism and reach a better understanding of the place of Jews in Christian theology, preaching and practice.

The Ecumenical Study Centre. "The Synagogue and the Church: Is There any Anti-Semitism in the Bible?" Hungarian Ecumenical Study Booklets (1993), Volume 5, 74 pp.
Christian theologians from the Ecumenical Study Centre surveyed the theological origins of anti-Judaism and the developments that have marked Jewish-Christian relations. Also explored is anti-Semitism in Hungary, especially as it influenced what happened during the Holocaust. The authors concluded, that though some Hungarian Church leaders assisted Jews, for the most part the

Churches failed to muster the resolve needed to oppose the Nazis. In the aftermath of the Holocaust, Christian Churches have felt compelled to reexamine the Church-Synagogue relation through dialogue between Christians and Jews.

Editorial. "Asking Forgiveness." America (March 25, 2000), Volume 182 Issue 10, pp. 3.
The author comments on the apology issued by Pope John Paul II on the first Sunday of Lent 2000 for the sins committed by Catholics over the last two millennia. The pope noted that Catholics have often broken faith with God's commands by "violating the rights of ethnic groups and peoples, and shown contempt for their culture and religious traditions." Though the response to the pope's apology was mostly positive, there were people who were uncomfortable or dissatisfied by the pope's statement. Some Catholics questioned the need for an apology for sins committed by past generations, others felt the pope neglected to ask forgiveness for present sins, and some wanted a more specific list of offenses. For example, Jewish leaders were understandably disappointed that the Holocaust was not mentioned. The author expresses the hope, that despite any perceived shortcomings in the pope's apology, future generations might well see this event as a positive step in reconciling the Church to people it has offended.

Editorial. "Christians, Jews and Anti-Semitism." First Things (March 1992), Issue 21, pp. 9-12.
This editorial argues, that it is important to reexamine the extent and nature of anti-Semitism in America every so often. The writer points to the importance of maintaining a "Judeo-Christian ethic" in this country, for those very words remind Christians of their dependence upon and required respect for Jewish tradition. He insists, this Judeo-Christian tradition does not require a common faith. "Jews should continue to be Jews and Christians be Christians", according to the editorial writer. However, both communities must remain alert to the evils of anti-Semitism, whether they are promoted from the conservative right or the liberal left. The article contends, it may be possible to recognize those who care little for Jews by pointing out those who care little for Israel, for this may provide a "firmer fix" on the current nature of anti-Semitism.

Editorial. "Cornwell's Popes." Commonweal (November 5, 1999), Volume 126 Issue 19, pp. 5-8.
The editor argues, that John Cornwell's book, *Hitler's Pope*, presents little in the way of new information and contends, some of the author's more sensational accusations do not stand up to scrutiny. The writer suggests, that when looking at Pius's record it might be helpful to compare the pontiff's attempts to use quiet diplomacy with Hitler, rather than overt opposition. In addressing the recent case of thirteen Iranian Jews arrested as spies for Israel, the editorial asks if

these Jews are better served by a strident and public protest of their arrests that might well anger the Iranian government, or a more prudent and behind the scenes diplomatic effort that could result in their freedom. Although this argument is intended to make Pius's actions seem more credible, the editorial decries the fact that books, like Cornwell's, put reasonable scholars in the unenviable position of coming to Pius's defense, when in fact they too feel the pope was negligent in offering adequate assistance to the Jews during the Holocaust.

Editorial. "Did Christianity Cause the Holocaust." Christianity Today (April 27,1998), Volume 42 Issue 5, 12-14.
A prominent group of Jewish spokesmen claims, the United States Holocaust Museum has misled visitors by linking Christian beliefs about Jews directly to Hitler's racist policies, and his intent to murder the Jewish population of Europe. The film *Anti-Semitism,* shown at the Holocaust Museum, they contend, uses too broad a brush in portraying the moral failures of Christianity in regards to the treatment of Jews. While Eliot Abrams, Michael Horowitz, and other Jewish intellectuals agree, Christians have plenty to regret and atone for, they insist that the Holocaust Museum has an obligation to present the Christian faith as it is, and should not engage in inaccurate stereotypes.

Eijk, A.H.C. van. "The Jewish People and the Church's Self-Understanding." Bijdragen (October-December 1989), Volume 50 Issue 4, pp. 373-393.
The author notes the theological revisions undertaken by the Catholic Church since Vatican II in relation to the Jews and Judaism. He asserts, that much of this change has taken place because the Church has come to better understand, that its identity is tied to Judaism and that any adjustment of its doctrines toward the Jews directly affects its own members. Eijk points out, that due to its common heritage with Jews the Catholic Church rejects any persecution of the Jewish people, and regrets actions of the past that led to Jewish suffering. The author asks whether or not other Christian churches share the same feeling of being bound to Jews and Judaism?

Eliach, Yaffa. "The Holocaust as Obligation and Excuse." Perkins Journal (November 16, 1979), Volume 9 Issue 181, pp. 1-3.
Eliach warns, that the Holocaust has been used to create a superficial identity for Jews in America. The author proposes, that many Jews regard the Holocaust, which was a common, but single tragic event, as their primary means for unification. Eliach suggests, this is a mistake and Jews should look to their rich heritage and traditions as a way to come together.

Ellis, Marc. *Beyond Innocence and Redemption: The Holocaust, Israel, and the Future of the Jewish People.* San Francisco: Harper & Row, 1990, 214

pp.
Ellis provides an overview of "Holocaust theology," or "that world view which places Jewish destiny within the parameters of the Holocaust and the state of Israel." He argues, that in their attempt to understand how a God of history could have permitted the murder of six million Jews, Holocaust theologians have essentially concluded there are no satisfactory answers. Thus for many, the rabbinic world of synagogue and prayer is no longer sufficient, and the religious duty of the faith must now include the survival of the Jewish people. Since only a sovereign and powerful state can guarantee such survival, "achieving power in Israel reaches the level of sacred principle." Ellis claims, a strong Israel is necessary to prevent a second Holocaust, and he helps readers understand the near-hysterical reaction of many in the Jewish community to criticism, especially when it comes to Israel's mistreatment of the Palestinians.

_____. *Ending Auschwitz: The Future of Jewish and Christian Life.* Louisville: Westminster/John Knox Press, 1994, 162 pp.
With regard to Israeli treatment of the Palestinians, Ellis charges that Jews use the memory of the Holocaust to further policies that oppress the Palestinian people. Ellis argues, Jews and their Christian supporters should stop using the Holocaust as a "blunt instrument against others, protecting our suffering as unique." Instead, the author proposes that Jews let that terrible event function "as a way of understanding and entering into the suffering of others." Ellis also contends, that the present state of Jewish-Christian dialogue in fact masks a religious-political collusion that furthers oppression of the powerless.

_____. *Revolutionary Forgiveness: Essays on Judaism, Christianity and the Future of Religious Life.* Waco, TX.: Baylor University Press, 2000, 337pp.
In a series of essays Ellis speaks to a variety of issues that will impact the future of both Jews and Christians. He criticizes Christianity for trying to minimize its role in the promoting anti-Semitism and for its complicity in the Holocaust. The author discusses the shortcomings of the Vatican in dealing with the Holocaust and in responding to Jews fairly in the aftermath of the atrocity. Furthermore, he condemns Christianity's failure to overcome its belief in its religious superiority. Ellis is also critical of Jews. He contends, that their grief for those who died in the camps and their insistence on assessing blame are insufficient responses to the tragedy and cannot be used to silence questions about the State of Israel's policies towards the Palestinians or anyone else. The author insists, both Christians and Jews turn to God and use the memory of the Holocaust in ways, which will avoid any future atrocities.

Enslin, Morton S. "The Parting of the Ways." The Jewish Quarterly Review (1960-61), Volume 51, pp. 177-197.
The author maintains, that though there was a parting of the ways between

Christians and Jews, Christians cannot overlook the traditions they inherited from Judaism. Enslin recounts some of the factors that contributed to the parting of ways and the invective that followed. He insists, any chance of the two faiths reuniting is slim, yet he is not bothered by that fact. The author concludes, that by coming together Christians and Jews would lose more than they might gain. Enslin recognizes, that both faiths have matured and that they should be able to co-exist peacefully with greater respect for one another and a better understanding of their similarities and differences.

Epstein, Jack. "Roots of Religious Prejudice." Journal of Ecumenical Studies (1968), Volume 5, pp. 697-717.
Epstein makes the case that *New Testament* texts with numerous anti-Jewish references must be revised. He takes issue with the view that these passages cannot be changed and insists, if the scriptures were translated according to their intent, and not by simple mechanics, much of the slander would be amended and made more understandable. Epstein insists if the modifications are not made Christians risk repeating their crimes against the Jews and imparting to the next generation the same anti-Jewish attitudes of the past.

Eron, Lewis John. "The Future of Judaeo-Christian Studies: A Jewish View." Journal of Ecumenical Studies (Winter 1993), Volume 30 Issue 1, pp.108-113.
The prominent role of Judeao-Christian studies is explored in an effort to note the steps needed to promote Jewish-Christian dialogue and to further improve the relationship between the two groups. The events surrounding the Holocaust are part of a discussion about interfaith education.

Eschwege, Helmut. "The Churches and the Jews in the German Democratic Republic." Leo Baeck Institute Year Book (1992), Volume 37, pp. 497-513.
A leading member of the Jewish community, living in the German Democratic Republic, Eschwege focuses his recollections upon the treatment of Jews in East Germany from the year 1945 to the German reunification in 1988. From the 1960's on, the Catholic and Evangelical Churches undertook a dialogue with the Jews to try to repent for the atrocities committed under Nazi governance. This was a direct challenge to the official East German government policy, which held that they too were victims of Hitler, since the Nazi's were West Germans.

Evans, Carl. "The Church's False Witness Against the Jews." Christian Century (May 5, 1982), Volume 99 Issue 16, pp. 520-537.
Evans maintains, Christians bear false witness against Jews because they fail to recognize that Judaism continued to develop as a religion with the *Talmud* and the *Mishnah*. He insists, Christians still believe the *New Testament* completes the promise of the *Old Testament*. Christians must re-educate themselves if they

hope to ever fully appreciate Judaism and the Jewish people.

Everett, Robert Andrew. *Christianity Without Anti-Semitism: James Parkes and the Jewish–Christian Encounter.* **Oxford: Pergamon, 1993, 346 pp.**
Everett follows the evolution of thought that James Parkes, an Anglican theologian, underwent when he pioneered Christian–Jewish dialogue and studied Christianity's influence in developing anti-Semitism. The author focuses upon Parkes' major works and examines the process which led the theologian to conclude, there was in fact a direct link between Christian teachings and the Holocaust. According to Everett, this conclusion led Parkes to call for Christian Churches to work toward a theology that was free from anti-Semitism.

_____. **"Dealing Honestly with Judaism and Jewish History: James Parkes as a Model for the Christian Community."** **Journal of Ecumenical Studies (Winter 1986), Volume 23 Issue 1, pp. 37-57.**
According to Everett, James Parkes', a prominent Anglican scholar and theologian, believed that anti-Semitism could only be countered if Christianity studied Judaism through the works of Jews. Parkes contended, Christianity's interpretations of Jewish sources simply distorted them. The theologian had come to understand that the teachings of Christianity through the *New Testament* had produced an inaccurate portrayal of Jews and Judaism, which resulted in anti-Semitic attitudes. Everett asserts, that Parkes works should be used as a basis for dialogue between Christians and Jews.

Fackenheim, Emil Ludwig. **"Concerning Authentic and Unauthentic Responses to the Holocaust."** **Holocaust and Genocide Studies (1986), Volume 1 Issue 1, pp. 101-120.**
The author takes issue with attempts to treat the Holocaust as an episode, which is unrelated to the histories and attitudes of Germans and Christians. Fackenheim claims, scholars engaged in attempts to provide an authentic response to the Holocaust realize that the Germans and Christian Churches must face their histories, and take responsibility for their role in perpetrating anti-Semitism and the Holocaust. Fackenheim suggests, that Jews must make certain that the memory of those who died at the hands of the Nazis is forever remembered, and that Jews must also reaffirm their commitment to life by committing their support to the Zionist cause.

_____. *Encounters Between Judaism and Modern Philosophy.* **New York: Basic Books, 1973, 275 pp.**
The author, a professor of philosophy at the University of Toronto, has written an inquiry into what standards and what conditions for choosing standards are to be employed in evaluating the cognitive contents of Judaism. In regard to the Holocaust, the author concludes, that Jewish messianic faith has not been falsi-

fied by Auschwitz, and that Jews continue to believe even after the death camps, thus demonstrating that Jewish faith conquers existence. Fackenheim asks, "If the Messiah did not die in the Holocaust, under what circumstances will he?"

____. *God's Presence in History: Jewish Affirmations and Philosophical Reflections;* **Containing the Charles F. Deems Lectures Delivered at New York University in 1968, 104 pp.**
The first lecture projects the concept of a root Jewish religious experience, whereby the author analyzes the instance of the Hebrews at the Red Sea, and asks how, after the Holocaust, can we find, in a similar way, God's presence in history. In his concluding lecture he considers the God who condoned the Holocaust.

____. **"The Holocaust and Philosophy." The Journal of Philosophy (October 1985), Volume 82 Issue 10, pp. 505-514.**
Fackenhiem offers reasons why philosophers have neglected to study the Holocaust. He maintains, that traditionally philosophers have avoided subjects, which are uniquely, related to Jews and negative in nature. According to Fackenhiem the Holocaust was "unique" and was "essentially (not accidentally) anti-Jewish." In this piece he examines the reasons why the Holocaust remains "unique" among other atrocities. In asking how the murder of six million Jews could take place in a "civilized world" the author examines the Christian tradition of portraying the Jews as devils, and the other factors that helped lay a foundation for the Nazi's unprecedented brand of racial anti-Semitism. Ultimately, Fackenhiem concludes, those who committed this unprecedented evil were "humans like ourselves." He notes, philosophers, when pondering the nature of mankind, must now add the element of unspeakable horror to their concept of man and what he is capable of doing.

____. *The Jewish Bible After the Holocaust: A Re-Reading.* **Bloomington: Indiana University Press, 1991, 134 pp.**
This book is based upon a series of the lectures presented by Emil Fackenheim at Manchester University in 1987. Fackenheim uses biblical text to show the relevancy of Judaism in a post-Holocaust world, as well as to examine the relationship between Christians and Jews after the Shoah.

____. **"Jewish Faith and the Holocaust: A Fragment." Commentary (1968), Volume 46 Issue 2, pp. 30-36.**
Fackenheim proposes, that the Holocaust, perpetrated by the Nazis, has no precedent in Jewish or non-Jewish history. The author takes issue with reasons offered for the genocide and insists that Jews and Judaism must survive, or otherwise Hitler claims a victory after death. Furthermore, Fackenheim calls for Christianity to come to terms with the reality of Jews and Judaism, and to com-

Christianity to come to terms with the reality of Jews and Judaism, and to commit itself to ensuring that the Arab nations are not allowed an excuse for repeating the mass murder of Jews.

____. *The Jewish Return Into History: Reflections in the Age of Auschwitz and a New Jerusalem.* **New York: Schocken Books, 1978, 296 pp.**
Written by the author between 1967 and 1977, this collection of essays is divided into three parts. Central to each essay in the section called " The Commanding Voice of Auschwitz," is Fackenheim' pronouncement of the 614th commandment, whereby, he argues, Jews are forbidden to grant Hitler posthumous victories. By this he means that to ensure that the Holocaust never be forgotten, every Jew, survivor or not, must consciously confront the enormity of the horror. In another essay, he argues, that although the Nazis were anti-Christian, their anti-Jewish policies would have been impossible without centuries of Christian anti-Semitism. Additional essays take up the implications of the Holocaust for Jewish faith and life as well as the ethical challenges successes, and failures for both Jews and non-Jews.

____. **"The Nazi Holocaust as a Persisting Trauma for the Non-Jewish Mind." Journal of the History of Ideas (1975), Volume 36 Issue 2, pp 369-76.**
The conclusion Fackenheim reaches is that non-Jewish writers have tried to confront, as well as evade, the trauma of the Holocaust. This is especially true as the atrocity is applied to Christian theology while it attempts to recognize the impact the murder of six million Jews has had on its morality. The author notes, that Christian writers, like Dietrich Bonhoeffer, A. Roy Eckadrt and Rosemary Ruether have confronted the issue of anti-Semitism. However, he insists, that even with the efforts of these scholars, the anti-Jewish attitudes of the past continue to be a matter that ordinary Christians must deal with and renounce.

____. *To Mend the World: Foundations of Future Thought.* **New York: Schocken Books, 1982, 362 pp.**
Using Baruch, Spinoza and Franz Rosenzweig as the foci of his theological construct, Fackenheim explores the possibility of *tikkun (redemption)* to mend the rupture of Jewish theology, which has occurred since the Holocaust. The author's purpose is to show how Jewish theology and revelation remain valid in the face of the Holocaust and to seek answers to the moral debasement humanity has witnessed in this century.

____. **"The People Israel Lives." Christian Century (May 6, 1970), Volume 87 Issue 18, pp. 568.**
This is an apology for not facing the enormous impact of the Holocaust earlier.

Fackenhiem insists, Jews be wary of ignoring the memory of Auschwitz or belittling it in any way. He suggests, that unless Jews renew and keep their covenant with God they risk betraying themselves, their children's future, and the memory of those who died at the hands of the Nazis. The author reminds us, that the threat to Jews did not end with the Holocaust, rather it continues. Despite the dialogue between Christians and Jews, elements of anti-Semitism remain. Christians still retain anti-Jewish attitudes and will continue to harbor them until they consciously face their prejudice and reject it.

____. *Quest for Past and Future: Essays in Jewish Theology.* **Bloomington and London: Indiana University Press, 1968, 336 pp.**
This volume is a collection of eighteen essays by the author, which reflect his more than twenty years of seeking an appropriate response after Auschwitz. His conclusion is "resisting rational, Auschwitz will forever resist religious explanation as well. No religious meaning will ever be found in Auschwitz, for the very attempt to find it is blasphemy."

____**and Michael Lewis Morgan.** *The Jewish Thought of Emil Fackenhiem: A Reader.* **Ed., Michael L. Morgan. Detroit: Wayne State University Press, 1987, 395 pp.**
This anthology of articles and excerpts from books examine the history of Christianity and how its theology is linked to the more modern forms of anti-Semitism, and its implications in the Holocaust. It also studies the uniqueness of the Holocaust, the unprecedented evil of the concentration camps, and theology in a post-Holocaust world.

Farmer, William R., Andre LaCocque and Sean McEvenue, eds. *The International Bible Commentary: A Catholic and Ecumenical Commentary for the Twenty-First Century.* **Liturgical Press, 1998, 918 pp.**
The editors of this volume challenge Christians to read the Bible in an informed manner. The issue of how the messages of evil, violence and anti-Semitism have been made part of Biblical interpretation is addressed, as well as other topics.

Fassching, Darrell. *Narrative Theology After Auschwitz: From Alienation to Ethics.* **Fortress Press, 1992, 198 pp.**
The author's aim is to help bring some understanding to the problem of how and why so many Chrisitans cooperated with the Nazis, or stood by and watched the murder of millions of Jews. The author's intent is to try and persuade Christians that ethics does not mean "blind obedience" to those in authority, rather to be truly ethical one must come to the defense of others even when it means questioning those in power.

____. *The Ethical Challenge of Auschwitz and Hiroshima: Apocalypse or*

Utopia? **Albany: State University of New York Press, 1993, 366 pp.**
Fasching argues, that we can prevent a future Auschwitz and Hiroshima only through constructing a narrative that will block the demonization of the other by elevating human rights, and human dignity to the ultimate level. The argument revolves around the basic distinction between the "sacred and the holy." By the "holy," Fasching means a narrative that constantly brings into question the present order, while at the same time challenging us to accept the other on his own term. The author writes that by weaving together the ideas from Jewish, Christian, Buddhist, and secular teaching, we can show what such a narrative might look like.

Fehrenbach, Ivan, John K. Roth (Afterword). *That Time Cannot be Forgotten.* **Indiana University Press: 2002, 224 pp.**
The written correspondence between Mr. Emil George Sold, a German Catholic born in 1920, and Paul Friedhoff, a German Jew born in 1907, focuses upon what both men felt was the most defining event of their lives; The Holocaust. Though these two men never met one another, the letters they exchanged decades after World War II bound them together in friendship. Their shared understanding of, and ideas about, the Holocaust were meant to help future generations avoid the same tragedy they were forced to confront. Taken in that light, the letters about the genocide provide some hope for the future.

Fein, Helen, ed. *The Persisting Question: Sociological Perspectives and Social Contexts of Modern Anti-Semitism.* **Berlin: Walter deGruyter, 1987, 430 pp.**
There are several chapters of this volume, which deal with the issue of the Christian connection to Anti-Semitism. For instance, Charles Glock points out the "Christian Sources of Anti-Semitism", and Rosemary Ruether examines "The Theological Roots of Anti-Semitism."

Feld, Edward. *The Spirit of Renewal: Finding Faith After the Holocaust.* **Woodstock, Vermont: Jewish Lights Publishing, 1991, 191 pp.**
Rabbi Feld explores the four key events that reshaped Jewish religious expression: The Babylonian exile, the Bar Kochba Revolution, the Holocaust, and the establishment of the State of Israel. Of particular note is the author's careful analysis of how the Holocaust differs from previous events in Jewish history, and how this atrocity forged a new theology of Judaism. Feld concludes by pointing out, that renewing faith after the Holocaust is difficult, but is also both possible and inevitable.

Feldblum, Esther. "On the Eve of a Jewish State: American-Catholic Responses." American Jewish Historical Quarterly (1974), Volume 64, Issue 2, pp. 99-119.
Catholic opposition to the formation of a Jewish state came together in the years

1945–1948. The resistance was based upon theological, psychological, and political considerations. It's own refugee problems, concern about Jewish control of the Holy Land, and the concern that creation of a Jewish state would push Arab populations into the communist camp, compelled the Vatican to resist Zionism.

Feldman, Egal. *Catholics and Jews in Twentieth Century America.* **University of Illinois; 2001, pp. 360.**
The author provides a summary of the relationship between Catholics and Jews in the twentieth century, with some reference to the last century and the medieval period. Feldman notes the improved communications that have developed between the two religious communities in the post-Vatican II era.

Fiedler, Peter. "Categories for a Correct Presentation of Jews and Judaism in Catholic Religious Teaching." Journal of Ecumenical Studies (Summer 1984), Volume 21 Issue 3, pp. 470-488.
Fiedler presents the materials for teaching Catholics about Jews and Judaism that have been produced for use in the Federal Republic of Germany. He contends, there are two important theological presuppositions that must be made in order to successfully revise the image Christians have of Jews and Judaism. First, it must be understood that Judaism is an "independent living body." Second, we must accept Christianity's exclusive relationship with the Jewish religion and people.

Finzi, Roberto. *Anti-Semitism.* **Maud Jackson, Translator. Interlink Publishing Group, Incorporated, 1998, 128 pp.**
Historian Robert Finzi examines the religious origins of anti-Semitism and explores how this anti-Jewish prejudice spilled over into secular society. The author notes, that for several centuries Jews have suffered hatred and persecution and he contends, that despite the Holocaust, aspects of anti-Semitism still persist. This concise history highlights the most significant ways in which anti-Jewish attitudes have been shown and acted upon.

Fisher, Edward. " The Holocaust and Christian Responsibility." America (February 14, 1981), Volume 144, Issue 6, pp. 118-121.
Christians, Fisher cautions, have just begun to answer questions about the extent to which they helped lay the basis for the Holocaust. He wonders how such a tragic event could be allowed to take place and warns Christian Churches against going too far and compromising their religious core, in an effort to atone for the atrocity committed against the Jews

Fisher, Eugene Joseph. "Bibliographic Update 1993-1999." Jewish-Christian Relations, http://www.jcrelations.net, 2002, 9 pp.

On the fiftieth anniversary of the liberation of Auschwitz, Fisher notes that Bishop's Conferences from a variety of countries have felt the need to issue statements concerning the Holocaust and the role played by the Catholic Church in that horrific event. In this article, the author reviews the statements and initiatives that these assemblages have produced. He also points out, that these meetings have had their share of debate over the issue of the Holocaust and the church's relationship to Jews and Judaism.

_____. "Research on Christian Teaching Concerning Jews and Judaism: Past Research and Present Needs." Journal of Ecumenical Studies (Summer 1984), Volume 21 Issue 3, pp. 421-451.
The author explores the studies, which have prompted religious leaders to issue statements in support of the ongoing dialogue between Christians and Jews. Fisher turns his attention to deciding whether or not these statements have been influential in creating a better educational process or teaching Christians about Jews. He concludes, there is both good and bad news. The textbooks that have been developed for teaching Christian students about Jews and Judaism are good. However, though well-intentioned, the instructors teaching the students are not sufficiently educated about their subject matter.

_____, Rosemary Radford Ruether and Anthony Bayfield. "Catholics and Jews Confront the Holocaust and Each Other." World Faiths Encounter (July 2000), Volume 26, pp. 3-23.
Fisher asserts, that since Vatican II Catholics have been intent upon improving their relationship with the Jewish community and that given the efforts of Catholics, Jewish criticisms are overstated. While he admits, the early church provided a foundation for the conflict that has existed between Christians and Jews, he insists that Christians held views that were religiously motivated, not racially inspired. Therefore, Christians cannot be held responsible for the Holocaust. Both Ruether and Bayfield take issue with Fisher's contentions. Ruether's response accuses Fisher of being too easy on Christianity and she points out, that he has failed to see the link between Christianity's brand of hostility toward Jews and the racial hatred of Jews that followed. Bayfield, in agreement with Ruether, maintains, that Jewish criticisms of Christians are justified, and he pushes for increasing the dialogue between the two faith communities

Flannery, Edward H. "Anti-Zionism and the Christian Psyche." Journal of Ecumenical Studies (1969), Volume 6, pp. 173-184.
The author proposes, that by looking at the Holocaust and Christian anti-Zionism it becomes clear that Christians may unconsciously harbor an antipathy toward the Jewish people. In support of his contention, Flannery notes that Church teachings prepared the way for the murder of six million Jews and Christians remained virtually silent when called upon to oppose the Nazi atroc-

ity. Now, according to Flannery, those same people resist the idea of a strong Jewish state. Therefore, the author suggests, that many anti-Zionist Christians are in fact anti-Semites. Flannery warns readers to use his theories carefully, yet hopes, his proposals will facilitate Jewish-Christian dialogue by making some Christians aware of their deepest prejudices.

____. "Anti-Semitism: A Spiritual Disease." Thought (Spring 1966), Volume 41 Issue 160, pp. 33-44.
Flannery examines the ways in which prejudice against Jews has been explained through the work of G.W. Allport, D.J. Levinson, and others. These men tie rigidity of thought, ethnocentrism, and anti-democratic ideas to anti-Semitism. The author also notes the work of Eckardt and Freud, as he points out, that Christians who hold Jews responsible for the killing of Christ are in fact guilty of deicide.

Fleischner, Eva. "The Christian and the Holocaust." Journal of Ecumenical Studies (1970), Volume 7, pp. 331-333.
Refuting Elwyn Smith's call to use the Holocaust as a basis for developing theology, Fleischner contends, that while the murder of six million Jews raises important theological questions, the Holocaust does not serve as a foundation for theology. Furthermore, though these moral questions should be asked, the author insists finding the answers may very well lie beyond human ability. Fleischner also asserts, that despite the pain the Holocaust caused it also provided a ray of hope for those who understand the resilience of the Jewish people. In the face of overwhelming odds, the Jews survived and have finally returned to Israel.

____. Judaism in German Christian Theology Since 1945. Lanham, Scarecrow Press, 1945, 205 pp.
The author questions how the Holocaust has affected German Christian attitudes towards Jews, since the war ended, given the long tradition of anti-Semitism in pre-Nazi Germany. The author attempts to show that since 1945 the Jews have been objects of proselytizing. After Auschwitz, however, Germans found this task difficult, and therefore the mission to the Jews has given way to dialogue. Fleischner, however, questions whether such an approach is merely a more subtle attempt to convert Jews.

____, ed. Auschwitz: Beginning of a New Era? Reflections on the Holocaust. New York: KTAV Publishing House, 1977, 469 pp.
This anthology consists of ten major themes addressed by twenty-six Jewish and Christian contributors. The essays explore the extent of responsibility that Christianity bears for the Holocaust, since Church teachings have fostered centuries of anti-Judaism. Some of the questions raised in this work, which is based on essays first presented at the 1974 International Symposium on the Holocaust in

New York, include the degree to which Christianity should revise those aspects of its doctrines that contributed to the Holocaust, as well as the level of guilt Christians should acknowledge for betraying their Jewish parent.

Flescher, Andrew. "Characterizing the Acts of Righteous Gentiles: A Matter of Duty or Supererogation?" The Journal of Religion and Society (2000), Volume 2, pp. 1-9.
Flescher points out, that although others proclaims that the Holocaust rescuers were heroic, they see themselves as merely having done what was morally expected. In other words, they simply did their "duty." The author suggests that we should take them at their word. This does not, according to Flescher, make their actions less important, but it demonstrates that these rescuers had a deep and ethically binding understanding of duty. Others who failed to help the Jews lacked this ethical underpinning, which they should have had if they considered themselves morally upright.

Fogel, Yehezkel ed. *I Will Be Sanctified: Religious Responses to the Holocaust.* Edward Levin, Translator. Northvale: Jason Aronson, 1998, 213 pp.
These essays by Jewish writers have been gathered in an attempt to understand the place of the Holocaust in Jewish history and religion. The editor has chosen essays that provide insight into the *halakhic* mind as it seeks to apply traditional Jewish religious law to situations of life and death, such as were manifested during the *Shoah.* Contributors, such as Hayyim Kanfo and Nissim Nadav, record acts of religious heroism during the Holocaust, whereby observant Jews defied the Nazis by maintaining their faith and religious rituals, despite oppression and suffering.

Fogelman, Eva. *Conscience & Courage: Rescuers of Jews During the Holocaust.* Wilmington: Anchor Books, 1994, 393 pp.
Explanations are offered, by the author, as to why the rescuers of Holocaust victims acted as they did. Fogelman divides rescuers into five categories; those driven by moral and ethical reasons, those who had special relationships with Jews, those who opposed the policies of the Third Reich and joined rescuer networks, those in professions such as medicine and social work who naturally provided assistance to the Jews, and children who became involved in rescue efforts through their families. Included in her survey is a discussion of the Christian Churches in rescuing Jews.

Frey, Robert Seitz and Nancy Thompson-Frey. *The Imperative of Response: The Holocaust in Human Context.* Lanham, MD.: University Press of America, 1985, 165 pp.
In light of their Holocaust studies, the authors converse about the moral and theological difficulties that have resulted from the murder of six million Jews.

They cite the need for a revision of Christian and Western ideology. The Frey's own conversion to Judaism serves as the context in which they base their ideas.

Friedlander, Albert H. *Riders Towards Dawn: From Holocaust to Hope.* **New York: Continuum Press, 1994, 328 pp.**
The book's title refers to those who strive for a new vision of hope and ethical reconstruction in the wake of the Holocaust. Among those included in this category are survivors such as, Paul Celan, Primo Levi, and Elie Wiesel as well as Righteous Christians such as Dieterich Bonhoeffer, Martin Niemoller, and postwar theologians such as Eugene Borowitz, Irving Greenberg, and Paul Tillich among others. The author compares the approaches used in coping with catastrophes, theologies of evil, sin and forgiveness, and the politics of remembrance and oblivion in both the Jewish and Christian traditions. Friedlander's book strives for a compassionate, humanistic understanding of the postwar reality, rather than complacent trivialization of the Holocaust.

Friedlander, Henry, and Sybil Milton, ed. *The Holocaust: Ideology, Bureaucracy, and Genocide--The San Jose Papers.* **Millwood: Kraus International Publications, 1980, 361 pp.**
Twenty-five papers comprise this book. All were given at the National Conference of Christians and Jews in San Jose, California in 1977 and 1978. Most of the essays skillfully synthesize large bodies of historical research and offer conceptually sophisticated generalizations about key problems in the history of the Holocaust.

Fry, Helen P., ed. *Christian-Jewish Dialogue: A Reader.* **Exeter: University of Exeter Press, 1996, 324 pp.**
Fry includes excerpts of theological documents and statements made by representatives from both the Jewish and Christian religions. These excerpts cover a variety of topics that impact upon Jewish-Christian dialogue. Included is a discussion of Christian anti-Semitism, the link it had to the Holocaust, the impact of the Holocaust on both faith communities, and the difficulties and misunderstandings that continue to surround Christian missionary activities.

Fumagalli, Pier Francesco. "The Church and the Jewish People: Twenty-Five Years after the Second Vatican Council (1963-65)." SIDIC (1992), Volume 25 Issue 2, pp. 18-27.
The author reviews the improvements made in the Jewish-Christian relationship over the past twenty-five years. He cites the positive outcome of Vatican II, which included the Church's rejection of anti-Semitism and affirmation of the Jews as a valued people who remain God's 'beloved." Fumagalli provides suggestions that may prove useful for Christian educators who are teaching about Jews and Judaism. He includes an appendix of fifty-one documents that track

Jews and Judaism. He includes an appendix of fifty-one documents that track the high points of the ongoing dialogue between Jews and Christians.

Funkenstein, Amos. "Theological Interpretations of the Holocaust: An Evaluation." Tel Aviv Review (1988), Volume 1, pp. 67-100.
Funkelstein traces the history of anti-Semitism and Christianity's role in promoting it to support his claim, that it is a fruitless endeavor to search for theological significance in the Holocaust. He suggests, instead, we should concentrate on the information that the Holocaust provides about man and his ability to commit evil. He concludes, that while Christian anti-Jewish attitudes played a role in the genocide of World War II, other factors were necessary for anti-Semitism to lead to the Nazi's "Final Solution to the Jewish Question." While the author is critical of Heidegger's theories, he views Primo Levi's ideas in a favorable light.

Gager, John G. "Judaism as Seen by Outsiders." *Early Judaism and Its Modern Interpreters*. Eds. Robert A. Kraft and George W.E. Nickelsburg. Atlanta, GA.: Scholars Press, 1996, pp. 99-116.
There are two parts to Gager's essay. The first addresses the debate since World War II surrounding the issue of whether or not the *New Testament* and Christianity have been historically anti-Semitic and therefore, bear responsibility for the development of modern forms of anti-Semitism. Gager cites the arguments of Jules Isaac and Rosemary Ruether, as well as their critics. Part two focuses upon the pagan perspective of Jews and Judaism. The author, through an examination of Hellenistic and Roman texts, concludes that while Jews were admired through antiquity, their militant nationalism and influence were a source of fear for non-Jews.

Garber, Zev. *Shoah: The Paradigmatic Genocide: Essays in Exegesis and Eisegesis*. Lanham: University Press of America, 1994, 213 pp.
In the essays included in this volume, Garber views the Holocaust as both a historical event and a theological watershed. The author argues for a critique of the collaboration of the Church and Nazi ideologies, and calls for a meaningful dialogue about the Holocaust with Christian interlocutors.

Garvey, John. "Facing Anti-Semitism." Commonweal (March 8, 2002) Volume 129 Issue 5, pp. 9.
Garvey responds to Daniel Jonah Goldhagen's article, "What Would Jesus Have Done? ", which was published in the January 21, 2002 issue of *New Republic*. The author argues, while there is vast agreement over the fact that the Catholic and Protestant Churches failed to meet their moral obligation during the Holocaust, Goldhagen has presented his evidence in a bigoted fashion. Garvey also discusses the problems present in Goldhagen's thesis and his dependence on flawed evidence taken from James Carrol's recent book, *Constantine's Sword*.

Gellman, Jack A. *A Brighter Future after 2000 Years of Christian Churches vs. Judaism: Why Pope John II Apologizes.* **Universe Incorporated, 2000, 198 pp.**
Gellman asserts, he is providing the reader with "the true story of two thousand years of the Roman Catholic Church's persecution of the Jews." The volume includes all of the anti-Jewish laws issued by the Church, the reasons why they were put forward, and the misery these edicts caused for the Jews. The author also contends, that Hitler used the Church's edicts against the Jews as models for his own anti-Semitic policies. These policies, which were taken to extremes that the Church never countenanced, culminated in the Holocaust. Gellman commends the Catholic and Protestant Churches for rejecting all types of anti-Semitic ideology and for their attempts to apologize to the Jewish community for past crimes.

Geras, Norman. *The Contract of Mutual Indifference: Political Philosophy After the Holocaust.* **London, New York: Verso Press, 1998, 181 pp.**
The author focuses on the "bystanders" of the Holocaust, those ordinary Germans, Poles, and others, who were guilty of inaction while Jews went to their deaths. For Geras, the bystanders exemplify what he terms "the contract of mutual indifference." The author's condemnation extends to the widespread indifference displayed when people "ignore" the torture, hunger and other varieties of suffering currently found in the world. The author argues, that a "mental turning away" is characteristic of the bystander mind-set. He also acknowledges, the natural human tendency to block out an unbearable reality. This, he insists, is a temptation that must be resisted if the "contract of mutual indifference" is to be broken.

Gershom, Yonassan. *Beyond the Ashes: Cases of Reincarnation from the Holocaust.* **Northvale: Jason Aronson, 1992, 276 pp.**
Rabbi Gershom is a Hasidic storyteller, teacher, and writer. He presents "compelling" evidence that people living today have died in past lives during the Holocaust.

_____. *From Ashes to Healing: Mystical Encounters With the Holocaust: Fifteen True Stories. Northvale*: **Jason Aronson, 1999, 281 pp.**
This book is a companion volume to the author's first book, *Beyond the Ashes: Cases of Reincarnation from the Holocaust* (1992). Both books deal with the subject of Holocaust reincarnation cases. The thesis in *From Ashes to Healing* is that the pain and suffering of those who died in the Holocaust still throbs as a psychic pain, even though the souls of these former victims have reincarnated into new bodies and new lives. The book details the stories of fourteen people who provide gripping first-person narratives about their mystical encounters with the Holocaust; past life memories of being in concentration camps,

earthbound souls still at the site of Auschwitz, and a group of spirit rabbis appearing in dreams and visions to heal lost souls.

Giacomini, George F. "We Remember." America (April 2, 2001), Volume 184 Issue 11, pp. 26-27.
The author discusses some of the recent books published about Pope Pius XII and his opposition, or lack of resistance, to the Nazis during the Holocaust. The author notes, that while most of these volumes charge Pius with having failed to act in an adequate manner to stop the extermination of the Jews, each author takes a different approach to his study of the pontiff. For example, while one writer focuses upon the pope's obsession with diplomacy, another examines Pius's high regard for all things German, or his intolerant attitude toward the Jewish people.

Gilbert, Arthur. "Jewish Resistance to Dialogue." Journal of Ecumenical Studies (1967), Volume 4, pp. 280-289.
In the past Christians have coerced, oppressed, preached to and manipulated Jews, and called this "dialogue." Given this tradition, when Christians desire and encourage true dialogue with Jews, they should not be surprised if Jews seem hesitant to welcome offers of open and mutual discourse. Gilbert notes, that many Christians still see Judaism as a precursor for Christianity and regard Jews as potential converts. Therefore, some Jewish leaders promote keeping followers of the two faiths at arms length. The author encourages those within the Jewish leadership to overcome their reservations and to enter into dialogue with Christians, but he also cautions Christians to understand why Jews might be fearful of meeting them halfway.

_____. " A Jewish Response." Dialogue (Summer 1967), Volume 6 Issue 3, pp. 176-183.
In this response to Harold Ditmanson's article, "Christian Declaration on Anti-Semitism" presented in _Dialogue_ (Summer 1967), Gilbert states, that despite the recent efforts and statements made by Christian Churches seeking dialogue with Jews, these churches still teach lessons that slander Jews and Judaism. The author maintains,that the relationship between Christians and Jews is unequal because "Christians hold the power and guilt on their side." Gilbert maintains, Jews have reason to be concerned about Chrisitan beliefs. He critiques the statements issued from church councils in the past few years.

_____. _The Vatican Council and the Jews._ Cleveland: World Publishing Company, 1968, 322 pp.
Rabbi Gilbert traces the evolution of the Catholic Church's teachings from the Fourth Lateran Council, which was presided over by Pope Innocent III in 1215, and crystallized the anti-Semitic tradition in Roman Catholicism, through to the

Second Vatican Council, which created and published "A Statement on the Jews."

Gillman, Nell. "Authenticity Without Demonization." Journal of Ecumenical Studies (Summer 1997), Volume 34 Issue 3, pp. 346-349.
Gillman reminds us that no one person has a "fix on God." Each human discovers God and then builds his/her own set of myths and images in order to make God more understandable. None of these images or myths, however, can be proved or disproved. They simply represent a plurality of human perspectives on God and God's word." Therefore we must teach our children "theological humility," which is the acceptance of differing beliefs, rather than the demonization of the religious ideas of others that differ from our own.

Glick, David. "Reflections on the Holocaust." Pastoral Psychology (September 1995), Volume 44 Issue 1, pp. 13-29.
Glick examines the divisions that exist between Christians and Jews and notes the impact of Christianity's "teachings of contempt" towards Jews. The author also reflects upon the Catholic Church's relationship with the Nazis as well as the Holocaust and its uniqueness in history.

Goldberg, Michael. *Why Should the Jews Survive?* New York and Oxford: Oxford University Press, 1995, 191 pp.
Goldberg's book discusses the problem of Holocaust-centered Judaism, which enshrines a view of Jews as the passive victims of a cruel anti-Semitic world that is closed to "divine salvific hope and redemptive possibility." The "cult" of the Holocaust, argues Goldberg, has preoccupied Jews with victim-hood, and an indifference to Judaism, focusing on an absent God to whom it seems absurd to pray. Goldberg suggests, that the way to survive this condition is to juxtapose the bitter Holocaust story with the alternative Exodus redemption story. Just as Hebrews were slaves to Pharaoh, Jews were slaves to Hitler, but in both cases God brought the Jews to freedom. The Exodus story, Goldberg argues, has all the resources Jews need to understand and to cope with the Holocaust.

Goldstein, David. "A Catholic Approach to Jews." The Ecclesiastical Review (July 1942), Volume 107 Issue 1, pp. 18-27.
American Catholics are challenged in this article to develop a national approach to converting the Jews. The author contends, sometime after World War II the initial feelings of remorse for anti-Semitism will dissipate and once that occurs new anti-Jewish movements will begin. The author cautions Catholics to resist becoming involved with these for that will harden Jews against the Catholic faith. Goldstein suggests, that the Church in America create a department to produce and provide educational programs about Catholicism for Jews. He maintains, Jews are "suffering a spiritual crisis" because they have refused to

are "suffering a spiritual crisis" because they have refused to accept Christ and it is the duty of Catholics to "lead them from spiritual darkness."

Gorsky, Jonathan. "Christian-Jewish Relations." *The Jewish Year Book.* **London: Valentine Mitchell, 2000, pp. 32-41.**
Gorsky traces the founding and history of the Council of Christians and Jews (CJC). He notes that when originally begun in 1942, Jews hoped the organization would serve as a platform for fighting anti-Semitism. However, Christians did not recognize a need to atone for their tradition of anti-Jewish teachings. In the post-war era joint activities were hampered by Jewish suspicions about Christian missionary efforts. Since those days there have been positive moves by many Christian Churches to repudiate anti-Semitism, and to end the work of the missions. Today the CJC is finally realizing its potential and is engaged in teaching groups about the dangers of anti-Semitism, racism, and the Holocaust.

Grace, Kevin Michael. "Libeling a Dead Pope." Alberta Report (November 8, 1999), Volume 26 Issue 41, pp. 60-62.
The author notes the revisionist views concerning Pope Pius XII's actions in assisting the Jews during World War II. Grace maintains, that views portraying Pius as "The devil's handmaiden" are inflammatory and libelous. He reports that Rabbi Daniel Lapin, author of *America's Real War,* has urged Catholics to "stop the apologies" and to "fight back against these heinous slurs." The Rabbi contends that "anti-Catholic" Jews are not representative of all Jews. He worries, that if those few "secular Jews" who have instigated the constant drumbeat of calling Christians to task for past offences do not stop their attacks, there could be a backlash against all Jews.

Greenberg, Irving. "Judaism and Christianity After the Holocaust." Journal of Ecumenical Studies (1975), Volume 12 Issue 4, pp. 521-551.
This article briefly sketches the dangers of allowing secular faith and religious humanism to overshadow the realities of history. Greenberg proposes, that Christianity has failed to face the reality of the Holocaust. He offers reasons for this failure, and prompts Christianity to acknowledge its shame and confront the Holocaust in a reasoned way.

Griffiths, Paul J. "CODA." Faith and Philosophy (1994), Volume 11 Issue 2, pp. 286-289.
Griffiths argues, that to contend Christianity is not responsible for anti-Semitic attitudes, because the differences concerning the doctrinal debate between Christians and Jews led to anti-Judaism, and not the sociological manifestation of anti-Semitism, is a mistake. According to the author, the distinction, if there is one, is very small.

Grondelski, John M. "Theological Literature in Poland on Catholic-Jewish Relations since the Auschwitz Convent Controversy, A Survey." Polish Review (1992), Volume 37 Issue 3, pp. 285-296.
Grondelski lists sources that scholars interested in the Holocaust should refer to when studying the ways in which the controversies surrounding the placement of a Carmelite Convent at Auschwitz have affected the relationship between Christians and Jews. The author concludes, that shared values provide a basis for reconciliation between the two communities.

Gushee, David P. "Learning From the Christian Rescuers: Lessons for the Churches." The Annals of the American Academy of Political and Social Sciences (November1996), pp. 138-155.
According to the author, the non-Jews who assisted Jews during the Holocaust provided an example of moral behavior for the Christian Churches that failed to respond appropriately or adequately to the murder of European Jewry. Gushee focuses in particular upon the lessons that hold specific import for religious tolerance towards the Jews, the Christian community, spirituality, the Bible, patriotism, and the development of character and moral leadership for Christianity.

_____. The Righteous Gentiles of the Holocaust: A Christian Interpretation. Minneapolis: Fortress Press, 1994, 258 pp.
The author states, that it is a "stunning" Christian failure that only one percent of European Gentiles risked their lives to help save Jews. Gushee asks whether anything useful can be learned from the tiny minority of rescuers, and offers an interpretation of their significance for Christian ethics and the church.

Gutman, Yisrael and Saf Avital, eds. Major Changes Within the Jewish People in the Wake of the Holocaust: Proceedings of the Ninth Yad Vashem International Historical Conference. Jerusalem: Yad Vashem, 1996, 754 pp.
Several of the papers that appear in this text address the role Christianity has played in anti-Semitism and the Holocaust. Included among the topics are studies about, the historical development of anti-Jewish and/or anti-Semitic attitudes, the problems surrounding atonement and forgiveness, the Christian perspective on the Holocaust, the creation of the State of Israel, and the recent attempts by some Christian Churches to revise their doctrines and teachings concerning Jews and Judaism.

Haar, Murray J. "Job After Auschwitz."A Journal of Bible and Theology (July1999), Volume 53 Issue3, pp. 265-276.
In using the Bible as a means to examine the theological implications of the Holocaust, the author rethinks the *Book of Job* and places it within the context of Hitler's plans to exterminate the Jews. Haar examines God's actions and the failures of Christianity and Judaism in connection with the Holocaust.

Haas, Peter J. *Morality After Auschwitz: The Radical Challenge of the Nazi Ethic.* **Philadelphia: Fortress Press, 1988, 257 pp.**
Haas carefully traces the intellectual and historical background that gave rise to the "Nazi ethic" by focusing, not on the question of how the Nazis and their collaborators could do what they knew to be evil, but rather on how they were able to redefine evil. He examines how their views came to dominate an entire nation, and how they acted out the logical implications of their own ethical theory. The author approaches the Holocaust as a problem in ethical theory. The thrust of his argument is that the Nazis created a coherent ethic that enabled them to justify their barbaric actions against the Jews.

Hackel, Sergii." The Relevance of Western Post-Holocaust Theology to the Thought and Practice of the Russian Orthodox Church." Jewish-Christian Relations, http://www.jcrelations.net, 2002, 13 pp.
The author notes, it has taken over thirty years for Russians to admit the Jews were singled out for persecution, in 1941, by the German army when it attacked Russia. Hackel commends the efforts that Jews, the Vatican, and other Christian faiths have made to increase religious dialogue. He credits these efforts with helping the Russian Orthodox Church to finally confront the tragedy of the Holocaust. The author admits, that progress has been slow and does not believe that Orthodox Christianity will hasten its efforts to reconcile with the Jews. However, Hackel contends that since the Russian Orthodox Church has begun to explore the theological implications of the Holocaust, there is every reason to hope the progress will continue.

Halff, Antione. 'Lutherans Rebuke Luther for Anti-Jewish Diatribes." Forward (May 20, 1994), Volume 98 Issue 30, 976, pp. 1.
Following months of discussion, the Evangelical Lutheran Church of America put forth a statement condemning Martin Luther's anti-Jewish rhetoric and teachings. The Lutheran Church had long denied that Church officials had ever taken Luther's diatribe seriously. Still it acknowledged the tragic effects Luther's rhetoric had on subsequent generations, and asked to be forgiven for these sins against the Jews. The author examines the way in which Luther's works helped shape more modern forms of anti-Semitism. Halff notes that while many Jewish leaders were heartened by the Lutheran Church's apology, there is still a lot of work to be done. The *New Testament* laid the foundation for Luther's anti-Jewish attitudes and, Halff insists, that until it is revised, the anti-Semitic messages in its texts still work to denigrate Jews and Judaism.

Halvini, David Weiss. *The Book and the Sword: A Life of Learning in the Shadow of the Destruction.* **New York: Farrar, Straus & Giroux, 1996, 224 pp.**
Halvini grew up in the town of Sighet in the Carpathian Mountains. This is the

same village where Elie Wiesel was raised. He is both a survivor of Auschwitz and a preeminent Talmudic scholar. The author recalls how his love for, and commitment to, the *Talmud* kept him alive and sane through his separation from his parents, his ordeals in Auschwitz, and the Gross Rosen concentration camps. Halvini also writes of his struggle for faith after the Holocaust.

Hargrove, Katherine T., ed. *Seeds of Reconciliation*. D and F Scott Publishing, Incorporated, 1996, 242 pp.
Hargrove has long played a prominent role in contributing to, and pushing forward, the dialogue between Christians and Jews. This volume is a collection of articles written by her counterparts. They cover a variety of the issues connected to the developing relationship between Christians and Jews.

Harrelson, Walter and Randall M. Falk. *Jews and Christians: A Troubled Family*. Nashville, TN. Abingdon Press, 1990, 208 pp.
A Jewish Rabbi (Falk) and Christian educator (Harrelson) discuss the problems that hamper the ongoing dialogue between Jews and Christians. They comment upon the anti-Jewish prejudice that has long infected Christianity, the Christian reactions to the murder of the Jews both before and after the Holocaust, the impact of the Holocaust on Christian theology, and the current state of Christian views about the conflict in the Middle East. Both men recognize the attempts by Christian Churches to overcome their age old, anti-Judaic feelings, and the efforts to positively engage with Jews.

Hartman, Geoffrey H, ed. *Bitburg in Moral and Political Perspective*. Bloomington: Indiana University Press, 1986. 284 pp.
This book consists of ten essays written on the occasion of former President Reagan's visit to the SS cemetery in Bitburg, West Germany in May of 1985. There are contributions by Theodor Adorno, Jurgen Habermas, Raul Hilberg, and Primo Levi. The essays, mostly critical of the President, are a response to Reagan's visit to Bitburg.

Hauerwas, Stanley. "Jews and Christians Among the Nations." Cross Currents (Spring 1981), Volume 31 Issue 1, pp. 15-43.
The author proposes, that the Holocaust could not have happened without Christian anti-Semitism, and that Christianity failed to oppose the Nazis in part because it recognized God as the Creator for Christians, rather than for all men. Hauerhaus insists, Christianity must radically alter its politics in order to finally achieve a true partnership with the Jews.

Haynes, Stephen R. "Changing Paradigms: Reformist, Radical, and Rejectionist Approaches to the Relationship Between Christianity and Anti-Semitism." Journal of Ecumenical Studies (1995), Volume 32 Issue 1, pp.

63-88.

Haynes discusses the changing ideas of twentieth century scholars who have chosen to study the connection between Christianity and anti-Semitism. Some have minimized the role of religion in promoting hatred of Jews. Others have acknowledged the guilt of Christianity in perpetrating anti-Semitism, while continuing to maintain that this prejudice had little to do with the Holocaust. After the 1960's a majority of scholars accepted the fact that anti-Semitism lays at the heart of Christianity. These "radicals" propose, that the Bible and other Christian liturgy must be cleansed of offensive passages. Despite this shift in thinking, some non-Christians believe these changes will probably not take place.

____. **"Christian Holocaust Theology: A Critical Reassessment." Journal of the American Academy of Religion (Summer 1994), Volume 62 Issue 2, pp. 553-585.**

Haynes focuses upon the small group of Christian Holocaust theologians, whom the author contends, are set apart from other theologians, in that they maintain the Holocaust holds great significance for Christian theology. These scholars admit the responsibility Christian anti-Judaism bears for the Holocaust, and criticize the remnants of anti-Jewish thinking that remain in the hearts and minds of some Christian clerics and theologians. However, according to Haynes, their recognition and assessment of a link between Christian hatred of Jews and Nazi anti-Semitism can prove to be historically troubling. Moreover, they are so far removed from the theological center, that most scholars inhabit, that their suggestions for reform are viewed, at best, as unworkable.

____. *Jews and the Christian Imagination: Reluctant Witnesses.* **Basingstoke, Hants:Macmillan, 1995, 221 pp.**

The author proposes, Christians have, through the ages, placed Jews in a theological role as witnesses to the validity of Christianity. Though this myth protected Jews through the Middle Ages, it also led to an escalation of anti-Jewish fervor. This hostility toward the Jews, spawned by Christianity, eventually found new outlets and ultimately played a role in the Nazis "Final Solution" for the Jews. Haynes contends, that although the Christian Churches of today would insist they harbor no anti-Semitic attitudes, remnants of this myth of the Jew as a witness to the Christian faith, remain intact. Even if it is presented as philo-Semitic, it is covertly anti-Jewish.

____."**Theology as Fiction and Fiction as Theology: Karl Barth and Percy Walker on "the Jews." Literature and Theology (December 1991), Volume 5Issue 4, pp. 388-407.**

In this article Haynes makes the case that despite their philo-Semitic intent the work of both Barth, the theologian and Percy Walker, the author of fiction, contain mythological depictions of the Jews that hinders their ability to live out a normal existence. Haynes insists, in the post-Holocaust world Christianity must rid itself of the myths it has constructed about the Jews so they can take the opportunity to create normal lives for themselves.

_____ **and John K. Roth.** *The Death Of God Movement and the Holocaust: Radical Theology Encounters the Shoah.* **Westport: Greenwood Publishing Inc., 1999, 176 pp.**
"Death of God" theologians represented one of the most influential religious movements of the 1960's, a decade in which theology underwent revolutionary changes. Four theologians who sparked radical changes---Thomas Altizer, William Hamilton, Richard Rubenstein, and Paul Van Buren---all considered the Holocaust to be one of the main challenges to Christian faith. This book asks the four radical theologians to reflect on how awareness of the Holocaust has affected their thinking, from the 1960's to the present.

Heinze, Andrew R. "Clare Boothe Luce and the Jews: A Chapter from the Catholic-Jewish Disputation of Postwar America." American Jewish History (2000), Volume 88 Issue 3, pp. 361-376.
Heinze explores the charge of anti-Semitism leveled against Clare Boothe Luce, a powerful Catholic writer and celebrity of the 1940's and 50's, in a 1948 article printed in *The American Scholar*. The article examines Luce's diaries and letters and determines that her attitude toward Jews was far more complex than the 1948 article states. In reality Luce, a Catholic convert, never totally accepted Catholicism's anti-Jewish stance.

Heschel, Susannah. "Anti-Judaism in Christian Feminist Theology." Tikkun (May-June 1990), Volume 5 Issue 3, pp. 95-97.
Feminist theology, according to the author, is replete with anti-Semitic beliefs. Heschel reports the three most important ideas that feminists embrace when indicting Judaism. First and foremost, they claim that the Jewish religion is responsible for patriarchy and that by replacing the "ancient goddess" image with a monotheistic faith, Jews destroyed the peaceful existence of society. They also maintain Christianity holds the solution to anti-feminist attitudes, and finally feminists support their contentions by showing that Christianity supported women by rejecting the negative treatment Jews afforded women in the first century. Some German women theologians have gone so far as to compare Judaism's treatment of women to Nazi policies. Though these women reject the theology offered by male Christians, they remain especially hostile toward the Jews and the Jewish faith.

Himmelfarb, Martin. "Some Attitudes Towards the Jews." Commentary (May 1963), Volume 35 Issue 5, pp. 424-429.
According to Himmelfarb, anti-Semtism still exists in the Soviet Union. The

author contends, that the Soviets may well deny accusations of anti-Semitic policies but, the facts show otherwise. The author also examines the irony in the fact that while Christianity throughout the centuries has demonized the Jews, its efforts led to two twentieth century anti-Christians (Hitler and Stalin) who took over the persecution of the Jews.

Holmgren, Frederick. *The God Who Cares.* **Louisville: John Knox Press, 1982, 144 pp.**
The author has written a guide for Christians who are unfamiliar with the teachings of Judaism. He takes some of the still widely held stereotypes about Judaism, such as the belief that Christianity is a religion of love, whereas Judaism is a religion of law, and holds these generalizations up to the light of honest scholarship to show the changes in Christian teaching and thinking since the Holocaust.

Huneke, Douglas K. *The Stones Will Cry Out.* **Westport, Conn: Greenwood Press, 1995, 232 pp.**
Huneke, a Holocaust scholar and parish minister, explains how encounters with the Holocaust have reformed his theology and informed his approaches to teaching, preaching, counseling, and social justice. He combines historical and theological insights with practical suggestions that show Christians how to respond to the Holocaust in ways that can mend the world.

Irwin-Zarecka, Iwona. "After the Holocaust: National Attitudes to Jews: Catholics and Jews in Poland Today." Holocaust and Genocide Studies (1989), Volume 4 Issue 1, pp. 27-40.
Though Poles currently discuss issues concerning Jews in a more open and moral way, according to the author, they do not address the issue of the Catholic Church's record regarding Jews historically, or during the Holocaust. The author contends, as Polish citizens come to better understand Jews the possibility for honest reflections about the Holocaust will emerge. This will bring about a recognition of broader moral responsibility for the crimes against Jews.

Jacobs, Steven L, ed. *Contemporary Christian Religious Responses to the Holocaust.* **Lanham: University Press of America, 1993, 336 pp.**
This selection of essays by prominent Christian theologians and intellectuals, such as the late Harry James Cargas and John Pawlikowski, is devoted to Christian theological self-exploration with regard to the Holocaust. The notion that Christianity must be rethought in the aftermath of the destruction of European Jewry provides the underlying theme for most of the essays.

___, ed. *Contemporary Jewish Religious Responses to the Shoah.* **Lanham: University Press of America, 1993, 264 pp.**

The volume includes essays by such eminent Jewish thinkers as Emil Fackenheim, Irving Greenberg, and Richard Rubenstein. The writings focus on the manner in which contemporary Jewry has been impacted by the Holocaust.

____. "A Jewish Response to Byron L. Sherwin's 'A New Jewish View of Jesus'." Journal of Ecumenical Studies (Spring 1995), Volume 32 Issue 2, pp. 225-232.
Jacob's welcomes Sherwin's ideas, yet suggests that he has not gone far enough in addressing how the issue of Jesus should be handled between Jews and Christians. Throughout history Jesus and his Crucifixion have been a basis for demonizing the Jews. Sherwin concludes, that Jews might well regard Jesus as a failed Jewish messiah but, according to Jacobs, that idea is too simplistic. However, he believes Sherwin's efforts might well prompt Jewish thinkers to begin developing a theology that deals with the thornier differences between the two faith communities.

Jaffee, Martin. "The Victim-Community in Myth and History: Holocaust Ritual, the Question of Palestine, and the Rhetoric of Christian Witness." Journal of Ecumenical Studies (Spring 1991), Volume 28 Issue 2, pp. 223-238.
The author discusses the distressing impact that the Jewish and Palestinian conflict has had upon the Jewish-Christian dialogue that has taken place in the post-Holocaust era. Jaffee notes, that each group has its own perception of what it means to have been victimized. Jews and Palestinians, in their current struggle, look to Christianity to provide an answer to their conflict that will render justice to both sides. Christianity, according to Jaffee, speaks out from the view that its God, in the body of a Jew, was victimized some two thousand years ago, and yet it must also address its long held role as the victimizer of Jews. Now Christians are caught in the dilemma of trying to find ways to make amends for its past anti-Semitism, but as it condemns hatred of the Jews (including the hostility that Islam harbors toward Jews), Christianity must also make certain the Palestinians receive fair treatment.

Jastrow, Morris Jr. "The Jewish Question in Its Recent Aspects." International Journal of Ethics (July 1896), Volume 6 Issue 4, pp. 457-479.
This article, written over one hundred years ago, presents problems facing the Jewish population externally and internally. The author contends, that the external problems for Jews appeared as Christianity evolved and took on its own identity. Religious conflict developed between the two groups. This religious conflict, according to Jastrow, has been replaced by more modern anti-Semitic ideologies. One aspect of this hatred holds that Jews and non-Jews should not mix so that racial purity can be preserved. The author contends, that notions of racial purity and national traits are "scientific myths." that must be rejected. In-

ternally the struggle for Jews, in Jastrow's view, centers on maintaining their identity and their relation to Judaism. The author offers no clear answers for Jews, but suggests that assimilation does not mean Jews must surrender their character, or their religious convictions.

Johnson, Luke Timothy. "The Church and Anti-Semitism." Commonweal (March 8, 2002), Volume 129 Issue 5, pp. 7-9.
Johnson presents a criticism of the Daniel Goldhagen article, "What Would Jesus Have Done?" (*New Republic,* January 21, 2002) condemning the Catholic Church for its role in the Holocaust. Johnson agrees, that the Church's record is dismal when it comes to the treatment of Jews, and stipulates that the facts surrounding its response to the Holocaust fell well short of what was needed. The author insists, however, the tone of indictment that seems to marking the latest publications on this subject is troubling. These works are less historical in approach than prosecutorial. In an effort to restore some civility to the discourse Johnson suggests the Catholic Church drop the issue of sainthood for Pius XII. He also proposes that Daniel Goldhagen tone down his rhetoric, that Cardinal Rattinger should "be quiet", and that James Carroll should table whatever personal disagreements he holds with the church. Ultimately, Johnson asks all parties to engage in serious scholarship in order to understand the complexities of the issues concerning Jews and Christians, and the Holocaust.

Jonas, Hans. *Mortality and Morality: A Search for the Good After Auschwitz.* Introduction by Lawrence Vogel. Chicago: Northwestern University Press, 1996, 218 pp.
The author, one of the most prominent philosophers of this generation, was a pupil of Martin Heidegger, whose mother was murdered at Auschwitz. Jonas discusses the role of reason, as well as the place of Auschwitz, in thinking about morality and God, the nature of modernity, and the place of the individual in the midst of the continuing dialect between reason and faith.

Kaminsky, Joel S. and Alice Ogden Bellis, eds. *Jews, Christians and the Theology of the Hebrew Scriptures.* Society of Biblical Literature, 2000, 450 pp.
The way in which Jews and Christians study the Bible in each others presence has changed during the years since the Holocaust. Scholars have therefore seen fit in this volume to address some of the difficulties posed by the scriptures, and to suggest possible solutions.

Kaplan, Harold I. *Conscience and Memory: Meditations in a Museum of the Holocaust.* Chicago: University of Chicago Press, 1994, 213 pp.
This text by Kaplan attempts to form an "interpretation of the philosophic and social factors contributing to the Holocaust and its implications for the body

politic and the human spirit."

Kaplan, Jacob and R. P. Michel Riquet. "Jews and Christians Since Vatican II." Revue des Travaux de l'Academie des Sciences Morales et Politiques and Comptes Rendus de ses Seances (1971), Volume 124 Issue 1, pp. 301-321.
The authors discuss the policy declaration put forward by the Second Vatican Council concerning the treatment of Jews and non-Jews. The statement did take positive steps in that it "repudiates" anti-Semitism. However, the authors contend, the document did not address, nor did it correct the charge of diecide, which indicts Jews as "murderers of God." Both authors, nevertheless, agree that Vatican II has created an increased atmosphere for understanding and opened the door to cooperation between Catholics and Jews.

Kasper, Walter. "The Good Olive Tree." America (September 17, 2001), Volume 185 Issue 7, pp. 12-15.
The declaration, *Dominus Iesus,* published in September 2000 by the Congregation for the Doctrine of Faith, in Kasper's opinion, has created misunderstandings between Catholics and Jews. The author contends the information upon which the misunderstandings are based has been misinterpreted. He insists, *Dominus Iesus* acknowledges the divine revelation in the Hebrew Bible, and declares that God's grace is available to all men (not only Catholics). Kasper maintains, that though the terms "evangelization" and "mission" are used within the document, they do not imply any attempt to "convert" Jews. The document was meant to further, not impede, relations between Catholics and Jews.

Kastning-Olmesdahl, Ruth. "Theological and Psychological Barriers to Changing the Images of Jews and Judaism in Education. Journal of Ecumenical Studies (Summer 1984), Volume 21 Issue 3, pp. 452-469.
The author attempts to address the various difficulties faced when trying to revise the way Christians teach about Jews. According to Kastning-Olmesdahl this will involve totally remaking Christianity's image of Jews and Judaism. It also, in her opinion, forces Christians to revise the way in which they regard themselves and their religious beliefs. The article proposes that in order for Christians to reach true accord with other faith communities, they must accept the fact that God hears more than one voice, and belief in Christ is not necessary for salvation.

Katz, Stephen T. *Historicism, the Holocaust, and Zionism: Critical Studies in Modern Jewish Thought and History.* New York: New York University Press, 1992, 315 pp.
Katz argues, in this collection of essays, that contemporary Jewish philosophy must emerge out of the concrete conditions of the Jewish religious experience,

meaning the interaction of God, Israel and the *Torah*. In Katz's view, the Jewish religious experience " has not been an area of great creativity since World War II." The reason for this, contends Katz, is the paralyzing heinous crimes of the *Shoah*, an event whose magnitude preoccupies all who attempt to make sense of the absurdity that allowed for the murder of six million innocent Jews. The need to comprehend the meaning of the tragedy in a post-Holocaust world, argues Katz, requires the answer to two questions; how could our contemporary fellow human beings perpetrate such a terrible crime, and how could God allow the *Shoah* to happen? What Katz demands is the necessary retrieval of pre-Holocaust Jewish theology in a post-Holocaust way.

___. *Post-Holocaust Dialogues: Critical Studies in Modern Jewish Thought.* **New York: New York University Press, 1983, 327 pp.**
Katz critiques modern Jewish thinkers, and in particular theological responses to the Holocaust.

Kauders, Anthony. "Catholics, the Jews and Democratization in Post War Germany, Munich 1945-65." German History (2000), Volume18 Issue 4: pp. 461-484.
The study of archived materials from the Bavarian state and a local Munich archdiocese reveal that both the Bavarian representatives of the Catholic Church and the leadership of the Catholic Christian Social Union avoided dealing with the connections between Germany's anti-Semitic past and the values associated with liberal democracy. However, since the 1960's the German Catholic leadership has begun to accept the responsibility all Germans share for the Holocaust.

Keith, Graham. *Hatred Without a Cause? A Survey of Anti-Semitism.* Carlisle, Cumbria: Paternoster Press, 1997, 301 pp.
The author takes issue with the allegation that Christianity was responsible for the development of anti-Semitism. He points out, that in the ancient world, prior to the birth of Christianity, there was hostility toward the Jews because they kept themselves separate in both the religious and civic arenas. Keith contends, that while there have been Christians who engaged in anti-Semitic rhetoric, the Christian Churches (Catholic and/or after the Reformation Protestant) never officially condoned it. According to Keith, the hostility toward the Jews expressed during and after the Enlightenment was much more vocal and dangerous than anything used by Christianity. He emphasizes the fact that during the nineteenth century the world became more anti-Christian as well as anti-Jewish and that Hitler hated Christianity as well as Jews and Judaism. Keith insists the Jews are no better or worse than any other group and therefore cannot be regarded as above criticism. He also maintains, that efforts to convert Jews to Christianity are not meant to be anti-Semitic and thus should not be viewed in that light.

Kenny, Anthony J. *Catholics, Jews and the State of Israel: Studies in Judaism and Christianity.* **New York: Paulist Press; 1993, 157 pp.**
Kenny discusses the delay in the Vatican's diplomatic recognition of the State of Israel. Kenny insists the reason was caution, not anti-Jewish sentiment. The author also contends, that the Catholic Church's attitudes towards Jews and Judaism are evolving in a positive manner. However, the theological issues that surround a Jewish return to Jerusalem have not been conclusively interpreted within Judaism to-date. Thus the church is reluctant to put forward any ideas on the subject because this could possibly be viewed as an attempt to impose its own theological view of these events on the Jewish faith.

Kessler, Edward. "God Doesn't Change His Choice." Church Times (March 8, 2002), http://www.jcrelations.net, 3 pp.
"Replacement theology", the idea that Christians have replaced the Jews in God's favor, has, according to Kessler, reared its controversial head once again. He suggests that the terrorist attacks of September 11, 2001 have encouraged Christians, and those of other faiths, to focus with greater awareness on their relationship with God. The author insists, that Christians are guilty of teaching "replacement theology", and Christians can only learn to repudiate this mistaken idea through educational programs that provide a better understanding of different faiths.

Kirsch, Paul J. "Another Look at Anti-Semitism." The Lutheran Quarterly (August 1972), Volume 24 Issue 3, pp. 227-240.
According to Kirsch, Christians must understand that anti-Semitism totally contradicts the tenets of their faith. The author asserts, that Christianity's "shame is staggering" because many Christians are anti-Semitic due to the teachings of their church. He warns that the "viciousness of anti-Jewish belief lies in its potential as ideology." For example, if one's faith dictates that God means to punish Jews then persecuting them is not only justified, but is also required. The author examines the Glock and Stark study of anti-Semitism and proposes some ways to overcome Christian anti-Semitism.

Klein, Charlotte. "From Conversion to Dialogue - The Sisters of Sion and the Jews: A Paradigm of Catholic–Jewish Relations." Journal of Ecumenical Studies (1981), Volume 18 Issue 3, pp. 388-400.
The Holocaust and the ecumenical movement have both had a profound affect on the aims of the Congregation of Our Lady of Sion. This religious order, founded by two converted Jews (the Ratisbonne brothers), had long been committed to the conversion of all Jews. In the wake of the reforms developed by Vatican II, and the growing realization that Jews were the victims of mass murder during the Holocaust, the sisters of this religious order have committed themselves to a revised mission. They now study Judaism, and their work has

helped move Jewish/Christian dialogue along by trying to increase our understanding of God's plan to redeem the world.

Klein, Emma and Jonathan Webber. *Battle for Auschwitz: Catholic-Jewish Relations on the Line.* **Valentine Mitchell Publishers, 2001, 86 pp.**
The author claims that Auschwitz serves as the most visible and recognizable image of the Holocaust. The dispute that has arisen between Catholics and Jews over the establishment of a Carmelite Convent on the perimeter of the concentration camp has hampered the dialogue between Christians and Jews. Moreover, the issue has rekindled tensions that had lessened over the last few decades. Many Jews find the erection of a cross over the site particularly offensive and see the subject as an attempt by the Catholic Church to co-opt and Christianize Auschwitz. Klein follows the history of the debate from its beginning to its apparent settlement in the year 2000.

Klenicki, Leon and Richard John Nuehaus. *Believing Today: Jews and Christians in Conversation.* **Grand Rapids: William B. Eerdmans, 1989, 108 pp.**
Issues of theology, which have been raised as the result of the recent dialogue between Christians and Jews, comprise part of this discussion undertaken by a Reformed Rabbi and Lutheran Minister. Among the theological topics discussed are pluralism, conversion and secularization. Other topics include the effect of the Holocaust on Christians and Jews, the beatification of Edith Stein, and the current state of anti-Semitism.

_____ and David Rosen, eds. *Catholics and Jews: A New Millennium.* **New York: Anti-Defamation League, 1999, 55 pp.**
The editors provide a compilation of documents that have been exchanged between the Vatican, Pope John Paul II and the State of Israel. The themes addressed in these diplomatic messages include; the Catholic Church's need to repent for its anti-Semitism and anti-Judaism, the renewal of the bond between Judaism and Christianity, the hope for continued dialogue and reconciliation, and the Church's efforts to revise its teachings about Jews and Judaism. The recent Vatican statement on the Holocaust, *We Remember: A Reflection on the Shoah* is also presented in this volume.

Kloner, William. *Which Jesus: The Docetic Influence in American Social History, (1894-1911).* **Dissertation, Columbia University, 1988, 346 pp.**
Kloner insists, that Christian doctrine is not the primary source of nativist or anti-Semitic attitudes. He contends, that Christian orthodoxy preaches compassion for the enemy and the less fortunate. Kloner maintains, the problem lies with the "heretical factors of Docetism (denial of the humanity of Jesus)." In support of his arguments the author studies Protestant attitudes towards five

with the "heretical factors of Docetism (denial of the humanity of Jesus)." In support of his arguments the author studies Protestant attitudes towards five groups (including Jews) residing in the United States. He concludes, that Christian Doctrine as a whole need not be attacked in order to change hostile feelings towards the Jews, Rather the concentration should be upon rectifying the image of Jews as those who rejected and murdered Christ.

Knight, Henry F. *Confessing Christ in a Post-Holocaust World: A Midrashic Experiment.* **Westport, CT.: Greenwood Press, 2000, 185 pp.**
The author attempts to answer questions posed by the Holocaust for faithful Christians. Knight has rooted his critical perspective in the *midrashic* framework of Jewish hermeneutics, which requires Christians to come to terms with the "significant other" in their confessional lives. By bringing Biblical texts and the history of the Holocaust face to face, the volume attempts to help Jews and Christians understand their own traditions and each another's.

____. "From Shame to Responsibility and Christian Identity: The Dynamics of Shame and Confession Regarding the Shoah." Journal of Ecumenical Studies (Winter 1998), Volume 35 Issue 1, pp. 41-62.
Knight maintains, that the shame and guilt Christianity has been forced to face due to its role in the Holocaust, has required Christians to reexamine past teachings that promoted persecution of the Jews. According to the author, this confrontation with its own crimes has led to a crisis of identity for Christianity. The hope that this crisis can be resolved through dialogue with Jews is a good first step in coming to grips with its failures. Knight insists, however, that shame alone is an inadequate basis for mending the past sins of Christianity.

Kolitz, Zvi. *Yossel Rakover Speaks To God; Holocaust Challenges to Religious Faith.* **New York: Pantheon Books, 1999, 110 pp.**
This powerful work of fiction was originally written for a Buenos Aires Yiddish newspaper in 1946. The novel allows the author to vent the pain and mourning that was becoming universal among Jews the world over in the aftermath of the Holocaust. The author, in writing a fictional account of the last moments of the Warsaw Ghetto, accepts his position as a Jew caught between God's veiling Himself from the world and the commensurate rise of evil in it. For Yossel Rakover, being a Jew means being the antithesis of the evil around him and holding steadfast to the *Torah* and the way of life it expounds. Once the author's protagonist accepts the authenticity of his belief in God, he is able to question the Almighty. The author asks God how long he can allow himself to remain hidden from the world.

Krajewski, Stanislaw. "The Jebwabne Service: A Grand Gesture with no Immediately Perceptible Consequences?" Dialogue and Universalism

(2001), Volume 11 Issue 5/6, pp. 135.
Though the author welcomes the "penitential prayer" made by Polish Catholic Bishops in an effort to accept moral responsibility for the role Polish Catholics played in the Holocaust, he contends that it is a good first step. The author also insists, there is much still to be done to make amends. Krajewski regards the actions of the bishops as a symbolic gesture that needs to be followed up with concrete actions. The author insists, that despite the prayer service no real change has taken place. As proof of this he notes the continued sale of anti-Semitic books in a store located in the basement of the same Church in which the penitential prayer service took place. Until changes in attitude occur, the author maintains, the sincerity of the bishops' words will not be fully acknowledged.

____. **"Steps to *Teshuvah.*" Dialogue and Universalism (2001),Volume 11 Issue 1-2, pp. 59-62.**
Teshuvah in Hebrew refers to a "repentance." In relation to the Catholic Church it denotes the process of repentance the church has undertaken. This process is evident in the Polish Episcopate's letter issued in August 2000. The statement asks for forgiveness for anti-Semitism and admits the need to overcome religious intolerance. Most Polish Jews welcomed the letter. However, the Beatification of Pope Pius IX and the declaration *Dominus Iesus* raised difficulties in the continuing dialogue between Catholics and Jews. Stanislaw contends, that some Jews, as well as Christians, hold the belief that they have the truest access to faith and that has also hampered efforts to promote healing.

Krell, Marc A. *Intersecting Pathways: Jewish Appropriations of Christian Motifs in the Twentieth Century.* England: Dissertation, Graduate Theological Union, 1998, 306 pp.
The author maintains, that four Jewish thinkers, Eliezer Berkovits, Irving Greenberg, Hans Richard Rubenstein, and Joachim Schoeps, consciously and unconsciously drew upon Christian motifs when attempting to redefine Jewish identity through polemics and dialogue. This was done in the context of the Jews relations to Christianity after anti-Semitism reached its apex in the Holocaust. Krell gives examples of how these Christian themes have been utilized and the impact this has had upon the ongoing Christian-Jewish dialogue. For example in Krell's view, Rubenstein, in a reaction to two centuries of Christian hostility towards Jews, attempted to destroy the myths that had been built up around both religious traditions. However by incorporating Christian anti-Jewish images into his work he actually perpetuated the mythology.

Kremers, Heinz. "The First German Church Faces The Challenge of the Holocaust: A Report." Annals of the American Academy of Political and Social Science (1980), Volume 450, pp. 190-201.

The Rhineland Evangelical Church, seeking to answer questions concerning the Holocaust, issued a statement following twenty years of studying Christianity's responsibility for the Holocaust. The resolution offered recognized the election of Israel, the role of the Jews as God's chosen people, and the importance of Jews and Christians coming together to bear witness to each other's religious faith. The statement was influenced by American studies about the Holocaust.

Kreutz, Andrej. *Vatican Policy on the Palestinian-Israeli Conflict: The Struggle for the Holy Land.* **Greenwood Publishing Group, Incorporated, 1990, 208 pp.**
This book details four decades of the Vatican's diplomatic policies and relations with the Middle East. The author addresses the Vatican's view of the Holocaust, its aftermath, and its impact on the creation of an Israeli State. He also examines the Palestinian refugee situation. Kreutz insists that the Vatican's policies have been misinterpreted and that in reality the Vatican's relationships focus upon more than religious ideology. According to Kreutz, they also mirror the economic, social, and political atmosphere.

Kung, Father Hans. *The Council, Reform and Reunion.* **Sheed and Ward; 1963, 242 pp.**
Though this book reacts to the hope for a reunion of Catholics and Protestants that has grown out of the Second Vatican Council, the author does address Jews and Judaism throughout the text. However, most of his references to Jews and Judaism are negative. For example, Kung accuses Jews of being "narrow" and takes Jewish law to task for being overly "bureaucratic" and a "burden." This text re-introduces anti-Semitic stereotypes at a time when the Catholic Church is working to reject them.

Kuper, Leo. "**Theological Warrants for Genocide: Judaism, Islam and Christianity.**" **Terrorism and Political Violence (Fall 1990), Volume 2 Issue 3, pp. 351-379.**
The author explores the religious aspect of genocide. Kuper contends that it is legitimized in the sacred scriptures of the largest religions, though the role of these texts in genocide is somewhat determinate upon the complexities and context of society. He asserts that modern Islamic anti-Semitism has its roots in the teachings of Christian Arabs. Although Christian doctrines do not give an outright justification for genocide, its negative stereotyping of Jews and Christian teachings, which are anti-Judaic in nature, helped pave the way for persecution of the Jews and the Holocaust

Lang, Berel. *Act and Idea in the Nazi Genocide.* **Chicago: University of Chicago Press, 1990, 258 pp.**
Nine chapters comprise this study, which is Lang's attempt to remedy the fact

that with few exceptions, professional philosophers have had little to say about the Holocaust. Some of the topics included are ethics, aesthetics, moral psychology, philosophy of language, and philosophy of history. Among the many arguments made in this important work are the author's contention, that the most significant and morally compelling treatments of the Holocaust are documentaries rather than literary recreations. Lang writes that when it comes to the evil unleashed by Hitler, the authenticity of the historical record makes a claim on our attention that no work of literature can. Lang also criticizes philosophers who ignore historical evidence and formulate theories of human behavior in the abstract. Elsewhere, Lang rejects any suggestion that the Nazis were operating in ignorance of their own goals, but rather the author insists the Nazis were engaged in a conscious effort to pursue evil. National Socialism's cruelty was total and universal and, states Lang, sought to eliminate Jews wherever they might be and at whatever cost might accrue.

Langer, Howard, J. *The History of the Holocaust: A Chronology of Quotations.* **Northvale, NJ.: Jason Aronson, 1997, 306 pp.**
This collection of quotations taken from a selection of articles, books, public statements, government documents and eyewitness accounts covers the history of anti-Semitism from early Christianity through 1932. Additionally, it examines the Holocaust, and the reactions and responses of Christian Churches as well as the rest of the world, to the murder of six million Jews. There is a section that deals with the aftermath of the Holocaust and reflections upon it.

Langer, Lawrence L. *Admitting the Holocaust: Collected Essays.* **Oxford : Oxford University Press, 1995, 202 pp.**
Langer examines how Western intellectuals and writers have sought to come to terms with the Holocaust.

_____. *Holocaust Testimonies: The Ruins of Memory.* **New Haven: Yale University Press, 1991, 216 pp.**
There is little "spiritual uplift" or optimistic rhetoric about the "resilience of the human spirit" in this analysis of some three hundred of the more than fourteen hundred Holocaust survivors interviewed by the author. The interviews were recorded for the video archive at Yale University. Those interviewed speak of complete powerlessness, of subjugation to the cruel capricious whims of their Nazi oppressors, and of the absence of rational behavior during their ordeal. Endurance and luck, rather than faith or heroism emerges as the key factors of survival. Langer points out that the inability to derive any meaning from their sufferings has had a profoundly deleterious effect on Holocaust survivors.

Langer, Ruth. "Teaching About the Shoah: An Inter-religious Conference."Journal of Ecumenical Studies (Summer/Fall 1999), Volume 36 Issue

3-4, pp. 501-504.
This article reports on a 1999 religious conference held in Baltimore. Inspired by the 1998 Vatican document *We Remember*, Catholic and Jewish educators met to compile guidelines for teaching about the Holocaust. Conferees agreed that effective education addresses history, theology, and the impact of the Holocaust on various groups of people.

Lapide, Pinchas E. "Jesus in Israeli Literature." Christian Century (October 21, 1970), Volume 87 Issue 42, pp.1248-1252.
The author reviews the ways in which Jesus has been portrayed in Jewish writings. Lapide notes that in view of the anti-Jewish invective that the Church employed Jews, were forced to place Jesus in some sort of context in their religion. Thus he has been referred to as a liar, someone who seduced Jews, and a pretender. The author points to the Jews recent 'rediscovery" process concerning Jesus. The spirit of ecumenism has prompted Jewish scholars to reexamine the issue of Christ in a more positive light.

Lapin, Daniel. "Misrepresenting the Holocaust." American Enterprise (May, 1999).
Rabbi Daniel Lapin criticizes Bill Clinton's remark at the National Prayer Breakfast that "Hitler preached a perverted form of Christianity." According to Rabbi Lapin this is untrue, for Hitler was an enemy of Christianity and a pagan. He questions where Clinton came by this misrepresentation of the facts and concludes that perhaps the origin can be found in Holocaust Museums and like-minded programs that exist throughout the country. Lapin notes the film shown at the Holocaust museum in Washington, D.C. and contends that it disseminates anti-Christian propaganda. He also points out that the actions of Christians who risked their lives during the Holocaust to rescue Jews are often afforded only fleeting attention. The author gives particular attention to the Ten Boom family, Dutch Christians who put their lives on the line to shelter Jews from the Nazis.

Leaman, Oliver. *Evil and Suffering in Jewish Philosophy*. Cambridge: Cambridge University Press, 1995, 257 pp.
The questions Leaman considers are: how could an omniscient and loving God permit the suffering of innocent humans and why did the Jews, as a chosen people, have to endure such a grim fate during the Holocaust? In order to find answers the author surveys Jewish philosophers ranging from Philo through Spinoza, and ends with Martin Buber, and post-Holocaust thinkers like Emil Fackenheim and Richard Rubenstein. Leaman concludes his study by contending that the Holocaust, as an unprecedented event, requires a "new theology" for the Jewish people.

Lee, Dorothy A. "Matthew's Gospel and Judaism." Jewish Christian Rela-

tions (2001) http://www.jcrelations.net/artic11/lee.htm; 7pp.
The author proposes that examinations of Matthew's Gospel in relation to Judaism will turn up inconsistencies that make analysis difficult. Lee points out the pro and anti-Jewish features of the Gospel. She suggests readers must understand Matthew's words in the context of the time. To do otherwise invites misinterpretation.

Leiter, Robert. "The Holocaust in Books." Commonweal (July 31, 1981), Volume 108 Issue 14, pp. 438-447.
Leiter examines many of the books that attempt to further our understanding of the meaning and causes for the Holocaust. At the heart of the book is a call for a more ecumenical spirit among men of all faiths so that a repeat of such an atrocity by humanity will never again be permitted to happen.

Levi, Primo. *If This is a Man (Survival in Auschwitz)*. Stuart Woolf, Translator. Orion Publishers, 1960, 157 pp.
This is the classic personal memoir of the Italian born Jewish chemist who survived a year of slave labor at the Auschwitz death camp. What raises this memoir above most accounts of suffering in the camps is the deep interest the author took in his fellow prisoners, as well his analytical description of the gruesome sociological structure of Auschwitz.

_____. *The Drowned and the Saved*. Raymond Rosenthal, Translator. New York: Random House, 1989, 205 pp.
A collection of essays detail Levi's role as a witness to the Holocaust while he was a prisoner at Auschwitz. The author tells us he took on the task of witness quite naturally, "whether out of a moral obligation toward those who were silenced or in order to free ourselves out of their memory."

Levkov, Ilya, ed. *Bitberg and Beyond: Encounters in American, German, and Jewish History*. Steimatzky/Shapolsky, Books, 1987, 734 pp.
Some two hundred primary and secondary documents, essays, and interviews relating to President Ronald Reagan's controversial 1985 Bitburg Nazi cemetery visit are contained in this volume. Although he presents a variety of views, Levkov condemns the Regan visit and concludes that the president sacrificed the moral high ground for short-term political gain.

Levy, David J. "Response to the Statement of the Evangelical Lutheran Church in Canada."Jewish-Christian Relations, http://www.jcrelations.net 2001, 6pp.
The Lutheran Church in Canada adopted a statement that was meant to improve its relations with the Jews of Canada in 1995. The author suggests ways to continue this initial positive step in furthering the dialogue between Jews and Chris-

tians. Levy proposes, the Canadian Lutheran Church must address issues like Martin Luther's anti-Semitism, the Holocaust and living the Christian faith in a way that shows love and respect for Jews.

Liberman, Serge, ed. *Anti-Semitism and Human Rights.* **Melbourne: Australian Institute of Jewish Affairs, 1985, 176 pp.**
These papers were presented as part of a seminar held in Melbourne in June of 1984. Though they cover a variety of the anti-Semitic ideologies from several countries, there are several that specifically address the role Christianity played in promoting hostility toward the Jews. For example there are essays concerning the state of "Jewish-Christian Relations"; "The Church and Anti-Semitism: The Beginning of a Tragedy", "The Religious Factor in Anti-Semitism", and two responses to "The Religious Factor."

Linafelt, Tod, ed. *Strange Fire: Reading the Bible After the Holocaust.* **New York: New York University Press, 2000, 300 pp.**
This volume of essays addresses the implications of the Holocaust for interpreting the Hebrew Bible and brings together a diverse and distinguished range of contributors, including Elie Wiesel. The contributors discuss theoretical and methodological considerations emerging from the *Shoah* and demonstrate their importance in the reading of specific Biblical texts. The book also addresses issues such as Jewish and Christian Biblical theology after the Holocaust, the ethics of the Christian appropriation of Jewish scripture, and the rethinking of Biblical models of suffering and sacrifice from a post-Holocaust perspective.

Littell, Franklin H. "Christendom, the Holocaust and Israel: The Importance For Christians of Recent Events in Jewish History." Journal of Ecumenical Studies (1973), Volume 10 Issue 3, pp. 483-497.
The historical role of the Jewish people since Christ's time is often ignored as a result of Christian religious anti-Semitism and therefore stands as "an affront to God." In this respect the anti-Semitism exhibited by Christianity fails to adequately come to terms with the Holocaust or the emergence of the State of Israel. The ways in which Christianity deals with these realities, according to Littell, will determine the future health of the Christian faith.

_____. *The Crucifixion of the Jews.* **New York: Harper & Row, 1975, 153 pp.**
Littell's book confronts Christendom with its massive betrayal of the Jewish people during the Holocaust. The author also charges that Christianity continues its unwillingness to admit that betrayal. The multifarious anti-Semitism that led both to the Holocaust, and to the church's response to the atrocity is traced to ancient but persistent errors in Christian thought.

_____, ed. *The German Church Struggle and the Holocaust.* Detroit: Wayne State University Press, 1974, 328 pp.
This is a collection of papers given at the Wayne State University International Scholars Conference on the Holocaust, held in 1970. The book brings together Jewish and Christian interpretations of the Holocaust, in which the contributors reflect aspects of the Nazi onslaught against the Christian Churches and the Jews of Europe.

_____. "Halting a Succession of Evil." Journal of Ecumenical Studies (Spring 1997), Volume 34 Issue 2, pp. 171-189.
The Christian concept of "apostolic succession" is used by Littell to advance the idea that there has been an "apostolic succession of evil" in Christianity ran from the persecution of Jews at the hands of the early Church through to the Holocaust. This "evil" against the Jews was later used as a political tool by governments, targeting the Jews and some others. The author claims we try to deny this thread of evil and "suppress it so we can get on with life." Littell insists, it is long past time we recognize tragic offenses like the Armenian Genocide and the Holocaust as crimes. He contends, that we have a moral imperative to remember the conditions that led to these atrocities. In the case of the Holocaust, these conditions were created through Christian anti-Judaism and government anti-Semitism. Littell warns, that religion and/or politics cannot be used to condone murder.

_____. "Holocaust and Genocide: The Essential Dialectic." Holocaust and Genocide Studies (1987), Volume 2 Issue 1, pp. 95-104.
Littell acknowledges that there are lessons about life and death that can be taken from the Holocaust, and that these are relevant for all people. Yet even though the author recognizes similarities between the atrocities committed against the Jews, and for example, the earlier Armenian genocide, he insists that the Nazi's attempt to exterminate the Jews remains "unique." Though this argument about the uniqueness of the Holocaust sometimes arouses controversy, Littell remains stalwart in his belief. Moreover he maintains that the murder of Jews during World War II represents a crisis of faith for Christians, who must once and for all put aside the idea that they hold the one true faith.

_____. "Repenting in a Passive Voice." Jewish Exponent (April 9, 1998), Volume 203 Issue 15, pp.5.
The author comments upon the Vatican Statement *We Remember.* Though Littell recognizes some value in the Church's document, he also notes a variety of shortcomings in the statement. For example, the Vatican fails to specifically mention anti-Semitism, or Nazism, admissions of guilt are vague and the document suggests a wrong-thinking moral equivalency between the way Catholics have treated Jews and the treatment of Catholics by Jews.

_____. **"Uprooting Anti-Semitism: A Call to Christians." Journal of Church and State (1975), Volume 17 Issue 1, pp. 15-24.**
The social and political affects of the Christian anti-Semitic idea that rests upon the theory that Jews were responsible for the murder of Jesus Christ provided a basis for implementing the Holocaust. The author points to writings of historian Arnold Toynbee as examples of this poisonous and influential line of thought.

Littell, Marcia Sachs, and Sharon Weissman Gutman _Liturgies of the Holocaust: An Interfaith Anthology_. Valley Forge: Trinity Press International, 1996, 199 pp.
The editors present examples of liturgies appropriate for the commemoration of _Yom Ha Shoah_ programs. These include commemorations that took place in the federal and state governments as well as branches of the military. Also included are liturgies that have been used in synagogue programs, by churches and interfaith groups, college campuses, and in general civic observances.

Livingston, Sigmund. _Must Men Hate?_ New York: Harper Press, 1944, 344 pp.
In this extensive study, Livingston comes to the conclusion that anti-Semitism "is not inherited, it is acquired." In this book he tries once again to dispel both the religious and secular falsehoods that have been used time and again to discredit the Jews. Generation after generation, according to the author, persist in teaching and reinforcing the same tired and ridiculous accusations that result in hatred of the Jew.

Locke, Hubert G. and Marcia Sachs Littell, eds. _Holocaust and Church Struggle: Religion, Power and the Politics of Resistance_. Lanham, MD.: University Press of America, 1996, 347 pp.
The following is a partial list of the contributors to this book. All of them presented papers at the 22nd Annual Scholars Conference on "The Holocaust and the German Church Struggle", which was held in 1992 at the University of Washington; Zev Garber, Steven Jacobs, Robert Krel, James F. Moore, Richard V. Pierard and, and Michael Steele. The topics covered include discussions concerning the role of Conservative Protestantism in anti-Semitism (especially the Christian Identity Movement), the impact of Christianity upon the formulation and reading of Holocaust literature, and the problem of Christian theology in a post-Holocaust world.

Lodahl, Michael E. "Christo-Praxis: Foundations for a Post-holocaust Ethical Christology." Journal of Ecumenical Studies (Spring 1993), Volume 30 Issue 2, pp. 213-26.
The article looks at selected biblical passages with an eye to providing a basis for a post- Holocaust consideration of the doctrine of Christology. It also exam-

ines the development of Christology within the ethics of Jesus Christ's words and actions.

_____. **"Rupturing the Judeo-Christian Tradition." Emory Studies on the Holocaust (1988), Volume 2, pp. 141-162.**
Lodahl contests, that there are many differences between Judaism and Christianity. Therefore it is foolish to argue that there is a commonly held "Judeo-Christian tradition. " The author uses the works of the Jewish scholars Arthur Cohen, Michael Goldberg, and Susan Shapiro to support his contentions. He argues any attempt to create a generally held belief in this so-called "tradition" ignores the fact that Christians have time and again tried to absorb Jewish history as a precursor to their religious doctrine. Christians have also purported that their religion is the fulfillment of the promise of Judaism. This idea, along with centuries of persecution of Jews, demonstrates clearly that Christians misunderstood Judaism's nature and history. Additionally, the sufferings inflicted upon Jews by Christians helped, to a degree, to lay the foundations for the Nazis plans to eradicate the Jews. The genocide that resulted further split the two religious communities. Though Lodahl supports the idea of improving Jewish-Christian dialogue and relations he insists the two groups cannot, as some have suggested, blend together.

MacDonald, Kevin. *Separation and Its Discontents: Toward an Evolutionary Theory of Anti-Semitism.* **Westport, CT.: Praeger, 1998, 326 pp.**
MacDonald asserts, that the widely held opinion that anti-Semitism is rooted in Western Civilization, and is dependent upon particular elements found in Christianity is wrong. As support for his contention MacDonald reminds readers that anti-Jewish attitudes have been in existence prior to Christianity and can be found in all places where Jews have resided. According to the author, by studying the development of hostility toward Jews in the Roman Empire, Medieval Europe and Germany, from the late eighteenth century through the Nazi regime, one can see that in each time and place there have been common aspects to anti-Semitic reactions. MacDonald proposes, that the tendency of Jews to remain culturally and genetically separate from broader society has contributed to the belief that they are different and outsiders. In addition, he maintains that competition between Jews and Gentiles over social resources has served to reinforce the separation of the two groups.

Madigan, Kevin. "A Survey of Jewish Reaction to the Vatican Statement on the Holocaust." Cross Currents, (Winter 2000/2001), Volume 50 Issue 4, pp. 488-503.
The author surveys the critical and positive responses issued by Jews reacting to the Vatican's document *We Remember.* Although there were positive comments expressed about the document's aims, many Jewish leaders had hoped for a

stronger and more specific acknowledgement of the Church's failures to treat the Jews fairly or honestly over the centuries. Additionally, the Vatican's efforts to defend Pope Pius XII disappointed many Jews. While some Catholics have insisted that criticisms of *We Remember* are due to misunderstandings, others believe that the Vatican missed an opportunity to truly confront its past persecutions of the Jews.

Maier, Paul L. "Who Killed Jesus." Christianity Today (April 9, 1990), Volume 34 Issue 6, pp. 16-20.
A group of Christian theologians known as the Jesus Seminar agree with Jewish scholars that the *New Testament* contains "the most dangerous anti-Semitic tract in history." They maintain, that all passages in the gospels that claim any Jewish responsibility in the Crucifixion are invalid and should be excised from the text. Maier insists this idea is almost as extreme as earlier claims that the Jews committed deicide. The author agrees Christianity should atone for past sins against Jews, but contends that repentance should not include tampering with the scriptures, even though the sacred texts should never be employed for "pejorative purposes."

Marcus, Paul, and Alan Rosenberg. *Healing Their Wounds: Psychotherapy with Holocaust Survivors and Their Families.* New York: Praeger, 1989. 304 pp.
Sixteen scholars discuss a range of approaches to helping Holocaust survivors recover and lead relatively normal lives. The methods include psychotherapy, self-psychology, family approaches, and pastoral counseling.

Marmur, Dow. "Christians, Jews, and Anti-Semitism Now." Jewish-Christian Relations, http://jcrelations.net, 2002, 8 pp.
Rabbi Marmur asserts, that despite "all the changes since rabbinic times, little has changed when it comes to the perception of Jews." The author insists, that Jews remain suspicious of attempts by Christians to open up a dialogue, because they believe that anti-Semitism originated within Christianity. He maintains, that only when Christians have adjusted their theology will any real progress be made in improving the relationship between Christians and Jews.

Maxwell, Elizabeth. "Why Should the Holocaust Be Remembered and Therefore Taught?" European Judaism (Winter 1988-Spring 1989), Volume 22 Issue 1, pp. 17-28.
Maxwell reports from a 1988 conference dedicated to "Remembering for the Future", that scholars are currently worried that the memory of the Holocaust has been threatened by revisionism and denial. Conferees proposed that the most effective way of combating this threat was through education. They discussed the fact that detailed documentation, conferences and publications can all serve

as elements to help keep the memory of the Holocaust alive for generations to come. In addition notable scholars like Roy Eckardt and Paul Van Buren discussed the responsibility that Christianity bears for the death of six million Jews, and the revisions needed in Christian doctrine if anti-Semitism and anti-Judaism are ever to be ended.

Maybaum, Ignaz. *The Face of God After Auschwitz.* **Amsterdam: Polak & Van Gennep, 1965, 265 pp.**
The author, a Jewish theologian and refugee from Nazi Germany in 1939, sees the salvation of humanity not in the political universalism of one world government or church, but in the universal application of the commandment to "love thy neighbor as thyself."

McGarry, Father Michael. *Christology After Auschwitz.* **New York: Paulist Press, 1977, 119 pp.**
By concentrating on post-World War II writings, the author attempts to show the impact of the Holocaust experience on three decades of Christian theology.

____. "Emil Fackenheim and Christianity After the Holocaust." American Journal of Theology and Philosophy (January-May 1988), Volume 9 Issue 1-2, pp. 117-135.
Emil Fackenheim insisted in his book *To Mend the World* that if Christians were ever going to be able to mend themselves in the aftermath of the Holocaust they would have to revise their theology by addressing three issues; the Jewishness of Jesus, the conflict of Jesus' being both God and man and whether Jesus was truly the Messiah. McGarry responds to Fackenheim's challenge by discussing the three subjects. He agrees, that Christianity bears a measure of responsibility for the Nazi's success in implementing the death of six million Jews, and while he does not think Christianity created National Socialism he does propose that Christian morality and courage might have stopped it. According to the author, in order to heal itself Christianity must come to terms with Jesus as Jew and must come to understand, respect, and appreciate the differences between the two faiths, rather than try to ignore them.

McMichael, Steven J. "The End of a Pilgrimage, An Acknowledgement of Guilt." America (January 2, 1999), Volume 180 Issue 1, pp. 14-16.
The author contends, that the Holocaust represents a tragedy for Christians as well as Jews. He insists, that this is true because of the anti-Jewish attitudes that Christianity taught for centuries. This hostility toward Jews undercut Christianity's basic tenet of faith; namely to love all our brothers and sisters. McMichael presents a brief history of some of the crimes Christianity committed against Jews over the years. He insists, that Christians must have the courage to admit their misdeeds and change their teachings about the Jews, in an effort to begin to

make amends for causing the Jewish people to suffer.

Melnick, Ralph. "Our Own Deeper Joy: Spiritual Resistance After the Holocaust." Journal of Religion (July 1995), Volume 75 Issue 3, pp. 392-401.
The author attempts to find comfort by exploring the possible spiritual meaning or implication of the Holocaust. Though the Holocaust provides a yardstick for measuring man's capability for evil, it also offers a possible re-affirmation of belief in God, and demonstrates the ability of Jews to use their spirituality to combat evil.

Merkle, John C. "Bound Together in God." Religious Education (Fall 1996), Volume 91 Issue 4, pp. 547-555.
Because of his relationships with Jews, the author, a Catholic, has come to understand that the reality of Jews and Judaism are far different from the manner in which Christians portrays them. Merkle admits that the Christian Church's historical anti-Judaism has provided the foundation for anti-Semitism. The author has discovered a way to be Catholic and still recognize the validity of Judaism. He hopes other Christians and their Jewish counterparts will find a way to ally themselves with one another.

Milchman, Alan, and Alan Rosenberg, eds. *Martin Heidegger and the Holocaust.* Atlantic Highlands: Humanities Press International Inc., 1995, 271 pp.
Fifteen essays explore the meaning of German philosopher Martin Heidegger's postwar silence about the Holocaust. Also examined is the meaning of his few enigmatic references to the extermination of six million Jews, in the light of his preoccupation with the nihilism that he believed to be the hallmark of the modern industrial world.

Millen, Rochelle, Timothy Bennett, Jack Mann, Joseph O'Connor, and Robert Walker eds. *New Perspectives on the Holocaust: A Guide for Teachers and Scholars.* New York: New York University Press, 1996.
This collection of twenty-five essays incorporates a wide range of topics dedicated to preserving the memory of the Holocaust through teaching, research, and dialogue. The book developed from an international conference, "Teaching the Holocaust," held at Wittenberg University in conjunction with *Yad Vashem* in 1993. The volume consists of three parts that includes essays by Jewish, Christian, German, and Israeli scholars. A common theme that links the essays is the emphasis placed on the tenacity of anti-Semitism which has been embedded in the language, culture and theology of the West. This prejudice is particularly found in the *New Testament,* the words of the early Church fathers, Martin Luther and beyond.

Misheff, Sue. "Why a Christian Teaches the Holocaust?" Moment (February 28, 1998), Volume 23 Issue 1, pp. 62.
Misheff, a Christian, explains her reasons for teaching students about the Holocaust. She notes, that some might consider the subject matter strange for a non-Jew, however she believes that by instructing her students about the atrocity committed by the Nazis she can lead them to a better understanding of the Jews, themselves and the world. Moreover, she contends she can help ensure that her pupils will work to make certain such a horrific occurrence cannot take place again without opposition. Misheff sees this as a way in which she can follow the teachings of her Christian faith, which prompts her to love God and her neighbor.

Moltmann, Juergen. "Theology in Germany Today." Observations on the Spiritual Situation of the Age: Contemporary German Perspectives. Ed. Juergen Habermas. Cambridge, Ma.: MIT Press, 1984, pp. 184-204.
The author focuses upon the religious life and attitudes in Germany today. Moltmann examines the state of Jewish-Christian relations in the aftermath of the Nazi regime's impact upon Germany's Churches. He notes the current efforts Christian Churches are making to reject anti-Semitism and rediscover those things they hold in common with Jews and Judaism.

Montefiore, Hugh W. "Radical Review of Christian Teaching." Christian Jewish Relations (March 1985), Volume 18 Issue 1, pp. 31-33.
In this article Montefiore expresses his frustration with the failure of Christianity to change the teachings about Jews that appear in the Holy Week Liturgy. He insists that anti-Semitism cannot be allowed to continue and that Christianity still has much to do to overcome the legacy of hostility it has fostered throughout the last two centuries.

Monti, Joseph E. *Who do You Say That I Am? The Christian Understanding of Christ and Anti-Semitism.* New York: Paulist Press, 1984, 98 pp.
Monti reviews the development of anti-Judaism in the early Christian Church through a theological context. He proposes possible changes for a "reconstructed Christology" that will include an appropriate response to the moral dilemma resulting from the legacy of anti-Judaism and anti-Semitism. He also suggests methods for making Christianity a more tolerant religion.

Moore, James F. *Christian Theology after the Shoah.* Lanham: University Press of America, 1993, 189 pp.
This book examines the nature of Christian theology before and after the Holocaust.

_____. "The Place of Teaching About Zionism in a Department of Christian

Theology." Shofar (Fall 1994), Volume 13 Issue 1, pp. 38-54.
The article examines the difficulties of teaching about Zionism in the Christian theological setting. The author suggests, that Zionism is best studied in the context of the nineteenth century when anti-Semitism was on the rise. He also believes it must be examined in connection with the Holocaust and its impact on the Jewish world and the world as a whole. Moore notes the problem that Zionism presents for ongoing Jewish-Christian dialogue, and the linkage of anti-Zionism to anti-Semitism in many minds.

_____. **"Re-Envisioning Christianity: A New Era in Christian Theological Interpretation of Christian Texts." Cross Currents (Winter 2000).**
In this article the contention is made that post-Shoah Theology must be founded upon dialogue and not on "received traditions." Moore claims that just as it is mistaken for Christians to hold onto theories about Christianity as a superior religion, it is also misguided to insist that the Holocaust is the "defining event under which all else must be subsumed." The author asserts that if we are ever to overcome our misunderstandings and improve the relationship between Christians and Jews we must move beyond long-held beliefs. He prompts Christians to put aside divisive traditions so that we need not defend them, rationalize them, or reconstruct the past in ways that makes sense in the current theological environment.

_____. **"Spectrum of Views: Traditional Christian Responses to the Holocaust." Journal of Ecumenical Studies (1988), Volume 25 Issue 2, pp. 212-224.**
Based upon sources compiled from a conference on the history of Judaism held in 1985, Moore surveys the traditional theological responses that Christians have had when confronted by the atrocities committed against the Jews during the Holocaust.

Mushkat, Marion. *Philo-Semitic and Anti-Jewish Attitudes in Post-Holocaust Poland.* Lewiston, NJ.: Edwin Mellen Press, 1992, 441 pp.
The author studies the roots of anti-Semitism and philo-Semitism in Poland from the Enlightenment period through World War II and after. Mushkat notes the part that Christianity played in forming negative attitudes toward Jews. He especially looks at the Polish Catholic Church's role in creating anti-Jewish feelings. The author examines the current existence of anti-Semitism in the post-Communist era.

Mussner, Franz. "Theology After Auschwitz: A Provisional Program." Jewish–Christian Relations (2001), http://www.jcrelations.net.
Mussner presents topics that need to be considered in formulating a "theology after Auschwitz" for Christianity. He contends, that in the wake of the slaughter

of six million Jews there must be a revision of theology and this must include thinking about Jews as God's chosen people, the Jewish origins of Jesus, the anti-Semitism of the Gospels, and why God allowed the Holocaust.

_____. *Tractate on the Jews: The Significance of Judaism for Christian Faith.* **Translator, Leonard Swidler. Philadelphia: Fortress Press, 1984, 339 pp.**
The author asks Christians to reexamine that part of their doctrine that helped develop an anti-Jewish climate. Mussner contends, that hostility towards the Jews has profoundly impacted the world and he insists that Christianity must re-evaluate its theology toward Jews and find ways to better understand them. To that end Mussner provides an explanation of Judaism on its terms, which is far different from the mythology developed about Jews by Christians.

Myers, Kenneth A. "Adjusting Theology in the Shadow of Auschwitz." Christianity Today (October 8, 1990), Volume 34 Issue 14, pp. 443.
This article examines the change in Christian theology in the last decades and the resolve of most Christian Churches to "retreat from embracing the task of evangelizing Jews." Myers contends, that this change, the result of adopting the "two covenant theology" that has grown out of Jewish-Christian dialogue, which places Judaism and Christianity on a parallel plane, is wrong. The author insists, that in meaning to do the right thing after the Holocaust, Christians have cut themselves and Jews off from God's redemption, which is only available through Christ.

_____. **"Do Jews Really Need Jesus?" Christianity Today (August 12, 2002), Volume 45 Issue 10, 3 pp.**
Myers criticizes Rabbi James Rudin's assertion that the Willowbank Declaration, issued from Bermuda in 1990, which supported the appropriateness of Christians evangelizing Jews, provided a "blueprint for spiritual genocide." According to Myers, the real genocide is committed when Christians fail to spread the news of salvation through Jesus Christ. The author claims that the "two-covenant" theology, which has been developed to place Judaism and Christianity on an equal footing, is problematic because it ensures "spiritual death" for those deprived of Christ.

Neff, David. "Faulty Memory." National Review (May 4, 1998), Volume 50 Issue 8, pp. 34-37.
In Neff's view, the Holocaust Museum's fourteen minute orientation film on anti-Semitism promotes the stereotyping of Christians. The author claims the film leaves viewers with the false impression that Nazi anti-Semitism was a direct result of Christian doctrine. Neff uses the research of Marc Saperstien (Professor at Georgetown University) to validate his contention that the Nazis drew from Christianity's ideas about Jews, but changed them to fit their racial ideol-

ogy.

Nether, Andre. *The Exile of the Work: The Impact of Christianity, Secularism, and Holocaust on Jewish Faith.* **Jewish Publication Society of America, 1981, 246 pp.**
Nether argues, that creation and covenant are exclusively fulfilled by the action of man; the responsibility of man necessitates the silence of God; and God's silence during centuries of pogroms and the Holocaust may be interpreted as His presence in suffering. The author also states "if God chooses to hide His face during the Holocaust so must man understand that no word about the *Shoah* and its consequences is thoroughly adequate and complete."

Neusner, Jacob. *Death and Birth of Judaism: The Impact of Christianity, Secularism and Holocaust on Jewish Faith.* **New York: Basic Books, 1987, 380 pp.**
Although the stated intent of the author is to examine the development of the various forms of Judaism as they existed in the past and present, there are two more apparent purposes for the book. The first is to expound upon what the author believes is his discovery of a non-linear and incremental view of history. The second is to espouse a particular and personal view of, and attachment to Judaism as a system of faith. Neusner argues,that there is "no single Judaism", hence, as a matter of hypothesis, no religious system recapitulates any other of its species, let alone the genus religion. Included in his Judaic systems is a discussion of what the author calls the Judaism of the Holocaust.

____. *The Jewish War Against the Jews: Reflections on Golah, Shoah, and Torah.* **New York: KTAV Publishing Corp., 1984, 149 pp.**
A collection of fouteen articles focused towards popular audiences, continues Neusner's ongoing ruminations about the myths and tensions inherent in *Diaspora* Jewish life, specifically the ambiguities involved in being a Jew, a Zionist, and an American all at once.

____. *Stranger at Home: The Holocaust, Zionism, and American Judaism.* **Chicago: University of Chicago Press, 1981, 213 pp.**
This group of essays written over a period of twenty years, confronts the social and psychological problems facing American Jews. Of particular interest are Neusner's essays concerning the implications of the two elements that constitute the mythic vision of contemporary Jewry that begins in death, with the Holocaust, and is completed by rebirth through the creation of the State of Israel.

No Author or Editor Listed. *Proceedings of the Second Biennial Conference on Christianity and the Holocaust: "Voices, Institutional and Individual Responses to the Holocaust."* **Lawrenceville, NJ.: Rider College, 1992, 599 pp.**

The following subjects provide a partial list of the contents of this text; Pearl Onliner examines the "Altruistic Responses to the Holocaust: Christian Voices", John Pawlikowski studies "Christian Leadership and the Holocaust: An Uneven Response", while John Morley explores 'The Prague Document and Its Impact Upon the Catholic Church" and Henry Huttenbach reviews the "Flaws in the Christian-Jewish Dialogue." Additional topics include a look at the way in which Pope John Paul has pursued better relations with Jews, and Christian America's response to the Holocaust.

Novak, David. "Jews and Catholics: Beyond Apologies." First Things: A Monthly Journal of Religion and Public Life (January 1999), Issue 89, pp. 20-26.
Reactions of Jews to Pope John Paul II's issuing of *"We Remember: A Reflection on the Shoah"* are examined, as well as the negative response many Jews have had regarding the pope's speech about *New Testament* interpretations of the Jewish people.

_____. *Jewish-Christian Relations in a Secular Age.* San Francisco: University of San Francisco, Swig Judaic Studies Program, 1998, 13 pp.
The Vatican's Statement *We Remember* is the author's focus in this article. Novak stresses, that any disappointment Jews may voice about the document is both unfair and unwarranted. He insists, that any apology would be rather irrelevant since those to whom the apology is owed are dead. He also admits, that repentance is appropriate, for Christians must come to terms with their collective responsibility for perpetuating anti-Semitism. Novak suggests, that perhaps the Vatican document tried to say too much and quite possibly was too far reaching in its efforts to portray Pius XII as a rescuer of Jews since that question remains the topic of intense debate and study. However, despite shortcomings, Novak commends Pope John Paul II for his efforts to reconcile with the Jews.

_____. "When Jews are Christians." First Things (November 1991), Issue 17, pp. 42-46.
Novak insists, that Jewish converts to Christianity pose a "unique" problem for both Church and Synagogue. These "Jewish Christians" maintain that they can play a special role by serving as a link between Christians and Jews the reverse is true. Yet they are troubling to Jews who feel they are being held up as role models for conversion. For the Christian community Jewish Christians, believing they have a special status, divide the membership into the privileged and non-privileged. Novak discusses the other problems posed by Jewish converts and then suggests that both Christians and Jews confront the problem and address it openly. He also cautions Christians not to assume that these converts "are the rule, for in fact they are the exception among Jews."

Oesterreicher, John Maria. *The New Encounter Between Christians and Jews.* **New York: Philosophical Library, 1986, 470 pp.**
The Vatican's issue of *Nostra Aetate* is commemorated by this compilation of essays and lectures, many of which trace the changes that took place within the Church prior to Vatican II. The author notes the hostile response that many conservative theologians exhibited when *Nostra Aetate* was put forward. In this article the author gives his own reactions to the declaration and insists that the Church must not only reject anti-Semitism, but should also acknowledge its roots in Judaism. He contends, that doing so would help improve the relationship between Christians and Jews.

O'Hare, Padraic. *The Enduring Covenant: The Education of Christians and the End of Anti-Semitism.* **Valley Forge: Trinity Press International, 1997, 195 pp.**
This book is the culmination of the author's fifteen years of sustained engagement in Jewish-Christian relations. His purpose for writing the text, is to speak about the Church's practice of anti-*Judentum* O'Hare focuses on "the holiness of the religious community," which he notes, can develop along triumphal, absolute, and exclusive lines.

Oldenhege, Tania. *Parables For Our Time: Re-Reading New Testament Scholarship After the Holocaust.* **Oxford University Press; 2002, 200 pp.**
The author notes the many ways in which the *New Testament* has been interpreted to encourage anti-Semitic attitudes. In the post-Holocaust world many Christians scholars have worked to dispel these anti-Jewish readings of *New Testament* texts. Oldenhege employs Holocaust memories in her effort to refashion Biblical hermeneutics.

Ostow, Mortimer. *Myth and Madness: The Psychodynamics of Anti-Semitism.* **New Brunswick, NJ.: Transaction, 1996, 191 pp.**
A study conducted by a group of psychoanalysts over a nine-year period concluded that group dynamics, rather than individual traits, bore the heaviest responsibility for the promotion of anti-Semitism. The author discusses the role that Christianity has played in formulating anti-Jewish stereotypes and myths. He also identifies Christian Churches political parties and parents as a source of anti-Semitic indoctrination. Ostow pinpoints promoting fear of a Jewish takeover as one of the ways to unify group members.

Paldiel, Mordecai. *Sheltering the Jews: Stories of Holocaust Rescuers.* **Minneapolis, MN.: Fortress Press, 1996, 224 pp.**
At *Yad Vashem,* Paldiel has served thirteen years as the director of the department that addresses the "Righteous among the Nations." In this volume the author recounts some of the inspiring stories of the efforts of individuals and

groups (many of whom were Christians) to save the Jews from the Nazis. Paldiel maintains that these were ordinary citizens who, when faced with an evil and murderous policy, risked there own lives for their neighbors'. They exemplify the best and most moral of human beings. The author insists, that the horror of the *Shoah* should never be forgotten, nor should the heroism of those who put everything on the line to help the Jews.

Patterson, David. *Sun Turned to Darkness: Memory and Recovery in the Holocaust Memoir.* **Syracuse: Syracuse University Press, 1998, 233 pp.**
This is a study of the role of memory in the lives of Holocaust survivors. Using fifty memoirs as a database, Patterson concludes, that memory performs three functions for Holocaust survivors. First, memory aids in the recovery of tradition. Second, memory assists survivors in their recovery from indifference. Finally, memory teaches survivors that recovery can never be complete, but rather remains an ongoing process.

___. *Pilgrimage of A Proselyte: From Auschwitz to Jerusalem.* **New Zealand: Jonathan David, 1993, 207 pp.**
The author, a convert to Judaism, has written a personal affirmation of his devotion to Judaism; "This affirmation comes by way of and in spite of a personal collision with the *Shoah* and a personal pilgrimage toward a light that even the *Shoah* cannot comprehend...." Patterson believes that he must be an observant Jew and maintain Jewish law and ritual, "if I'm to meet my responsibilities for the life around me. And if I'm to refuse the Nazis a posthumous victory."

Pavlat, Leo. *The Treatment of Jewish Themes in Czech Schools.* **New York: American Jewish Committee, 1998, 47 pp.**
Although there was an introduction of some Jewish topics into the curriculum of Czech schools after the fall of Communism, the author contends, that this was an insufficient and biased approach to the subject. Pavlat notes, that lessons addressing Judaism still teach it as being inferior to Christianity. Moreover, even though the Holocaust receives significant coverage the facts about earlier and other forms of Jewish persecution are largely ignored. The author contends, that Czechs are currently trying to address this problem of bias and reject what is viewed as Christian indoctrination.

Pawelczynska, Anna. *Values and Violence in Auschwitz.* **Los Angeles: University of California Press, 1980, 201 pp.**
This book examines what life was like inside the Nazi death camp, Auschwitz. The author, a sociologist and Auschwitz survivor, places events in neo-Marxist categories, and concludes that prisoner resistance and survival were due exclusively to group solidarity. She also includes the nature of the camp structure, the socio-economic defense mechanism employed by the prisoners and their strate-

gies of adaptation and self-defense.

Pawlikowski, John T. *Christ in the Light of the Christian-Jewish Dialogue.* **New York: Paulist Press, 1982, 168 pp.**
Pawlikowski's volume surveys the thoughts of the major theologians concerned with Christian-Jewish dialogue. The author also provides a response to the charge made by Rosemary Reuther that "anti-Semitism is the left-hand of Christology." The final section of the book discusses the impact of the Holocaust on contemporary Christianity thought.

____. **"Developments in the Liturgy of Holy Week." Common Ground, http://www.jcrelations.net/articl1/pawlikowski.htm., 2001.**
Pawlikowski insists, that all Christians must commit to the positive vision of *Nostra Aetate* by working to strengthen Jewish-Christian relations. One way of doing this is to focus upon and change Holy Week services. The author notes the difficulties encountered when trying to rid Holy Week Liturgy of negative Jewish imagery and suggests that one method is to look at the common bonds Jews and Christians share. He also contends, that the Jewish historian Ellis Rivkin appropriately felt the emphasis of Holy Week should be shifted from the question of "Who crucified Jesus?" to "What crucified Jesus?"

____. **"Honesty Breeds Integrity." Dialogue and Universalism (2001), Vol. 11 Issue 1-2, pp. 53-58.**
The author attempts to explain the intent behind the Jubilee Letter issued by the Polish Episcopate, which asked forgiveness for the anti-Semitic and nationalist attitudes that negatively impacted past relations between Polish Catholics and Jews. According to Pawlikowski, this statement was in keeping with the efforts of Pope John Paul II. The author claims, that the Catholic Church must recognize its Jewish roots in order to understand its own identity and must admit that some have left the Catholic fold due to the Church's failings.

____. **"***Nostra Aetate*** : Its Impact on Catholic-Jewish Relations." Thought (1992), Volume 67 Issue267, pp 71-385.**
On the twenty-fifth anniversary of the issuance of *Nostra Aetate,* Pawlikowski examines the document's effects on Catholic education, theology and liturgy. The document officially prohibited Jewish stereotypes and called for reinterpretations of the *Old and New Testaments.*

____. **"The Vatican and the Holocaust: Putting *We Remember* in Context." Dimensions (1998), Volume12 Issue 2, pp. 11-16.**
The author offers a brief look at the actions of Pope Pius XII during the Holocaust. He suggests, that though the Vatican's statement *We Remember* was limited it did take a necessary step in admitting the wrong done by the Catholic

Church when it failed to act on behalf of the Jews during the Holocaust.

___. *What are They Saying About Jewish-Christian Dialogue?* **New York: Paulist Press, 1980, 165 pp.**
The author refutes the notion that Jewish-Christian dialogue is "dead," and contends that a new and hopeful stage requires a candid discussion of the differences between Christians and Jews on all levels. Pawlikowski divides the current conversation into six parts, including the deicide charge, *New Testament* anti-Semitism, and theological perspectives on the Nazi Holocaust.

Peck, Abraham J., ed. *Jews and Christians after the Holocaust.* **Philadelphia: Fortress Press, 1982. 111 pp.**
This is a collection of papers presented at a November 1980 symposium concerning Religion in a Post-Holocaust World, which was sponsored by the Hebrew Union College Institute of Religion in Cincinnati. The symposium brought together Jewish and Christian scholars to " evaluate the place of religious values in a world which has forever been changed by...the Holocaust." The volume includes a foreword by Elie Wiesel and includes essays by Allan R. Brockway, John Conway, Yaffa Eliach, Irving Greenberg, Rosemary Reuther and, David Tracy.

Perdurant, Daniel. *Anti-Semitism in Contemporary Greek Society.* **Jerusalem: Hebrew University, Vidal Sassoon International Center for the Study of Anti-Semitism, 1995, 21 pp.**
The author insists, that the most common way that Greek society deals with the subject of anti-Semitism is to ignore it and claim it has no hold in Greece. However, in Perdurant's view, Greek society in the 1980's and 90's still harbors prejudices against the Jews. Perdurant notes that the Orthodox Church condemns anti-Semitism, yet there are those within the Church that retain anti-Jewish sentiments and use anti-Zionism as a way to mask these attitudes. The author also discusses the retention of anti-Semitic ideas in school texts and negative attitudes against Jews that remain part of politics.

Perlmutter, Phillip. "Catholics and Jews." America (October 21, 2002), Volume 187 Issue 12.
Perlmutter insists, that the relationship between Christians and Jews has greatly improved over the last few decades. He contends, that the remaining gap between the two faiths has been reduced and that reports to the contrary are mostly exaggerations meant to help sensationalize media coverage.

Perry, Barbara J. "Defenders of the Faith: Hate Groups and Ideologies of Power in the United States." Patterns of Prejudice (July 1998), Volume 32 Issue 3, pp. 32-54.

Hate groups in the United States, according to Perry, rely upon Christianity's hostility toward the Jews and racism as justification for their rejection of the Jews. They identify Jews as a threat to Christianity and because they view the United States as a "Christian" nation, meant for "whites", they perceive Jews to be a subversive force that is responsible for the ills of the country.

Perry, Marvin and Frederick M. Scweitzer, eds. *Jewish-Christian Encounters Over the Centuries: Symbiosis, Prejudice, Holocaust, Dialogue.* **Peter Lang Publishing, 1994, 436 pp.**
The authors have chosen for this volume a selection of the essays read in 1989 at a conference sponsored by Manhattan College, Baruch College, and CUNY. Among the topics covered were; "Jesus was a Jew"; "Paul the Pharisee"; "The Jews in Reformation Theology"; "Medieval Images of Jews"; and "The Holocaust and Christian Thought."

Petuchowski, Jacob J. "Jewish Survival" and Anti-Semitism." Judaism (Fall 1984), Volume 33 Issue 132, pp. 391-401.
Petuchowski recognizes, that the phrase 'Jewish survival" can be interpreted in a variety of ways. For example it can mean the preservation of religious heritage, of ethnicity or culture. At the same time, others might insist that only in a secure Israel can Jews survive. The author, in this article, examines survival at its basic biological level. He concludes, that Jews, faced with two centuries of Christian anti-Semitism, which promoted persecution and culminated in the Holocaust, have proven they are adept at managing to survive on a physical level. In addition to their ability to survive despite adverse conditions, some Jews have managed to retain their commitment to Judaism and its spiritual and intellectual tradition. That Judaism still exists moves the author to admiration and to the hope that the future challenge will be "Jewish survival without anti-Semitism."

Phayer, Michael. "The Postwar German Catholic Debate Over Holocaust Guilt." Kirchliche Zeitgeschichte (1995), Volume 8 Issue 2, pp. 426-439.
Phayer traces the attitudes of German bishops about the Holocaust as they have changed from 1945 to1965. The statement made at Fulda in 1945, states the author, are very different from their admission of guilt and responsibility for the Holocaust made in 1965.

Plank, Karl A. *Mother of the Wire Fence: Inside and Outside the Holocaust.* **Louisville: Westminster/John Knox Press, 1994, 169 pp.**
Plank's book attempts to bridge the gap between Holocaust survivors and those who seek to understand their experience, particularly Christians. The author weaves together poetic/photographic images from the *Shoah*, with biblical passages and eyewitness accounts in order to evoke the experience of perpetrators, victims, and bystanders. For Plank the possibility that the "inside" may touch the

"outside" is crucial because the connection enables ethical and spiritual transformation. The author contends, that Holocaust images may bring the "onlooker to a point where humility, compassion, and vigilance might begin and thereby transform the outsider (Gentile) with the scar of the insider (Jewish victims of the Holocaust)."

Pollefeyt, Didier, ed. *Jews and Christians: Rivals or Partners for the Kingdom of God? In Search of an Alternative for the Theology of Substitution.* **Eerdmans, William B. Publishing Company, 1998, 153 pp.**
Christian Churches, according to Pollefeyt, have tried for centuries to validate their religious foundations by challenging Judaism. Christians have traditionally claimed that the Jews have been set aside as God's "chosen People" and that Christianity has replaced them. The author maintains that this assertion that Christians have become central to salvation has resulted in persecution of the Jews. In the aftermath of the Holocaust, Pollefeyt contends that Christian theology must be revised. The contributors to this collection discuss the problem from a variety of perspectives and propose possible solutions.

Polish, David. "The Statement on the Jews: An Inadequate Document." Christian Century (December 1965), Volume 82 Issue 48, pp. 1475-77.
The author concludes the Vatican's document is inadequate since there is no true sign of contrition or repudiation of anti-Semitism contained in the statement concerning Jews.

Polonsky, Antony, ed. *My Brother's Keeper?: Recent Polish Debates on the Holocaust.* **Routledge Press, 1990, 242 pp.**
The volume is a series of responses by Polish writers and intellectuals to an article written by Jan Blonski, which was published in a 1987 Krakow-based Catholic weekly. Blonski called upon Poland to admit not only moral guilt for the Holocaust, but also its indifference to the Jewish genocide.

Radcliffe,Albert. "How Dialogue with Jews has Transformed the Holy Week Liturgy." CommonGround, http://www.jcrelations.net/
Though Radcliffe, an Anglican minister, professes a deep spiritual feeling regarding the commemoration of Holy Week, he also acknowledges that the liturgy used during Holy Week services is tainted by its long held antipathy towards the Jews. Radcliffe specifically takes issue with one Collect, which is a prayer used on specific occasions. The Collect recited during Holy Week accuses the Jews of ignorance and "contempt for the word of God." The author suggests, that while theologians have made revisions in the "form" of prayers, they have not addressed the "spirit" of new prayers.

Ramras-Rauch, Gila. *Aron Appelfeld: The Holocaust and Beyond.* **Bloom-**

ington: Indiana University Press, 1994, 21 pp.
This book is the first English language publication of the writings of Aron Applefeld, Israel's foremost Holocaust writer.

Rausch, David A. *A Legacy of Hatred: Why Christians Must Not Forget the Holocaust.* Chicago: Moody Press, 1984, 222 pp.
Rausch underscores the inherent contradictions and dangers of white supremacist and other racist groups who assert their theology in the name of Christianity. The Holocaust, states the author, must teach Christians that there is no choice but to accept successfully the challenge of approaching all other peoples and religions in humility and love.

_____. "Chosen People: Christian Views of Judaism are Changing." Christianity Today (October 7, 1988), Volume 32 Issue 14, pp. 53-59.
In his recounting of conferences held between Jews and Christian Evangelicals in 1975, 1980, and 1984 Rausch concludes, that while these meetings had a positive impact upon the relationship between the two groups, there are still very serious issues that must be addressed. He notes three recent statements in which prominent evangelical ministers have declared that Jews "need to repent and be born again in Christ in order to be saved." The author discusses the worry that some evangelicals have expressed over Christian Churches who have reaffirmed the position of Jews and Judaism in God's plan. Evangelicals suggest that these Christians have in effect "given away the theological store." Rausch recognizes the concern that statements like these cause for Jews and proposes that if there is to be any progress in Jewish-Christian dialogue it will take place at the grassroots level among everyday people who work, live, and recreate together.

___. "Evangelical Zionism: The Vicious Debate Among Evangelicals." Jewish Frontier (May 1977), Volume 44 Issue 5, pp. 28-30.
Protestant evangelicals are split over the issue of Zionism. While fundamentalists support the Jewish state, liberal evangelicals do not. Two authors, William Hendriksen and John Walvoord, delineate the different approaches in their books that bear the same title, *Israel in Prophecy.* Hendriksen opposes anti-Semitism as un-Christian. He urges Jewish conversion and considers the Jews return to Israel as unbiblical. Walvoord, while not dismissing the idea of Jewish conversion, accepts Jews as God's chosen people and views their return to Israel as part of the Almighty's plan.

_____. *Fundamentalist Evangelicals and Anti-Semitism.* Trintiy Press International, 1992, 264 pp.
This is a comprehensive study of the relationship between fundamentalist Christians and Jews from the nineteenth century, through the Holocaust years of the twentieth century, and beyond. The author explores such issues as, whether or

not the more fundamentalist the Christian, the more anti-Semitic he/she becomes.

Reese, William L. "Christianity and the Final Solution." The Philosopher's Index (1984), Volume 16, pp. 138-147.
Reese makes the claim that Christianity bears overwhelming responsibility for the Holocaust. The author contends the *New Testament* portrays Jews as the murderers of Christ, and this left them vulnerable to persecution. The Holocaust was the final step in a long line of atrocities committed against Jews as a result of Christianity's intolerance and prejudice.

Rittner, Carol, and Dorothee Solle, et al., eds. *The Holocaust & the Christian World: Reflections on the Past, Challenges for the Future.* New York: Continuum Publishing Company, 2000, 296 pp.
The role of the Christian Churches during the Holocaust, and its consequences for Christian thought and practice in the contemporary world, are examined in this book of essays. The volume presents a broad range of perspectives from European, North American, and Israeli scholars, as well as accounts from heads of state and church, to rescuers and survivors.

____and John Roth, eds. *Confessing Christ in a Post-Holocaust World.* Westport, Conn.: Greenwood Publishing Group, Incorporated, 2000, 192 pp.
Rittner and Roth have compiled essays that examine how Christians and Jews engage one another in a post-Holocaust world, given the diversity of religious traditions. This volume seeks to provide pathways intended to make the relationship easier. The essayists explore methods by which Christians can shed the supercessionist traditions that have long been part of their "teaching of contempt" toward Jews and Judaism.

____. *From the Unthinkable to the Unavoidable: American Christian and Jewish Scholars Encounter the Holocaust.* Westport, Volume 4: Greenwood Publishing, 1997, 232 pp.
Essays by American and Jewish scholars, such as Michael Berenbaum, Eva Fleischner, John T. Pawlikowski, and Richard L. Rubenstein, reveal the effect life stories and personal experiences of the Holocaust have had on their thinking, and the issues and questions that engage them. The fifteen topics in this collection include post-Holocaust Jewish reflections on German theology.

____. *Good News After Auschwitz? Christian Faith in a Post-Holocaust World.* Mercer University Press, 2001, 215 pp.
Scholars argue, that in the aftermath of the Holocaust Christians must confront their culpability in the destruction of Europe's Jewish community. Roth and

Rittner contend, that Christianity must discover and emphasize the positive difference it can make in the world by renouncing and repenting the anti-Semitic
teachings of the past, by eliminating the idea of Christian exclusiveness from its
teachings, by developing an appreciation for the Jews and Judaism, and by accepting God's command "to love one's neighbor as oneself."

____. *Memory Offended: The Auschwitz Convent Controversy.* **Westport:
Greenwood Publishing Group, Incorporated, 1991, 312 pp.**
The book is a compilation of fourteen essays discussing various aspects of the
1984 controversy that surrounded the construction of a Carmelite convent at a
site near the Auschwitz death camp. The essayists examine how the issue of the
convent affects the current state of Jewish-Christian relations, as well as what
can be learned from this problem and applied to solving other disagreements
between the two faiths. Contributors to this volume include Robert McAfee ,
John Pawlikowski, Richard Rubenstein, and Elie Wiesel.

____ **and Julius Simon, eds.** *History, Religion and Meaning: American Reflections on the Holocaust and Israel.* **Westport, CT.: Greenwood Publishing
Group, 2000, 138 pp.**
The editors assembled a group of scholars, whose essays deal with assessing
whether or not American Christians displayed even a minimum level of ethical
behavior when confronting the "Jewish Question " during the twentieth century.
In the aftermath of the Holocaust and the debate that has surrounded the establishment of an Israeli State, the editors believe that this an area that requires
study.

____, **Stephen D. Smith and Irena Steinfeldt, eds.** *The Holocaust and the
Christian World: Reflections on the Past; Challenges for the Future.* **New
York: Kuperad Publishing, 2000, 296 pp.**
Nine sections of essays deal with different aspects of the European churches
response to the persecution of the Jews and the Holocaust. Contributors include
Michael Berenbaum, Hubert Locke, John T. Pawlikowski, Michael Phayer, John
K. Roth, and others. Two themes characterize this collection of essays; the frank
admission of the role Christianity played in the Holocaust and the current project
of completely ridding Christianity of all anti-Judaism.

Robinson, Jacob. *And the World Crooked Shall Be Made Straight: The
Eichmann Trial, the Jewish Catastrophe, and Hannah Arendt's Narrative.*
New York: MacMillan Publishers, 1965, 406 pp.
Ostensibly a book about the Eichmann trial, Robinson devotes a great deal of
space to refuting the arguments made by Hannah Arendt in her own book on the
trial, *Eichmann in Jerusalem.*

Rosenberg, Alan, and Gerald E. Myers, eds. *Echoes From the Holocaust: Philosophical Reflections on a Dark Time.* **Philadelphia: Temple University Press, 1988, 453 pp.**
The volume consists of twenty-three essays written mostly by professional philosophers on moral themes, on aspects of Western society, and on challenges to the understanding that requires urgent and sustained philosophical attention against the background of the Holocaust. The intent of the volume is to initiate some self-examination of philosophy in the light of the Holocaust, and to explore how the discipline might contribute to better understanding the implications and probable effects of the Nazi genocide.

Rosenberg, Bernhard, and Fred S. Heuman., eds. *Theological and Halakhic Reflections on the Holocaust.* **New York: KTAV Publishing House, Inc., 1996, 363 pp.**
This collection of articles represents the theological response of modern Orthodox Judaism, a generation after the Holocaust. It also represents a rejection of the "God's judgment theory," a view which holds that the Holocaust was God's judgment on an erring people. Contributors include Rabbis Norman Lamm, Emmanuel Rackman, Joseph B. Soloveitchik, and others.

Rosenfeld, Alvin H. *A Double Dying: Reflections on Holocaust Literature.* **Bloomington: Indiana University Press, 1980, 210 pp.**
This study of Holocaust literature uses as its theme the words of Elie Wiesel who wrote, "At Auschwitz, not only man died, but also the idea of man." Rosenfeld traces the implications of that "double dying" in a highly selective group of diaries, novels, poems, and one play. Without posing explicitly theological questions, his book is a thoughtful meditation on the meaning of speech after Auschwitz.

_____ and Irving Greenberg, eds. *Confronting the Holocaust: The Impact of Elie Wiesel.* **Bloomington: Indiana University Press, 1979, 239 pp.**
Rosenfeld and Greenberg's volume considers the impact of Elie Wiesel on the field of Holocaust studies. In their introduction, the editors state that " for a generation Elie Wiesel has stood as the interpreter of the Holocaust from a religious-theological perspective, raising issues about the covenant of God with His people, the nature of man and the universe." The thirteen essays in this volume are devoted to an examination of Wiesel's work from the vantage point of divergent perspectives as reflected in the editor's introduction.

Roth, John K. *The Consuming Fire: Encounters with Elie Wiesel and the Holocaust.* **Louisville, Westminster: John Knox Press, 1979, 191 pp.**
Roth, a Christian theologian, writes to help heal the centuries old rift between Christians and Jews, by providing a personal response to Elie Wiesel as author

and teacher. The author, through his examination of Wiesel's thought, attempts to discover what Christians can learn from Jewish suffering during the Holocaust.

____. "On the Impossibility and Necessity of Being a Christian: Reflections on Mending the World." The Philosopher's Index (1988), Volume 9, pp. 75-97.
Roth reminds readers that Jean Amery, a highly regarded philosopher and Holocaust survivor, believed that the Holocaust provided Jews with a true existential point of reference. With this in mind, Christians should try to understand how this reference point affects them. Roth attempts to pinpoint some of the implications that the Holocaust holds for Christianity.

____. "Talking About Religion in Public." American Journal of Theology and Philosophy (1993), Volume 14 Issue 2, pp. 189-204.
This essay, which emphasizes the work of philosopher John E. Smith, raises questions about Christianity in lieu of Auschwitz and the horror of the Holocaust. For example, Roth questions whether words like atonement, salvation and redemption assume new meanings after the extermination of Jews by Nazis, or if there is any hope that the alienation and hate which fostered such a crime can be overcome.

____. and Michael Berenbaum, eds. Holocaust: Religious and Philosophical Implications. Paragon House Publishers, 1991, 570 pp.
The essays included in this volume attempt to explore the religious and philosophical implications of the destruction of European Jewry. Contributors include Terence DePres, Richard Rubenstein, and Elie Wiesel.

Rousseau, Richard W. Christianity and Judaism: The Deepening Dialogue. Scranton: University of Scranton Press, 2000, 217 pp.
The author has pulled together fifteen essays on the relationship between Christianity and Judaism, in which both the Christian and Jewish contributors discuss such issues as anti-Semitism, the Holocaust and the State of Israel.

Rubenstein, Betty R., and Sus Garber. What Kind of God?: Essays in Honor of Richard L. Rubenstein, Vol. 11. Lanham: University Press of America, 1995, 524 pp.
This book is a Festschrift in honor of Richard L. Rubenstein. Half of one text consists of critical responses to Rubenstein's work. The balance of the book deals with the issues of the Holocaust, inter-religious dialogue, and theology not specifically keyed to Rubenstein's work.

Rubenstein,L. Richard. After Auschwitz: History, Theology, and Contempo-

rary Judaism. **Baltimore: Johns Hopkins University Press, 1992, 358 pp.**
Rubenstien has given readers a revised edition of his controversial 1966 collection of essays. This updated volume includes ten new chapters that address issues from the Auschwitz convent controversy to the connection between genocide and modernization.

_____. *After Auschwitz: Radical Theology and Contemporary Judaism.* **New York: Bobbs-Merrill Publishers, 1966, 287 pp.**
This landmark book set the agenda for the development of a "Holocaust theology", in which Jewish theologians could wrestle with the Holocaust as a question about traditional Jewish views of election and theodicy. Rubenstein asks whether the traditional view of God, as a "God of providence" in charge of history, is believable after Auschwitz. A God who could allow the Holocaust, states Rubenstein, as a means of "chastisement" for his people could only be a "cosmic sadist, not a God to be honored and worshiped."

_____. **"After the Holocaust: National Attitudes to Jews: Waldheim, the Pope and the Holocaust." Holocaust and Genocide Studies (1989), Volume 4 Issue 1, pp.1-13**
Kurt Waldheim, as the newly elected President of Austria, was invited to meet with Pope John Paul II at the Vatican. Rubenstein maintains, that their controversial meeting highlighted several ongoing problems between Jews and the Catholic Church. For example, when the Pope entertained Waldheim, he knew the newly elected leader was a war criminal, who had cooperated with the Nazis. Therefore it seemed clear that the Church was still putting its own political interests ahead of moral concerns like the Holocaust. Additionally, Waldheim had been elected to office in a Catholic country and had campaigned on a Catholic party ticket. Austrians supported him, claims Rubenstein, because they were indifferent to his anti-Jewish past. According to Rubenstein, Austrians, like Waldheim have long refused to acknowledge their complicity in the Holocaust.

_____. **"Religion and the Uniqueness of the Holocaust." Book Chapter Abstract (1996), pp. 11-18.**
The author contends, that the Holocaust is regarded as unique in western Civilization due to the fact that it is viewed as a modern "Holy War" perpetrated by a state that opposed Christianity. Therefore,while non-Christian, Asian scholars perceive the Holocaust as just another atrocity, Westerners remain focused upon it because it calls into question God's presence in history for both Jews and Christians.

_____. **'Should Jews Talk to Christians." Dialogue (Summer 1967), Volume 67 Issue 3, pp. 184-190.**
Although Rubenstein encourages Jewish-Christian dialogue, he recognizes the

difficulty of going forward with discussions. In this article he explores the attitudes of the conservative leaders on both sides and presents their reasons for opposing efforts to pursue a relationship. He notes, that each side believes his religious doctrine is rooted in "divine truth", and both worry that compromise and open dialogue pose threats to their faith. The threat is especially strong for Jews for they have suffered much at the hands of Christianity. Keeping the difficulties in mind, Rubenstein presents his reasons for promoting continued dialogue among Christians and Jews.

____ and John Roth. *Approaches to Auschwitz: The Holocaust and its Legacy.* **Louisville and Westminster: John Knox Press, 1987, 422 pp.**
This book covers the historical sources of the Holocaust, its realization in Nazi Germany, and responses to the Holocaust both during and afterwards. A recurring theme that runs throughout the book is that the Holocaust was one of the twentieth century's enduring monuments to rationality, albeit demented.

Rudin, Arnold James. "Christian-Jewish Relations in the United States: The Central Issues." Amerikanisches Judentum: Eine Tagung in der Hamburger Tagungsstaette (1987), Volume 19-20 Issue 6, pp. 28-42.
Three issues are emphasized in this piece. First, the author contends that the longstanding Christian teaching of "contempt for Jews" has resulted in more modern types of anti-Semitism that continues to infect much of Christianity. He calls for Christian Churches to rid themselves of all elements of hostility against Jews and Judaism. Second, Rudin discusses the controversy over conversion efforts that continue to hinder the improvement of Jewish-Christian relations. He contends, that Jews see conversion efforts as hostile, while Christians view proselizing as a way to complete Judaism. Third, the author insists that Israel should not be held to a different standard than other countries when policies are at issue.

____. **"Rabbi: Will Painful Tale Find Catholic Reception." The National Catholic Reporter (February 2, 2001), http//www.natcath.com .**
Since 1965, Rudin claims, there have been more positive encounters between Christians and Jews than in the previous four centuries. The author notes that *Nostra Aetate* repudiated anti-Semitism. Though he admits that books recounting the history between Christianity and Judaism places Christians in an extremely unflattering light, he maintains that the future holds the promise of better relations between the two faiths.

____. **"Reflections on the Vatican's *Reflection on the Shoah*," Cross Currents (Winter 1998), Volume 48 Issue 4, pp. 518-531.**
In Rabbi Rudin's view, *We Remember: A Reflection on the Shoah,* the long awaited statement by the Catholic Church about the Holocaust, raised more

questions and created more problems than it solved. This article details Rudin's criticisms of the document. For example, the document defends Pius XII, lumps several twentieth century atrocities together with the Holocaust, and makes a distinction between the Church's anti-Judaism and the secular forms of anti-Semitism that have been practiced. Although he regards the Pope's statement as "well intentioned" he also notes, that its message is "compromised and ambivalent". Rudin also worries, that this document will be the conclusion and not the beginning of the Catholic Church's examination of the Holocaust.

Ruether, Rosemary R. "Anti-Semitism and the State of Israel: Some Principles for Christians." Christianity and Crisis (September 26, 1973), Volume 33 Issue 20, pp. 240-244.
In this article Ruether discusses the difficulty that Christians face when confronted by the evidence of Christian anti-Semitism and are asked to consider the State of Israel. The author notes, that due to their guilt over the past role they played in promoting anti-Jewish sentiment, Christians feel compelled to equate any criticism of Israel with anti-Semitism. Ruether recognizes, that given these circumstances Christians find it hard to take a neutral stance in the dispute between Israel, the Palestinians, and the rest of the Arab world. She proposes a new start wherein Christians and Arabs alike recognize the right of Israel to exist. Furthermore she asserts, that Israel must face the reality that counter-attack is not a strategy that guarantees long-term survival. Ruether challenges Christians to take up the role of fair and just arbiters in this dispute.

____."Anti-Semitism in Christian Theology." Theology Today (January 1974), Volume 30 Issue 4, pp. 365-389.
Ruether argues, that there has been nothing accidental in Christianity's anti-Judaic stance. She states, that it was theologically necessary for Christians to show that the Jews, in rejecting Christ, had been rejected by God. Given this rejection any contentions Jews made about Jesus could be ignored. Since Jews were discredited, any acceptance of their ability to properly interpret scripture was open to challenge. Christians, according to Ruether,had positioned themselves as the true heirs of God's promise of salvation and Jews were perpetrators of evil and murder. Christians welcomed the word of God while Jews had always killed God's messengers, including Christ the "Messiah." Ruether examines the ways in which Christianity validated these contentions of a superior Christian faith and an evil Jewish history through the scriptures. She also traces the hardening of this Christian concept through the centuries and notes the conflicts that occurred as a result of it.

____. "Jesus as One Word of God to Us. A Response to Isabel Wollaston." MC (1992), Volume 34 Issue 2, pp. 38-40.
Ruether responds to Isabel Wollaston's article "Faith and Fratricide" printed in

MC (1991, Volume 33). Ruether admits, that Wollaston correctly notes that Ruether's book *Faith and Fratricide* contends "there is continuity and disconti- nuity in the relation of Christian anti-Judaism to modern racial anti-Semitism." Furthermore, this means there is a connection between the Christian tradition of Jewish persecution and the Holocaust. She also agrees, that Wollaston correctly assessed the idea that Christianity must reject claims of superiority or exclusiv- ity in terms of faith if it is to overcome its traditional prejudices against other faiths. She takes issue, however, with other claims made by Wollaston. Ruether contends, that by accepting Jesus as the messenger bearing "one word" of God to those of Christian faith, Christians reinforce anti-Semitism. However, Ruether is not proposing, that as Wollaston suggests, "Christians should dilute their faith,, or feel that the word they receive is meaningless." She maintains that her contention simply allows that Christians can hear God's message in a particular way, and yet accept that there are other valid religious messages. Ruether likens this to speaking in different languages and regarding them all as valid means of communication, even though one may be more understandable for us than oth- ers.

_____and Herman J. Reuther. *The Wrath of Jonah: The Crisis of Religious Nationalism in the Israeli-Palestinian Conflict.* New York: Harper and Row, 1989, 277 pp. (2nd ed, Minneapolis: Fortress Press, 2002, 296 pp.).
The Ruethers reject the idea proposed by other Holocaust theologians that in order to condemn anti-Semitism one must be uncritically supportive of Israel, and that when viewed in that light any criticisms about Israeli policy toward the Palestinians are tantamount to anti-Semitism. The Ruethers' examine the rela- tionship that exists between Christians, Jews and Palestinians. The authors re- view the development of Christian theology's claim to superiority and exclusiv- ity, the traditional anti-Jewish and anti-Zionist attitudes of Christianity, and the change in theology and feeling that has developed within the Vatican and The World Council of Churches in the past few decades.

Rylaarsdam, J. Coert. "The Disavowal of the Curse." Dialogue (Summer 1967), Volume 6 Issue 2, pp. 190-199.
The author proposes, that Judaism has faced both death and rebirth in the Holo- caust and in the creation of the State of Israel. Thus despair has been "matched by hope" and yet Jews still feel threatened. Christians, according to Rylaarsdam, are uneasy because they feel culpable for the Holocaust. Many Christians have come to understand that the persecution of the Jews is rooted in church teach- ings that claim God has placed his chosen people under a "perpetual curse" and their only escape from this curse is to convert to Christianity. Christians, desir- ing to make amends, confess and ask forgiveness for past offenses. However, Jews remain wary of Christian professions of guilt because they have endured so much Christian hostility. The author suggests, that Christianity must disavow

anti-Semitism, cast aside all its old theological beliefs about Israel, revise perceptions of the Jews, and begin anew to develop relations with Jews and Judaism.

Sacks, Jonathan. *Crisis and Covenant: Jewish Thought after the Holocaust.* Manchester and New York: Manchester University Press, and St. Martin's Press, 1992, 294 pp.
Written by the Chief Rabbi of the United Kingdom and the Commonwealth, this book is a defense of Orthodox Judaism. Sacks views the last two hundred years as centuries wherein Judaism and the Jews have been buffeted by crisis; Enlightenment and Emancipation at the beginning of modernity, and later the Holocaust. The author surveys the broad spectrum of modern Jewish life and thought from the time of Jewish emancipation through to the present day.

Sandmel Samuel, Malcolm L. Diamond, A. Roy Eckardt and Manfred Vogel. "Symposium on the Contemporary Jewish-Christian Encounter." Journal of Bible and Religion (April 1965), Volume 33 Issue 2, pp. 101-13
Each author tackles an aspect of the ongoing dialogue between Christians and Jews. Sandmel deals with the problem of a total theology for Judaism and proposes that the nature of Judaism determines that its theology remain uncompleted. Diamond, in writing about the dialogue between Christians and Jews, questions the honesty of the encounter and discusses the complicity of Christians in promoting anti-Semitism. Eckardt wonders if there can be an effective reconciliation between Jews and Christians because the Jews have been persecuted for such a long time, and anti-Judaism lays at the heart of the Christian Gospels. Vogel maintains, that Christians and Jews must admit that neither can claim to hold divine truth, for they each have relied upon man for assurance of their religious truth.

Sandri, Luigi. "Not all Religions Equal, Declares Pope John Paul II." Christianity Today (February 7, 2000), Volume 44 Issue 2, 4 pp.
Pope John Paul II, in a speech given before the cardinals, bishops and theologians who comprise the Congregation for the Doctrine of Faith stated, that Jesus Christ is the "unique Savior" of the universe. He then spoke of the Church as the "royal road" to God's saving grace. This statement led non-Catholic, and some Catholic scholars, to the conclusion that other faiths are not equal to or as complete as the Catholic faith. Though the Pope did not single out any one group or person, Sandri states, that he meant to respond to the theories of Jesuit theologian Jacques Dupuis. Dupuis has asserted, that divine revelation extends beyond the Church's teachings. Vatican officials insist, that the Pope's words were not meant to be offensive toward Jews.

Schafler, Samuel. "Anti-Semitism in Historical Perspective." Journal of

Jewish Communal Service (1984), Volume 60 Issue 3, pp. 250-255.
The author insists, that the lines between the different types of anti-Semitism should not be blurred, and that the anti-Semitic attitudes promoted by Christianity laid the foundation for Hitler, even though Hitler is regarded as post-Christian. According to Schafler, valid criticisms of Israeli policy do not signal anti-Semitism, but ideology which refutes the right to an Israeli State is anti-Semitic in nature. He contends, that anti-Semitism is ultimately irrational, no matter who its proponents are.

Schlant, Ernestine. *The Language of Silence: West German Literature and the Holocaust.* **New York: Routledge Press, 1999, 277 pp.**
Schlant argues, that since the end of World War II, German novelists have produced a "literature of silence" in regards to the Holocaust and the general treatment of Jews during the Nazi years.

Schusler-Fiorenza, Elizabeth and David Tracy, eds. *The Holocaust as Interruption.* **Edinbergh: T. & T. Clark Publishers and Philadelphia: Fortress Press, 1984, 88 pp.**
This slim volume is a compilation of articles that describe the impact of the Holocaust for Christian theology.

Schuster, Ekkehard, ed. *Hope Against Hope: Johann Baptist Metz and Elie Wiesel Speak Out on the Holocaust.* **New York: Paulist Press, 1999, 106 pp.**
The book focuses on Elie Wiesel, who was interned at Auschwitz, and Christian theologian Johann Baptist Metz, who was drafted into the German army at the age of fifteen. Both came from religious backgrounds only to have their lives broken by the horrors that they witnessed during WWII. Metz and Wiesel share the belief that the Holocaust was a rift in history, after which nothing could ever be seen in the same way as before.

Schwarzschild, Steven S. "Judaism, Scriptures, and Ecumenism." Judaism (Summer 1964), Volume 13 Issue 3, pp. 259-273.
Schwarzschild claims, that the ecumenical movement offers nothing to Jews. In his opinion, Christians, understandably and out of necessity, view ecumenism as one more attempt to convert Jews. Therefore, Christians and Jews are divided even when dealing with "Scripture." If any progress is to be made between the two groups, the author insists, that Jews must prompt Christians to undertake a serious and long-term study of rabbinic Judaism.

Schwartz,Daniel. *Imagining the Holocaust.* **New York: St. Martin's Press, 1999, 353 pp.**
The author contends, that to vicariously experience the Holocaust means to address critical philosophical questions. To ignore these questions and to concen-

trate only on emotional content is to risk not understanding the little that can be understood about the murder of European Jewery.

Scweid, Eliezer. *Wrestling Until Daybreak.* Lanham: University Press of America, 1994, 367 pp.
This book is devoted to a systematic and a more fragmentary reflection proceeding from the midst of the Holocaust experience. Scweid focuses on the thought of Rabbi Leo Baeck, Shimshon Drenger, Abba Kovner, and others who displayed uncanny insight when articulating the ever-so-limited ethical-existential and religious alternatives available to victims of the Holocaust. There is also discussion about the post-Holocaust writings of Eliezer Berkovits, and Emil Fackenheim. Their "614 commandment," that Jews are absolutely forbidden to give Hitler posthumous victories, is rejected by the author as an example of how "radical" theologians seized on the uniqueness of the Holocaust as a basis for a redirection of the normative basis of Jewish commitment.

Seager, Frederic. *The Jewish Challenge, or the Vicissitudes of Judaism in the West.* Montreal: Picard, 1996, 277 pp.
This survey of Jewish history covers many issues. Among those addressed that deal with the relationship between Christianity and anti-Semitism are; the development of Christian anti-Judaism, the hostility against Jews during the Middle Ages, the evolution of nineteenth century anti-Semitism, anti-Semitic attitudes in Russia, Hitler's rise to power and the Holocaust. Sager also discusses two responses in the aftermath of the Holocaust that he regards as important. He contends, that although there seems to be a lessening of anti-Semitic ideology, and many have come to accept the tie that exists between the anti-Jewish feelings disseminated by Christianity and the Holocaust, there will always be elements of anti-Semitism in Christianity. The author also maintains, that Jewish missionary activity would help combat anti-Semitism.

Section: Explorations and Responses. "Christians and Jews: A Declaration of the Lutheran Church of Bavaria." Journal of Ecumenical Studies (Summer/Fall 1999), Volume 36 Issue 3-4, pp. 480-85.
This is a translation of a statement issued by representatives of the Lutheran Church of Bavaria following meetings that spanned the years 1992 through 1995. Within these meetings the topic "Christians and Jews" was examined. The statement focuses upon the importance of relations between Christianity and Judaism, accepts complicity for the Holocaust, and highlights the common elements of the two faiths.

Section: Sign of the Times. "Church Examines Conscience in Treatment of the Jews." U.S. Catholic (December 1997), Volume 62 Issue 12, pp.9.
Catholic Church officials in France issued a statement apologizing to Jews for

the Churches inaction and silence during the Nazi's deportation of Jewish Citizens to concentration camps, and for the murder of the Jews. The statement accused French bishops of being "stuck to an attitude of conformism, caution, and abstention", while the Holocaust took place.

Section: Sign of the Times. "Don't Lift the Cross so High." U.S. Catholic (November 1998), Volume 63 Issue 11, pp. 8-12.
The argument surrounding the erection of crosses commemorating the murder of non-Jewish Poles at Auschwitz is the focus of this article. Jews contend, that although gypsies, non-Jewish Poles and Russians were killed by the Nazi's in the death camp, Jewish victims far outnumbered others and so the "character of a Jewish cemetery should be respected."

Shanks, Hershel. "Silence, Anti-Semitism and the Scrolls." Biblical Archaeology Review (March-April 1991), Volume 17 Issue 2, pp. 54-60.
The author asserts, that John Strugnell, chief-editor of the *Dead Sea Scrolls,* in a 1990 interview with an Israeli reporter made comments that show he is anti-Semitic. Shanks claims that Strugnell believes Christianity is superior to Judaism. Colleagues working with Strugnell defended him and claimed his comments were made at a time when he was ill. They contend his work has shown no evidence of prejudice against the Jews. The author also notes, that while Israel gained control over the *Scrolls* in 1967, it was not until the 1980's that any Israeli scholars were made part of the team working on the *Scrolls*. Scrugnell has already been replaced as chief editor of the project, but Shanks takes issue with the rest of the teams failure to deal with the charge that an anti-Semitic bias pervades the assignment.

Shapiro, Edward S. "American anti-Semitism and the Historians." Congress Monthly (June-August 1994), Volume 61 Issue 4, pp. 12-15
The contention made by Shapiro, is that only one Gentile historian has addressed the subject of American anti-Semitism in any significant manner. Furthermore, he maintains that Jewish historians generally disagree over how important anti-Semitism is within American Jewish history. Recent books by Fredric Jaher and Leonard Dinnerstein offer support for the argument that anti-Semitism has been deeply rooted in America. Both authors also assert that the origins of anti-Jewish feelings in the United States can be traced to Christianity's role in the history of this country. According to Jaher and Dinnerstein, in the private world of religion, a pool of hostility toward Jews lays waiting to be tapped.

Sherbok, Dan Cohn. *God & the Holocaust.* Harrisburg: Morehouse Publishing, 1987, 212 pp.
This book asks, "Where was God when six million died?" The author explores

the work of eight major Holocaust theologians and argues that all fail to reconcile, as they must, the reality of suffering with the loving kindness of God.

Shereshevsky, Esra. "The Lesson of the Holocaust: A Jewish Point of View." Journal of Ecumenical Studies (Fall 1980), Volume XVII Issue 4, pp. 665-669.
The author suggests, that Jews have put much of their energy into memorializing the Holocaust, therefore they are not working to do away with anti-Semitic attitudes that exist today and threaten Jews. According to the author, the Holocaust was not the beginning of anti-Semitism. Rather it was the culmination of it. Jews must invest their resources into revitalizing and " immortalizing" life, not death.

Sherman, Franklin. "Speaking of God After Auschwitz." Jewish-Christian Relations, http://www.jcrelations.net, 2002, 13 pp.
Sherman, a Lutheran minister, notes that among most religions, including Judaism, there are debates about the meaning of the Holocaust. He reviews the different approaches that have been taken in trying to understand how Auschwitz fits into God's plan for humanity. Sherman admits that Christianity bears guilt for the treatment of the Jews, both prior to and during the Holocaust. He contends, that when speaking of God, after the death of six million Jews, there can be no reference to "triumphalism" by Christians. He prompts all Christians and Jews to work toward a greater understanding of each other's religious traditions.

Sherwin, Byron L, and Susan G. Ament, eds. *Encountering the Holocaust: An Interdisciplinary Survey.* Chicago: Impact Press, 1979, 502 pp.
The bibliographical essays about the Holocaust included in this volume are addressed to college and university instructors. The book examines all branches of literature on the subject, including historical, theological, judicial, and the social-psychological perspectives.

Short, Geoffrey. "Teaching the Holocaust: The Relevance of Children's Perceptions of Jewish Culture and Identity." British Educational Research Journal (1994), Volume 20 Issue 4, pp.393-406.
In order to help develop an effective method for teaching eleven-to-fourteen year old British students about the Holocaust the author interviewed seventy-two children as a way to determine what they understood about Jewish culture and identity. In this process policy implications were formed and obstacles were identified. The study noted, that teachers would have to ensure that students know the Holocaust was a crime against humanity and that pupils must be made to recognize the power of anti-Semitic ideas and racist attitudes.

Siegle-Wenschkenewitz, Leonore. "The Contribution of Church History to a Post-Holocaust Theology: Christian Anti-Judaism as the Root of Anti-

Semitism." *The Holocaust as Interruption*. Eds. Elisabeth Schuessler Fiorenza and David Tracy. Edinburgh; T. and T. Clark, 1984, pp. 60-64.

The author contends, that after World War II the German Confessing Church claimed to have been victimized by the Nazis and asserted that it had come to the defense of the Jews when targeted by Hitler. However, over time Christian Churches have admited, that their theology is in some part complicit in the atrocities committed by the Nazis. The author maintains, that despite this move to accept some responsibility for the Holocaust, academics teaching theology avoid mentioning Christian guilt for having cooperated with Hitler. They ignore the fact that their compliance with Nazi policies occurred at a time when they believed they could hide their aim to rid Christianity of all Jewish influence.

Siefman, Henry. "Christian-Jewish Relations: Still a Way to Go." Judaism (Winter 1986), Volume 35 Issue 1, pp. 25-28.

The author contests the theory that greater understanding of religious doctrine has caused a growing tolerance and respect between Jews and Christians. Rather, Siegman claims the ecumenical spirit that permeates Jewish-Christian relations stems from the revulsion experienced when the horrific consequences of anti-Semitism were understood. He contends, that Christian Churches must continue to work at realizing their role in promoting anti-Jewish attitudes and act to reject them once for all.

_____. "Christianity and Judaism: The Unfinished Agenda." Christian Jewish Relations (March 1986), Volume 19 Issue 1, pp. 57.

The article demands that the pope do more to fight anti-Jewish feelings in Poland and elsewhere. Siegman claims, that the Vatican's refusal to recognize Israel diplomatically is partly due to the Catholic Church's long history of anti-Judaism and the idea that the Jews homelessness is God's punishment visited upon them. The author asserts, that the Church must accept its complicity in perpetrating hatred of the Jewish people.

Signer, Michael A. "Can Jews Trust Catholics." Commonweal (January 12, 2001), Volume 128 Issue 1, pp. 12-15.

The author contends Jews need not fear that by opening themselves up to the overtures of Pope John Paul II and the Catholic community they are betraying their heritage and ancestors. In the Jubilee 2000 year the pope has called for Catholics to repent for the anti-Jewish attitudes and actions of the past and put an end to the enmity that has existed between Jews and Christians over the centuries. According to Signer, preserving anger over sins of the past will not ensure the preservation of the Jewish community.

_____. *Humanity at the Limit: The Impact of the Holocaust Experience on Jews and Christians*. Bloomington: Indiana University Press, 2000, 478 pp.

The purpose of this volume is to bring together Jewish and Christian thinkers from Israel, Germany, and Eastern Europe, as well as the United States and Canada in order to confront the legacy of the Holocaust and its continuing impact. This study is done from the perspectives of a variety of disciplines. An unresolved question discussed by the contributors is what, in view of the crimes of the Holocaust, is the nature of human nature?

Silva, Antonio Barbosa. *Is There a New Imbalance in Jewish-Christian Relations? An Analysis of the Theoretical Presuppositions and Theological Implications of the Jewish-Christian Dialogue in the Light of the World Council of Churches and the Catholic Church's Conceptions of Inter-Religious Dialogue.* **Upsala: Upsala University, Department of Theology, 1992, 339 pp.**
The contention is made that an imbalance in the Jewish–Christian dialogue has been developing since 1967, and this has led to difficulties in the relationship. Silva notes that there are three factors that have created this problem; first that Christians must renounce anti-Semitism, second that attempts to convert Jews must stop, and last that Christians must recognize the right of Israel to exist. The author studies Rosemary Ruether's theory that anti-Judaism is tied to anti-Semitism and that if Christians are forced to reject anti-Semitism and wipe it out of the *New Testament* it could ultimately help Christianity. Silva argues, that the Holocaust and anti-Semitism, in any form, are both anti-Biblical and anti-Christian.

Simon, Ulrich. *A Theology of Auschwitz: The Christian Faith and the Problem of Evil.* **Louisville: John Knox Press, 1979, 160 pp.**
Ulrich seeks to interpret the problem of Auschwitz in terms of that other dimension revealed in Jesus Christ, particularly his (and the Jews') arrest, trial, and arrival at the place of the skull (Auschwitz), death and resurrection. It is admitted that it is God, not humankind, who incorporates the terror of Auschwitz into a pattern of meaningful sacrifice. It can then be understood that such a transformation is believable only if we accept "that God has himself entered human history in the sacrifice of Jesus."

Slaybaugh, Dennis L. **"Review Essay: The Work of the German Academies." Journal of Ecumenical Studies (1989), Volume 26 Issue 4, pp. 722-724.**
Nine of the ten papers contained within the book *Offene Wunden- Brennende Fragen:Juden in Deutschland von 1938 bis Heute* are reviewed by Slaybaugh. These papers were originally presented at a 1988 conference commemorating *Kristallnacht* and each offers the hope that German Christian theologians will accept Christianity's responsibility for the Holocaust. By admitting its culpability it is proposed that Christianity can lessen any chance for re-establishing dangerous anti-Semitism in Germany.

Smiga, George M. *Pain and Polemic: Anti-Judaism in the Gospels.* **New York: Paulist Press; 1992, 210 pp.**
The author studies the role of the *New Testament* in Jewish-Christian relations. He takes note of the Biblical texts that negatively portray the Jews and Judaism. Smiga categorizes the polemic statements, which helps provide a comprehensible basis for analysis. Although addressed to Christian audiences, the book should also prove helpful to those outside the faith, and might well advance dialogue between Christians and Jews.

Smith, David Norman. "The Social Construction of Enemies: Jews and the Representation of Evil." Sociological Theory (November 1996), Volume 14 Issue 3, pp. 203-240.
Smith develops a seven-part argument about why "hate" continues to plague our world and relationships. He focuses upon the fact that anti-Semitism seems to be growing again some fifty years after the Holocaust. The aurthor also explores the "social construction" of "anti-Semitic demonology" and tries to understand it through a series of written works.

Smith, Elwyn. "The Christian Meaning of the Holocaust." Journal of Ecumenical Studies (1969), Volume 6, pp. 419-422.
The author argues, that the Holocaust is "rich in meaning " for both Jews and Christians. For followers of Christ it stands as a symbol and a reminder of Christianity's failure to "love thy neighbor." Smith maintains, that the Holocaust prompts Christians to ask some probing questions about their religious theology. The author suggests, that whether or not Jews would have been saved if Christians had loved their neighbors, and opposed Hitler, is not pertinent. Rather Christians should understand, that no matter the result, it would have been far better if they had embraced their theological underpinnings and stood with Jews during the Holocaust.

Sobosan, Jeffrey G. "The Jews and Christian Ingratitude." Dialogue (Spring 1977), Volume 15 Issue 2, pp. 42-44.
The author points out, that the spirit of ecumenism, which supposedly has brought Christians and Jews closer together has not effectively filtered down to the laity. There are still Christian laypersons that read the *New Testament* and, through misinterpretation, accept the negative imagery of Jews as divinely inspired. There are Christians that resist the idea of a Jewish return to Israel because they view Jews as the murderers of Christ. Sosbosan contends, that many followers of Christ fail to acknowledge the past crimes that were committed against the Jews in the name of religious belief. Additionally, Christians do not appreciate the heritage of faith they have received from Judaism. The author insists, that it is time to admit how much has been learned, and can be learned from the Jews.

Special Edition: "The Fate of European Jews, 1939-1945: Continuity or Contingency." Studies in Contemporary Jewry (1997), Volume 13.
Articles contained in this special edition address the topic of how to present the Holocaust, and whether long-term or short-term, specific or universal factors should be highlighted. While some of the articles are general in nature, others provide a more philosophical view of the causes for the Holocaust. Some of the pieces included in this edition examine the responsibility Christianity bears for the murder of six million Jews. For instance, Gavin Langmuir explores Christian anti-Judaism and its ties to modern anti-Semitism, while Steven Katz points out how Christian nationalist and Nazi hostility toward the Jews differed.

Special Issue. "The Holocaust: Remembering for the Future." The Annals of the American Academy of Political and Social Science (November 1996), Volume 548, 200 pp.
This is a special edition of the journal, which includes a selection of the papers presented at the March 1994 conference "Remembering for the Future." The focus of the conference was to present ideas about the role that education could play in preventing future genocides. Some of the papers address the Holocaust as a "Holy War" which harkens back to the role of Christian anti-Judaism in the atrocity, the impact of Christian rescuers on Holocaust studies, and the influence of the Catholic Press on the "Jewish Question" in Poland. Yehuda Bauer, David Gushee , Ronald Modras, Carol Rittner, and Richard Rubenstein are among the contributors to this edition.

Special Issue. "Teaching Jewish-Christian Relations in the University Classroom." Shofar (Summer 1988), Volume 6 Issue 4.
The contents of this special edition of *Shofar* deal with teaching effectively about Jewish-Christian relations within University classrooms. The following are some of the topics included; exploring the past and understanding it in the context of the relationship between Jews and Christians, the teaching of the *New Testament*, the impact of the Holocaust upon Jewish-Christian dialogue, and Christianity and the State of Israel.

Steele, Michael R. *Christianity, Tragedy, and Holocaust Literature.* Westport, CT.: Greenwood Press, 1995, 192 pp.
Steele contends, that due to the influence of Christianity there is a lack of a connection between literature concerning the Holocaust and tragic literature. He asserts that tragedy has always been an important part of Western culture and history and that it was Christianity's view of itself as having surpassed Judaism that helped develop the preconditions that made the Holocaust possible. This idea of Christian superiority must be revised, according to the author, "if we are ever going to come to terms with the Holocaust. Once we truly confront the Holocaust the literature that has come from it will be placed in the proper con-

text and will be better understood."

Stern, David H. *Restoring the Jewishness of the Gospel.* **Jewish New Testament Publications, Incorporated, 1989, 96 pp.**
This short text introduces Christians to the Jewish roots of their faith. The author examines some of the conventional issues that exist between Christians and Jews, and addresses some of the questions that crop up in discussing the dialogue between the two religious groups.

Stoehr, Martin. "Against Forgetting." Christian Jewish Relations (Winter 1991), Volume 24 Issue 1-2, pp. 43-45.
In a 1991 lecture given in Essen the call went out for Christians to become aware of anti-Semitism, fight against any evidence of it and to undertake a new assessment of its theology. The author prompts Christians to reject the negative stereotypes of the past and examine any beliefs that might have contributed to the Holocaust, or other persecutions of Jews over the ages.

Stone, Ronald. 'The Zionism of Paul Tillich and Reinhold Niebuhr." Christian Jewish Relations (September 1982), Volume 15 Issue 3, pp. 31-43.
Stone examines the ideas of Paul Tillich and Reinhold Niebuhr, and finds that both men incorporated theology and politics into their Christian Zionist attitudes. Each repudiated anti-Semitism, provided aid to Jewish refugees, and acknowledged the need for a Jewish homeland. Their acceptance of Israel was on the grounds that Jews needed a safe haven for Holocaust survivors. These two also recognized that there would be problems with the Palestinians and suggested ways to bring about peace.

Subcommittee on Jewish-Anglican Relations. *From Darkness to Dawn: Rethinking Christian Attitudes toward Jews and Judaism in the Light of the Holocaust.* **Toronto: Anglican Church of Canada, 1989, 67 pp.**
This study produced by the Subcommittee on Jewish Anglican Relations, focuses upon the problem of Christian anti-Semitism throughout the centuries. The Committee admits that years of Christian anti-Jewish teachings led a majority of Christ's followers to remain silent in the face of Jewish persecution at the hands of the Nazis. Christianity's lack of moral courage during the Holocaust hinders attempts to improve the relationship between Christians and Jews.

Sullivan, Robert, Daren Fonda, Mimi Murphy and Joshua Simon. "Journey to the Past." Life (April 2000), Volume 23 Issue 4, pp. 50-60.
Sullivan discusses the visit of Pope John Paul II to the Middle East. He notes the importance of this trip to Christians and Jews and to their ongoing dialogue. The author examines the fact that some Jews worried, that in light of his Polish background the pope might harbor some of the anti-Semitic attitudes that have

been prevalent in Poland. They were relieved at finding John Paul an advocate of reconciliation between the two faiths. He remembered the pain and evil of the Holocaust. Though some Jews fault him for not going far enough in apologizing for the role the Catholic Church played in Jewish suffering, still others believe him to be a friend to the Jewish people and commend him for his visit.

Sultanik, Kalman. "Anti-Semitism a Malady of the Past?" Midstream (June-July 1992), Volume 38 Issue 5, pp. 14-15.
The author contends, that *Nostra Aetate* and the United Nation's decision to finally renounce Resolution 385, which equated Zionism and racism, are not sufficient actions to combat anti-Semitism. Sultanik reviews the role Christianity played in developing anti-Semitic attitudes and insists that many countries still harbor hostility toward the Jews. He demands, that every effort be made to eradicate anti-Semitism throughout the world.

Swidler, Leonard. "A New Hocuth?" Journal of Ecumenical Studies (1965), Volume 2, pp. 469-470.
Swidler maintains, that despite the work coming out of Vatican II there are still powerful elements in the Catholic Church that remain anti-Semitic. Some Catholic prelates have vehemently opposed the Council's attempt to put forward a statement rejecting anti-Jewish attitudes within the Church. This offers proof that a reconciliation between Jews and Christians will be difficult. Swidler also contends, that the Arab states are exerting enormous pressure on Christians to resist Zionism. The author proposes, that if Vatican II officials fail to clearly affirm their rejection of Anti-Semitism they provide material for a future Hochuth.

_____."Catholic Statements on Jews: A Revolution in Progress." Judaism (Summer 1978), Volume 27 Issue 3, pp. 299-308.
This author focuses on the impact the statements issued from Vatican II have had upon Jewish-Christian relations. The author observes the evolution in the dialogue between Christians and Jews, since the Catholic Church repudiated anti-Semitism and rejected the charge of deicide against Jews.

_____. "Germany, Christianity and the Jews: From Diatribe to Dialogue." Leonard Swidler, Editor. *Breaking Down the Walls Between Americans and East Germans: Jews and Christians Through Dialogue*. Lanham, MD.: University Press of America, 1987, pp. 39-61.
This excerpt from the book discusses German (mostly West Germany) Protestant and Catholic Church activities in pursuing Jewish-Christian dialogue since the end of World War II. Swidler notes, that while Protestant Churches in Germany accepted a measure of responsibility in 1950 for what happened to the Jews before and during the war, the German Catholic Church waited until 1975

to address the issue. According to the author, even though both the Catholic and Protestant Churches are intent on removing anti-Semitism from German society, it still persists.

Talmadge, Frank. "Christian Theology and the Holocaust." Commentary (1975), Volume 60 Issue 4, pp. 72-75.
The author examines the writings of A. Roy Eckardt, Franklin Littel and Rosemary Ruether. Talmadge explains, that these writers do not believe that Judaism was superceded in God's plan for mankind by Christianity. He also notes, that each of these scholars advocates educational programs that will help offer new methods with which Christians can develop and improve their relationship with Jews.

Terman, David. "Anti-Semitism: A Study in Group Vulnerability and the Vicissitudes of Group Ideals." Psychohistory Review (Spring 1984), Volume 12 Issue 4, pp. 18-24.
Terman explains the history of Christian, as well as other forms of anti-Semitism in terms of the psychological workings that take place in groups who feel that their ideology is threatened. The author examines the earliest origins of conflict between Jews and Christians and demonstrates the steps that made Christians regard Jews as dangerous. He follows suit with other groups who have attacked Jews.

Thorne, Edward. "We Cannot Hide You From Jesus." Commonweal (March 9, 1990), Volume 117 Issue 5, pp. 141-143.
The Vatican Document *Nostra Aetate* is examined in this article. The article describes the manner in which Catholics have tried to overcome anti-Semitism and work within the teachings of Christ in order to assist Jews.

Todorov, Tzevetan. *Facing the Extreme: Moral Life in the Concentration Camps.* **New York: Metropolitan Books, 1996, 307 pp.**
Using memoirs by survivors of Nazi and Soviet concentration camps, Todorov reflects upon possibilities for moral life in extreme situations. The survivor's memoirs show classical heroism. Todorov concludes, that in an age of depersonalization and fragmentation, the seemingly banal act of caring can redefine morality.

Unsworth, Tim. "Cassidy's Open Ears a Sign of Hope for Dialogue." National Catholic Reporter (May 14, 1999), http://www,natcath.com.
This article details Cardinal Bernadin's efforts to bring Catholics and Jews closer together with a conference dedicated to exploring the Vatican's statement *We Remember: Reflections on the Shoah*. The author notes the tensions that were evident between the Catholic and Jewish scholars in attendance. The

document has caused a great deal of controversy. Cardinal Edward Cassidy spoke to the assemblage and while he noted the improvement in Jewish-Catholic relations, he also stated that there was a good deal left to be done if we intend to bridge the gap between the two faiths. Furthermore, he walked a fine line between crediting Pope Pius XII for some of his efforts on behalf of Jews during the Holocaust and maintaining that the pope's case requires more study before any final conclusions about his activities can be reached. Unsworth is quick to recognize, that despite areas of agreement between Catholics and Jews it will be a long time before the distrust and animosity between the two groups is completely overcome.

Van Buren, Paul M. *According to the Scriptures: The Origins of the Gospel and of the Church's Old Testament.* **Eerdmans, William B. Publishing Company, 1998, 151 pp.**
Van Buren calls for a reevaluation of the *Old Testament* and its role in the church. The author contends, that the church must recognize the claim of the Jews to these sacred scriptures and yet find a way to claim the text as its own because, in Van Buren's view the *Old Testament* plays an important role in Christian faith. This book honestly criticizes Christian anti-Semitism and shows that there is no need to denigrate one another's faith. According to the author, both Christians and Jews can read Biblical texts differently and still respect one another's interpretations. Van Buren's efforts in this volume are directed toward fostering the dialogue between Christians and Jews.

____. **"Authenticity Without Demonization." Journal of Ecumenical Studies (Summer 1997), Volume 34 Issue 3, pp. 341-345.**
The author questions how Christians could believe that demonizing the Jews enhanced the authenticity of their faith, for this ignored the fact that Jesus was Jewish and lived and worked among the Jews. If Christians were called by God to love their enemies, was it not easier to love the people of Christ? Van Buren maintains, that it is the differing interpretations of Biblical text that each side uses that invites disagreement. He suggests, that for too long Jews and Christians have asked the wrong questions of one another. They should put aside the Holocaust and Christ, and ask whether or not God is generous and "large" enough to call more than one group "his beloved." By concentrating on God, each community returns to its roots and has no reason to demonize the other.

____. *A Theology of the Jewish-Christian Reality: A Christian Theology of the People of Israel.* **University of America Press, 1995, 362 pp.**
This three-volume set provides a systematic theology for Christians that stresses the relevance that the continued existence of the Jewish people has for Christian belief. Van Buren makes it clear that it has been a mistake for Christians to ignore or denigrate Jews. In his three books, the author traces the theological roots

of Christianity, gives insights into how Christianity has drawn upon Jewish thought for its theology, and argues that the covenant between God and the Jews remains intact. Van Buren calls upon the Church to recognize and respect that covenant.

____. *Discerning the Way: A Theology of the Jewish Christian Reality.* **New York: Seabury Press, 1980, 207 pp.**
In recognizing the uniqueness of Jewish and Christian theology, the author uses the burden of the Holocaust and the significance of the State of Israel as corner-stones for the reconstruction of Christian theology.

Vawter, Bruce. "Are the Gospels Anti-Semitic?" Journal of Ecumenical Studies (1968), Volume 5, pp. 473-487.
The author contends, that the Gospels, which have been the source of Christian anti-Jewishness, have often been misunderstood and oversimplified. He puts forward facts that influenced the tone of the Gospels, and makes the case that the Scriptures must be interpreted in context. Vawter insists the promotion of hostility toward the Jews due to uncritical readings of scripture must end. He also asserts, that anti-Christian writers must stop linking the Gospels to anti-Semitic atrocities.

Vernoff, Charles Elliot. "After the Holocaust: History and Being as Sources of Method Within the Emerging Inter-Religious Hermeneutic." Journal of Ecumenical Studies (Fall 1984), Volume 21 Issue 4, pp. 639-663.
Given the fact that Christianity's teachings about the Jews influenced Nazism, in the aftermath of the Holocaust, Christians sensitive to the suffering of the Jews insist that they have a moral obligation to change the relationship their faith has had to Jews and Judaism.

Vogel, Manfred H. "The Problem of Dialogue Between Judaism and Christianity." Journal of Ecumenical Studies (1967), Volume 4, pp. 684-699.
Vogel asserts, that "kinship and difference" are the two elements necessary for a successful dialogue to take place. He makes the case that despite the history of Christian anti-Judaism both these factors can be identified as part of the evolving association among Christians and Jews. Ultimately the author sees mutual benefit in an open relationship between members of the two faiths. In an increasingly secularized world these Christianity and Judaism will "strengthen each other through dialogue."

Volf, Miroslav. "Kneeling to Remember." Christian Century (July 1, 1998), Volume 115 Issue 19, pp. 653.
The author recounts the ideas that came to mind during a sermon he was listening to in a Christian service celebrating Memorial Day. He notes the contention

made by Elie Wiesel in his book, *All Rivers Run to the Sea* that "...salvation can only be found in memory....certain events will be omitted, especially those episodes that might embarrass friends and, of course those that might damage the Jewish people." Volf relates these lines to the Catholic Church's document *We Remember*. Although he commends the Church for issuing the apology, he recognizes its failings. The author speculates, that perhaps the church is reluctant to admit the full extent of its complicity in the Holocaust because of the embarrassment it would cause. Yet he warns, that by doing this the Church continues to do damage to the Jewish people.

Walker, Graham Jr. *Elie Wiesel: A Challenge to Theology.* **Jefferson: McFarland and Company, 1988, 184 pp.**
His Christian world shattered by the Holocaust, Walker, a Southern Baptist theologian, began a reconstruction of his faith and its connection to the *Shoah* through studying the writings of Elie Wiesel. Four images dominate this book: the "wandering Jew," the "survivor," the "God who listens," and the "ambiguous God." The volume also explores the thoughts of two Christian theologians, Paul VanBuren and Jurgen Moltmann. These two have struggled with the same kind of questions as the author.

Washington, Harold C. **"The Lord's Mercy Endures Forever: Toward a Post-Shoah Reading of Grace in the Hebrew Scripture."** **Interpretation (April 2000), Volume 54 Issue 2, pp. 135-145.**
Washington discusses how Christians and Jews can preserve the integrity of their respective traditions while reaffirming "that God's mercy toward Israel endures forever." The author examines Christianity's effort in the post-Holocaust world to reject and fight any vestiges of anti-Semitism that may still linger in its doctrine. He suggests reliance upon the Bible as a way to work toward repentance. The author specifically turns to Exodus for examples that can be used to demonstrate "Divine forgiveness and the message that God's blessings are meant for all people." Thus the Jews retain the blessing God intended for all religions and people.

Wasserstein, Bernard. *Vanishing Diaspora: The Jews in Europe Since 1945.* **London: Hamish Hamilton Press, 1996, 332 pp.**
The author's study shows, that the Catholic Church in France has much to account for during the Holocaust. Wasserstein's charges against the church include "that it actively collaborated with the regime, pressured Vichy in favor of its anti-Semitic policies, and proclaimed loudly its own continued "teaching of contempt" for Jews as "Christ-killers." After the war, writes the author, the church aided the so-called "rat-line" for the rescue of Nazi war criminals that was maintained by Croatian Catholics in France. In addition, Wasserstein condemns the French church for its stubborn refusal to return the Jewish children, who

were converted to Catholicism, while entrusted to Catholics during the war.

Webber, Jonathan, ed. *Jewish Identities in the New Europe.* **London: Littman Library of Jewish Civilization, 1994, 307 pp.**
A partial list of the essays compiled for this book that addressing the topic of interfaith relations in the aftermath of the Holocaust includes; the impact that Auschwitz and Vatican II have had on Christianity's ideas about Jews and Judaism, and the new relationship of "New Europe".

Weingrad, Michael. "Jews (in Theory): Representations of Judaism, Anti-Semitism, and the Holocaust in Postmodern French Thought." Judaism (Winter 1996), Volume 45 Issue 1, pp. 79-98.
The author reviews the ideas of three French postmodern thinkers about Jews and anti-Semitism. Weingrad demonstrates that each of the three theorists show in their work a lack of accurate knowledge of Jews and Judaism. He notes their occasional use of traditionally held negative stereotypes about Jews that Christianity helped develop. Moreover, the author claims that two of the theorists retain the belief that Christianity is superior to Judaism.

Wiesel, Elie. *A Journey of Faith: A Dialogue between Elie Wiesel and His Eminence John Cardinal O'Connor.* **New York: Fine, 1990, 87 pp.**
Sharp disagreements emerge concerning such diverse subjects as, the actions of Pope Pius XII during World War II, original sin, and the meaning of suffering.

___. *All Rivers Run to the Sea.* **New York: Alfred Knopf Publishing, 1995, 432 pp.**
The first volume of Wiesel's memoirs, reveals much about his childhood, his religious upbringing, and his experiences in the Nazi camps. His life is brought up to the post-war period, when he decided to live in France and become a journalist.

___. *And the Sea is Never Full: Memoirs.* **New York: Alfred Knopf Publishing, 1999, 429 pp.**
This is the second volume of Wiesel's autobiography, which traces his life and thought up to the early 1990's. The author has much to say about matters relating to history, politics, ethics, and religion. Of special interest is the section that deals with his relationship with Simon Wiesenthal, President Ronald Reagan's trip to the Bitburg cemetery, and the politics behind the construction of the United States Holocaust Memorial Museum.

___. *From the Kingdom of Memory: Reminiscences* **New York: Schocken, 1990, 250 pp.**
In this collection of personal essays and speeches, the author reflects on his life

and faith before and after the Holocaust. In the concluding essay, Wiesel compares the suffering of the Jewish people with that of Job, and writes of Job's suffering as an example for post-Holocaust Jews to emulate, "Did he ever lose his faith? If so, he rediscovered it within his rebellion...the source of his hope was memory, as it must be ours. Because I remember, I have the duty to reject despair. I remember the killers and I despair; I remember the victims, and on their behalf and for their sake and for their children's sake, I must invent a thousand and one reasons to hope."

____. *The Trial of God* (*as it was held on February 25,1649, in Shamgorod*) **New York: Schocken, 1979, 177 pp.**
Ostensibly, this work is a play about three itinerant actors who arrive in an eastern European town to perform a *Purim spiel* (Purim play) and are horrified to learn that all but two of the residents have been killed in a recent pogrom. The actors decide to stage a mock trial of God, indicting Him for allowing such things to happen to His children. The plays' intent is to ponder the question, where was God during the Holocaust?

____. *Twilight*. **New York: Schocken, 1988, 217 pp.**
This is the story of Raphael, a professor of literature and a Holocaust survivor, whose search for the man who rescued him from the Nazis brings him to an asylum, where the patients' delusions spring from the Bible. Amid patients calling themselves Adam, Cain, Abraham, Joseph, Jeremiah and God, Raphael's search for his rescuer forces him to confront the meaning of his own survival.

Wieseltier, Leon. "Slander." New Republic (February 4, 2002), Volume 226, Issue 4, pp. 42.
Wieseltier responds to an article by Andrew Sullivan that criticized an earlier piece writtwen by Daniel Goldhagen called, "What Would Jesus Have Done?", which appeared in the *New Republic* in January of 2002. Sullivan criticized, what he viewed, as an unfair attack on the Catholic Church's actions during the Holocaust. Wieseltier, on the other hand, takes issue with Sullivan's views. He claims, that he and other Jews have nothing to discuss with the Church. Any guilt Catholics feel for their behavior towards Jews, or repentance they desire to make is their own problem. He credits Goldhagen for his work and criticizes Sullivan for trying to distinguish between Catholic anti-Jewishness and the Nazi's racial brand of anti-Semitism. In Wieselter's opinion, each contributed to the pain and suffering of the Jews.

____. **"Washington Diarist." New Republic (February 9, 1998), Volume 218 Issue 6, pp. 42, 1 pp.**
The author is highly critical of recent attacks on the film about the origins of anti-Semitism that is shown at the Holocaust Museum in Washington, D.C. He

claims, that those who bemoan the fact that the film slanders Christianity as the originator of anti-Semitism are trying to rewrite history in order to soothe their own consciences. According to Wieseltier, the Holocaust Museum is correct in laying blame for anti-Semitism on Christianity, even if it is troublesome or "inconvenient" for Christians to hear.

Wiesenthal, Simon. *The Sunflower on the Possibilities and Limits of Forgiveness.* **New York: Schocken Books, 1997, 271 pp.**
The author employs various features of Holocaust memoir, fiction and oral testimony to pose this incomparable moral dilemma: "You are a prisoner in a concentration camp, and a dying Nazi soldier asks for your forgiveness. What would you do?" The query taps the deepest recesses of the post-Holocaust imagination, as well as the nature of forgiveness. It also forces the reader to contemplate the following question; "How would I have acted in the Holocaust?"

Wigoder, Geoffrey. *Jewish-Christian Interfaith Relations: Agendas for Tomorrow.* **Jerusalem: Institute of the World Jewish Congress: Policy Forum 1998, 52 pp.**
Though the author notes the progress that has been made over the last few decades in interfaith relations, he contends, that the dialogue between Christians and Jews has been more evident within the Catholic Church than with the Protestant and Orthodox Churches. The author, an Israeli delegate to the International Jewish Committee for Inter-religious Consultations, summarizes this groups' work under three issues that must be dealt with; anti-Semitism, theological dialogue and the State of Israel. Wigoder also claims, that because of the advances made in removing "the teaching of contempt" about Jews from Christian theology the dialogue should now focus its concentration on the relationship between Christians and Jews at the "parish or communal level."

____. *Jewish-Christian Relations Since the Second World War.* **Manchester and New York: Manchester University Press, 1988, 176 pp.**
Through a survey of the state of Jewish-Christian relations over the past forty years, Wigoder documents the increased sensitivity of Christians to the theological roots of anti-Semitism.

Williamson, Clark M. " The Church's Mission and the People of Israel."
Christian Century October 10, 1993, Volume 110 Issue 28, pp. 974-979.
This article targets the anti-Judaism that remains in the Christian Church, the relationship of the Christians to Jews, and the issue of any mission to convert Jews to Christianity. According to the author, Christian Churches need to revamp their teachings regarding Jews and Judaism.

____. *A Guest in the House of Israel: Post-Holocaust Church Theology.* **Lou-**

isville: Westminster/John Knox Press, 1993, 344 pp.
Williamson asks; if the Holocaust indicates that God does not stand by His covenant with Israel, why should Gentiles expect God to be faithful to the church? The author's response is that a properly revised ecclesiology regards the church as unintelligible apart from the God of Israel...and as " pursuing a common mission with the Jewish people: to bring to the world the call and claim of the God of Israel." The author also surveys confessional statements from denominations that accept Christian complicity in the Holocaust.

Willebrands, Cardinal Johannes Gerardus Maria. *Church and Jewish People: New Considerations.* **New York: Paulist Press, 1992, 288 pp.**
The volume represents sixteen years of writing by the author, former head of the Vatican Secretariat for Promoting Christian Unity and the Pontifical Council for Religious Relations with the Jews. This is a selection of the author's addresses and articles, which reflect on Catholic-Jewish relations since Vatican II. Two themes run through this volume; the Jewish people have at long last been recognized by the Church as a living and creative reality, and Catholics have affirmed that in order to understand the Jews, the essential traits delineated by the Jews for their own identity have to be affirmed unquestionably. Willebrands also stresses the bond between the church and the Jewish people due to Christianity's Judaic roots

Willis, Robert. "Christian Theology After Auschwitz." Journal of Ecumenical Studies (1975), Volume 12 Issue 4, pp. 493-519.
The author suggests ways in which Christianity can mount valid theological responses to Judaism, given the fact that Christian prelates have failed thus far to recognize the moral consequences of the Holocaust.

____. "Why Christianity Needs an Enduring Jewish Presence." Journal of Ecumenical Studies (Winter 1988), Volume 25 Issue 1, pp. 22-38.
Willis maintains, that the Holocaust and the founding of the State of Israel provide the context within which a conversation can be held about how important a Jewish presence is for Christianity. The long history of Christian anti-Semitism makes these two events necessary topics. The author contends, that in order for Christianity to revitalize itself it must reject the anti-Semitic notion of superiority over Judaism, and must come to recognize that the covenant between God and the Jews is still valid. Ultimately Christians must recognize that Jews can and must define themselves and their State.

Wilson, John. "In the Beginning Was the Holocaust?" Christianity Today (April 8, 2002), http.//www.Christianitytoday.com.
The author discusses the large number of books dealing with the Holocaust that have been produced over the last fifty years. He asserts, that many of these vol-

umes are spurred by rage directed at God and Christianity and warns that the rage can be "seductive." He contends, that simple answers do not provide a true or helpful examination of the Holocaust. For example, he criticizes Daniel Goldhagen's claims that the Catholic Church bears the brunt of the responsibility for anti-Semitism. Wilson prods authors and readers to look deeper into the evidence in order to formulate more complete theories and to increase the possibility that the Holocaust will be long remembered by Jews and non-Jews.

Wolf, Arnold Jacob. 'Anti-Semitism and Reunion." Christian Century (May 29, 1963), Volume 80 Issue 22, pp. 709-710.
Jews view the reunion of all Christians with ambivalence. On one hand a united Christianity provides the possibility of a powerful ally, while on the other, Jews have often suffered at the hands of Christians and so they could be a threat. Jews have overwhelmingly supported the ecumenical spirit that has come from the Second Vatican Council, but unfortunately books like Father Hans Kung's, *The Council, Reform, and Reunion,* have added to the concern of Jews. The book deals with the subject of Catholic-Protestant rapprochement. Though it does not directly concern Judaism it, does contain elements that tread dangerously close to anti-Semitism.

Wollaston, Isabel. "Faith and Fratricide: Christianity, Anti-Semitism, and the Holocaust in the Work of Rosemary Ruether." MC (1991), Volume 33 Issue 1, pp. 8-15.
The author critiques Rosemary Radford Ruether's contentions in her book *Faith and Fratricide.* According to Wollaston, Ruether contends, that Jesus' message was free of anti-Judaism, but the early Christian Church revised this message and used an anti-Jewish theology as a means for validation. Ruether also asserts, in Wolliston's view, that while Christians worked to protect the Jews as witnesses to Christ, they also believed the Jews should be made to suffer and survive, so they could eventually accept Christ. In Ruether's opinion, even though Christian anti-Judaism was related to the racial anti-Semitism of the Nazis, there was also a "disconnect" between the two beliefs. Christians never meant to eradicate Jews, they wanted to convert them. Wollaston, in examining Ruether's arguments, insists the theory that Christian anti-Judaism "developed as the left hand of Christology," means that in order for Christianity to reject anti-Jewish attitudes it must revise its message concerning redemption, the resurrection, and the cross. She concludes, that if the Church follows Reuther's prescription the Christian message is completely diluted. According to Wollaston, this means "rejecting Christianity and exploring alternative avenues" of faith.

____. "Sharing Sacred Space? The Carmelite Controversy and the Politics of Commemoration." Patterns of Prejudice (1994), Volume 38 Issue 3-4, pp. 19-27.

The controversy between Catholics and Jews that developed in 1985 over the placement of a Carmelite convent on the grounds of Auschwitz is the focus of this article. Wollaston maintains, that this issue has highlighted the differences that exist in the way Jews and Christians perceive the Holocaust and this has hindered the Christian/ Jewish relationship.

Wolpe, David. *"Hester Panim* in Modern Jewish Thought." Modern Judaism (1997), Volume 17 Issue 1, pp. 25-56.
Wolpe examines "death of God " theologies and how they tie into the idea of Hester Panim or "the eclipse of God." He discusses the ways in which these two movements are defined and the differences between the two. The author also looks at how the Holocaust figures into the two theories. Wolpe concludes, that the idea of God's absence is a condition of the human heart and not a "pronouncement of divine disregard."

Wood, Karen Louise. *The Partnering God: A Constructive Christian Theology in Conversation with Liberal American Judaism.* Cambridge MA.: Dissertation; Harvard University, 1998, 195 pp.
Wood notes the advances that have been made in the relationship between Christians and Jews since 1964. She reviews the fact that Christianity has examined its role in perpetrating the anti-Semitic attitudes that made the Holocaust possible. The author claims, that as a result of the dialogue Christian theologians have renounced the "teaching of contempt", accepted that the covenant between God and the Jews remains intact, and that Jesus provides Gentiles a way to salvation. Wood contends, that the shift in Christian theology has opened the door to the idea that God elects the saved and the Jews are witnesses to his truth. However, she proposes, that the idea of election does not fit well in the modern world. She suggests that, based upon the work of others, religion should move to a view of "God as partner." This would solve a host of difficulties by countering Christian anti-Semitism premised upon the idea of religious superiority and would open the door to multiple partnerships between God and man.

Yaseen, Leonard C., and Billy Graham. *The Jesus Connection: To Triumph over Anti-Semitism.* New York: Crossroad Publishing Company, 1985, 192 pp.
Included in this volume are separate introductions by Billy Graham (Protestant), Theodore M. Hesburgh (Catholic), and Marc H. Tannenbaum (Jewish). The book examines the historical influences leading to anti-Semitism, and also underscores the anti-racist teachings of Vatican II. The author emphasizes the commonalities between Jews and Christians.

Yovel, Yirmiyahu. "Sublimity and Resentment: Hegel, Nietzsche, and the Jews." Jewish Social Studies (July 31, 1997), Volume 3 Issue 3, pp. 1-13.

Yovel discusses the ways in which the philosophers Hegel and Nietzsche dealt with the "Jewish question" in their work. Both men undertook the task of presenting a philosophical understanding of the modern world and each displayed mixed ideas about where the Jews fit into the world. Hegel, presenting his ideas in the early nineteenth century, held strong anti-Jewish feelings that were rooted in Christianity. Though he came to recognize that Judaism had some value and he supported Jewish emancipation politically, his philosophical view remained centered on Christianity. The Jews, however, were central to Nietzche's plan to promote a "revolution in values" that would root out the corruption of Christianity. Neitzsche, working to combat the decadence of the modern world as it was developing in the latter half of the nineteenth century, was not philo-Semitic. Rather he defended the Jews as the catalyst for his new Europe and believed their education and experience made them strong and stable enough to play a dominant role in changing humanity.

Zakim, Leonard P. *Confronting Anti-Semitism: A Practical Guide.* **Ed. Janet Ditchik. Hoboken, NJ.: KTAV, 2000, 157 pp.**
This volume makes the case that even though anti-Semitism has sharply declined in the United States, there are still elements of it to be found. Zakim reviews the ways in which it is still evident and suggests responses and methods for combating the prejudice. He includes statements issued from a variety of Christian Churches in condemning anti-Semitism and the Holocaust. He pays special attention to the Catholic councils and conferences that have spoken out about these issues. The author also incorporates the essays of several other scholars in this book. An example is Padraic O'Hare's "Anti-Judaism, Anti-Semitism: History, Roots, and Cures."

Zanicky, Martin. *Anti-Judaism in Contemporary Christian Preaching.* **Princeton, NJ.: Princeton Theological Seminary, 1997, 219 pp.**
The author charges that anti-Semitism remains a part of Christian preaching. He buttresses this contention by reviewing Christianity's anti-Judaism and connecting it to anti-Semitism. He surveyed over a three-year period the sermons and suggestions provided by four journals that address the issue of preaching. He also met with congregants to discuss and analyze sermons for their anti-Jewish content. Zanicky's work identifies six categories in which anti-Judaism is evident; the idea that Judaism is passé or inferior; references to the Pharisees without noting the derogatory context; the failure to qualify anti-Judaic terms; the concept of a superior Christian faith; presenting the Jews as being unable to properly interpret the scriptures; and the charge of deicide.

Zanicky, Robert, Stephen King Wright. *The Vengeance of Our Lord: Medieval Dramatizations of the Destruction of Jerusalem.* **Toronto: Pontifical Institute of Mediaeval Studies, 1989, 233 pp.**

This book explores the medieval tradition of the Passion Plays that focused upon the siege and destruction of Jerusalem in 70CE. These plays were extremely popular with audiences in Spain, Germany, Italy, France and England from the fourteenth through the sixteenth centuries. Wright provides an explanation for how these dramatizations began and presents details about the anti-Jewish stereotypes that were employed by the Christians who put on these plays. Many of the plots included the charge of deicide and the theory that the Jews received punishment from God because they rejected Christ.

Zimmels, H.J. *The Echo of the Nazi Holocaust in Rabbinic Literature.* **New York: KTAV, 1977, 372 pp.**
Zimmels tries to correlate the phases of the Holocaust with Jewish ritual, as well as the community problems raised by the Nazi campaign of destruction. Using rabbinic *responsa*, Zimmels presents the Holocaust in light of its impact on Jewish law and Talmudic interpretation.

Glossary

Abraham
In Biblical history Abraham is the patriarchal figure. He is presumed to have lived about 2000-1700 B.C.E. Abraham was the father of Ishmael and Isaac.

Aktion Reinhard
Named after Reinhard Heydrich, after his assassination in May 1942. Heydrich presided over the Wannsee Conference, at which the Nazi's plans were laid for the "Final Solution". This term, honoring the fallen leader of the SS, was the German code name for the Nazi's murder of the Jews in Europe.

Aktion T-4 (Tiergarten Strasse 4)
The Nazi's used this as the code for the Third Reich's Euthanasia program and was named for the address of the Reich Chancellery building, where the offices of those in charge of the Euthanasia Program resided.

Allies
The United States, Britain, the Soviet Union and the Free French under the leadership of DeGaulle were the Allied coalition, who fought against the Axis governments during World War II. The Axis nations were Germany's Nazi regime, Italy and Japan.

Anti-Semitism

Wilhelm Marr coined the word in 1879. In literal terms it denotes opposition to Semites. This would include Arabs as well as other Semitic populations. However, it's meaning is usually connected with the hostility felt toward Jews. Marr intended that the word distinguished between Christianity's aversion to the Jews, and a repugnance toward Jews based on race.

Aryan

This linguistic term was originally used to designate Indo-European languages. Later the meaning was distorted to refer to the populations that spoke those languages. The Nazi's regarded these people as superior to Semitic groups and through this perversion of the term Aryan came to describe persons who could be proven to be non Jews.

Aryan Paragraph

Once the Nazi regime had consolidated its power in Germany, in an attempt to purge the German churches of all influence, it issued the Aryan Paragraph which held that "no priest could be of Jewish extraction and no non-Jew could marry a Jewish woman." The German Churches took issue with this decree because they believed the government was challenging Christian theology by denying the efficacy of baptism.

Ashkenazi Jews

Jews from middle and eastern European background (including Russia) with their specific religious practices and social customs were referred to as Ashkenazi.

Auschwitz

First established as a concentration camp in 1940, Auschwitz later became an extermination or death camp in 1942. The camp, located in Poland consisted of three sections: Auschwitz I, which served as the main camp; Auschwitz II, also known as Birkenau, which was the extermination camp and Auschwitz III, which was the I.G. Farben labor camp.

Bar Kokhba Revolt

The revolt was the last and one of the most successful of the Jewish uprisings against the Romans. The rebellion, which took place in 132-135 CE, was led by Simeon ben Kosiba, who died in battle when the Romans finally proved able to defeat the revolt.

Beatification
The process in which popes declare that a person having lived a saintly life or suffered a heroic death (martyrdom) can be designated "Blessed". This is a long process and one of the steps toward Canonization.

Bible
This is the designation given to the Jewish scriptures, plus the New Testament.

Birkenau
Also known as Auschwitz II, this was the death camp (or extermination camp) of the Auschwitz site, which was located in Poland.

Black Death
This is a form of the plague. During the Middle Ages Christians accused Jews of having poisoned wells in order to spread the plague among Christ's followers.

Blood Libel
Blood libel allegations were made against Jews during the thirteenth century and later. These accusations charged Jews with murdering Christian children in order to use their blood for the purpose of making unleavened bread. It has been suggested that an occasional red mold found growing on the bread gave rise to this myth.

Bolshevism
The term is synonymous with Soviet Communism and refers to the dictatorship established by Lenin in Russia in 1917.

Boycott (Anti-Jewish)
The Nazis organized this action against the Jews in Germany on April 1, 1933 in order to induce them to leave Germany. The boycott began as a response to the threat of a restriction on the use of German goods by American Jewish and non-Jewish groups, who were concerned about the anti-Jewish policies employed by the Nazi regime. The official Nazi boycott lasted only one day because the government feared that to prolong it would hurt Germany's image abroad.

Buchenwald
Located north of Weimar and constructed in 1937, Buchenwald was originally used as a camp for political prisoners. However, after the horrors of *Kristallnacht* the facility was used to imprison thousands of Jews. After 1945, when the Germans commenced the dismantling of Auschwitz, thousands of Jews were transferred to Buchenwald, where they were used for "medical experiments." This concentration camp was one of the largest on German soil.

Bystanders
These included governments, institutions, churches and individuals who either refused to aid the Jews or responded with indifference while the Nazi's persecuted and murdered European Jewry.

Canonization
This is the solemn declaration by the Pope that a person is now in heaven and is accorded the full honor of the Church. This is a two-step process in which a persons' cause must be presented and accepted by the appropriate Church committee for consideration. This is followed by an examination and reexamination of the person's life and of the required miracles attributed to the candidate. If the procedure is successful then a declaration of Canonization is made.

Chelmo
This extermination camp, built in 1941 in the western region of Poland, was the first camp where mass executions were carried out with gas. Over 300,000 people were murdered at Chelmo.

Concentration Camps
When the Nazi's took power in Germany in 1933 they quickly established concentration camps for the imprisonment of their "enemies". Jews were targeted for incarceration merely because they were Jewish. Others regarded as problematic for the Nazi state included gays, gypsies, Jehovah's Witnesses and political opponents. Initially, the concentration camps were distinguished from the death camps, but as the war drew to an end, these camps became sites of mass deaths, as Jewish prisoners transferred from the death camps outside Germany were crowded into the concentration sites.

Concordat of 1933
This was the treaty drawn up between the Catholic Church and the Third Reich government in 1933. Cardinal Eugenio Pacelli negotiated the pact, which laid out the terms of agreement for the Church's continuance of its mission to care for the souls of Catholics in Germany under Hitler's rule. However, once the treaty was signed it became clear that Hitler had no intention of abiding by it, and eventually his regime mounted a campaign of repression and terror against German Catholic clerics, that severely minimized the influence of Catholicism in Germany.

Confessing Church
Once it became clear that the Nazi government intended to exercise strict control over all German Churches, the Confessing Church mounted opposition to Hitler's aim to interfere with Christian theology and rites. Though these

Christians fought Nazi attempts to expel converts from their congregations, they remained mostly silent about the persecution of the Jews.

Covenant

A covenant is a pact or a promise between two parties. In Judaism the concept of covenant is very theologically important for it denotes the eternal bond the Jews share with God. Jewish scriptures note two primary covenants; God's agreement with Abraham and the covenant made between God and the people of Israel with Moses at Mount Sinai. Christianity proposed that its followers had established a new covenant with God that replaced the bond between the Almighty and the Jews.

Crusades

Pope Urban II rallied Christians to recover the Holy Land and the Sepulcre of Jesus from the Moslems in 1066. The armies of Christian peasants and noblemen were referred to as Crusaders and the "holy war" they engaged in was called a Crusade. Christians marching toward Israel invaded Jewish communities, took Jerusalem in 1099 and massacred the non-Christian population residing there.

Dachau

Erected in 1933, this Nazi concentration camp located in southern Germany, was used mainly to imprison political opponents until 1938. After that time groups of Jews, gypsies, Jehovah Witnesses and homosexuals were incarcerated there. Though construction was begun on a gas Chamber at Dachau it was never operational, however Nazi doctors and scientists did use many of the prisoners for experimentation.

Death Camp

These were the extermination centers where the Nazis murdered Jews and non-Jews as part of Hitler's policy to achieve a "Final Solution" to the Jewish problem.

Death Marches

Towards the end of the war, the Nazis leveled the death camps in Poland and began moving their victims by forced marches over long distances and under intolerable conditions to camps in Germany, where the prisoners were treated brutally and had little chance of escape because of the heavy security employed. These prisoners were transported from one camp to another to meet labor needs or to be put to death.

Deicide
Deicide is the charge of having killed God. Christians leveled this accusation at Jews. For centuries Christians insisted Jews had murdered Jesus Christ, the only "Son of God."

Deportation
The process of transporting and resettling Jews in the Nazi occupied regions of Europe to the labor or death camps.

Diaspora
This word is the Greek translation for "scattering", or exile. The term is used to describe the Jewish communities who lived among Gentiles outside of the holy lands.

Displaced Persons (DPs)
Of the eight million Europeans driven from their countries during World War II, two million were unable to return home after the war. These displaced persons were placed into camps run by the United Nations Relief and Rehabilitation Administration. Of the DP population approximately 50, 000 were Jews, who had been liberated from camps throughout Nazi occupied Europe. These internees were sometimes the objects of anti-Semitic taunts from their Allied liberators.

Doctrine of Choseness
Jews, according to the *Torah,* were Chosen by God to receive his word and to serve as a "Light Unto the Nations" and spread God's word among them.

Ecumenical (Ecumenism)
Worldwide or universal in extent, the word has come to describe the movement toward greater understanding and improved relations between religious faiths.

Einsatzgruppen
Accompanying the German army during its invasion into the Soviet Union in 1941, these four mobile units of Security Police and SS were ordered to kill all Jews, Soviet officials and other "undesirables or defectives". The victims were murdered and buried in mass graves.

Emancipation (Jewish)
From antiquity through the Middle ages Jews were forced by law to live in ghettos separated from the rest of European society. With Enlightenment thought came the growing demand for the equality of all men during the eighteenth century. This was especially significant for Jews. In France the "Jewish Question" was dealt with through revolution and emancipation was

granted. In the nineteenth century Jews were emancipated in most of central and Western Europe.

Encyclicals
Though the word refers to a circular letter, in modern times it has come to identify a specific type of papal document. Encyclicals addressed to the world's bishops are generally concerned with issues that affect the welfare of the Church as a whole, although some encyclicals have been issued to the prelates of a specific country. These written statements from the pope are not necessarily considered infallible.

Eugenics
Francis Galton first used this term in 1883. Eugenics drew upon Darwin's principles and in this context proposed a scientific method of breeding out undesirable characteristics that might otherwise be passed on to the next generation.

Euthanasia
Originally associated with providing a painless and easy death for the terminally ill. Hitler's Euthanasia Program, however, incorporated theory of eugenics. He used so-called mercy deaths for those considered undesirable in society so that their unacceptable characteristics would not be inherited.

Euthanasia Program
This program, initiated in 1939, was designed to weed out those who were deemed socially or genetically defective for death. Hitler's goal was to create a super race of Germans who were devoid of any undesirable mental, physical or social traits.

Extermination Camps
The six death camps in Poland were established to serve as the means for the Nazis Final Solution. They were Chelmo, Belzec, Sobibor, Auschwitz-Birkenau, Treblinka and Majdanek.

Final Solution
This was the euphemism used by the Nazi's to refer to their plans for the mass murder and annihilation of European Jews.

Fuhrer
This was Adolpf Hitler's title in Germany during the Nazi Regime. It means "leader".

Gas Chamber
First used in the Nazi euthanasia Program in 1939, the gassing of victims was later applied to the death camps, where the Nazis systematically and efficiently implemented their plan to exterminate European Jewry.

Genocide
This word refers to the entire, or almost entire, destruction of a religious, racial or national group. Hitler targeted the Jews of Europe for genocide with the Final Solution. In 1944, Rudolf Lemkin coined the term. The Final Solution, or Holocaust marks the most extreme form of genocide.

Gentiles
The term is used to refer to non-Jews. Both Jews and Christians have also used the word "gentile" as a designation for "pagans".

German Christian Church
When the Nazis assumed power in Germany in 1933 they immediately tried to transform the Churches by ridding them of any Jewish influence. The radical wing of the German Lutheran church, which supported Hitler's attempt to create a "Positive Christianity" devoid of any Jewish inspiration. This so-called German Christian Church began to synthesize Christian doctrine with Nazi anti-Semitic ideology.

Gestapo
The Gestapo's chief function was to persecute Jews and political dissidents. This group served as the Nazi's Secret State Police and under the direction of Himmler became a major force in bringing about the Holocaust.

Ghetto
Ghettos were sections of cities where Jews were forced to reside in order to separate them from the rest of the population. Used during the Middle Ages, the Nazis revived this practice and moved the Jewish population into sealed areas in which conditions were horrific.

Gypsies
Living a nomadic lifestyle, gypsies first appeared in Europe during the fifteenth century and were believed to have emigrated from northern India. Gypsies often suffered as much persecution as the Jews and subsequently were targeted by the Nazis for death.

Halakah
Jewish law as established or ratified by rabbinic jurists and teachers.

Haskalah
The term denotes the eighteenth and nineteenth century Jewish "enlightenment". The Jews who engaged in this secular study helped facilitate the acculturation of Jews to Western culture and society.

Holocaust
Taken from the Greek "burnt offering", this term is used to identify the Nazi's policy to annihilate the Jewish people during World War II. It is estimated that six million Jews were murdered.

Inquisition
This was the judicial system or ecclesiastical tribunal used by the Catholic Church for the discovery, examination and punishment of heretics.

Jehovah's Witness
A religious group that began in the United States, the Witnesses believe in the Bible and reject the need for official ministers. They refuse to salute the flag, take up arms, or participate in government affairs of any kind. Therefore they were at odds with the Nazi government and were persecuted.

Judeophobia
The hatred of Jews.

Kaddish
This Jewish prayer is recited by those in mourning during the first year after the death of a parent or child and on the anniversaries following the loss.

Kiddush Hashem
This is the Jewish term for martyrdom in the name of God.

Kristallnacht
In German this means "night of broken glass". The term is used to reference the night of November 9-10, 1938 when the Joseph Goebbels organized a nationwide pogrom bent upon the destruction of synagogues, Jewish homes and businesses. Before the night ended ninety Jews were killed and another thirty thousand were targeted for arrest. This night's brutality demonstrated clearly the Reich's acceptance and promotion of violence directed toward Jews.

Lebensraum
Hitler's *Mein Kampf* argued for the German need for lebensraum, which meant increased "living space." He planned to obtain this additional territory for Germany by conquering Eastern Europe and using it as an empire from which Germany could expand her population, draw needed food supplies and gain raw

materials. The ideology of German racial superiority was also part of this plan, for Hitler deemed the Slavic people "inferior" and sought to use them as a source of cheap labor.

Madagascar Plan
This early option for ridding Germany of its Jewish population proposed in 1940 for evacuating them to Madagascar over a period of four years. This plan was dropped because of the Nazis inability to defeat Great Britain, which controlled the sea-lanes to North Africa. Those who argue that this plan proves that Hitler did not always intend to murder the Jews, must admit that given the lack of sufficient infrastructure to sustain life in the colony, it is not unreasonable to conclude that the plan was a prescription for genocide.

Majdanek
Located in eastern Poland, this Nazi death camp was at first used as a labor camp for Poles and a prisoner of war camp for Russians. Later it became a site for the mass murder of Jews. It is reported that some 250,000 Jews were gassed there.

Marranos
During the medieval era Jews in Spain, who had converted to Christianity, but remained secretly tied to Judaism, were referred to as marranos, which in Spanish meant "swine."

Mein Kampf
While imprisoned in Landsberg prison after the 1923 "Beer Hall Putsch" Hitler wrote this autobiographical book. In its pages Hitler's ideas about the German state, its future, foreign policy, and need for *lebensraum* are clearly outlined. Each aspect of his ideology is infused with his racial beliefs, which were premised upon the myth of an Aryan master race and his hatred for the Jews. Those who compare his speeches with the book, recognize his radical anti-Semitic ideas , as well as his extremist solutions for Germany's "Jewish problem."

Messiah
For Jews, the 'anointed one' or messiah to come, who would restore the kingdom of Israel and usher in an age of peace, justice and plenty. Christians applied the title to Jesus Christ who they insisted had come as the "Redeemer" for mankind.

Mischling
According to the Nuremberg Laws of 1935, Mischlings were Germans of mixed Aryan and Jewish ancestry.

National Socialism (Nazism)
The party was founded in 1919 in Germany. Its platform was based upon a militaristic, racial, anti-Semitic and nationalistic ideology. Having started out as a small movement, the Party's membership and influence grew dramatically in the late 1920s and early 30s. Hitler's use of propaganda, mass rallies, demonstrations and violence helped promote Nazism's appeal to the German populace.

New Testament
This refers to the portion of the Bible that details the life and teachings of Jesus Christ and his followers. The words New Testament are taken by Christians to mean a new contract or covenant with God. The twenty-seven books of the New Testament explain this covenant.

Nuremberg Laws
In September of 1935 two anti-Jewish statutes were enacted in Nuremberg. The Reich Citizenship Law, the first of the two, deprived German Jews of their citizenship and related rights. The second, The Law for the Protection of German Blood and Honor, forbade the marriage of non-Jews to Jews, held that Jews could not employ German women of childbearing age and prohibited Jews from flying the German flag. Additional regulations were added to the original statutes and through these the Nazis were able to effectively cut Jews out of German economic, political, and social life. Importantly, the Nuremberg Laws established definitions about who was or was not a Jew.

Old Testament
This is the name Christians traditionally give to the Jewish scriptural writings. Together with the New Testament, it forms the whole of the Christian Bible.

Pope
For Catholics the pope is the visible head of the church founded by Jesus Christ.

Papacy
This is the office of the pope who is head of the Roman Catholic Church. The pope as the Bishop of Rome is regarded as the successor to St. Peter and is therefore the Shepard to all Christians and Christ's representative.

Passion Play
Passion Plays are religious dramas centering on the Passion of Jesus Christ. The most famous of these is the Obergammu Passion Play in Bavaria. The charge has been made that much of the play's content is anti-Semitic.

Pogrom
The term is taken from the Russian word for "devastation." It denotes the unprovoked state-sponsored attacks upon Jews by non-Jews.

Protocols of the Elders of Zion
This forgery was purported to be an eyewitness account of a meeting in a cemetery, where rabbis and other Jewish leaders unfolded their plan to rule the world. First published in Czarist Russia, the *Protocols* were soon disseminated throughout Western Europe and the United States. Hitler was able to use the forgery as support for his accusations against the Jews.

Reformation
The sixteenth century Protestant Christian movement, which sought to rectify the corruption of the Catholic Church is known as the Reformation. Those championing reform sought to return the church to its earliest traditions.

Renaissance
This name is given to the fourteenth and fifteenth century period in which there was a "rebirth' of classical learning in Europe.

Righteous Gentiles
These are the non-Jews who tried to save or give aid to the Jews suffering at the hands of the Nazis during the Holocaust. These Gentiles risked their lives to hide Jews from deportation to death camps. Though many of the names of these heroic persons are unknown, Israel has honored more than eight thousand people who have been designated "Righteous."

Ritual Murder
The accusation made during the Middle Ages, that Jews used the blood of murdered Christians in their religious rites, particularly in the preparation of unleavened bread for Passover.

Sanhedrin
This was the judicial body within early Judaism. Traditionally the Jewish court, or Sanhedrin consisted of seventy-one members.

Scapegoat
This is the word used to denote a person or group that bears the blame for the acts of others.

S.S. or Schutzstaffel
As an elite organization within the Nazi Party, the SS carried out many of the tasks that were essential to the success of the Final Solution. Heinrich Himmler,

as the head of this unit, was able to make it the most powerful wing of the Nazi Party, as well as its tool of terror. Racial pedigree and ideology were institutionalized in the SS. Membership in the SS required that recruits and their wives, prove that their "racial purity" extended back as far as the year 1700.

Shoah
The word Shoah means catastrophe in Hebrew. In the post-war world the term as been used to designate the mass murder of Jews, by the Nazis, during World War II

Sobibor
Located in eastern Poland, Sobibor was established in 1942. Over 200,000 Jews were killed there before the camp closed in 1943.

Social Darwinism
Darwin's biological theory as applied to society was part of Hitler's ideological worldview. He firmly adhered to the aspect of the theory that noted the "survival of the fittest."

Star of David
The Jews were forced to wear a patch of this six-pointed star on their sleeves or on the front and back of their shirts during the Holocaust so that they were easily recognized.

Supersessionism
This is the Christian teaching that claims Christianity has replaced the Jews in God's plan of salvation. It holds that Judaism has become an outdated religion.

Survivors of the Holocaust
The definition of a holocaust survivor refers to any Jew who lived under the Nazi regime or German occupation, or in a state that collaborated with the Germans or was its ally. It is estimated that the number of Holocaust survivors range from between eight hundred thousand to less than a million Jews.

Swastika
An ancient symbol that originated in India, the Nazis claimed the swastika as a symbol for Aryan superiority.

Synagogue
The word Synagogue takes its root meaning from the Greek term for "assembly". This is the most widely recognized name for a Jewish house of worship.

T-4
This was the code name for the Nazi's Euthanasia Program, which killed more than one hundred thousand people, who were defined as "unworthy " of life.

Talmud
The body of Jewish civil and religious law, as well as the commentaries that are not included in the Pentateuch

Third Reich
Reich means "regime or empire". The designation Third Reich referred to the Nazi Regime in Germany, which lasted from 1933 through 1945. The First Reich was the Holy Roman Empire of the medieval era. This lasted until 1806. The Second Reich included the German empire from 1871 to 1918.

Torah
The term refers to the five books of Moses and to the entire body of sacred literature.

Treblinka
Established in 1942, Treblinka located in northeast Poland served as a death camp. The camp operated until 1943 and within that time over 800, 000 people were murdered by the Nazis.

Vatican
The residence of the Pope, which is built on Vatican Hill in Rome is referred to as the Vatican. In recent times the word has been used to denote the papal authorities or the system they represent.

Vichy Government
This was the French government of Marshall Phillipe Petain, which collaborated with the Germans and cooperated in the efforts to deport French Jews to Auschwitz. The headquarters was located in Vichy, the capital of unoccupied France.

Volk (Ethnic People or Nation)
During the Nazi era this term took on an especially specific meaning. It referred to the German people who were "joined by blood." The Nazis employed the word to exclude Jews, Gypsies, and other non-Aryan people from their rights as German citizens.

Wannsee Conference
This meeting, of Nazi officials, called by Reinhard Heydrich on January 20, 1942, was held in the Berlin suburb of Wannsee. The officials in attendance

worked to coordinate the efforts of all the government agencies needed to carry out the Final Solution. The policy outlined called for using Jews first as forced laborers, and then those who survived the rigors of work would be treated "accordingly", a euphemism for their murder.

Warsaw Ghetto
This walled ghetto was established in 1940 and it housed approximately 500,000 Jews. Overcrowding, starvation, forced labor and unsanitary conditions caused the deaths of 45,000 Jews in the first year alone. In 1943 Jews within the ghetto revolted. This uprising lasted for about a month before the Nazis were able to end it.

Weimar Republic
Following World War I this was Germany's political structure. The governing power rested with the country's Chancellor, the German President retained a veto power and performed ceremonial duties, while the German Parliament or *Reichstag* provided more of an advisory role than legislative one. The Weimar government retained power until Hitler and the Nazi Party gained control of Germany in 1933.

Yad Vashem
The Holocaust Museum in Israel, this museum commemorates the Holocaust, Jewish resistance and the Righteous Gentiles, who risked their lives to save Jews.

Yellow Badge
The Nazis made the Jews wear this symbol in order to designate them from the rest of German society.

Yeshiva
Talmudic Jewish academies of higher learning.

Zionism
Mount Zion has historically been a symbol for Jerusalem. The word Zion or Zionism became bound up in the goal to create a Jewish homeland. Although the idea of Zionism, or the return of Jews to Palestine, had been proposed by several nineteenth century personalities, it was Theodor Hertzl, an assimilated Hungarian Jew, who became credited as the founder of the Zionist movement.

Author Index

Subject Index

About the Authors

JACK R. FISCHEL is the author of two books, *The Holocaust* and *Historical Dictionary of the Holocaust* and editor of seven other books. He is the chair of the History Department at Millersville University and editor of *Congress Monthly*.

SUSAN M. ORTMANN is married with three children and resides in Landisville, Pennsylvania. She is a Graduate Student at the University of Delaware.